Commodifying Plunder

Commodifying Plunder

Unequal Exchange and the Hidden Logic of Imperialism

CRELIS RAMMELT

MERLIN PRESS

First published in 2026 by
The Merlin Press Ltd,
Central Books Building,
Freshwater Road,
Dagenham
RM8 1RX
www.merlinpress.co.uk
ISBN 9780850368086

A CIP record of this book is available from the British Library.

Commodifying Plunder is a sign that the political economy of imperialism is back on the agenda again after fifty years in the shadow of neoliberal globalization. The book unveils the hidden logic of imperialist value transfer. Crelis Rammelt's understanding of unequal exchange is firmly rooted in Marx's theory of value. By combining the economic and ecological aspect of imperialism, he brings the theory of unequal exchange into the 21st century.

Torkil Lauesen, anti-imperialist activist, member of the Arghiri Emmanuel Association, and author of *Unequal Exchange, Past, Present and future.*

Finally! An engaging, accessible introduction to a vitally important set of analytical tools for understanding the roots of socio-environmental exploitation. A must read for anyone interested in a sustainable planetary future.

Robert Fletcher, Personal Professor of Political Ecology, Sociology of Development and Change

This book is a clear and accessible map of the current geopolitical condition. A must read for all those who wish to understand today's neo-imperial mutations of capitalism and its instable militarized geopolitics. Crelis Rammelt first shows us why imperialism exists and how it works. He exposes the ever-pressing needs of the minority world to exploit, enslave, dispossess, and abuse of the human and environmental wealth of the majority world. He also provides us with concrete tools to contest it.

Federico Savini, Associate Professor in Environmental Planning, Institutions and Politics

I loved your chapter that we read during the course. Your writing style is really fun to read and I appreciate how it is a text for all and not only other academics.

Geira Sol, Master Student, International Development Studies

Unequal exchange – in both its economic and ecological forms – lies at the root of modern imperialism, explaining how one country can grow at the expense of another under modern capitalism. However, such inequalities in exchange are to a large extent hidden by the operation of the price system, only revealed via Marxian value analysis. Among the numerous works written on this subject in recent years, very few are at once theoretically comprehensive, empirically sophisticated, and widely accessible. Among these Crelis Rammelt's *Commodifying Plunder: Unequal Exchange and the Hidden Logic of Imperialism* is quite possibly the best.

John Bellamy Foster, author (with Fred Magdoff) of *Grand Theft Capital: What Workers Should Know About the Affordability Crisis*

Commodifying Plunder presents an urgent and compelling argument, backed up by rigorous research and a stringent logic. It challenged me as a reader with its level of complexity, but that complexity never felt pretentious or gratuitous: all steps were clearly explained so that I could follow along even without any specific technical knowledge. I genuinely feel that I have developed a much better understanding of how capitalist trade works, and I'm grateful for that!

Valentina Carraro, Assistant professor, Political and Economic Geographies

Acknowledgments

This book has been a long time in the making and has benefited from countless conversations with people to whom I am deeply grateful.

To my students: your critical questions, insistence on clarity, and keen eye for weaknesses in the arguments challenged me to strengthen the reasoning, examples, and evidence found in these pages. A special thank you to those who joined me in exploring unequal exchange through your own academic research.

I am also grateful to my colleagues, who contributed to this project in many different ways: by giving me the opportunity to explore unequal exchange through teaching; by collaborating with me on research on unequal exchange; by helping me untangle some of the more intricate theoretical knots; by providing feedback on individual chapters or the manuscript as a whole; and by offering generous endorsements.

My thanks also go to the Governance and Inclusive Development research group as well as the Department of Human Geography, Planning, and International Development for funding research assistance and data access; to the Amsterdam Institute for Social Science Research for the grant that supported the final stages of writing and the open-access electronic edition; and to Merlin Press for its support and guidance throughout the publication process.

Finally, I want to express my gratitude to my family: thank you for all the encouragement.

Milena and Julius, may you grow up in a world that is more just.

CONTENTS

ABOUT THE AUTHOR

Dr Crelis Rammelt is an associate professor in environmental geography and development studies at the Faculty of Social and Behavioural Sciences, University of Amsterdam in the Netherlands. His research and teaching focus on forging links across disciplinary divides – mostly in the areas of political ecology, post-development, and systems science. He has also been involved in establishing the Dutch degrowth platform *Ontgroei* and in leading an action research and social justice programme in Bangladesh.

LIST OF ABBREVIATIONS

DVA – Domestic Value Added
ERDI – Exchange Rate Deviation Index
FVA – Foreign Value Added
GVC – Global Value Chains
HICs – High-Income Countries
IPL – International Poverty Line
LICs – Low-Income Countries
LMICs – Lower-Middle-Income Countries
MELT – Monetary Expression of Labour Time
MEN – Monetary Expression of Nature
MFA – Material Flow Analysis
MOC – Means of Consumption
MOP – Means of Production
NELT – Natural Expression of Labour Time
PPP – Purchasing Power Parity
UMICs – Upper-Middle-Income Countries

LIST OF DIAGRAMS

LIST OF TABLES

LIST OF GRAPHS

1. GENERAL INTRODUCTION

OPENING REMARKS

How can wealthy countries increase their material wealth at the expense of other, less wealthy, countries without resorting to genocide and pillage? By forming trade alliances under the guise of economic cooperation and mutual benefit. Such an answer might vex a good many people, but it must be considered. International trade is, and always has been, a form of violence, even if its methods and justifications have evolved.

'There can be no trade without war, and no war without trade,' said Jan Coen, officer of the Dutch East India Company in the early seventeenth century.[1] Coen employed ruthless tactics and orchestrated the massacre of thousands to establish a monopoly on valuable commodities from the East Indies – a pattern all too familiar from five centuries of European imperial expansion.[2] Such operations reflected a dominant Eurocentric vision of the world as a vast repository of material and human resources merely awaiting appropriation and exploitation.

This core vision persists today, and its execution remains violent, whether through direct military intervention, the threat of force, or the deliberate fuelling of conflict. The Russo-Ukrainian war which began in 2022 has become a bargaining tool for American and European states seeking access to Ukraine's mineral wealth.[3] That same war pushed up global gold prices, which contributed to a new wave of killings, extortion, and displacement around Peru's gold mines,[4] with violence spreading through the supply chain from extraction to transportation. The United States, meanwhile, has threatened military intervention to maintain control over the Panama Canal, a key artery of global trade.[5] And elsewhere, trade sustains the very violence it incites by ensuring a steady flow of arms and oil. This is the case, for example, in Western support for Israel, which has enabled genocide in Palestine, due to Israel's role in the global arms trade and its strategic ties to Middle Eastern oil producers.[6]

In the pursuit of economic expansion, violence and commerce intertwine. Contemporary corporations and their owners – equipped with wealth, influence, and empowered by dominant states and global institutions – embody a newer version of that old colonial ruthlessness. All of which, of course, unfolds behind the 'civilised' veil of so-called development and progress.

Violence riddles today's global production networks, not only in the form of overt genocide and pillage, but also through routinised sweatshop labour, environmental degradation, resource grabs, lost livelihoods, and other gradual, structural inflictions of harm. Textile factories in Bangladesh, Vietnam and India, for example, have been associated with child labour, exploitation, abuse, hazardous working conditions, the violent suppression of labour movements, and so on.[7] Few of us would steal food from a starving three-year-old or abduct their mother to exploit her in a such a factory, and yet our everyday participation in the economy has the same effect.[8]

Strip away all the fully overt violence, and contemporary trade is still plunder, just neatly commodified and concealed. Lengthy and complex supply chains obscure the conditions in which products are made, along with the machines and materials used to make them. Each node in these global chains involves the expenditure of human effort; directly through the labour operating machines and handling materials, and indirectly through the labour that created those machines and materials. Normal trade siphons this embodied effort away, draining it from one corner of the globe to enrich another in a process that Greek-French Marxist theoretician Arghiri Emmanuel calls 'unequal exchange.'[9]

GLOBAL DISPARITIES

Conventional economic perspectives consider unequal exchange to be an oxymoron:[10] Trade would not occur without mutual benefits. People simply walk away from a bad deal. 'The most important single central fact about a free market is that no exchange takes place unless both parties benefit,' Milton Friedman claimed.[11]

This conviction goes back to David Ricardo's theory of comparative advantage,[12] later refined by economists Eli Heckscher and Bertil Ohlin.[13] In essence, countries should specialise in exporting those goods that they can produce efficiently, from relatively abundant and inexpensive resources (even if other countries might be able to produce the same goods more efficiently). A burger chef may be better than the kitchen porter at both cooking and cleaning, but much better at cooking. If the former cooks, and the latter cleans, the restaurant's return increases. Countries benefit from trade in the same way: by specialising where their resources give them the greatest advantage.

One such advantage could be abundant cheap labour, which economic logic deems fit to exploit.[14] In the words of a World Bank senior vice president:

'When a labour-abundant developing country follows its comparative advantage to develop labour-intensive industries, it can also exploit the advantage of backwardness [sic] to reduce the cost of innovation.'[15] Why invest in automated sewing machines when you can hire hundreds of low-wage seamstresses?

Specialised trade presumably leads to gains for everyone involved. Some might gain more than others, but the fundamental premise is that trade never produces outright losses.[16] Even workers in the labour-intensive industries of low-income countries are supposed to benefit. According to a previous advisor to the United Nations Secretary-General, life as a seamstress in a Dhaka textile factory represents 'a step on the way to economic opportunity that was unimaginable in the countryside in generations past.'[17]

Such assumptions greatly influenced the Bretton Woods institutions (International Monetary Fund (IMF) and World Bank),[18] which have shaped global economic, financial, and trade policies for the past eighty years and continue to do so today.[19] As the IMF recently declared, 'at the aggregate level, trade is a win-win game.'[20]

What can we say after eighty years of this pro-trade narrative? In one sense, it has been a huge success. Of the 9.6 trillion hours of global labour performed in 2021, 2.1 trillion was spent producing internationally traded goods and services.[21] In other words, 22 per cent of all work is export-oriented. Measured in volume, global trade grew twelvefold from 1970 to 2022 (see left Graph 1).[22] It even outpaced global Gross Domestic Product (GDP), which had grown to about five times its 1970 levels by 2022 (see right Graph 1). This trend tells us that economies rely increasingly on

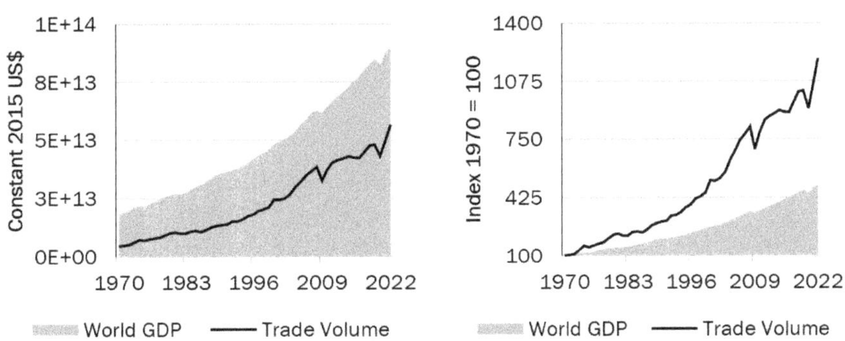

Graph 1. Increasing Trade and Economic Growth.
Both graphs use the same data. The left graph shows the global GDP (the sum of all national GDPs) and total trade volume in absolute monetary terms. The right graph indexes these values to 1970 (set as one hundred per cent) to highlight the relative growth rates of each variable.

imports to meet domestic demand. At the current rate, the monetary value of internationally traded goods will surpass that of domestically produced and consumed goods by 2048.[23]

At the same time, the relevance of labels such as 'Made in the USA' or 'Made in China' has progressively fallen, such that 'Made in the World' better represents much of what we consume today. Over time, companies fragmented their production processes across national borders to capitalise on each country's specialised advantages, giving rise to global value chains (GVCs). The proportion of GVCs in total trade flows rose from 24 per cent in 1965 to fifty per cent in 2022.[24] Another study estimates that trade in semi-finished goods now comprises up to two thirds of the global total.[25]
The pro-trade narrative has been successful to the point of absurdity. For instance, nations simultaneously import and export various brands of toilet paper. Trucks transport bottles of San Pellegrino from Italy to France, and bottles of Evian in the other direction. Despite abundant timber resources, the United States imports safety matches from Japan, which are sourced from forests in Indonesia, while Japan imports chopsticks from the United States.[26] For someone, somewhere, these absurd arrangements presumably make good economic sense.

It should be recognised that trade is one element of a larger project of assimilation into the world system. Countries grow increasingly entangled through personal remittances, incoming investments, outgoing profits, and wealth, as well as non-financial ties such as military involvement and technology exchange. For example, between 1990 and 2022, foreign investment, foreign debt, and remittances received by low-income countries all increased – by 1,515 per cent, 159 per cent, and 665 per cent respectively.[27]

Now, what has been the effect of this remarkable growth in trade? Challenging the win-win assumptions of mainstream trade theories, this increase has not led to a reduction in economic disparities between different regions of the global economy (per World Bank categories). The per capita GDP of low-income countries (LICs) increased by 42 per cent from 1950 to 2022, while that of high-income countries (HICs) increased by 385 per cent (see left Graph 2). At best, this reveals a win-more, win-less dynamic.

The gap widens further when within-country inequalities are taken into account (see right Graph 2). In 2022, when measured at Purchasing Power Parity (PPP) which controls for differences in cost of living,[28] the poorest forty per cent of the world population only accounted for about six per cent of total global income. Meanwhile, the richest ten per cent earned roughly 44 per cent of global income.[29] Zooming further in, the richest one per cent earned as much as the total income of the poorest fifty per cent (roughly ten per cent of total income). In 2023, our seamstress in Dhaka earned $1.50 (at PPP) per hour.[30] That same year, Jeff Bezos made $7.9 million an hour – earning a lifetime's worth of the seamstress's wages in little over a minute.[31]

The inequalities would have been greater still had we not corrected for differences in costs of living.[32] Uncorrected, the seamstress makes just $0.40 an hour, so that Bezos earns the equivalent of about three lifetimes of her wages in a single minute. This gives a better sense of the purchasing power of nations and is a more appropriate method for measuring the distribution of income generated by the global economy.

Moreover, individual-based global inequality has worsened since 1950, with the average income of the richest ten per cent growing 19.6 times more than that of the poorest fifty per cent between 1950 and 2022 in absolute terms. That same period saw the average income of the richest one per cent grow 48.2 times more than that of the poorest fifty per cent (see right Graph 2).[33]

Some claim that the inequality is driven not by trade, but by a lack of it. However, the evidence suggests otherwise. Beyond income inequality, there is a wide and growing gap in the distribution of returns from participation in global value chains (GVCs), measured as 'value-added.' I will discuss this in greater detail later in the book, but just to give an impression: In 2018, high-income countries captured 275 times more returns from trade than their low-income counterparts, up from 37 times more in 1990.[34] Importantly, this gap has continued to grow despite the increased participation of low-income countries in GVCs.[35]

From a class perspective, labour's share of GDP remained fairly constant until the 1980s, since when it has declined. Between 2017 and 2021, only 51.6 per cent of global GDP was captured by workers as wages, down from

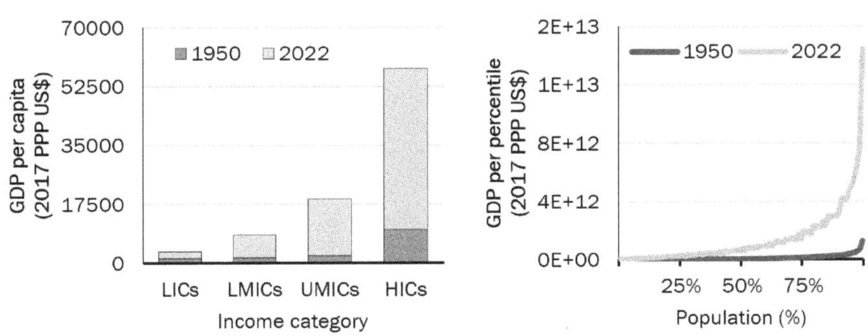

Graph 2. Income Inequality.

The left graph shows international inequality in 1950 and 2022, with countries grouped by income level. The right graph shows individual inequality,organised by global population percentiles for the same two years.

54.7 per cent in 1995–1999. The labour share is relatively lower in the Global South where workers captured just 47.5 per cent of GDP between 2017 and 2021, compared to 54.7 per cent in the Global North.[36] The remaining share, though also produced by labour – as we shall come to understand – was captured by others, mainly capitalists, as profit to be invested in the accumulation of wealth.

Indeed, wealth inequality is even more extreme than income inequality. The richest one per cent accumulated half of all new wealth produced in 2010-2020. This accelerated to almost two thirds of all new wealth since 2020, six times more than the bottom ninety per cent of humanity. By 2023, the top one per cent owned a staggering 45.6 per cent of global wealth, while the poorest half owned only 0.75 per cent. A mere 81 individuals held more wealth than fifty per cent of the world combined.[37] This drops to only eight individuals, when accounting for indebtedness.[38]

Such dense concentrations of wealth drive patterns of power and authority in global economic systems, for they allow the wealthy to subvert democratic processes through increasingly powerful lobbies and enhance corporations' ability to externalise costs, minimise liability, and obstruct structural change. These economic and political hegemonies are mutually reinforcing and perpetuate uneven development trends worldwide. We will discuss this in detail in the forthcoming chapters.

The financial inequalities described thus far reflect all sorts of material inequalities: In 2018, high-income countries consumed 23.5 times more energy and 10.2 times more raw materials, and emitted 17.1 times more greenhouse gases per capita, than low-income countries.[39]

Measuring material footprints in tons per capita, which calculates raw materials consumed to meet final domestic demand, reveals significant differences between income clusters. In 2022, low-income countries, lower-middle-income countries, and India had mean raw material footprints of 3.1, 7.3, and 5.0 tons per capita respectively, while upper-middle-income countries, high-income countries, and China had 11.6, 24.7, and 24.8 tons per capita. All clusters have increased their footprints since 1992, with low-income countries rising least (sixteen per cent) and China showing a 290 per cent surge.[40]

Turning our attention to emissions, the richest ten per cent accounted for half of total emissions in 2019. The richest one per cent (77 million people) were responsible for sixteen per cent of global consumption emissions. It would take someone in the bottom 99 per cent roughly nineteen years to produce emissions equivalent to what a member of the one percent emits in a single year.[41]

While few contest the reality of such growing inequalities today, many continue to seek reassurance in the supposed reduction of extreme poverty.[42]

They point to the fact that, based on the current International Poverty Line (IPL) target of $2.15 (2017 PPP), global poverty fell from 1.99 billion in 1981 to 684 million in 2024 (see Graph 3).[43] Based on this evidence, one could assume that the rising tide of global capitalism lifts all boats, unequal though the lifting may be. This assumption would, however, be incorrect.

One reason is that the current IPL is far too low: No one can survive on a daily allowance of $2.15 (2017 PPP). For example, a person needs on average $6.9 (2017 PPP) just to afford a healthy diet.[44] Others propose an 'ethical poverty line' of $10 (2017 PPP) per day, beyond which further increases in income cease to increase life expectancy significantly.[45] On this basis, the number of people in poverty rose by 136 per cent, from 3.3 billion in 1981 to 4.6 billion in 2024, or 56 per cent of the world population. Still others propose an 'escape from poverty' threshold of $15 (2017 PPP) per day, which would reduce the probability of falling back into poverty to ten per cent.[46] Based on this threshold, poverty increased to 5.5 billion in 2024 (see Graph 3).

It is common for defenders of the current system to shift attention towards the share rather than the number of people in poverty. For example, the percentage of those living in households with consumption or income per person below $15 (2017 PPP) dropped from eighty per cent in 1981 to 67 per cent in 2024. In my opinion however, this means nothing to the 5.5 billion, including an additional 1.9 billion since 1981, who face the insecurity of sinking into poverty.

These facts tend to be ignored. Poverty has only been eradicated from the minds and narratives of those who govern and control the world economy, and of their intellectual allies. Worse still, they insist that an abundance

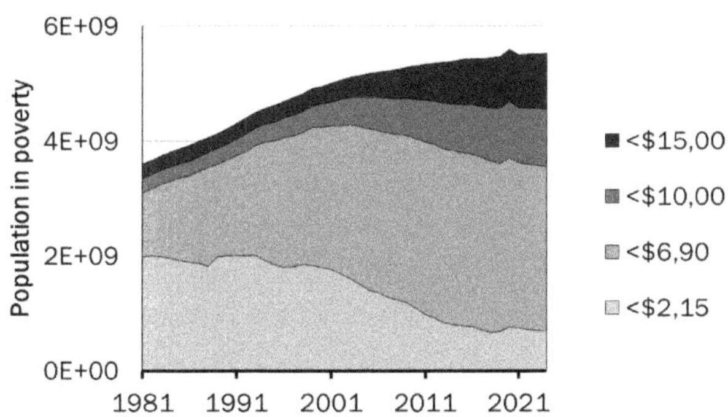

Graph 3. Extreme Poverty.

Extreme Poverty. The graph shows the global population living below four poverty lines (measured in dollars per day and adjusted for cost-of-living differences) from 1981 to 2024. Each successive poverty line includes everyone counted under the lines below.

of 'poor people' constitutes a comparative advantage in trade. But let's be clear – cheap labour presents no advantage to cheap labour. The employer's comparative advantage is simply the worker's disadvantage.

So far, we have observed growing disparities in a world increasingly interconnected through investment, production, and trade. Clearly, someone, somewhere, has drawn the short straw – and it's getting shorter! The simultaneous increase in wealth and poverty reveals a win-lose dynamic. These observations alone do not prove that impoverishment occurs as an inverse result of others' enrichment. However, we can safely say that while global economic incorporation in the neocolonial period may have generated a great deal of wealth and profit, it did not succeed in reducing the disparities – contrary to the expectations and narratives advanced to justify it.

As we will discover, pro-trade arguments build on flawed assumptions about capital mobility and wage rates dating back to Ricardo. More importantly, these arguments overlook the fact that the distribution of financial gains from trade does not align with the distribution of embodied effort across countries. Standard trade statistics obscure this reality because prices mask the seemingly paradoxical truth that products requiring more effort tend to be cheaper. Not only is someone drawing the short straw, but it is even shorter than it appears!

With the right analytical tools, we can better understand this unequal exchange not as arbitrary, but as an inherent feature of the world system. The systemic unidirectional transfer of embodied effort is a key explanation of the enduring global disparities in material wealth, and consequently the unequal power dynamics that perpetuate the system.

Although it may initially seem like just another academic jigsaw puzzle, unequal exchange carries profound practical implications. The development strategies that we choose rely heavily on an understanding of the mechanisms driving global wealth and power disparities. Their persistence points to the inadequacy of global trade as a means of fostering genuine mutual benefits. It is important to note that it is not trade in general that unequal exchange theory puts on the stand but specifically trade under capitalism. Trade existed long before capitalism, long before it started moving different brands of toilet paper back and forth in the name of profit. As noted, trade has long been bound up with violence; in Part 2, we examine how this violence manifests in capitalist trade. Capitalism is of course a big word, so let me offer some general contours to get us started.

CAPITALISM

There is someone who can help us get to grips with the salient features of capitalism, regardless of whether one embraces his political ideologies and strategies, or trusts his revolutionary predictions. You know who I mean. His name alone rattles people, as if uttering the moniker 'Beetlejuice' three times grants the malicious ghost access to the mortal world where he will wreak havoc: 'Marx, Marx, Marx!' But fear not, for summoning his ideas yields constructive insights. As the economic historian John Kenneth Galbraith notes, 'Marx is much too valuable a source of social insight to be left as the exclusive property of the Communists.'[47] While Marx wasn't right about everything, and his ideas have been used to justify brutality, his framework still proves highly useful today.

The capitalist system – whatever it is – coexists and interacts with a host of other ways of creating, delivering, and utilising goods and services, by such actors as states, households, or cooperatives.[48] However, we can label an economy 'capitalistic' when it prevails over and encroaches on other coexisting economic activities.

All economies produce, distribute, and use goods and services. The question, therefore, is: What do those activities look like under capitalism, as opposed to socialism, feudalism, or totalitarianism? Before answering this, however, we must first ask: Are we attempting to describe the system that operates out there in the world, or the one that exists only in our minds? I say both.

American author and philosopher Ayn Rand may be right on one point: 'A pure system of capitalism has never yet existed.'[49] However, she then takes this claim to fuel sheer speculation. She blames meddlesome regulators for hindering the true and noble potential of capitalism, which she refers to as 'the unknown ideal'. Unlike an unrealised dream, though, capitalist forces do operate in the world, even if political and institutional hindrances 'get in the way'. It is reasonable, therefore, to attempt to describe these forces. At the same time, nothing stops us from reflecting on how a theoretically unhindered ideal-typical system might behave.

We should explore capitalism as it is – subject to red tape, lobbying, subsidies, monopolies, militarism, and so on – as well as capitalism as it is envisioned by its champions – voluntary, free, deregulated, competitive, privatised, and so on. This second version, of course, is theoretical; capitalism depends on an interventionist, militarised state, and always has.

Describing capitalism is a challenge: We are like fish in a bowl, oblivious to the fact that we are swimming in it. We struggle to perceive the order around us precisely because it saturates nearly every facet of our lives. To paraphrase Roger Kint from *The Usual Suspects* (1995): 'The greatest trick capitalism ever pulled was convincing the world it didn't exist'. Let's try bringing it into the light, nonetheless.

In essence, capitalism is a system where goods and services are produced for profitable exchange; where human labour power is treated as a commodity to be sold on the market; where the means of production are owned by a class that the labourers do not belong to; where investments are made with the expectation of a return; where a monetary system facilitates the provision of bank credit; and where private property rights are upheld by law.[50] Supported by the state, these private property rights are institutionally created, violently enforced, and zealously protected.

Over the past few centuries, capitalism has undoubtedly evolved, and today's statist Rhineland variant differs from its more rampant neoliberal Anglo-Saxon sibling, or indeed from the more recent Chinese version of state capitalism. However, certain foundational features remain true across contexts and specific manifestations. As the saying goes, 'the more capitalism changes, the more it stays the same'.[51] It is crucial, therefore, that any critique of capitalism addresses its foundations, rather than focusing solely on its different manifestations.

To use an analogy, psychopathic personalities can exhibit a range of traits: Some display greater levels of callousness and manipulation, while others are more pretentious and promiscuous. However, both sets of behaviours fit the overall profile of a psychopath. Similarly, neoliberalism can be seen as a specific form of capitalism characterised by reduced welfare states, deregulated markets, widespread use of flexible contracts, and the presence of tax-evading oligopolies. While these issues, commonly associated with the adjective 'neoliberal,' are certainly significant, we must not overlook the fundamental problems associated with the noun 'capitalism,' such as dispossession, disconnection, domination, destruction, and death.[52]

Whether neoliberal, social democratic, imperialist, fascist, or crony, capitalism's multiple personalities all share one important trait: the pursuit of economic growth, or capital accumulation. Some progressive thinkers like to propose inclusive, responsible, or green models of capitalism,[53] but these cannot alter the system's fundamental compulsion: 'Accumulate, accumulate! This is Moses and the Prophets!'[54] As I will argue, this compulsion is inherently antisocial and ecocidal, for in the name of growth, capitalism frantically converts 'nature into products, communities into markets, citizens into consumers, and relationships into services.'[55]

It is worth mentioning that productivist forms of socialism and communism also display the compulsion to grow. Not all systems based on growth are capitalistic, but all capitalistic systems are based on growth. Similarly, not all manipulative people are psychopaths, but all psychopaths are manipulative. Max Weber contends that although the pursuit of profit may exist outside of capitalism, the latter does not exist without the former.[56] So let's not get distracted by those other systems and keep close to the system at hand.

It is not just any form of growth that capitalism seeks, but specifically capital accumulation, a relentless and self-perpetuating cycle of appropriation and control. Accumulation arises as a compulsion: The system has no choice. As political thinker Murray Bookchin observes, '[c]apitalism can no more be "persuaded" to limit growth than a human being can be "persuaded" to stop breathing.'[57] Any deceleration would destabilise capitalism's inner workings. Indeed, when accumulation falters, innovation stops, companies are outcompeted, recessions loom, banks collapse, businesses foreclose, people lose jobs, and governments default on their debts. That said, it's not just the threat of collapse that drives accumulation, but the potential rewards of expansion too.

This compulsion is rooted in social interactions driven by conflicting interests rather than cohesion.[58] Perhaps the most obvious conflict is over profits and wages, but there are many others. Cost-cutting wars among capitalists lead to bankruptcies and consolidation into oligopolies. Competing workers accept precarious jobs and low pay. Conflicts also erupt between retailers (e.g., Amazon versus Alibaba), buyers and sellers (e.g., 'market for lemons'),[59] producers and middlemen (e.g., over service fees), shareholders and stakeholders, taxmen and businessmen, borrowers and lenders, and so on. 'Everywhere we are encouraged to fight for wealth and social position like stray dogs over a dustbin,' writes George Monbiot.[60]

These struggles also have an international dimension, with countries competing for global market shares, resource access, foreign investment, capital flows, sovereign loans, favourable exchange rates, skilled workers, and so on.

What causes these ubiquitous conflicts? By turning work and its products into commodities – that is, by converting human effort as embodied in goods and services into money – the system creates conflict. At its core, this conflict stems from the system's appropriation of one group's labour time for another's monetary gain. As a lecturer, I have less time per student because the university seeks to earn more while spending less. Unsurprisingly, labour struggles often centre on time: working hours, weekends, holidays, breaks, overtime, travel time, time for training, for example.

And what do such conflicts lead to? The structures of capitalism – privatised services, liberalised markets, bank credit, multinational corporations, stock shares, etc. – reward self-interested profit-maximisation, expansion, and accumulation. They also punish a lack of ruthlessness on the part of economic actors. Some may act out of greed, but that is not most people's dominant motivator. Indeed, many struggle simply to stay afloat in this dog-eat-dog world, hoping to secure a job, save up, redeem debts, etc. In the words of David Graeber, '[w]hile humans may be justly accused of having a proclivity to accuse others of acting like conquistadors, few really act this way themselves.'[61]

The capitalist structures within which we all operate are strengthened when such behaviours as dominance, competition, and ruthlessness pay off. The compulsion to accumulate arises precisely from this mutual interaction between social behaviour and the system.

CAPITALIST TRADE

Having laid out some basic characteristics of capitalism, let me now introduce capitalist trade, or exchange – the focus of the book.

Capitalist trade functions primarily to generate profit, with the satisfaction of an increasingly diverse range of consumer needs and desires being a secondary aim at best. The costs and benefits of this expansion, in terms of human effort and its remuneration, are unevenly distributed. I began this introduction by stating that normal capitalist trade is, in fact, unequal exchange. What exactly legitimates the use of the term 'unequal' here? And if trade is indeed unequal, what are the forms, magnitudes, patterns, and trends of those inequalities? These questions are the basis of the inquiry pursued in this book.

Please note that I use 'Global North/South' loosely in the first part of the book, acknowledging its limitations as a simplistic binary sometimes fixed colonial history or geography. Later, when the argument demands it, I will introduce 'centre' and 'periphery' – concepts better suited to discussing shifting positions of dependency and dominance between and within countries.

Briefly, 'unequal' typically denotes an imbalance in quantity or amount. However, an exchange that withdraws more resources than it returns is not, in itself, necessarily unfair. It becomes socially unfair when it supports development in the Global North at the expense of the Global South. What's more, the latter often needs the exchange to address immediate socioeconomic concerns, yet the underlying structural barriers to its development persist. For example, while mineral extraction and exports provide the dollars needed to import essential goods or service debts, they seldom change the South's underlying dependence on extractivism.

I therefore understand unequal exchange as encompassing all three dimensions: quantitatively unbalanced, socially unfair, and structurally unjust. It systemically enriches some groups and regions by impoverishing others.

Marxists have long argued that enrichment through impoverishment happens via the globalised forces of capitalist accumulation, which they blame for the interconnected and uneven patterns of development in the world system. One particular school of Marxist thought, beginning with Otto Bauer, Henryk Grossman, and Arghiri Emmanuel,[62] proposes unequal exchange as the main culprit.

Unequal exchange is firmly rooted in the Marxist value framework, which I will discuss in detail after this introduction. As mentioned above, this framework allows us to reflect on the source of value in (global) capitalism: human effort, specifically average labour time. It also reveals how (labour) value and price can diverge, where some commodities are sold above their value and others below (reflecting an average conversion factor between the two). Such divergences occur not only between firms and sectors, but also between nations. Emmanuel, who pioneered the theory of unequal exchange, was inspired by Marx's insight that '[t]he favoured country recovers more labour in exchange for less labour'.[63] As we shall see, these divergences can be attributed to either productivity or wage gaps, which in turn cause a drain of value (in the form of average labour time) from Global South to Global North.

The distribution of value cannot be understood through traditional money-based inequality and poverty statistics such as those reviewed earlier. These statistics, though they provide important observations, offer no explanations. Marx's framework, however, delves deeper into the distribution of value, elucidating how enrichment occurs through impoverishment and how capitalism thrives on this disparity. While we need the concept of value to grasp these dynamics, the fact that we cannot ignore money represents a challenge: Not only do prices and profits significantly influence our thinking; they also hold genuine importance within Marx's framework, as I will clarify.

At this point, I want to shift focus somewhat to recognise that the framework would lose its relevance if it did not also address the pressing environmental harms and conflicts of our time. Thus, Chapter 7 will explore the unjust allocation of natural resources and environmental risks, as well as the unequal distribution of responsibility for these risks. I will examine how these inequalities are deeply interwoven with the book's central theme of unequal exchange.

The seemingly endless capitalist accumulation goes hand in hand with growing biophysical exchanges with nature, understood as 'social metabolism,'[64] as shown in Graph 4.[65] Despite a decline in energy consumption per unit of economic output globally, total primary energy consumption has been on the rise for decades. Similarly, improvements in

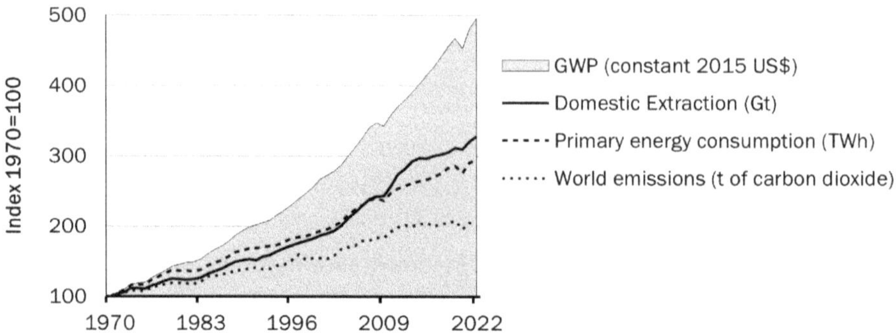

Graph 4. Metabolic Growth.
This graph shows the growth of three biophysical variables against that of the global economy (measured as global GDP) from 1970 to 2022. All data are indexed to one hundred per cent in 1970.

energy's carbon intensity have failed to offset rising greenhouse emissions. While transitioning to renewables may offer a potential solution, the pace is insufficient to avert climate breakdown,[66] nor will it curb the escalating use of material resources. In fact, global raw material extraction started outpacing world economic growth a couple of decades ago.[67]

Growth of the world economy correlates almost perfectly with global energy production since 1971 (correlation coefficient of 0.997), atmospheric CO_2 since 1960 (0.998),[68] and many other environmental variables.[69] These correlations mean that increased social metabolism intensifies during periods of high economic growth and eases up only during periods of low economic growth or recession.

Global capitalism resembles a gargantuan beast, a superorganism,[70] that devours resources on a planetary scale and discharges mountains of waste back into its habitat. By failing to restrain its gluttonous impulses, the beast has destabilised the Earth's climate system, nutrient cycles, biodiversity, freshwater reserves, and so on.[71] In so doing, it also threatens its own existence. Indeed, whether because of excessive depletion, pollution, or the rising costs of extraction and clean-up, global capitalism will eventually stop growing.[72] Until then, however, the system's growing social metabolism will continue to inflict often abrupt and irreversible harm to life on Earth.

We have entered what some call the 'capitalocene,' an alternative designation for the current geological epoch which locates capitalism and its associated modes of production, distribution, and accumulation as the primary drivers of planetary and environmental change.[73]

As I will explore in the book's final chapter, this growing metabolism creates unevenly distributed burdens and benefits. World trade has resulted not only in a tremendous outflow of resources from the poorest areas of the world,[74] but a corresponding inflow of waste back into them.[75] These flows have deprived the poor of vital resources and damaged their local ecosystems, while wealth continues to accumulate for a small minority.

In recent years, some have therefore started thinking about unequal exchange as an ecological process – a drain not of value as average labour time, but as uneven metabolic flows of resources through trade. I will describe the ways in which this ecological form differs from the original Marxist interpretation of unequal exchange. Moreover, the ecological version is yet to be embedded in the Marxist value framework. I will argue that doing so would help distinguish, as well as connect, unequal exchange as an appropriation of value in the Marxist sense (average labour time) and ecologically unequal exchange as an appropriation of use values, that is, the material wealth produced through labour involving natural resources. I believe that making this connection is key to forging alliances between class-based, social, and environmental justice movements.

CLOSING REMARKS

Following this introduction, Part 1 begins by explaining the Marxist value framework, including key concepts such as use value, value, and surplus value. I also explore the relationship between value and money in order to understand the dynamics of price and profit in relation to value and surplus value. The chapters of Part 1 not only provide necessary tools for analysing unequal exchange later on, but also, serve as a concise and accessible summary of the Marxist framework.

Marxist writing can be opaque, the source of an inordinate amount of squabbling about what Karl may or may not have said or meant to say. I will not cover any of that. Instead, I want to make his theory more accessible to a wider audience, particularly the transformation of value into price and surplus value into profit, which, I feel, has not been clearly presented elsewhere. Summarising Marx necessarily excludes many details and presents a selective perspective, here focused on the tools needed to unravel unequal exchange in Part 2.

If you already have a good grasp of Marxist theory, you may choose to skip Part 1 and proceed directly to Part 2. However, I strongly recommend reading the section on price and profit, which addresses Marx's transformation problem of values into prices (and surplus value into profit). He takes this essential step in the third volume of *Capital*, abandoning his assumption of price-value alignment throughout the preceding volumes to recognise that higher prices no longer coincide with more value. Without this crucial piece, his puzzle is liable to misinterpretation. If all of this sounds like gibberish to you, as it did to me when I began my journey into Marxist theory, you will probably need to read Part 1.

I draw references and quotations from Marx's works from the editions available on the Marxists Internet Archive.[76] I provide relevant information on volumes, parts, and chapters in the endnotes.

After the value framework, Part 2 consists of three distinct chapters related to unequal exchange, covering its historical context, fundamentals, and its ecological version. The first of these chapters provides a general outline of the causes of uneven development. Its aim is twofold: to provide some historical context for understanding unequal exchange, and to differentiate between losses resulting from unequal exchange from other losses affecting the Global South. Mine is a condensed analysis, as many other works cover the topic in much greater detail.

While the theory of unequal exchange may seem outdated to some, its resurgence in recent years underscores its enduring relevance for issues concerning international trade and development. It is worth stating that I do not provide a comprehensive overview of the literature on unequal exchange, nor does this book constitute a critique or review of existing critiques. I primarily focus on the work of Arghiri Emmanuel, supplemented by key insights from other sources and without too many distracting nuances and discussions.

Finally, I conclude by weaving together various strands and synthesising the main themes examined. You can find this summary in Chapter 8 if you'd like to see a map of the book upfront.

Unequal exchange emerges as a critical factor in explanations of uneven development, yet, despite its resurgence, it remains a rather obscure notion. While several publications deal with the topic, they are often limited to specialised academic contexts. At other times, the theory is either simplified or ignored. This is neither a textbook, nor a lightweight primer, nor a popular science book, but something in between. It aims to be a compendium-like resource for both academic and non-academic audiences, that is, intellectually serious without drowning in academic opacity and accessible without sacrificing depth.

In a way, I have written this examination of these theoretical complexities for my past self. I have sought to keep it simple, but I must warn you that this is not light reading – it will get theoretical. At the same time, the desire for simplicity means that the book is inevitably incomplete, and it may contain occasional inaccuracies. I must also warn you that the book relies on algebraic formulas – abstract at first, then empirical – to reveal hidden relationships, counterintuitive insights, and the scale of unequal exchange. No advanced math is needed, so I hope the approach stays relatively accessible.

Importantly, I also hope that this work speaks not only to academics, but also activists, practitioners, community organisers, frontline defenders, policymakers, and others engaged in international solidarity, social justice, and environmental struggles. Through this theory, I aim to offer a lens that exposes an important yet neglected part of the system responsible for the violence of global capitalist exchange and its – impacts on impoverished populations and vulnerable environments worldwide.

I'm not suggesting that those on the front lines lack this understanding – they know the realities and violence of the system more intimately than most. But theory might offer an additional layer to support that consciousness and make connections across struggles through shared analysis. I say this because tensions often arise between movements facing a common adversary: farmers' protests versus climate actions; green energy initiatives versus anti-extractivist campaigns; national labour struggles versus international solidarity. These conflicts reflect the deeper contradictions of a system that ultimately needs transformation.

I recently attended a conference where a speaker offered an ecological critique of the wasteful surge in electric bikes despite the critical raw materials crisis. An audience member countered from a feminist perspective, arguing that e-bikes offer cleaner, safer mobility for vulnerable groups, especially women in remote areas. The speaker clarified that he was criticising their unnecessary adoption by European youth. Another feminist voice countered, asking whether e-bikes simply accelerate women's integration into an exploitative and productivist economy. Then a participant called out the Eurocentric framing altogether, reminding the room that anti-mining activists in their home country are being killed for resisting the extraction of the very materials needed to produce the e-bikes. This dialogue revealed the internal tensions that exist even in spaces built on shared progressive principles.

At first glance, such tensions might appear irresolvable. However, they arise from the same system, which creates these contradictions and fractures resistance. As stated by a prominent figure in the *Gilets Jaunes* movement, a French citizens' group protesting a diesel tax that would raise the costs of living for the working class even further: 'The social and ecological emergencies are inseparable. The fights against the end of the world and the end of the month are the same.'[77]

If these movements have a common enemy, why are their struggles not more unified? One reason, I believe, stems from the lack of a compelling shared framework that lays bare the entire system – particularly the violence it inflicts and conceals through complex global entanglements, as the e-bike incident illustrates. Ongoing academic debates, especially those related to theories of (ecological) unequal exchange, often deepen divisions rather than building consensus. It is time to move beyond these impasses. Greater theoretical clarity might help bring movements closer together. With this book, I hope to make a modest contribution to developing ideas and constructing a framework to bridge divides, ease tensions, or at the very least, illuminate aspects of the system that remain hidden to many.

This book is less interested in offering solutions than exposing the system and understanding that the transformations required must be systemic. However, critique without action is mere observation. If nothing changes, global exploitation and appropriation will only accelerate. To sustain their wealth and power, the ruling classes will demand ever more labour and resources, which will lead to an escalation in social and ecological injustices, while deepening patterns of dispossession, appropriation, exploitation, and so on. The more violent the system becomes, the more some groups resist, the more other groups double down with violent forms of repression. For example, the Dutch and UK governments are discussing plans to criminalise public support for so-called 'terrorist organisations' and to ban certain 'extreme protest groups.'[78] Such plans threaten the democratic space for peaceful social and environmental activism.

Perhaps more than anything, this book is about driving home this simple message: This system does not end well unless *we* end it. The oppressed, together with those in solidarity, must break it before it breaks everything. And theory, among other tools, can serve as a guide. As Leonardo da Vinci put it: 'He who loves practice without theory is like the sailor who boards ship without a rudder and compass and never knows where he may cast.'

Part 1. Value Framework

2. Value

OPENING REMARKS

> How lucky! A nugget of gold, right there in my path! I placed it in my bag and continued my journey. When I looked inside the bag after some time, the nugget had magically transformed into a pouch brimming with cash. So much more convenient, I thought. A little later, I looked inside again to find the pouch had turned into a pack of rice. One less errand to the market, I rejoiced. When I eventually got home, my treasure metamorphosed once again, unveiling its true nature as a shape-shifting spirit. As it fluttered off, I thanked my lucky stars for having witnessed such a mystical creature.[79]

What is value? A precious ingot, a sum of money, a consumable item, or an intangible experience? Karl Marx would have answered that value is manifest in all these things – like a shape-shifter metamorphosing from one form to another. Unfortunately, many economists reject this intriguing premise, along with Marx's elaborate underlying value framework, and turn to the epiphenomenon of price rather than probing the nature, origin, movement, and accumulation of value. Marx encourages us to dig deeper.

In what follows, I use a shorthand system based on initials to explain the Marxist framework. Table 1 lists the main variables, their abbreviations, and brief descriptions. I'll explain each as we go, but the table serves as a quick reference.

The equations shown in the table and employed when explaining the theory rely only on basic arithmetic and use simplified measures of labour time and money. The analysis builds gradually: from a sector with two firms, to an economy with two sectors, to a world with two economies. To keep the logic clear and the maths easy to follow, I've chosen numbers that divide and multiply cleanly, even if that means sacrificing a degree of realism. The numbers are intentionally unrealistic – they're pedagogical tools. Later in the book, I turn to an empirical analysis with real-world data.

Variable	Initials/Formula	Description
Capital Invested	C = c + v	Total capital invested, comprising constant capital and variable capital
Constant Capital	c	Capital invested in machinery, tools, and materials
Variable Capital	v	Capital invested in labour power
Organic Composition of Capital	OC = c / v	Ratio of constant to variable capital; indicates "capital intensity" of production
Surplus Rate	s′ = S / v	Rate of surplus value extracted from labour; measures the degree of labour exploitation
Surplus Value	S = s′ × v	Excess value created by labour; dependent on surplus rate and variable capital
Value Produced	V = C + S	Total value of output, composed of capital expended and surplus value created
Output (firm)	o	A firm's output measured in physical units over a production period
Breakeven Price (firm)	BP = C / o	A firm's capital cost per unit; its expended capital divided by its output
Market Price (sector)	MP = ΣV / Σo	The sector-wide average selling price; the sector's total value divided by total output
Markup (firm)	MU = MP - BP	The difference between a firm's breakeven price and the sector-wide selling price
Revenue (firm)	R = MP × o	A firm's income from selling commodities at the sector-wide market price
Profit (firm)	P = R - C = MU × o	A firm's profit; the difference between its revenue and expended capital, or the total markup on all output
Average Profit Rate (economy)	P′ = ΣS / ΣC	The economy-wide average rate of return; the economy's total surplus value divided by total invested capital
Profit (sector)	P = C × P′	A sector's profit, proportionate to the amount of invested capital and the economy-wide average profit rate
Revenue (sector)	R = C + P	A sector's income incorporating the expended capital and profit, expressed in monetary terms
Surplus Profit	SP = P - S = R - V	Gap between profit and surplus value, or between revenue and value
Profit Rate	p′ = S / C	Return on total capital invested, expressed in value terms
Monetary Profit Rate	m′ = P / C	Return on total capital invested, expressed in monetary terms
Monetary Expression of Labour Time	MELT = R / V	Converts labour-time into monetary units; links value to monetary magnitudes

Table 1. Glossary of Key Variables and Definitions

VALUE IN MOTION

'Value' holds a range of meanings in everyday language, but Marx and other classical economists related it specifically to human labour. My pillow's value equals the labour-time expended in its production, not the quality of my sleep. This focus on labour time doesn't reflect Marx's personal opinion; it's the system's fundamental logic. As already pointed out in the introduction, labour time plays a pivotal role in the various social struggles under capitalism.

Let me directly address three common reactions to this narrow definition of value. First, while it ties value under capitalism to labour time, it doesn't exclude other 'valuable' contributions from nature, households, or communities, known as use values. In fact, as we will see, there would be no value without use values. Workers need their tools. Furthermore, many use values do not have value in the Marxist sense. For example, a spring naturally provides water without any human labour. Finally, not everything that we value, in the colloquial sense, must be useful: Although today's economy favours timber plantations, I assign intrinsic value to biodiverse woodlands.

Second, although articulated in these specific terms, value remains largely hidden, contingent on production techniques, management methods, labour exploitation, etc. Unlike shape or colour, labour time invested can't be seen just by looking at an object. 'So far no chemist has ever discovered [value] either in a pearl or a diamond.'[80] Marx does not propose an instrument for measuring value; rather, he offers a means to understand it.

Third, an object's value as labour time diverges from its price, as price merely reflects value, and often inadequately. We intuitively feel this when we buy a t-shirt for five euros. While most of the world's population invests tremendous labour time in production and receives meagre compensation, a privileged minority contributes minimally yet reaps substantial rewards. To illustrate: In 2021, workers in the Global South provided ninety per cent of the world's labour power but received only 21 per cent of global income.[81] The divergence between price and value is precisely what enables wealth accumulation for the few from the toiling of the masses.

We will delve into these complexities later, but fundamentally, value emanates from human labour during production, not user satisfaction, relative demand, or a price tag. In all subsequent references to value, you can therefore mentally append the suffix '...as labour time normally invested in production' to represent the way Marxists approach the concept.

However, as this chapter's opening parable suggests, value in the labour form also shape-shifts to the money form. After it has been sold on the market, a product acquires a price – a specific monetary amount that more or less reflects its value. Marx refers to the goods and services produced for sale as commodities. Commodities therefore have a value and a price.

Now that we've established the origin of value in labour, what is its subsequent path?

First, value flows through the production of commodities. The infusion of value into commodities resembles the convergence of tributaries within a watershed. As illustrated in Diagram 1 (best read from bottom to top), a bushel of grain derives its value from the direct expenditure of labour time during cultivation, as well as the value of the farm equipment, such as a tractor. The tractor acquires value through the labour time and machinery involved in its production; a portion of its value is then transferred to the grain as indirect labour time. These various tributaries merge to form more substantial rivers, in much the same way that all labour time, both direct and indirect, combines to constitute a product's value.

The value of the product therefore represents human labour 'incorporated,' 'embodied,' or 'materialised,' or, in Marx's terminology, as 'a congealed mass of human labour.' Given the complexity of supply chains behind something as ostensibly simple as a bag of grain, its true value is ultimately unknowable and can only be approximated. Let me also flag that for value to pass into the product, labour itself must possess value. We will return to the source of this value in labour power in Chapter 3.

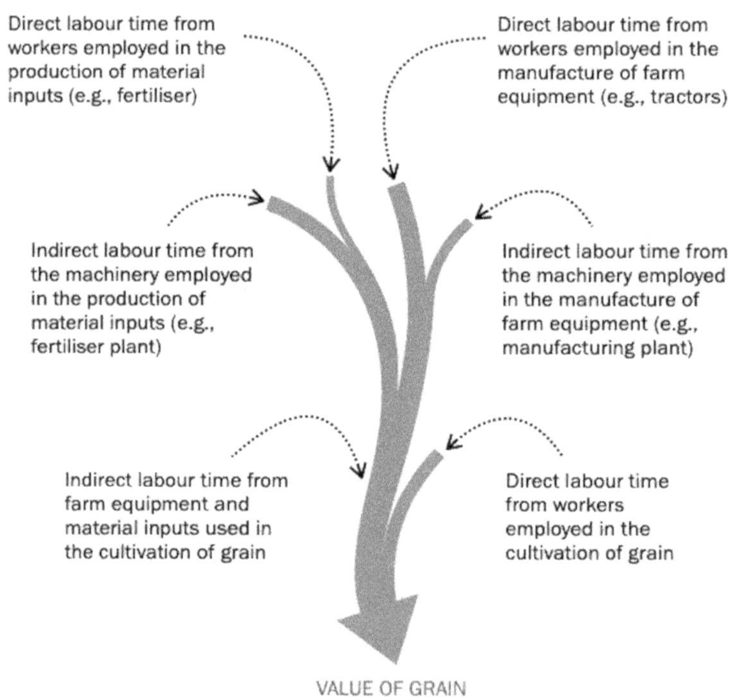

Diagram 1. Value from Production

Here's another example. Let me introduce Bob the burger chef. To understand the value of one of his hamburgers (say ten minutes of labour time), we must consider Bob's direct work in the kitchen (say, an average of eight minutes per hamburger), which Marxists sometimes refer to as 'living' labour time (see Diagram 2). Additionally, we should account for the indirect 'dead' labour time dedicated to making all the necessary tools and ingredients (say, two minutes per hamburger).

This last point may be less intuitive, and I will develop it more later, but for now imagine the following scenario: If 20,000 minutes of labour time are devoted to producing Bob's kitchen appliances, and those appliances can be used to produce 10,000 hamburgers before breaking down, then a single hamburger inherits two minutes of value as 'dead' labour time from those appliances.

Diagram 2. Living and Dead Labour

Now that we've seen how value flows through the production of commodities, let's look at how value flows through exchange (the Marxist term for trade). Exchange takes various forms, such as commodity-to-commodity exchange (co→co): direct barter without money. You might knit a pair of socks and trade those for a bunch of tomatoes from your neighbour.

However, as anthropologist David Graeber convincingly reveals, such exchange never actually existed; barter always involved (in)formal accounting to document the debt owed – what some call 'virtual' money (not physically existing). This allows you to trade warm socks in winter for tomatoes in the summer. Humans didn't start with barter, discover money, and then establish credit systems, but went precisely the opposite way.[82] Hence, the typical exchange followed a pattern of commodity-to-money-to-commodity (co→mo→co). A commodity sells for money, which is then spent to acquire another commodity. Money appears 'virtually' in barter as a unit of account and a store of value, allowing people to save and defer consumption.

Under capitalism, money also holds those functions but appears as currency rather than virtually. In fact, you likely engage in co→mo→co exchanges regularly: selling your labour (co) for a wage (mo), which you then spend on food, rent, etc. (co) (see Diagram 3). As with barter, this wage represents a debt. However, in this case, society at large owes you compensation for your labour, instead of the neighbour with whom you exchanged socks for tomatoes. A government-issued twenty-pound note in your pocket constitutes legal tender, meaning that you are entitled, by law, to goods or services worth twenty pounds. Money thus asserts a (usually solid) claim over present and future value.

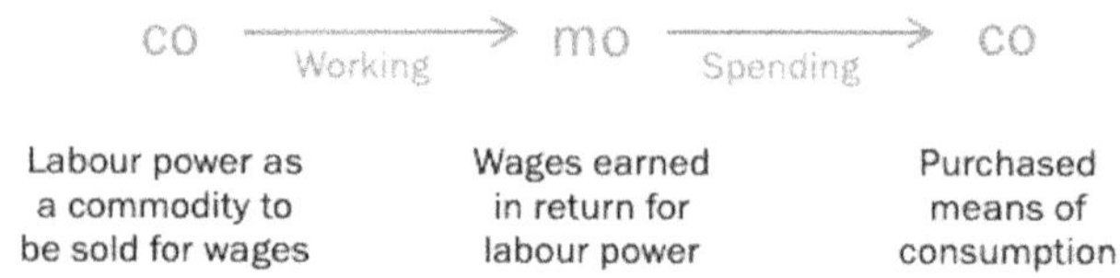

Diagram 3. Labour Circuit

To be clear: In the co→mo→co circuit under barter, money serves as payment for goods or services between independent producers; under capitalism, it is a wage, a payment for labour time. In this context, the circuit disconnects labour from its fruits. As the theorist André Gorz puts it, capitalism turns the worker/producer into a worker/consumer:

> [T]hat is, the social individual who produces nothing she or he consumes and consumes nothing he or she produces; for whom the essential objective of work is to earn enough to buy commodities produced and defined by the social machine as a whole.[83]

This disconnection represents a glaring form of alienation, or estrangement, depriving individuals of agency and control over what the system produces. Capitalism introduces a 'compulsion to trade:' autonomous producers choose when to engage, but wage-workers must trade or starve.[84]

The co→mo→co circuit contrasts sharply to the money-to-commodity-to-money (MO→CO→MO') circuit, in which only a small group operates: capitalists. They invest money (MO) to produce commodities (CO) to yield more money (MO'). The commodities' 'value exceeds that of their component parts,' Marx writes, 'and therefore contains the capital originally advanced plus a surplus value.'[85] There is a difference, as we'll discuss in Chapter 3, but for now, you can think of surplus value (S) as the extra labour time that gets realised as monetary profit, then reinvested for more production and profit. We therefore equate S to MO' minus MO (see Diagram 4).

Consider one last form of exchange. In the MO→CO→MO' circuit, capitalists invest money capital to produce and sell tangible goods and services. By contrast, financial capital represents money invested to increase

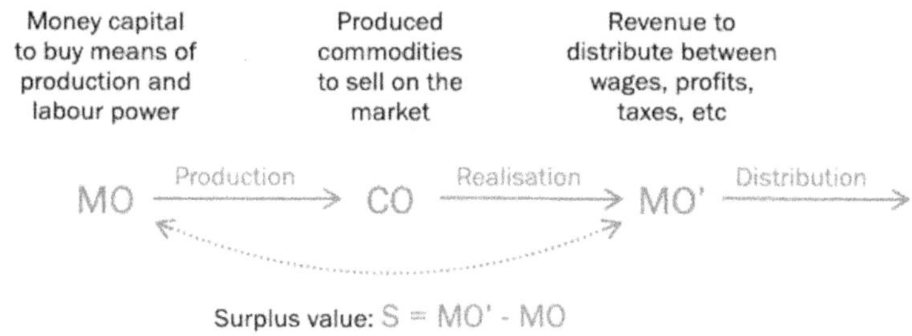

Diagram 4. Capitalist Circuit

monetary returns. For example, I could invest in a housing fund, wait for prices to rise, and sell my share for a profit. This money-to-money (MO1→MO1') circuit propels financial innovation and speculation intended only to multiply money. There is nothing productive about this circuit. In fact, it often destabilises the productive system by causing periodic crises.[86]

This is not a new phenomenon: Banks and industrial capital have long been intertwined, forming a financial oligarchy. To maximise profits beyond the domestic market, this merger creates finance capitalism to drive capital export and investment in the Global South,[87] as explored in Part 2.

Financial capitalists accelerate accumulation by modifying the traditional circuit of productive capitalists, shifting from MO→CO→MO' to MO1→(MO→CO→MO')→MO1'.[88] Here, MO1, a portion of the total capital invested (MO), is borrowed from a bank. Ultimately, MO1' is returned to the bank in the form of interest and loan repayments. MO1 can also originate from the profits of a firm unable or unwilling to reinvest in its own production. In this way, idle money capital becomes active, ensuring that capital continues to circulate and fostering accelerated accumulation. This is the essence of financialisation (see Diagram 5).

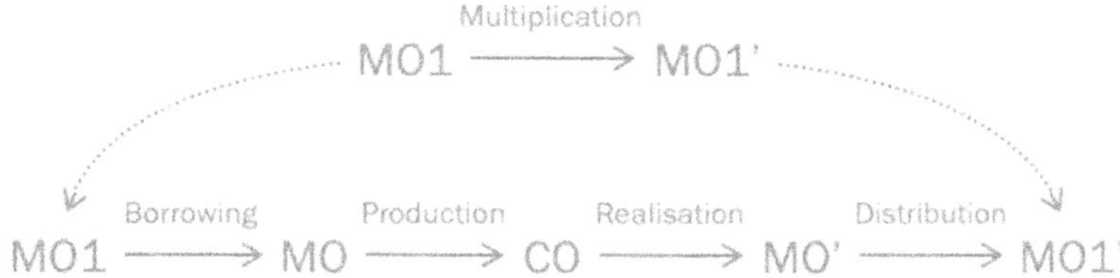

Diagram 5. Financialisation

Value therefore moves through exchange (co→mo→co and MO→CO→MO'). It is important to remember that exchange does not create value. Its creation arises from labour time in production, as per the watershed analogy (see Diagram 1).

MO→CO→MO' forms a cornerstone of Marxist theory, rather like Einstein's 'E = mc^2' in the domain of special relativity. The three moments are connected: commodity production from MO to CO; revenue realisation from CO to MO'; and revenue distribution from MO' onwards, then back to production. Through these connections, value isn't confined to money or material possession but flows between them. Hence why 'capital is not a thing;' it is a circulation process.[89]

'This cycle, in which the same phases are continually gone through in succession, forms the circulation of capital,' Marx tells us.[90] Harvey likens this circulation to water in the hydrological cycle, which 'depicts H_2O passing through different forms and states at different rates before returning to the oceans to start all over again. This is very similar to how capital moves.'[91] H_2O is the common substance in the hydrological cycle; capital plays a similar role in the economic cycle. It flows from monetary investment to means of production, then to output, revenue, profit, before finally returning as reinvestment. The cycle therefore includes the 'watershed' from Diagram 1, as well as a return of capital to the upstream source.

However, this analogy comes with a caveat: 'The volume of capital in motion is constantly expanding at a compound rate,'[92] Harvey warns. In Marx's own words, '[capital] expands itself as the subject of the circle and thus describes a self-expanding circle, a spiral' (see Diagram 6).[93] Capital doesn't merely circle like water; it expands. Herein lies the foundation of exponential economic growth, or more specifically capital accumulation: a self-amplifying mechanism that generates increasing surplus value with each iteration.

Capitalism? It's not pressing shift on a keyboard to make a letter big, as Vince in *Champions* joked – it's capital constantly hitting the self-expanding key to grow ever bigger. We're dealing with the system's internal drive itself, not yet the social or environmental constraints that might be imposed on it.

If value derives from production rather than exchange, so too does surplus value. Money (MO) may superficially appear to generate more money (MO') through risky ventures, innovative ideas, and entrepreneurial spirit. However, Marx uncovers a more profound process by linking the labour circuit (co→mo→co) to the capitalist circuit (MO→CO→MO'), as shown in Diagram 7.

Marx proposes that employees generate more value – surplus value (MO' minus MO) – in a workday than the value that they can claim with their daily wage (mo). Put simply, a McDonald's staff member may generate ninety dollars' worth of burgers per hour (produced commodities, CO), yet earn only around fourteen dollars per hour, allowing them to buy roughly

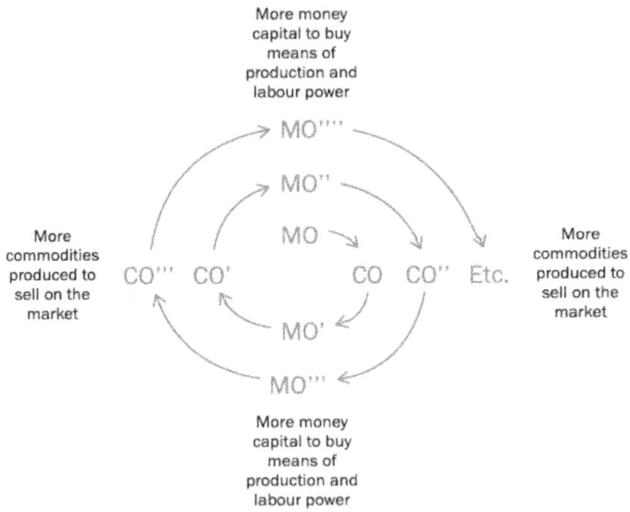

Diagram 6. Spiralling Value

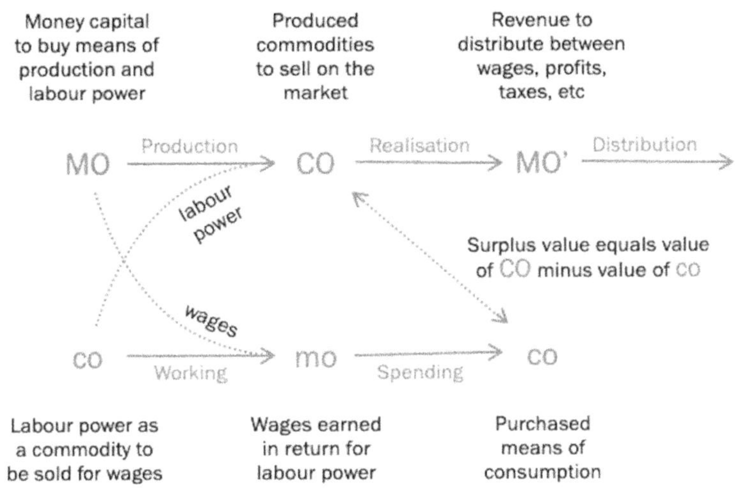

Diagram 7. Connecting the Capitalist and Labour Circuits

fifteen per cent of the value they create (purchased means of consumption, co) – leaving 85 per cent to be captured as surplus value by the company.[94] While this is a simplified explanation (as surplus value technically differs from profit), it suffices to clarify the source of surplus value.

Marx's *Capital* does not present an overview of value creation and motion but rather works through the process step by step. Each volume then homes in on different sub-systems: production, realisation, and distribution. The three combine to make up Marx's system. David Harvey turned this into a diagram,[95] which I've simplified further in Diagram 8.[96] Any such attempt will inevitably omit a great amount of detail, so see it as a rough sketch of what's to come.

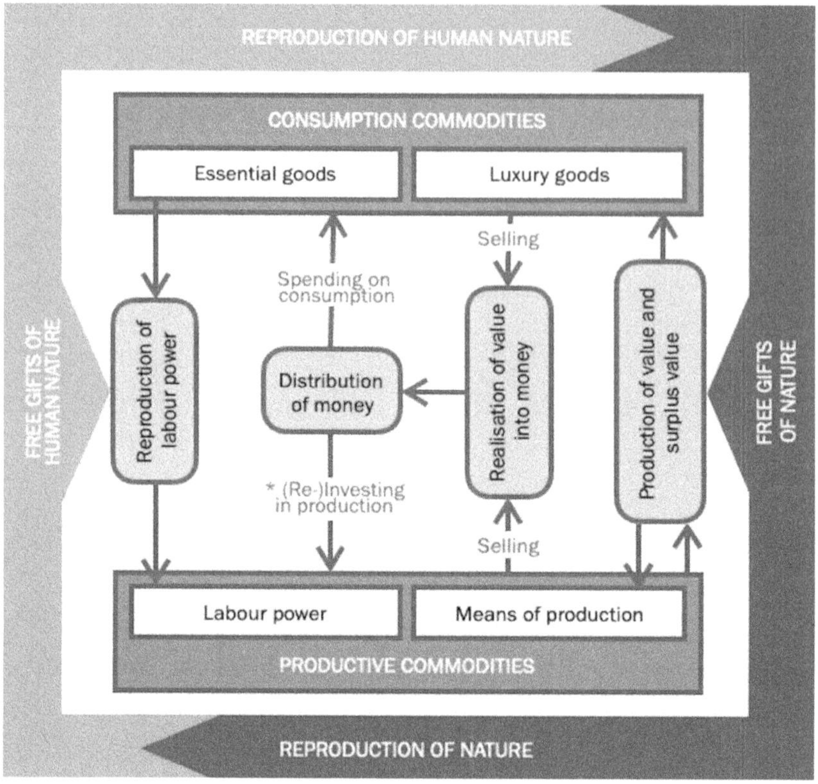

Diagram 8. Mapping Capital

Beginning at '*,' capitalists invest in capital (C) consisting of two productive commodities: labour power (termed 'variable capital,' v, by Marx) and means of production ('constant capital,' c), such as tools, supplies, or fuel. This investment (C = v + c) produces two other categories of commodity (broadly speaking): new means of production for other capitalists and commodities for consumption, encompassing essential goods for workers and luxury goods for the bourgeoisie, or capitalist class.

To generate a profit, value produced (V = c + v + S) must exceed the initial investments in productive commodities (C = c + v) by an amount that equates to surplus value (S). Diagram 9 shows how these elements connect. Surplus value can only arise when a productive commodity generates more value than the value needed for its (re)production – an attribute unique to labour power, as the McDonald's example illustrated. Constant capital can only transfer its value, its dead labour time, to the output of production; it cannot create value.

As mentioned previously, a commodity gets its value (including surplus value) during production. This value exists regardless of whether the commodity is sold. It is only after production that, through sale, this value is realised as revenue (R) (see Diagram 9). Then comes distribution, as revenue is allocated to stakeholders: wages to labour, taxes to government, interest to bankers, rents to landholders, dividends to shareholders, and profits to capitalists. The cycle then begins again, with capitalists reinvesting profits, labourers buying essential goods, and the bourgeoisie spending their fortunes on luxuries. I'm caricaturing here, as capitalists include small business owners who consume like regular people too.

Diagram 9. Revisited Capitalist Circuit

Like the collection of water in a watershed, with small streams forming a primary watercourse, value accumulates in commodities during production (see Diagram 1). At the same time, water evaporates from the ocean to form clouds, in a way that we can compare to the transformation of value: The liquid form (value) undergoes a transition into vapour (money). This then circulates back upstream, ready for reinvestment in further value production, akin to rain or snowfall in the watershed's recharge area.

I'd like to make one final observation regarding Diagram 8. Capitalism relies on two essential reproduction systems. Constant capital would not exist without the 'free gifts' of nature, while variable capital relies on the 'free gifts' of human nature. Capitalism not only squeezes surplus value from labour through exploitation, but also appropriates these gifts, often to the detriment of their underlying systems of reproduction, as I will describe later.

To bring this section to a close, let us recall the spirit shape-shifting from a gold nugget to a money pouch, a pack of rice, and eventually an intangible experience. The metamorphosis of value within capitalism begins with money capital being transformed into an outlay of constant and variable capital (c + v). Production transfers this value into new commodities, with labour contributing surplus value on top (V = c + v + S). Through exchange, value then transforms into prices and surplus value into profit, ready to shape-shift back into new outlays of variable and constant capital.

USE VALUE AND EXCHANGE VALUE

Marx's *Capital* isn't a pleasant tale of shape-shifting spirits; it is a stark revelation of the origins and evolution of real, profound, global disparities. The system under scrutiny relentlessly and unapologetically funnels wealth to a privileged minority, and it shows neither the capacity nor the intention to address the impoverishment of the majority. Moreover, the relative gains of the working classes in high-income countries have come at the expense of their counterparts elsewhere – a serious charge on capitalism that we will revisit later.

The book's general introduction already provided evidence for this, particularly of wealth inequalities. In those statistics, wealth was understood as covering money capital for production (MO→CO→MO'), financial capital for speculation (MO1→MO1'), and the market price of real estate, factories, land, and other privately-owned tangible assets. This accumulates in the hands of an ever-smaller group.

Marx's definition of wealth excludes money and encompasses only useful objects – referred to as 'use values' – created through human labour from natural resources. Examples of use values include a chair for relaxation, a bicycle for transportation, timber for producing chairs, or welding machines for producing bicycles. Non-human species also create use values, such as honey or medicinal plants. Furthermore, labour power itself stands as a use value for employers, namely the capacity to produce commodities that embody value and surplus value.

For Marxist theorists, use value points to an object's tangible, practical, sensory, or symbolic qualities. For instance, a tree offers practical use values such as shade and shelter, while fashionable clothing provides both the sensory use values of warmth and comfort along with symbolic use values of self-adornment and status (see example in Diagram 10). Moreover, use value applies not only in objects, but also to such organisms and experiences as bees, labour, and music, according to the uses made of them by humans.

Diagram 10. Value and Use Value of a Burger

Why exclude money from the definition of wealth? As previously discussed, money is a debt owed (MO in MO→CO→MO', as well as mo in co→mo→co). As Frederick Soddy notes, someone can own two pigs, but not 'minus two' pigs. One can of course owe someone two pigs, but that would denote a debt.[97] We must therefore see wealth as a tangible positive quantity and debt as an imaginary negative quantity.

This distinction helps to understand why certain segments of society can accumulate wealth while others cannot. A worker on a pig farm without pigs of his own typically exchanges his labour for wages to be spent on self-sustenance (co→mo→co). Another household might own some pigs but expend all disposable income on maintaining the farm (also co→mo→co). Yet another household with twenty pigs may hire a farm worker, generate profits, and augment their wealth (MO→CO→MO'). Some might even amass enough profit to invest in someone else's farm and earn a dividend (MO1→MO1'). The issue here is not one of scale, but of fundamentally different types of economic activity, with wealth and money playing very different roles in each scenario.

Wealth as use value takes us back to the moment our ancient ancestor first picked up a stick to use as a spear. Use values, therefore, shed little light on capitalism's specific workings. Things become interesting when we consider the dominant form of wealth in capitalist societies: commodities. As explained above, these are specifically produced for market sale, as opposed to wealth produced for the direct use or consumption of the producer. For instance, the burger that Bob fries for his lunch represents only a use value. If Bob fries it with the intention of selling it, the burger becomes a commodity.

To capitalists, use values only matter to the extent that objects perceived as useless can't be sold. In addition to use value, then, commodities must possess another identity: exchange value, that is, the potential to fetch a good price on the market. A burger from Bob's private kitchen has a use value, while a burger from his restaurant possesses both use value and exchange value. As a consumer, I appreciate the burger for its use value, but as a capitalist, I would solely be concerned with its exchange value and whether I can make a lucrative sale. Marxists therefore refer to these as the 'opposite poles' of a commodity.[98]

Why introduce the concept of exchange value instead of simply referring to price? Marxists will tell you that price in modern markets expresses a commodity's exchange value. But what exactly is meant by 'express'? How does price differ from exchange value?

Exchange value reveals the ratios governing the barter of commodities. For instance, Bob might estimate that one of his hamburgers is worth, in terms of labour time, one hundred of Rick's toothpicks, where one toothpick corresponds to one hundredth of a burger (see Diagram 11). If Bob and Rick actually swap a burger for toothpicks, the burger's exchange value equals a given number of toothpicks. However, if the burger is traded for money rather than toothpicks, its exchange value equals its price. The question is: Does price adequately reflect value?

Based on these ratios, in the hypothetical perfect market where a burger costs one dollar, a toothpick should cost \$0.01 (\$1 × 1 / 100) (see Diagram 11). Because it homogenises and simplifies the comparison and exchange of diverse commodities, Marxists refer to money as the 'universal equivalent' of exchange value.

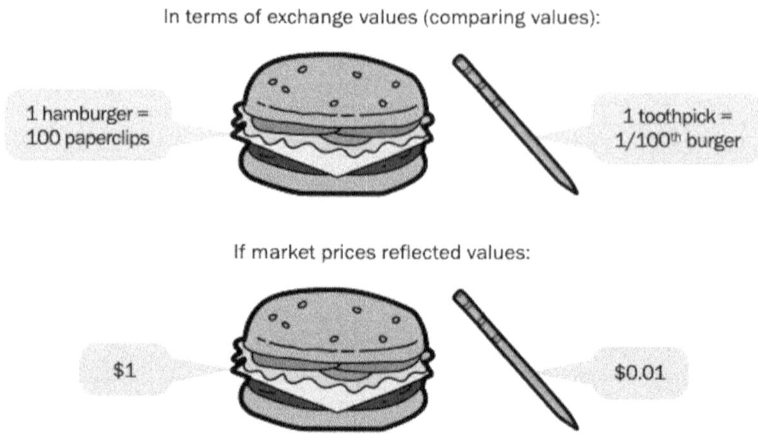

Diagram 11. Aligned Values and Prices

In a local economy where producers and buyers are well-informed about production methods, an item's exchange value based on relative human effort may be easier to estimate. It's easy enough for you and your neighbour to agree on how many tomatoes to trade for a pair of socks. Relative prices may then also better reflect exchange value. In today's globalised world, however, tracing the sources of value through complex supply chains is nearly impossible, making prices a highly imperfect representation of exchange value proportions.

Prices are subject to supply, demand, elasticity, negotiation, speculation, inflation, delays, monopolies, pandemics, and myriad other factors that have nothing to do with the commodities' inherent exchange values. Consequently, a commodity's price can vary from one exchange to the next. Middlemen who stockpile goods and wait for demand to rise are well aware of this. The resulting price-value gaps imply situations where a buyer obtains either more or less value than their payment warrants.

Reflecting on a commodity's exchange value therefore involves taking the following two dimensions into account:[99] its relative value in exchange, and the price measurement of this value. Capitalists might care about exchange values; for instance, Bob must sell one burger to buy one hundred toothpicks. However, as values are unknown, capitalists care only about prices; Bob simply aims to buy toothpicks inexpensively and sell burgers expensively.

For classical economists, human labour was the source of value; this then influences commodity prices (along with other factors). Neoclassical economists disagreed, believing that price reveals consumer sentiment towards a product – the satisfaction or 'utility' that they derive (or anticipate) from it. So, rather than unravelling the origin of value and its effect on price, the neoclassical school simply presumed that price is a good measure of a commodity's value, and that we need look no further.

The supposed equivalence of use value and exchange value therefore means that one or other can be dropped from the neoclassical lexicon.[100] Their definition of value conflates use value and price, by assuming that a consumer's perception of a product's use value determines its price (and therefore its exchange value). Representing greater use value, a burger arguably costs more than a toothpick.

This is, of course, fairly intuitive. We choose products based on our needs, wants, and desires, and our collective shopping behaviour influences prices. However, treating this as the whole story is deeply problematic. Moreover, a narrative that focuses solely on price is ultimately inconsistent. Let me explain.

The neoclassical view that prices reflect use values creates a paradox:[101] Essential use values can cost considerably less than decadent ones. A one-carat diamond costs more than twelve Olympic-size swimming pools' worth of life-sustaining water.[102] Economists have worked around this paradox by asserting that people prioritise indispensable needs such as potable water over trivial desires such as blowing soap bubbles. Each additional unit of water consumed adds satisfaction, but incrementally less. However, this tempering effect is less pronounced for scarce commodities such as diamonds. In other words, the added satisfaction from acquiring additional diamonds surpasses that of water, resulting in higher prices for diamonds than water.

Economists call this convoluted logic the 'theory of marginal utility,' where 'marginal' means the last unit of something: that 'one more cookie' a parent reluctantly agrees to. Marginal utility is thus the supplementary utility accrued from consuming that last unit.[103] As price reflects marginal utility, a diamond's utility – and price – exceeds that of water. Paradox resolved. Or so it seems, for this reasoning is flawed.

The theory of marginal utility tortuously circles back to a labour time notion of value, though this is not typically something its proponents concede. In a competitive market, prices tend to settle where consumers' willingness to pay for one more unit equals the marginal cost of producing it. Scarce goods generally have higher marginal costs: Obtaining an additional diamond typically requires a greater investment of (direct and indirect) labour time than obtaining an additional quantity of water.[104] In this sense, the diamond's exchange value exceeds that of water, which partly explains their relative prices (though the relationship is not straightforward, as we shall see in Chapter 4).

In the Marxist value framework, the paradox never existed: Use and exchange value can move in different directions. While water has a lower exchange value, its use value is far greater (more universal and fundamental) than a diamond's, whose use value lies largely in their role as signs of wealth and status.

The marginal utility reasoning is also deeply problematic. It assumes a direct relationship between utility and price, without considering economic disparities. Soap bubbles, much like golf course sprinklers, private swimming pools, and other extravagant uses of water, exist alongside and even contribute to severe shortages of potable water. The affluent, with more disposable income, indulge in such lavish uses, which in turn drive up water prices. Meanwhile, individuals facing dire shortages undoubtedly desire the potential utility of water but cannot afford it. As sociologist and economist Thorstein Veblen explains, the pricing of certain goods is influenced more by symbolic than practical use value.[105]

Likewise, grain prices do not accurately reflect grain's use value for the undernourished poor. Among other factors, grain prices are raised by the demand for fodder crops destined for meat and dairy production, primarily to cater to better-off consumers. Were it not for this heightened demand, these prices would be lower. The economist Amartya Sen suggested that this outcome shouldn't surprise us: 'Market demands are not reflections of biological needs or psychological desires, but choices based on exchange entitlement relations.'[106] He famously revealed that famines often occur after market forces siphon food away from destitute regions to markets with greater purchasing power, thus exposing the stark mismatch between food's potential use value and its price.

But enough about this mad theory of marginal utility. The water-diamond paradox exposes the superficial grasp and potential inconsistencies that come with theories centred on market prices. Marx classified the neoclassical fixation on the market as 'vulgar economics.'[107] His value framework unravels the origin of value before considering its effect on exchange value, and only then its effect on price, as we will see. His fundamental premise: If the exchange value of a toothpick equals, for instance, one per cent of the exchange value of a burger, then these two commodities must share an intangible attribute that they possess to varying degrees – value as labour time invested in production. So, let us now go deeper into this notion of labour time.

VALUE AS LABOUR TIME

A commodity's value in capitalism originates from human effort. Specifically, value equals the average time, or socially necessary labour time, directly and indirectly needed to produce the commodity. A burger is 'worth' more than a toothpick (in the theoretical, not colloquial, sense) because, on average, it takes more labour power to produce. A diamond is worth more than millions of gallons of water, because of the greater amount of labour time involved in discovering, extracting, and processing the mineral. Some of its value also comes from the labour time involved in producing the mining equipment and infrastructure (see earlier Diagram 1). This logic equally applies to the value of intangible services, such as health care or education.

Crucially, it takes different producers different lengths of time to produce the same commodity. Value therefore arises from the average time required to produce a commodity under normal conditions in the context in question. It therefore averages or homogenises the hours of skilled and unskilled workers. Otherwise, a chair made by a slower, inexperienced carpenter would be worth more than that of their faster, expert colleague. Similarly, if Bob gets tired and asks his daughter to take over in the kitchen, her halving the time it takes him to cook a burger does not make her burger half as valuable.

We know that looking at a burger cannot reveal the direct and indirect hours it took to make, the number of workers involved, or their working conditions. All we see is its price, a mere expression of its value. Marx was interested in understanding what drives value in capitalism, how it is produced, who accumulates it, and how it affects prices. To do this, we must look beyond the façade of prices and markets, and into the realm of value and production.

Critics point out that commodity prices rarely align with the labour time needed to produce them. The difference can be substantial. The relative prices of a Picasso painting and one of mine (if I painted) don't stem from Pablo spending heaps more time at the easel than me. Indeed, prices do not adequately reflect value. Rather, capitalists and merchants attach price tags, which express – often quite badly – their products' value.

Without a doubt, prices and values frequently diverge, but this does not invalidate the theory. In the first two volumes of *Capital*, Marx deliberately simplifies by assuming that prices do in fact align with values. However, in the third volume, he abandons this simplification precisely to investigate their deviation.

Prices fluctuate for reasons that have nothing to do with values: a blocked shipping lane, a consumer craze, a war. Still, it is important to comprehend values because they both attract and repel prices, much like orbital motion, where gravity pulls the Earth towards the Sun while the centrifugal effect pushes it away. This doesn't mean that value represents an equilibrium at which prices eventually settle. Values themselves change all the time as we develop new production techniques and skills. As a result, the system never reaches equilibrium; it never rests.

You might still be wondering about this price-value gap and the earlier claim that buyers receive more or less value than what they paid, especially since it involves comparing labour time to money across commodities, such as the value of apples and the price of pears.

We will look more closely at such intricacies later (see Chapter 4). For now, let's return to burgers and toothpicks. Ignoring dead/indirect labour for the sake of simplicity, and focusing on living/direct labour, suppose it takes Bob a thousand minutes of labour to produce burgers that sell for a total of one hundred dollars. This results in a ratio of total price to total value of \$0.1 per minute (= \$100 / 1,000m). This price-to-value ratio is called the 'Monetary Expression of Labour Time' (MELT).

To be clear, MELT isn't a wage rate, but the price of a unit of value. A commodity's price should cover not just wages, but also profits, taxes, and so on. In MELT, this price is divided by total labour time expended in production. As said, this would normally also include indirect labour time, but I am keeping it simple for now.

In Scenario 1, Table 2, where prices align perfectly with values and MELT consistently remains at \$0.1 per minute, a single burger, requiring ten minutes of labour to produce, should be priced at one dollar. Similarly, a toothpick, requiring 0.1 minute, should be priced at \$0.01 (see also earlier Diagram 11). In this scenario:

- Unit Values (UV): 1 UV_{burger} = 100 $UV_{toothpick}$ (1 × 10m = 100 × 0.1m)
- Market Prices (MP): 1 MP_{burger} = 100 $MP_{toothpick}$ (1 × \$1 = 100 × \$0.01)

Discrepancies between values and prices come about if, for some reason, commodities sell below or above their value. Scenario 2 shows different MELTs for burgers (\$0.05 per minute) and toothpicks (\$0.15 per minute). However, when considering the aggregate, the total hours of labour expended remains ten times greater than total prices paid. For this scenario, I made adjustments only to the market prices, without altering the quantities produced or labour times involved. Now, prices and values misalign:

- Unit Values (UV) as before: 1 UV_{burger} = 100 $UV_{toothpick}$ (1 × 10m = 100 × 0.1m)
- Market Prices (MP): 1 MP_{burger} = 33 $MP_{toothpick}$ (1 × \$0.5 = 33 × \$0.015)

From this, we can deduce that disparities between values and prices occur when certain commodities sell below their value (burgers in Scenario 2), while others sell above it (toothpicks in Scenario 2). It's crucial to grasp this logic because, as we will see, commodities with high MELTs are traded globally for commodities with low MELTs – an asymmetry that monetary trade statistics fail to show, and the essence of unequal exchange.

Having established this way to understand the exchanging of commodities above or below their value, let's turn to a deeper exploration of value itself.

	Scenario 1: Prices and values align			Scenario 2: Prices and values misalign		
	Burgers	Toothpicks	Total / Ratio	Burgers	Toothpicks	Total / Ratio
Unit Value (UV)	10m	0.1m	100/1	10m	0.1m	100/1
Output (o)	100	10,000	1/100	100	10,000	1/100
Value (V = UV × o)	1,000m	1,000m	2,000m	1,000m	1,000m	2,000m
Market Price (MP)	$1.00	$0.01	100/1	$0.50	$0.02	33/1
Revenue (R = MP × o)	$100	$100	$200	$50	$150	$200
MELT (R / V)	0.10$/m	0.10$/m	0.10$/m	0.05$/m	0.15$/m	0.10$/m

Table 2. Monetary Expression of Labour Time

The burger-toothpick economy symbolises the reality for many disparate goods and services. The human work needed to produce them also differs greatly but, through exchange values and prices, the system homogenises and ignores the idiosyncrasies of the specific tasks and concrete experiences involved.

Marx would, therefore, designate Bob's work as he chops vegetables, fries beef, and slices buns as 'concrete labour.' In contrast, 'abstract labour' pertains to the work that imparts commodities with quantities of value. In the capitalist economy, a hamburger's exchange value isn't determined by the concrete tasks that Bob undertakes, but rather by the average labour time required for burger production. His labour has become abstract or homogenous,[108] because ten minutes spent by Bob preparing a burger equates to ten minutes spent by Rick producing one hundred toothpicks. Technically speaking, average ('socially necessary') labour time therefore consists of abstract, not concrete, labour.

In short, the dual character of the commodity (as use and exchange value) corresponds to a dual character of labour. Labour's use value is concrete and qualitative: farming, building, trucking, etc., while its exchange value is abstract and quantitative: labour time. In concrete labour, time for working overlaps with time for living. Abstract labour severs the latter. Indeed, the system often makes it painfully clear just how easily we can be replaced, how abstract our work really is.

So far, our burger sector has consisted only of Bob. Let's bring in some competition. Imagine Bob tries to sell his burgers at two dollars apiece, a rate that he deems fair compensation for his concrete efforts. Regrettably, his burgers go unsold as the prevailing market price stands at one dollar. Bob must act to stay in business. To lower his price, he could discipline himself into working faster than his competitors, or procure cheaper ingredients from producers that work faster than their competitors. Price variations are therefore partly driven by variations in labour time, including its exploitation – which Bob must inflict upon himself to compete. This is how we have all internalised the master's whip. Being relatively slower at producing burgers, Bob must either step up or bow out. Until then, he will be forced to sell burgers at the prevailing price, even if it means accepting below-average profits. The point here is that competition forces more intensive and/or productive work. Allow me to clarify the difference.

Various factors affect labour time, including work environment, skill, motivation, discipline, and technology (an account of natural resources will come later). In short, an increase in the quantity of goods produced over a given period can be attributed to either the productivity of technology or the intensity of labour power.

Suppose Bob looks for someone to replace him in the kitchen. The standard daily wage for a burger chef stands at one hundred dollars. A piece rate of one dollar indicates that an average chef, with average skills and utensils, would produce one hundred burgers a day,[109] whereas a skilled chef may demand a higher wage but make two hundred burgers with the same tools, through greater work intensity. The work can also be made more intensive by optimising workflow processes to eliminate inefficiencies and distractions.

Alternatively, automating production would increase productivity by enabling a higher output per worker in a certain timeframe. Bob could invest in an electric food processor, allowing the average chef to chop, slice, and dice vegetables more rapidly, thereby upping their daily output to two hundred burgers. This enhancement increases productivity, not intensity. Machines represent important use values in capitalist production as they boost the worker's capacity to produce more. Therefore, one should speak of the productivity of technology rather than that of labour.

Often, increased productivity and intensity go hand in hand. We see this clearly illustrated in the film *Modern Times* (1936), in which Charlie Chaplin plays a factory worker tasked with tightening bolts on a conveyor belt. In one iconic scene, Chaplin is equipped with a feeding device that eliminates lunch breaks. Together, the conveyor belt and feeding machine increase productivity and intensity, respectively. Amazon distribution centres, the modern equivalent of Chaplin's factory, increase intensity by enforcing strict bathroom breaks and prohibiting workers from sitting down, outside of their unpaid thirty-minute lunch break. Amazon also increases productivity with automated conveyor belts and individual productivity goals, which boost workers' output per unit of time.[110]

In a nutshell, Bob can boost output by either having a chef work more intensively with the same tools, or more productively with new ones. Either way, more commodities are produced in the same time. However, only increased intensity generates more value per unit of time. This is something of a puzzle, so let's go through it step by step.

If Bob's chef spent less time chatting with customers and more time preparing burgers, he would be working more intensively and producing more value. By contrast, a new food processor would allow him to work more productively and prepare more burgers in the same length of time. However, this would also mean that the value of each individual burger decreases. Increased productivity only leads to an increase in quantity, while the value embedded in each unit falls. Indeed, a commodity's unit value, though directly related to the average labour time required to produce it, is inversely related to productivity: '[M]ore intense labour produces more use-values and more value; more productive labour produces more use-values but the same value.'[111]

This may sound counterintuitive but remember that machines do not create value. Instead, as they depreciate during their productive life, machines convey their value, bit by bit, to whatever they produce. The food processor's value gradually transfers to Bob's burgers. Previously, I drew a parallel between the infusion of value into commodities and the convergence of tributaries within a watershed (see Diagram 1). Bob's chef contributes direct, living labour time to the burger; the food processor, along with the burger's ingredients, contribute indirect, dead labour time.

A final note on the link between intensity and productivity. In a capitalist system, technical innovations increase productivity and expedite work by eliminating interruptions and fostering discipline. This also heightens the intensity of labour. A knitter using a machine can complete in one hour what would take a manual knitter ten hours – or up to twelve when factoring in breaks. Despite their close connection, intensity and productivity remain separate factors that impact a commodity's value in different ways.

COMPONENTS AND COMPOSITION OF CAPITAL

These are the basic components of capital discussed thus far:

- Constant capital (c) refers to the value gradually transmitted by machines, materials, and other productive inputs to their output. This value represents past, dead labour time and contributes nothing more than its own value. Constant capital encompasses the following:
    - Instruments of production (ci): This category includes buildings, tools, and equipment. Their value is gradually transferred to the commodities produced in accordance with the instruments' rate of depreciation.
    - Materials of production (cm): This category comprises raw materials, supplies, and energy consumed in the production process. The entirety of their value is transferred to the commodities in accordance with their rate of consumption (minus the value of inevitable waste materials).
- Variable capital (v) refers to the immediate, living labour time expended during production and subsequently infused as value into the output. The term 'variable' signifies that the imparted value varies depending on the rate of exploitation (we will get to this later).
- The total capital invested equals the sum of constant and variable capital (C = c + v).

Consider the following quantitative illustration (see Table 3). For simplicity's sake, let's assume a monetary expression of labour time (MELT) of one dollar per hour. A capitalist invests fifty dollars' worth of capital to establish a burger restaurant (depicted as 'MO' in Diagram 4). With a MELT of one, this capital (C) embodies fifty hours' worth of value. The investment is allocated as follows: Forty dollars is spent on a chef (v = 40h), six dollars invested in a grill (ci = 6h), and four dollars spent on ingredients, water, gas, and related expenses (cm = 4h). With that, the investment in constant capital (c = ci + cm = 10h) amounts to ten dollars. Using Marx's notation system, which involves the suffixes c, ci, cm, or v to indicate value compositions, the capital invested can be expressed as: 50C = 10c + 40v = (6ci + 4cm) + 40v.

The relative proportions of these components tell us something about the level of technological advancement within a firm, sector, or economy.

Money capital (MO = C × MELT, with MELT = 1$/h)	$50
Capital invested (C = c + v), including:	50h
Variable capital (v)	40h
Constant capital (c = ci + cm), including:	10h
Instruments of production (ci)	6h
Materials of production (cm)	4h
Organic composition (OC = c / v)	0.25

Table 3. Components of Capital

Marx provides a measure for this advancement in the concept of the 'organic composition of capital' (OC), calculated as the ratio of constant to variable capital (c / v), or machines to workers. In this case, OC = 10c / 40v = 0.25 (Table 3). A higher organic composition indicates that constant capital makes up a more substantial portion of total capital. In neoclassical terms, this translates to a more 'capital-intensive' production process. Conversely, a lower composition signifies a more 'labour-intensive' process. As noted earlier, Marx uses the terms 'capital' and 'intensive' differently. Transportation and telecommunications typically have higher organic compositions of capital than, say, healthcare and hospitality.

The goal of adopting more mechanised and automated production methods may be to increase productivity. Increased productivity implies a higher organic composition, as more machines and materials are deployed. However, the reverse isn't always true: An increase in the organic composition of capital doesn't necessarily mean higher productivity and might simply reflect changes in the value of constant or variable capital. For instance, Bob might use a high-end cooker that embodies more value but performs no better than his competitor's cheaper model. That's more constant capital, not more output. Or he might hire a certified chef with years of training, while his competitor employs an equally productive but self-taught cook. That's more variable capital, not more productivity. In both cases, the organic composition changes without any impact on productivity.

Let me end this section with a note about the use of materials. It is important to distinguish between virgin natural resources and the materials of production (cm) discussed so far. Marx refers to natural resources as 'furnished by Nature gratis,'[112] to reflect the tendency to treat the natural prerequisites of production, such as underground minerals and soil fertility, as free gifts (see Diagram 8).

Consider crude oil. It is not the product of human labour but the result of ancient sunlight and photosynthesis. While it clearly possesses use value, crude oil holds no value in the Marxist sense until it enters the labour process. When oil companies acquire it, they do not pay the biosphere for having created the oil; they pay landowners for accessing it. This rent may reflect the relative ease or difficulty of extraction (factors tied to labour, energy, and technology) but the oil itself, in its natural state, is essentially 'on the house.'

The key point is this: It is only through human labour that this 'free gift' can be transformed into gasoline, plastics, and chemicals. In doing so, labour confers value upon the crude oil and integrates it into the production process, specifically as constant capital, in the form of materials of production (cm). We will discuss this in greater detail in Chapter 7.

CLOSING REMARKS

Let's recapitulate. In capitalism, a commodity's value is not determined by its practical use value, which is the subjective utility it has for the end user, nor by its commercial exchange value, which is the proportion in which it can be exchanged with other commodities. Instead, value is determined by socially necessary labour time: the average time involved, directly and indirectly, in its production.

The recognition that commodities possess both use and exchange value predates capitalism. In the fourth century BC, Aristotle observed that '[e]very article or property has a double use… [A] shoe may be used either to put on your foot or to offer in exchange.'[113] What distinguishes the commodity under capitalism is not this dual character, nor even its embodiment of surplus value – this, too, was extracted in earlier societies, occasionally through the exploitation of hired labour, but mostly through direct coercion, such as tribute, corvée, or slavery. No, what sets capitalist commodities apart is that they are produced systematically to generate surplus value, which is extracted primarily through 'free' wage labour and realised as profit through market exchange. Once converted into profit, it can be reinvested, thereby fuelling accumulation.

The next chapter will further scrutinise this concept of surplus value, as well as its relation to the exploitation of labour, its distinction from profit, and its role in the so-called expanded reproduction of capital.

3. Surplus Value

OPENING REMARKS

In 1948, the McDonald brothers started selling burgers for half the price and in half the time of competing restaurants, replacing waitresses with self-service counters and keeping pre-cooked burgers warm under powerful heat lamps. Although such practices are now commonplace, the brothers found a way to boost their profits and jump ahead of the entire fast-food sector.[114]

Business magazines and blogs teem with this kind of success story: capitalists making killer profits by outwitting their rivals. These stories breed a belief in 'the power of the profit motive to deliver profits,'[115] to quote one investment strategist.

While firms may indeed amass profits at the expense of others, as we will discover, these stories fail to acknowledge that surplus value, the source of all profit, arises from labour – not from the clever minds of entrepreneurs. Brief reminder: Capital invested equals constant plus variable capital ($C = c + v$), and value produced exceeds initial investment by an amount of surplus value ($V = c + v + S$). Surplus value arises from the difference between the value created by workers and the value that their wages mean they can afford.

Or, to put it plainly: Capitalism's exploitative dynamic relies on employers monopolising the means of production and extracting as much surplus value as possible from propertyless, wage-dependent employees. This is precisely what prompted overworked and underpaid fast-food workers to issue formal complaints against their employers.[116] Triumphant portrayals of the competitive game ignore this dark underbelly.

SURPLUS FROM LABOUR

While capitalist accumulation originates in surplus value, accumulation can only occur after surplus value has metamorphosed into monetary profit that can be reinvested. One cannot reinvest labour time. And then, surplus value can only metamorphose into profit once capitalists successfully sell their goods (and value metamorphoses into price). In Chapter 5, we'll see how a firm's profits can either exceed or fall short of its surplus value (in the way prices diverge from values, as illustrated earlier in Table 2). For now, let us assume that they align.

For surplus value and its offspring, profit, to come about – indeed, for capitalism to exist at all – labour must exert greater effort than in a hypothetical economy where goods are sold at prices that match invested capital. Such an economy reproduces itself but doesn't accumulate. Accumulation requires that extra effort.

Consider slavery. All the value (V) produced by plantation slaves in a given day immediately belongs to the master. The master allocates a portion to the slaves in the form of shelter, sustenance, and clothing, thus securing their labour for the next day (v). Another portion maintains the plantation's equipment and restocks supplies (c). The remainder accrues to the master as surplus value (S).

Capitalism today differs from slavery in that, generally speaking, bosses do not directly dispense the necessities required by workers to reproduce their labour power. Instead, workers must purchase these goods from them by first earning a wage. Capitalism thus commodifies work, not the worker. As a commodity, labour power therefore possesses an exchange value, represented by a wage.

Historically, of course, slavery was foundational to capitalism.[117] Marx understood that 'the turning of Africa into a warren for the commercial hunting of black-skins [sic], signalised the rosy dawn of the era of capitalist production.'[118] And despite its formal abolition, slavery persists in multiple forms today. Indeed, an estimated 28 million people are victims of modern slavery, with 63 per cent engaged in forced labour within the private sector – a number that continues to grow.[119]

While the systems differ in their reproduction of labour power, capitalism clearly also takes after slavery, as both systems extract surplus value from the worker. Moreover, both systems divide the working day into periods of so-called necessary labour and surplus labour.[120] During the necessary part of the workday, workers produce a value equivalent to the value that they will purchase with their wages (or receive in kind in the case of slavery). The surplus part generates capitalist surplus value.

As a 'free' employed academic, I could just walk out halfway through a two-hour lecture, calculating that by that point, my employer will have accrued from student fees (minus operational costs) precisely what it owes me in wages. After all, I have already fulfilled the necessary labour for which I am to be compensated. However, my contract obliges me to contribute an additional hour of 'unpaid' surplus labour to conclude the lecture and generate a surplus for the university. 'The Roman slave was held by fetters: The wage labourer is bound to his owner by invisible threads.'[121]

In a sense, we already work overtime during official working hours. I'm not referring to the usual concept of overtime, which happens outside official hours. In 2024, for example, workers in Europe were logging an average of 9.2 hours of unpaid overtime every week.[122]

Technically speaking, in the above example, the rate at which I'm being exploited is one hundred per cent: My two-hour lecture consists of one hour of paid necessary labour plus one additional hour of unpaid surplus labour (1h + 1h × 100% = 2h). So, for every 'paid' hour, I 'volunteer' another, as depicted in Graph 5. In other words, if the rate of surplus value is one hundred per cent, I must work two hours to afford goods embodying one hour of average labour time. My employer appropriates the remaining hour as surplus value. Earlier, Diagram 7 depicted this surplus value as the difference between the value embodied in 'co' (commodities consumed by labour) and 'CO' (commodities produced by labour). I don't mean that my employer pays me from nine to ten in the morning and appropriates my time from ten to eleven, but rather that every moment, whether a month, an hour, or a second in length, consists of both types of labour.

How does my situation differ from that of a lower-paid teaching assistant? In that case, Graph 5 shows that a rate of three hundred per cent would mean half an hour of necessary labour and one and a half hour of surplus labour (0.5h + 0.5h × 300% = 2h). Marx refers to this percentage as the rate of surplus value, or the rate of labour exploitation. I'll refer to it simply as surplus rate (s'). It is important to emphasise that I am subject to the surplus rate, irrespective of my ability to measure it and my awareness of its existence.

I'll revisit this later, but the value created by the lecture isn't measured purely by clock time – or 'concrete labour,' as defined in Chapter 2. Workers' concrete time impart different amounts of value based on training and

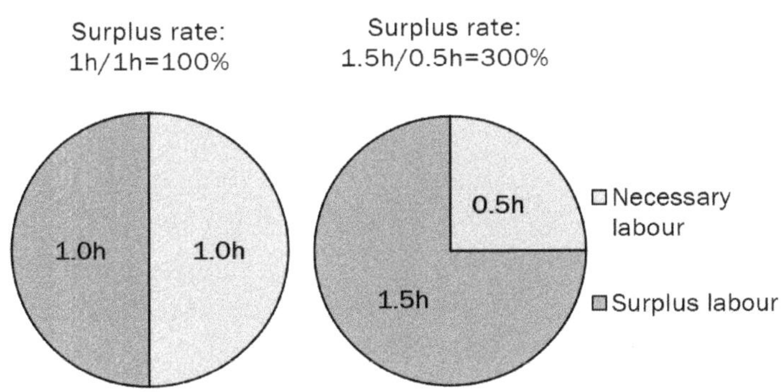

Graph 5. Surplus Rate.
This graph shows the distribution of necessary and surplus labour in a two-hour lecture for two different surplus rates.

experience. Thus, my hour of surplus labour and my teaching assistant's one and a half hours aren't directly comparable: I might still impart more surplus value. But let's leave that for now.

It is also important to emphasize that my exploitation begins not in production but in exchange, with the contract for the purchase of my labour power that fixes my wages and working hours. At this point, I know only my earnings (the 'nominal' wage); its purchasing power (the 'real' wage) becomes apparent only later, when I purchase consumption goods.[123] Only then does the difference between the two hours of labour I perform and the one hour of value my wage commands arise.

Employers typically seek to increase surplus labour, the wellspring of profit. They have two ways to do this. Let's consider a workday divided into six hours of necessary labour time and three hours surplus labour time, as shown in row I in Graph 6.

Firstly, employers can increase surplus labour within the same nine-hour workday, as shown in row II. When we increase the surplus rate from fifty to one hundred per cent, we get a 1.5-hour increase in what is known as 'relative' surplus labour, and an equivalent drop in necessary labour. Employers achieve this through wage cuts or contracting low-wage producers. For example, outsourcing call centre services from Australia to India lowers the hourly minimum wage rate from $17.5 to $0.27.[124] As I will explain later, relative surplus labour can also increase without any reduction in wages, namely through an increase in productivity. This will become clear after a few further conceptual steps.

Secondly, employers can extend the workday, or outsource to countries with longer working hours, while maintaining the same surplus rate. Row III shows a workday that is three hours longer than in row I. With the same surplus rate (s' = 50%), surplus labour increases from three to four hours – a one-hour increase in what is referred to as 'absolute' surplus labour. For example, the average working week in India is 46 hours, compared to 32.8 in Australia.[125] Increasing the intensity of labour (as explained in Chapter 2) also leads to an increase in 'absolute' surplus labour, for example by shortening or eliminating breaks during the working day.

Lastly, row IV depicts a scenario where employers increase both surplus rate and work duration. Here, surplus labour increases from three to six hours, as a combination of increased relative and absolute surplus labour. While Australian workers might fall under the scenario in row I, Indian workers align with row IV, enduring both lower wages and longer working hours.

I already pointed out that capitalism can only exist when labour produces more value than the value they purchase with their wages. I wish to note here that global trade allows some higher-wage earners to actually consume more value than they produce – a contentious issue to which I return in Chapter 6.[126] Under capitalism, this can only occur when goods are imported from places where lower-wage earners consume much less value than they produce.

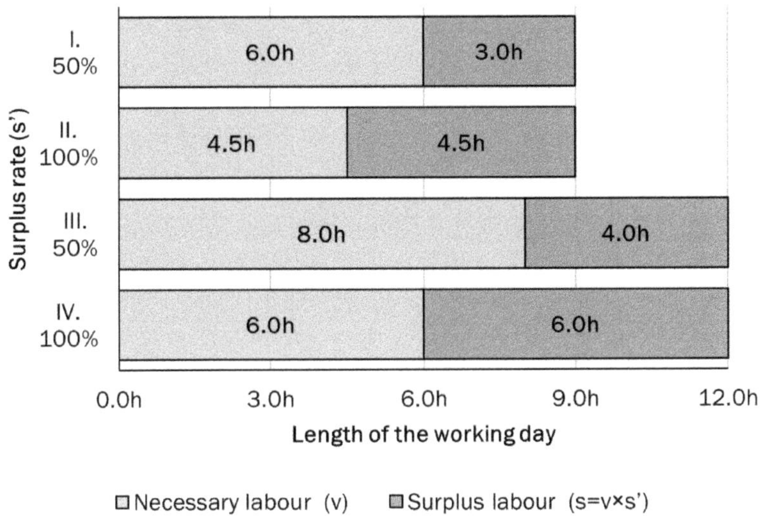

Graph 6. Increasing Surplus Labour.
This graph illustrates an increase in surplus labour achieved through either relative surplus labour (I→II), absolute surplus labour (I→III), or a combination of both (I→IV).

The surplus rate, i.e. the ratio of surplus labour to necessary labour, indicates the proportion of surplus value going to capitalists and value going to labour (s' = S / v). Or, in terms of money (assuming price-value alignment): the proportion of profits to wages.

It may be helpful to distinguish between the rate of surplus value (s') and its amount, or 'mass' (S) in Marxist terms. An analogy might be the flow of interest payments into a savings account (expressed in dollars per year) versus the rate of interest that determines the magnitude of the interest payments (expressed as a percentage of the savings stock). A fixed five per cent rate on savings of one hundred dollars will yield a 'mass' of interest of five dollars per year.

Building on Table 3 from before, a fifty per cent rate of surplus value on forty hours of variable capital adds a mass of twenty hours of surplus value, as shown in Table 4. Or, to use Marx's notation system: 40v × 50% = 20S. The distinction helps convey the possibility that a lower rate does not automatically imply a lower mass, such as in: 100v × 20% = 20S. These units are expressed in both dollars and hours, as we continue to assume a monetary expression of labour time (MELT) of one dollar per hour.

Money capital (MO = C × MELT, with MELT = 1$/h)	$50
Capital invested (C = c + v), including:	50h
Constant capital (c)	10h
Variable capital (v)	40h
Surplus rate (s')	50%
Surplus value (S = v × s')	20h

Table 4. Rate and Mass of Surplus

For a more complete picture, I should add that although all surplus value arises from workers, not all workers give rise to surplus value. Take slavery again. The master must allocate a portion of the surplus extracted from the slaves' work to support various other roles, including servants and guards, all of whom work to uphold the master's dominion over the plantation.[127]

In capitalist societies, many derive their livelihoods from the surplus value generated by others. Marx categorised this group as 'unproductive labourers,' since they don't directly generate surpluses (not because they don't work hard).[128] They might include real estate agents, police officers, postal workers, office cleaners, and so on. The term also applies to a managerial class whose primary function is to serve the interests of capitalists by expediting surplus value creation,[129] by for example intensifying work to accommodate budget cuts. Still others, who work in sales, marketing, and retail, accelerate turnover time in the sphere of realisation (as discussed in Chapter 2), thus expediting the capitalists' return on investment.

It is worth noting, however, that Marxist theorists have not yet reached a consensus on what should be classified as (un)productive.[130] It would seem logical to extend the logic of the surplus rate to cleaning services provided by a firm whose profits are derived from the surplus value produced by its employees. Should they not therefore be labelled 'productive' after all?

Also important to acknowledge is that this classification doesn't imply moral judgment: 'unproductive labour' can still produce vital use values, such as firefighting, therapy, or nursing, while productive labour performs many 'bullshit jobs' (according to those that hold them).[131] Nowhere does Marx suggest that the distinction depends on the social usefulness of the labour's content: Productive and unproductive labour alike create both necessary and superfluous commodities. With these categories, Marx simply adopts the capitalists' productivist viewpoint. Only capitalists purchase productive labour power with the specific aim of generating surplus value, whereas capitalists, states, and households all regularly acquire use values produced by unproductive labour.

As discussed above, productive labour power possesses a concrete use value – its ability to generate value, including surplus value, for the capitalist class. Labour power also possesses its own value, referred to as abstract value. I promised I would return to this question: If a product's value originates in labour, where does the abstract value of labour power itself come from? The answer is the socially necessary labour time needed to (re)produce the worker's capacity to expend labour power. This also explains the difference in value between a two-hour lecture by me and one by my assistant. Let me break this down by starting with Marx's own formulation:

> If the owner of labour-power works today, tomorrow he must again be able to repeat the same process in the same conditions as regards health and strength. His means of subsistence must therefore be sufficient to maintain him in his normal state as a labouring individual.[132]

To (re)produce their, mental, and intellectual capacities, workers must eat, rest, learn, commute, shop, and more. Capitalism commodifies these activities by stripping workers of control over production (though not fully, as they also rely on unpaid social reproduction, as discussed later). And here lies the core message: The abstract value of labour power corresponds to the average labour time invested in producing these essential commodities, which allow the worker to return to work every day. Labour brings this abstract value to work, embodying it in the commodities' value as variable capital (v).

Logic implies that an hour of skilled labour yields greater value than an hour of unskilled labour. However, this greater value does not come from the increased productivity of skilled labour. Enhanced productivity, as described previously, is a result of the machinery employed by skilled labour, whereas the relatively greater abstract value of skilled labour comes from the greater labour time needed to acquire the requisite skills and knowledge themselves. The time invested in university education or vocational training increases graduates' abstract value.

Near the end of his life, Picasso was dining in a restaurant when a fan approached and asked if he would draw something on a napkin. Picasso obliged, then said, 'That'll be ten thousand dollars.' The fan protested, 'But it only took thirty seconds!' Picasso replied, 'No – it took me eighty years.' This is just an illustrative example; in reality, the sketch's price stems more from its status as a monopolised cultural commodity than from Picasso's abstract value.

With this understanding of abstract value, I can return to the earlier unfinished claim that the surplus rate can rise with increasing productivity through an increase in 'relative' surplus value (from row I to row II in Graph 6). Productivity does so by reducing the value of labour-power. Since the value of labour-power depends on the value of the means of subsistence, rising productivity in the sectors producing these goods lowers their value. As explained in Chapter 2, higher productivity does not increase the total value created in a given working time; rather, the same value is distributed over or diluted across a larger output, so the value per unit falls. As the means of subsistence embody less value, the value of labour-power declines, shortening necessary labour and expanding surplus labour within an unchanged working day. In the Global North, this effect is offset by an expansion in the bundle of goods and services normally consumed by labour. Indeed, the richest twenty per cent of the world population enjoys a bundle 42 times larger than that of the poorest twenty per cent (derived from Graph 2 in Chapter 1, which adjusts for price level differences).

As we are dealing with multiple concepts that sound highly similar to one another, let me recap the main points:

- 'Variable capital' represents the capitalists' investment in labour power, compensated through wages.
- Capitalists compensate workers for an length of time on the job, divided into 'necessary labour' and 'surplus labour.'
- 'Necessary labour' denotes the time spent by workers to produce value equivalent to what's needed for the reproduction of their labour power.
- 'Surplus labour' constitutes the additional time beyond necessary labour, during which surplus value is generated.
- During production, the entire value of 'variable capital,' known as 'abstract value,' transfers into the commodity, along with additional 'surplus value' generated through 'surplus labour.'
- The price of 'variable capital' (wages) differs from its 'abstract value.'
- 'Abstract value' corresponds to the average labour time required to produce the means of subsistence consumed and utilised by the worker to regenerate their labour power.

This leads to a number of important questions, including: What happens when wages are too low to cover sufficient commodities to regenerate labour power? And how do different costs of living and wage levels affect labour's abstract value around the world?

Similar to price-value misalignments, gaps exist between abstract value and wages. However, the two variables also maintain a close correlation through interaction. Historical labour struggles in late-industrial capitalist economies led to higher wages, consistently exceeding abstract value over long periods of time.[133] Workers gradually grew accustomed to this increased purchasing power, and today typically own cars, dishwashers, high-end electronics, in addition to handling such significant expenses as mortgages, energy, and childcare. This way of life tends to be factored into a 'subsistence' wage in the Global North. As the means of subsistence and their value increased over time, abstract value followed suit.

History thus initiates a self-reinforcing cycle: Higher wages increase abstract value, further driving up wages (assuming wages fluctuate around abstract value). Here, we see the price-value gravitational force in action, particularly in relation to the price and value of labour power as a commodity.

However, this represents only a general tendency, as many other factors are also at play. For instance, developments in public healthcare, childcare, and education can alleviate the financial burdens associated with the reproduction of labour power, thereby weakening the relationship between abstract value and wages. Conversely, heightened access to these services empowers workers to negotiate higher wages, potentially leading to increased consumption and, consequently, abstract value.

Furthermore, the simultaneous increase in both the price and value of labour fails to bridge the divide between the returns to labour and those to capital. For instance, consider the case of the Netherlands, where disposable income has stagnated over the past forty years, despite a growing economy.[134] This indicates a diminishing share for labour (see Chapter 1), and implies persistent poverty for thousands of households.[135]

In contrast to the Global North, the interplay between the price and value of labour power in Global South countries has been more sluggish and even moving backwards for certain groups. The persistent combination of meagre wages (see Chapter 1) and rising prices has led to reduced spending on essential goods, particularly for food.[136] This pushes down the abstract value of labour power. At some point, labour power can even be remunerated below its own abstract value, meaning that wages cannot even cover the bare necessities. Living on below-subsistence incomes compels underpaid households to forgo meals or healthy food, reduce heating at home, drink contaminated water, and so forth. Brazilian Marxist Ruy Mauro Marini refers to it as 'super-exploitation.'[137] This also occurs in the Global North, albeit less severely and widely.

This exploitation also propagates internally: Many industrial workers in Global South countries rely on an underpaid 'South within the South' –

rural labourers, peasants, and informal service workers whose unpaid or low-paid care and subsistence labour that enables low industrial wages.[138]

While wages and abstract value mutually reinforce each other, rising and falling together in dynamic interplay, the strength and direction of this relationship vary between countries. This leads to significant international divergences, with equally skilled labourers earning vastly different wages in different nations.[139] In short, we generally see an upward-moving virtuous cycle in the price and value of labour power in the Global North, and a downward-moving vicious cycle in the South (see Diagram 12), with exceptions.[140]

Diagram 12. Two Spirals

People cope with low wages not only by cutting back on spending but also by working longer hours. For instance, the average worker in Bangladesh toils 168 per cent more hours per year than their equivalent in the Netherlands, but earns a mere 8.4 per cent of the income.[141] This discrepancy can be vividly illustrated via an international comparison of the hours of minimum-wage labour required to afford a McDonalds Big Mac at local prices:[142] about twenty minutes in Australia, 42 minutes in the United States, an hour in Portugal, and over nine hours in Sri Lanka.[143]

When compared to their counterparts in wealthier nations, low-wage earners in less affluent countries must work significantly longer to afford similar commodities. However, whether or not longer working hours do in fact result in an equivalent increase in paid necessary labour – and not simply more surplus labour – depends on the rate of exploitation.

Another striking indicator of these divergent trajectories is the sizable disparity between various nations' officially defined poverty lines (as opposed to the international poverty line discussed in Chapter 1). For instance, while poverty in Luxembourg is defined as living on less than $46.4 per day, in the Democratic Republic of the Congo (DRC) the threshold is set at $1.5 per day.[144] To be clear: The dollar unit used here has been adjusted to account for differences in purchasing power between countries. This adjustment implies that a 'poor person' in Luxembourg can afford 31 times more food, water, energy, and other essential items than a 'poor person' in the DRC, i.e., their abstract values differ by a ratio of 31:1. Official poverty lines demonstrate how governments normalise these divergences.

Most underpaid and overworked households will also try to mitigate the impacts of below-subsistence wages through uncompensated housework, which feminist scholars refer to as social reproduction. This term encompasses the caregiving work carried out within households and communities to reproduce the workforce and its labour power. Such work, which is distinctly gendered,[145] includes raising children, providing healthcare, imparting knowledge, and so on. Social reproduction revitalises our bodies, creativity, focus, and other essential faculties.

For the philosopher and political scientist Nancy Fraser, the production of commodities by commodities (paid labour) takes place against a backdrop of non-commodities in the sphere of social reproduction.[146] Fraser emphasises that the capitalist economy freerides on social reproduction, treating it as a wellspring of 'free gifts' of human nature (see Chapter 2).

The more the system exploits its workforce, the more it appropriates these free gifts. To live below subsistence means being unable to cover the costs of reproducing labour power through wages alone and becoming increasingly reliant on informal support from a spouse, children, or elderly relatives. If a household can't afford heating, its members will have to gather fuel for fire. Likewise, if they can't afford transportation, they'll have to walk their children to school. Exploited workers exert greater pressure on social reproduction. Fraser therefore characterises the encroachment on and appropriation of social reproduction as a self-destructive, cannibalising process, given capitalism's utter dependence on the very social system that it undermines.[147]

To conclude, the abstract value of labour power – that is, the average (socially necessary) labour time required to reproduce labour power – not only reveals the source of value in commodities but also uncovers the origin of surplus value. As explained, labour power holds a distinct use value for employers: It creates surplus value. While we work, the value that we produce surpasses the value that we obtain through wages, and which then becomes the abstract value of our labour power. The difference constitutes surplus value. For instance, the average burger chef may work eight hours a day, while their abstract value gets produced (by other workers in the system) in just two hours, on average. This allows the restaurant owner to capture six hours' worth of surplus value.

Marx begins with an unprovable yet plausible assertion that value and surplus value emerge from average labour time. Based on this premise, he advances a compelling explanation of how capitalism functions, who performs the work, and who appropriates the surplus.[148]

In this explanation, Marx goes beyond the realm of market exchange into the darker recesses of production, with the intention of unveiling capitalism's dirty secret: accumulation through exploitation.[149] Capital expands precisely by not fully compensating labour time. As wealth accumulates for the capitalist class, misery accumulates for the working class. The two are connected through exploitation. In Marx's words:

> [A]ll methods for the production of surplus value are at the same time methods of accumulation; and every extension of accumulation becomes again a means for the development of those methods. It follows therefore that in proportion as capital accumulates, the lot of the labourer, be his payment high or low, must grow worse [...] Accumulation of wealth at one pole is, therefore, at the same time accumulation of misery, agony of toil, slavery, ignorance, brutality, mental degradation, at the opposite pole, i.e., on the side of the class that produces its own product in the form of capital.[150]

Crucially, the combined accumulation of wealth and poverty is an international process. The two spirals shown in Diagram 12 are linked through unequal exchange. Whether consumed directly by labour or used by capital to produce goods for labour's consumption, most commodities are globally traded and therefore embody value produced in faraway places. Consequently, the abstract value of labour power rises or falls with the types and quantities of commodities that wages can command, and with the often distant sites of their production. Labour power itself, however, is the one commodity that is not freely traded internationally, or only very weakly so, sustaining persistent international wage gaps. As will become clear in Part 2, these asymmetries generate systematic transfers of value from the South to both capital and labour in the North – that is, unequal exchange.[151]

CREATION OF VALUE

Now that we understand what (surplus) value means, let's turn to how it is produced. I'll refer to the entire sequence from the investment of money capital to the production of value as a 'turnover.' Diagram 13 schematises a turnover, starting with an initial capital outlay of constant and variable capital (C = c + v). As discussed, constant capital (c) consists of the instruments of production (ci) and the materials of production (cm). Variable capital (v) represents labour power. Bob's burger restaurant started with the following investment: 50C = 10c + 40v = (6ci + 4cm) + 40v (see Chapter 2). Let me remind you that we use the suffixes C, c, ci, cm, v for value compositions, expressed in dollars or hours (assuming one dollar equal to one hour of value).

Each input has its own lifespan. For instance, Bob need not replace his appliances, utensils, and other instruments of production (ci) annually; they transfer their value to the commodities gradually, in line with their depreciation rates. A grill worth 6ci that lasts six years conveys 1 unit of value to the burgers in a year. Conversely, materials of production (cm) such as ingredients, gas, and other consumables require more frequent restocking. Similarly, wages are dispensed monthly, resulting in twelve variable capital expenses annually.

The amounts of constant and variable capital used and consumed within one turnover represent what Marx calls cost-price, a breakeven price that covers only production costs for that turnover. Due to the varied lifespans of inputs, cost-price naturally differs from the initial capital outlay. Moving forward, let's assume that all invested capital is entirely depleted and requires replacement after a single turnover, an unrealistic but useful simplification that will not alter the underlying logic I intend to convey. In this scenario, cost-price equals capital outlay. The entire value of both constant and variable capital investments gets transferred into the production of burgers in one turnover.

Constant capital gets its name from the fact that it does not add new value during production. As we know, production transfers the existing value of the instruments and materials of production into the product, e.g., from the grill or bread bun to the finished burger. Meanwhile, variable capital, i.e. labour power, gets its name from its ability to create more value than it represents: v + S.

Previously, we assumed that Bob's hired chef (Bob himself ceased working in the kitchen) performs three hours of 'unpaid' surplus labour for every six hours of 'paid' necessary labour: a surplus rate (s') of fifty per cent. Given a yearly variable capital investment of 40v, Bob's chef produces a surplus value of 20S (40v × 50%).

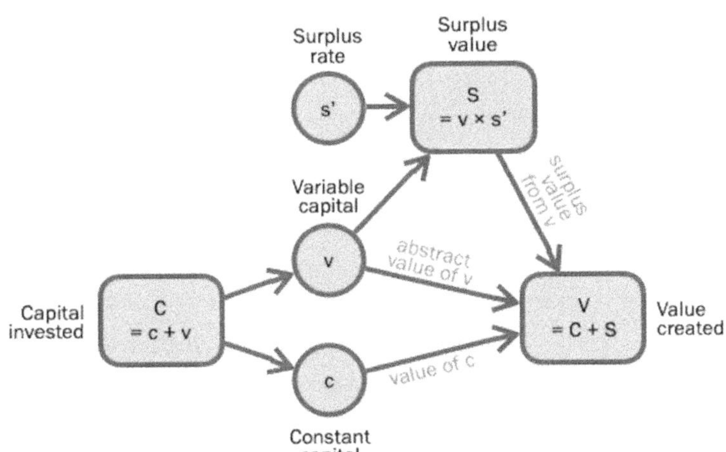

Diagram 13. (Surplus) Value Creation

Bob invested in 50C units of value at the start of the year (including durables, consumables, and labour power) and ended with 50C + 20S = 70V units of value at the end of the year. (Remember that, in this scenario, all invested capital is consumed in one turnover. Otherwise, we would need to replace 50C in the above formula with whatever the cost-price is.) From 70V, 40v units went to the chef and 10c went on inputs. The remaining 20S surplus value is potentially available for the next production phase, minus what Bob decides to pocket and spend on personal consumption. The entire logic is presented in Table 5.

Capital invested (C = c + v), including:	50h
Constant capital (c)	10h
Variable capital (v)	40h
Surplus rate (s')	50%
Surplus value (S = v × s')	20h
Value produced (V = C + S)	70h

Table 5. (Surplus) Value Creation

In short, a single turnover begins with a phase of production where invested money capital (C) metamorphoses into produced value (V), including surplus value (S).

Let's begin to move away from the realm of value, and towards the realm of money. As mentioned, capital travels from one to the other, through processes of production and exchange, respectively. In the realm of money and exchange, we must take an intermediary step and engage in a conceptual reflection on prices in an ideal-typical economy, free from the messiness of the real world. In this pristine market, let's christen the currency 'limbo' (Ł).

It's quite obvious that monopolies, market frictions, weather, war, and various other real-world 'distortions' inevitably cause actual prices to deviate from hypothetical limbo prices. But what's more intriguing: Limbo prices also deviate from values in the ideal-typical economy. In fact, if capitalism operated as intended, prices and values would necessarily deviate. This constitutes a central enigma that Marx aims to unravel. Graph 7 illustrates how ideal (Ł) prices might deviate from values (h), and real ($) prices fluctuate around ideal (Ł) prices.

Just as value differs from price, surplus value differs from profit. The distinction may seem unnecessary: Aren't they both simply the difference between the exchange value of labour power (wage) and the exchange value of what has been produced (revenue)?[152] The answer is no: Profit and surplus value do differ, and the difference is very important.

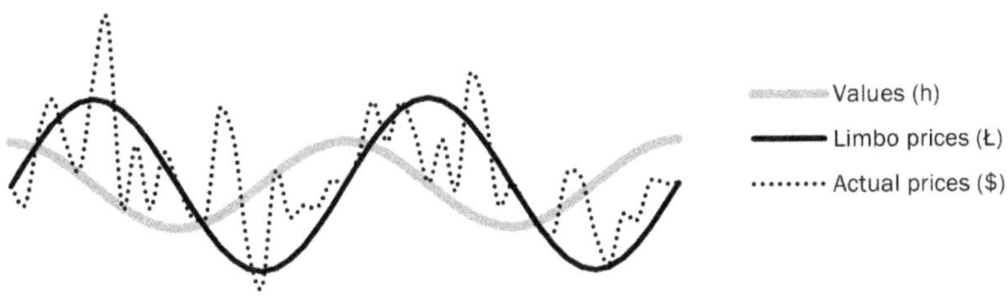

Graph 7. Price-to-Value Deviations.
This graph conveys the idea that actual dollar prices fluctuate around hypothetical limbo prices, which themselves deviate from the underlying values.

Labour generates surplus value during production, prior to market exchange. This surplus value then becomes part of the commodity's value, whether the commodity is sold or not. By contrast, profit only appears at the point of sale – not as the fruit of market exchange, but rather through the transformation of value into money. Profit represents surplus value realised in money form. This may sound somewhat metaphysical but basically means that surplus labour went into making a product before it was sold for a profit. (It's worth recalling that aside from profit, surplus value must also cover interest, rent, and various other claims, as mentioned earlier. Here, I have simplified the situation by focusing only on profit.)

For capitalists to turn a profit, they must sell their goods at a price that exceeds capital invested (C). This is obvious, but what might be less obvious is that they can make a profit even when selling the commodity below its full value (V = C + S). Consider Bob's production of 70V = 50C + 20S, and a monetary expression of labour time (MELT) equal to one limbo per hour. Imagine that Bob has invested Ł50 as his initial capital (50C × MELT = Ł50, meaning that price and value align). If he sells burgers for a total of Ł70, equal to their value (70V × MELT = Ł70), Bob will have transformed his entire surplus value of 20S into Ł20 of profit (Ł70 - Ł50 = Ł20 = 20S × MELT). If, for some reason, the burgers sell for a price lower than their value, say Ł60, Bob will still have managed to transform half of the surplus value into a profit of Ł10 (Ł60 - Ł50 = Ł10 < 20S × MELT).

Importantly, the value of the commodity remains unchanged (70V, including 20S), and so Bob's customers receive 10S for free, calculated as the difference between price and value (Ł60 / MELT - 70V = 10S), or between profit and surplus value (Ł10 / MELT - 20S = 10S). If, however, the burgers sell for Ł80 instead of Ł70, Bob will have secured a profit of Ł30 instead of Ł20, exceeding 20S surplus value by Ł10 (Ł80 - Ł50 = Ł30 > 20S × MELT). In this case, Bob's customers will have paid Ł10 more for the same value.

In summary, commodities can be traded at prices above or below their value, resulting in profits either above or below surplus value. Divergences between profits and surplus values can be the result of various external factors, such as when effective marketing entices customers away from competitors, pandemic-related lockdowns disrupt supplies, or competitors engage in price-fixing. However, in the ideal-typical world of limbo money, these things don't happen. Here, divergences between the two follow some internally-driven dynamic, as we'll soon discover. Similar to how values affect prices, surplus values exert a magnetic influence on profits. They may sometimes draw closer or drift apart; rather than arbitrary, such variations are governed by forces within the ideal-typical model (see Chapter 4).

By suggesting that money represents surface appearance while value acts as a kind of underlying magnetic force, I am not trivialising the significance of the realm of money. Marx's approach may feel distant from the everyday world of price tags, discounts, and paycheques. As workers and employees, we are often overworked, undervalued, or even underpaid, yet we do not consciously contemplate our own necessary and surplus labour, the labour time invested in reproducing our own abstract value, or the surplus value we contribute to commodities.

The same is true of our employers, for whom wages merely compensate a day's work. They, too, are unable to differentiate between necessary and surplus labour. Concepts such as surplus value or surplus rate typically don't occupy their thoughts; instead, capitalists are primarily concerned with the profitability of their invested capital.[153]

Investors, too, react to changes in profit rather than surplus value. This fact will be crucial when examining the distribution of value within and between countries and has to do with the equalisation of profit rates, which I will discuss in the next chapter.

Now that surplus value has metamorphosed into money (in Ł currency), it is ready to be reinvested in the next MO→CO→MO' turnover, or rather MO'→CO→MO''. This brings us one step closer to understanding how the system reproduces itself at an ever-widening spiral (see earlier Diagram 6) – in other words, how accumulation occurs. Next, I will present a series of increasingly complex schemes to illustrate how surplus value from one turnover (Table 5) is reinvested in the next. This quantitatively demonstrates the process of accumulation over time and lays the foundation for exploring falling profit rates in Chapter 4 – a key driver of the ever-widening unequal exchange examined in Part 2.

REPRODUCTION

Once upon a time, a farmer, a blacksmith, and a steelmaker united to establish a local economy. They employed labourers who worked for wages. The steelmaker's workers transformed ore into iron and sold it to the blacksmith, whose workers crafted ploughs and then sold those to the farmer. The farmer's workers, in turn, cultivated and sold food, fuel, and fibre to the workers in all three industries.

While engaging in trade, these three entrepreneurs set prices based on the typical time required to produce their respective goods. Workers received wages commensurate with the average direct and indirect time needed to satisfy their daily requirements of food, fuel, and fibre.

Workers dedicated more hours than required to meet their combined daily needs, resulting in a surplus that their employers appropriated for personal indulgences, such as extravagant jewellery and spices from foreign markets. As a result, they never reinvested more money than they had initially.

Things took a turn, however, when the steelmaker decided to invest some of his extra earnings into increased iron production, which he took to the blacksmith. Recognising the opportunity, the blacksmith scaled up plough production and persuaded the farmer to buy more ploughs to grow more food. This led to the conversion of more farmland, the recruitment of additional workers, and an increased consumption of food, fuel, and fibre – an endless spiral of further expansion, employment, and consumption.

How might such an economic and social arrangement persist over time, that is, reproduce itself? Value circulates between capitalist firms, which enables the continuous renewal of commodities, including labour power. Value also self-accrues, leading to accumulation from one turnover to the next. For now, let us look at this process for a closed, advanced capitalist economy. We will get to the process for open economies engaged in global trade later.

The driving force behind accumulation undoubtedly lies in the creation of surplus value. However, the pace of accumulation depends on how society allocates surplus value between productive and non-productive purposes.

If all capitalists spent all of their surplus value on non-productive pursuits such as luxury vacations, art collections, and philanthropic charities, the capital remaining after each turnover would consistently match subsequent investment. In this scenario, known as simple reproduction, the economy maintains its size without expansion or contraction. Of course, given the competitive push for accumulation, this scenario is unrealistic; it simply conceptualises an initial step towards understanding expanded reproduction, where a portion of the surplus value is invested productively after each turnover. Let's delve further into both scenarios.

We start with a self-contained economy consisting of two distinct 'departments' (i.e., sets of sectors): one dedicated to the production of machinery, materials, factories, or other means of production (MOP), the other producing the means of consumption (MOC). This includes 'essential goods' such as loaves of bread and pairs of trousers, as well as 'luxury goods' such as gold-flaked champagne and diamond-encrusted watches. The category could easily be made to include arms and military equipment.[154] As capital accumulates, the luxuries enjoyed by the wealthy expand, driving an increased demand for arms and other mechanisms for safeguarding wealth and its continued accumulation.

The division between the MOP and MOC departments reflects the way in which capitalism takes ownership of the means of production away from the primary producers, the workers. Consequently, workers become dependent on waged employment to access the means of consumption.

I will now apply the scheme originally devised for Bob's restaurant to the collective capitals of firms operating within MOC. For simplicity's sake, I will combine instruments and materials into a single constant capital variable (ci + cm = c). To distinguish between the two departments, MOP will work with relatively more constant capital (40c instead of 10c) and less variable capital (10v instead of 40v). Both departments will maintain the same surplus rate (s' = 50%).

Output after the first production phase amounts to:

- MOP: 40c + 10v + 5S = 55V
- MOC: 10c + 40v + 20S = 70V

Exchange follows production. Workers in both departments acquire consumer goods from MOC firms, while capitalists in both purchase machines and materials from MOP firms. Thus concludes the first turnover (t = 1), as shown in Table 6.

As mentioned, the scale of accumulation depends on how much surplus value capitalists allocate between productive investment and unproductive consumption. In the context of simple reproduction, the amount of surplus value reinvested is zero. Consequently, neither capital invested (C) nor output (V) will grow. The arithmetic logic for this form of reproduction is as follows (see also Table 6):

At the end of t = 1, MOP generates 55V, including 5S. For now, let's assume that MOP sells only 50V, failing to realise any of its surplus value as profit (I will introduce non-productive luxury spending of profit shortly). MOP sells this 50V for Ł50, given a MELT of one limbo per hour. Of this, Ł40 come from internal sales to firms within MOP, and Ł10 comes from sales to MOC firms. At the start of t = 2, MOP reinvests these Ł50 earnings into 40c and 10v (as it did at the start of t = 1). Meanwhile, at the end of t = 1, MOC generates 70V, selling 50V and leaving 20V unsold. It sells 50V for Ł40 within MOC and Ł10 to MOP. At the start of t = 2, MOC reinvests its Ł50 into 10c and 40v (also, as it did at t = 1).

Under these conditions, the value of goods exchanged between the two departments remains constant, establishing a dynamic equilibrium without accumulation. This logic continues in subsequent turnovers, if we were to expand Table 6.

This scheme builds on three assumptions, all of which will be abandoned later: that prices and values align (50V is sold for Ł50, given a MELT of one limbo per hour); that there is no distinction in the surplus rates (s') between the departments; and that there is no evolution over time in the departments' organic composition, i.e., in the ratio of constant to variable capital.

	t = 1		t = 2	
	MOP	MOC	MOP	MOC
Capital invested (C = c + v):	50	50	50	50
Constant capital (c)	40	10	40	10
Variable capital (v)	10	40	10	40
Organic composition (c / v)	4	0.3	4	0.3
Surplus rate (s')	50%	50%	50%	50%
Surplus value (S = v × s')	5	20	5	20
Value produced (V = C + S)	55	70	55	70
Unsold value	5	20	5	20

Table 6. Simple Reproduction

This simple reproduction scheme reveals an oversupply, where the surplus value generated in one turnover cannot be fully realised as profit for reinvestment in the next. By contrast, the ideal-typical system supposedly balances supply and demand, as outlined earlier. This discrepancy suggests that the reproduction scheme functions primarily as a conceptual stepping stone rather than a comprehensive understanding of how the system works.

One solution would be to adjust the scheme so that MOP sells its entire 55V for Ł55, with MOP capitalists spending their Ł5 profit unproductively on luxury consumption. In the same way, MOC would sell 70V for Ł70, with MOC capitalists unproductively spending their Ł20 profit. To complete this adjustment, the scheme should be adjusted by splitting MOC into a department that produces essential goods and another that produces luxury goods, as proposed by Marxist theorists Paul Baran and Paul Sweezy. The luxury goods department would also produce its own surplus value, which, once realised as profit, would again be spent unproductively on luxury goods in the context of simple reproduction. This approach, shown in Table 7, achieves a balance between supply and demand while ensuring that no value remains unsold.

	t = 1			t = 2		
	MOP	MOC		MOP	MOC	
		Essential goods	Luxury goods		Essential goods	Luxury goods
Capital invested (C = c + v):	50	50	25	50	50	25
Constant capital (c)	40	10	5	40	10	5
Variable capital (v)	10	40	20	10	40	20
Organic composition (c / v)	4	0.3	0.3	4	0.3	0.3
Surplus rate (s')	50%	50%	50%	50%	50%	50%
Surplus value (S = v × s')	5	20	10	5	20	10
Value produced (V = C + S)	55	70	35	55	70	35
Unsold value	0	0	0	0	0	0

Table 7. Three Departments

Alternatively, or additionally to spending profits on luxury, we could also consider capitalist spending on so-called unproductive labour (supported by the surplus value produced by productive labour, as discussed earlier). In recent times, the rise of labour employed in the circulation process, such as delivery drivers, online customer service workers, or shopping platform developers, has become a particularly salient means of disposing of surplus value.

Rather than adding complexity, let's go back to the simpler two-department model, and increase reinvestment.

In the context of expanded reproduction, a certain amount of surplus value is realised and reinvested. At the end of t = 1, MOP generates 55V, including 5S, which could potentially realise Ł5 in profit. However, if for some reason the sector sells only 52.5V for Ł52.5 at the end of t = 1, it will only realise fifty per cent of its surplus value (5S × 50% = 2.5S) as profit (Ł2.5), leaving 2.5S unrealised, as shown in Table 8.

At the start of t = 2, we assume that MOP reinvests its Ł52.5 in constant and variable capital in the same proportions as at the start of t =1, that is, without introducing technical progress or changes in the organic composition of capital (c / v = 4.0). The new outlay of capital then becomes: 52.5C = 42c + 10.5v.

Understanding MOC's reproduction involves a few additional logical steps. As MOP firms invest in 10.5v of variable capital at t = 2 – meaning they pay Ł10.5 in wages to their workers – those workers purchase an equivalent amount of consumer goods from MOC firms. With Ł10.5 revenue from those sales, MOC firms can acquire an equivalent amount of constant capital from MOP firms, totalling 10.5c. To maintain its own organic composition (c / v = 0.25, rounded to 0.3 in the table), MOC firms must also invest in 42v variable capital (= 10.5c / 0.25).

Compared to simple reproduction, MOC now realises 2.5S as profit, leaving 17.5S unrealised (20S - 2.5S). A calculation of MOC's accumulation rate would be thirteen per cent (2.5S / 20S). This rate is endogenously determined (for MOP it was exogenously set at fifty per cent).

Table 8 shows how the process can continue indefinitely with additional investments in each turnover. In this scheme, both departments experience a consistent five per cent compound growth in value per turnover (calculated as: [57.8V - 55V] / 55V for MOP).

	t = 1		t = 2	
	MOP	MOC	MOP	MOC
Capital invested (C = c + v):	50	50	52.5	52.5
Constant capital (c)	40	10	42	10.5
Variable capital (v)	10	40	10.5	42
Organic composition (c / v)	4	0.3	4	0.3
Surplus rate (s')	50%	50%	50%	50%
Surplus value (S = v × s')	5	20	5.3	21
Value produced (V = C + S)	55	70	57.8	73.5
Unsold value	2.5	17.5	2.6	18.4

Table 8. Expanded Reproduction

'Accumulate, accumulate!' We've heard this before, but then Marx adds: 'Therefore, save, save, i.e., reconvert the greatest possible portion of surplus value, or surplus-product into capital!'[155] Table 9 shows a scenario in which capitalists heed the call and invest the greatest possible amount of surplus value. The MOP department now doubles its reinvestment rate to one hundred per cent. Applying the above equations, the MOC department can save and reinvest 25 per cent, also doubling its previous rate. Therefore, both departments accumulate twice as fast. Value grows at around ten per cent in this maximum reproduction scheme (calculated as [61V - 55V] / 55V), twice the rate of the first expanded reproduction scheme.

	t = 1		t = 2	
	MOP	MOC	MOP	MOC
Capital invested (C = c + v):	50	50	55	55
Constant capital (c)	40	10	44	11
Variable capital (v)	10	40	11	44
Organic composition (c / v)	4	0.3	4	0.3
Surplus rate (s')	50%	50%	50%	50%
Surplus value (S = v × s')	5	20	5.5	22
Value produced (V = C + S)	55	70	60.5	77
Unsold value	0	15	0	16.5

Table 9. Maximum Reproduction

Let's briefly examine two adjustments in this last scheme: (1) to account for rising wages, and (2) to account for additional sources of credit.

We assumed constant wages throughout the reproduction period. In reality, workers and unions in the Global North have successfully pushed for higher pay. We can account for this in Table 10 by drawing inspiration from Arghiri Emmanuel's work.[156] Emmanuel explains that an increase in variable capital can stem from multiple sources: employing more workers, lengthening the working hours of a fixed workforce, or increasing wages for a fixed workforce with fixed working hours. In the latter case, the rise in variable capital must coincide with a reduced surplus rate. Why? Because capitalists pay the wage bill. When wages increase, necessary labour rises while surplus labour decreases, resulting in a lower surplus rate. Any addition to variable capital must thus take away from surplus value. For instance, MOP's variable capital increased from 10v at t = 1 to 11v at t = 2, as shown in Table 10. For this increase to mean an increase in wages (and not in number of workers or hours), the additional 1v at t = 2 should be compensated by a reduction in 1S. MOP's surplus value therefore decreases from 5S at t = 1 to 4S at t = 2.

Extending this logic over time results in a falling compound growth rate of value. For example, MOP's growth rate falls from ten per cent at t = 1 ([55V - 50V] / 50V) to seven per cent at t = 2 ([59V - 55V] / 55V). It would continue to decline if Table 10 were extended further in time. As we'll observe later, this fall may trigger efforts by capitalists to compensate for the higher wage bill by cutting other costs, such as foreign inputs.

	t = 1		t = 2	
	MOP	MOC	MOP	MOC
Capital invested (C = c + v):	50	50	55	55
Constant capital (c)	40	10	44	11
Variable capital (v)	10	40	11	44
Organic composition (c / v)	4	0.3	4	0.3
Surplus rate (s')	50%	50%	36%	36%
Surplus value (S = v × s')	5	20	4	16
Value produced (V = C + S)	55	70	59	71
Unsold value	0	15	0	12

Table 10. Wage-Corrected Reproduction

Let me introduce one final adjustment. Even under conditions of maximum reproduction, growth is limited. The MOP department can reinvest only its own surplus value, restricting accumulation for the MOC department which relies on a limited supply of MOP commodities. Bank credit plays a crucial role in overcoming this limitation (as well as destabilising the system, though that is not the point here[157]), as we saw in the MO1→(MO→CO→MO')→MO1' circuit in Diagram 5. I will integrate credit into the reproduction scheme by drawing on the approach developed by Samir Amin.[158]

Looking again at the maximum reproduction scheme from before, MOP can reinvest no more than Ł5 after the first turnover. In proportion to its organic composition, MOP allocated Ł4 to constant capital (4c), leaving Ł1 for variable capital (1v) and ultimately for MOC to earn (see earlier logical steps). However, with Ł20 to invest, MOC could potentially purchase up to 4c and 16v (in proportion to its organic composition). Since MOP cannot meet this additional demand from its own reinvestment alone, it turns to credit to increase production. By taking on a loan, MOP will also require additional variable capital, that is, to hire more people, which raises the demand for MOC commodities. Consequently, MOC also relies on credit to meet growing consumer demand, and so on.

Let's incorporate this into the reproduction scheme. As shown in Table 11, MOP produces means of production worth 55V at t = 1. MOP firms within the department purchase an amount of those commodities worth Ł44, and MOC firms purchase the rest for Ł11 (to keep the same distribution between departments as in the previous turnover). Similarly, MOC produces means of consumption worth 70V at t = 1, selling these for Ł56 to MOC workers and Ł14 to MOP workers. This reproduces 56v and 14v of labour power for the departments to employ at t = 2. With this there is no unabsorbed surplus left (MOP's V at the end of t =1 equals the sum of constant capital investments at the start of t =2, and MOC's V at t =1 equals the sum of variable capital investments at t =2).

	t = 1		t = 2	
	MOP	MOC	MOP	MOC
Capital invested (C = c + v):	50	50	58	67
Constant capital (c)	40	10	44	11
Variable capital (v)	10	40	14	56
Organic composition (c / v)	4	0.3	3.1	0.2
Surplus rate (s')	50%	50%	50%	50%
Surplus value (S = v × s')	5	20	7	28
Value produced (V = C + S)	55	70	65	95
Unsold value	0	0	0	0

Table 11. Debt-Fuelled Reproduction

From this, we can conclude that financialisation catalyses the process of expanded reproduction, as shown in Graph 8.

For these reproduction schemes, I assumed that prices and values align, meaning that 50V sells for Ł50 (with MELT equal to one limbo per unit of value, in both departments), and kept the organic compositions stable (except when introducing the possibility of credit, see Table 11). I will modify these assumptions and introduce more complexity in later chapters, but for now I simply want to acknowledge that these schemes are simplistic constructs that can be improved, such as to include the luxury goods department mentioned previously.

In another adaptation of Marx's schemes, Rosa Luxemburg incorporated technical progress by increasing the organic composition of capital over

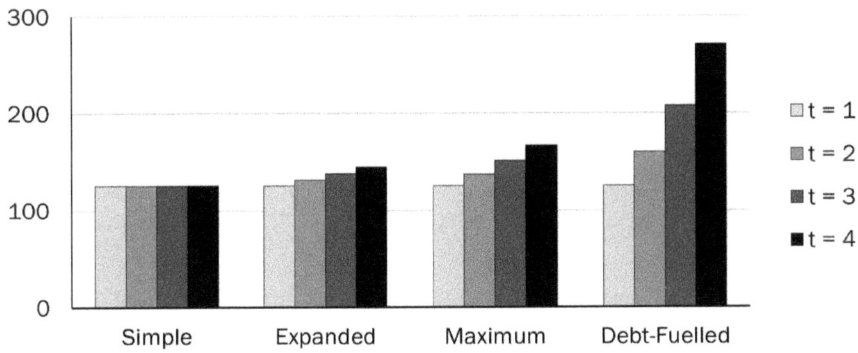

Graph 8. Comparing Reproduction Schemes.
This graph depicts the accumulation of total capital (the sum of both sectors) over time from t=1 to t=4 under four scenarios: simple, expanded, maximum, and debt-fuelled reproduction.

time.[159] Her Intensive Reproduction scheme revealed overproduction in the MOC department and underproduction in the MOP department.[160] Luxemburg argued that this discrepancy leads to a crisis, resolvable only through colonial expansion into non-capitalist economies. Such expansion would absorb MOC's excess output and address MOP's limited supply.

There is much to consider here, and we will revisit this question later, but let me just flag the fact that colonial expansion is driven less by overproduction so much as by a falling profit rate, as we shall see. Furthermore, MOP's underproduction already features in the maximum reproduction scheme (before technical progress is even 'added'), and then those shortages disappear once we transform value into price, as we will see in Chapter 4.

What's more, capitalists have many other strategies to address over- and underproduction besides colonial expansion (or its current form: unequal exchange with peripheral economies). These include planned obsolescence, aggressive marketing, luxury and military spending, and so on.

However, dwelling on these details may not be the most productive use of our time. The schemes were never intended to accurately depict the system's trajectory, but rather to illustrate capitalism's inherent drive toward accumulation and to provide an essential foundation for what follows. Misunderstanding this limited purpose can lead to fruitless debates. Both maximum and debt-fuelled expanded reproduction are hypothetical scenarios because, in reality, the accumulation is disrupted by internal contradictions that lead to economic crises – something Marx understood well. The schemes are therefore 'half-baked,' as they do not yet account for prices and profits. That's fine, though, because they are still in the oven, so to speak. The schemes will be refined one final time in Chapter 4 to reveal a key driver of unequal exchange: the tendency for profit rates to fall over time.

Returning to our proto-capitalist society, the mechanism of expanded reproduction is set in motion by the farmer, who increases production to meet rising demand from growing wages in the economy. This triggers more demand for ploughs and steel, amplifying both wages and the demand for food. The cyclical process then continues, with each producer mutually reinforcing the expansion of the others.

This dynamic might evoke the familiar image of preparing pancake mix: too little milk, add more, too runny; add flour, too dense; add milk, and so on. Similarly, firms try to prevent imbalances and constraints, which occur when one sector cannot absorb enough of the output of another, or when one sector doesn't produce enough of the input needed by another. That's also when finance steps in, to add fuel to the fire beyond maximum expanded reproduction.

CLOSING REMARKS

We can therefore depict a commodity's value under capitalism as $V = c + v + S$, where:

- c denotes the value (average labour time) objectified in the means of production;
- v denotes the value produced by necessary labour;
- S denotes the surplus value produced by surplus labour.

Constant capital can only transfer value that has already been produced, while labour power can create additional value. Workers add surplus value to a commodity on top of the value of the labour power advanced as variable capital. For the capitalist, $c + v$ indicates what the commodity costs the capitalist, which is to say the value spent on its production, i.e., its cost-price ($c + v$, if all capital inputs get used up in a single turnover).

Capitalism depends on commodities selling for more than they cost to produce. Where does the profit come from? Behind the hype of the McDonald brothers and other clever entrepreneur lies a simple truth: Labour creates the surplus that becomes profit. Surplus value (S) is the excess value produced by labour above a commodity's cost-price, and is appropriated and reinvested by capitalism to fuel its expansion. Of course, before it can be reinvested, surplus value must first be transformed into profit – labour time into money. We will now turn our attention to this transformation.

4. Price and Profit

OPENING REMARKS

Saying that McDonald's profited by outwitting its competition in the fast-food sector hardly explains anything. Upon closer examination, we see that labour power is the true wellspring of profit, of which McDonald's managed to snatch some at the expense of its competitors. This may sound strange, and the logic behind it involves several steps.

When McDonald's first innovated fast-food production, it enjoyed a monopoly advantage over traditional burger establishments. Typically, a company that adopts a new cost-cutting method can charge the prevailing market rate and essentially 'steal' money from customers, or it can lower its price and 'steal' customers from the competition. However, this monopoly position is fleeting in ideal-typical capitalism, as rivals swiftly adopt similar methods of their own. In the fast-food war, technological developments are constantly reducing the relative production cost of a hamburger, undercutting the average. Here's where things get puzzling: Early adopters can pocket more profit while actually producing less surplus value.

But things get even more puzzling: Can a lucrative sector such as fast-food benefit at the expense of an entirely different but less lucrative sector, such as toothpick manufacturers? Yes, says Marx, who would postulate that, when buying toothpicks, the fast-food sector hijacks surplus value that was created by toothpick workers.

Marx refers to difficulties in converting values into prices (and surplus values into profits) as the transformation problem. In this chapter, we will explore how this problem plays out within national capitalist economies, to prepare us for the international perspectives of subsequent chapters. Let's dive in, considering both intra-sector dynamics (transfers of value between similar firms within a sector) and inter-sector dynamics (transfers of value between different sectors).

INTRA-SECTOR DYNAMICS

Deviations between values and prices can arise from monopolies, pandemics, wars, trade barriers, and other real-world messiness. In my previous explanation, I adjusted prices arbitrarily to illustrate the point (see Table 2 in Chapter 2).

As we shall see now, even in the ideal-typical world of unobstructed and undisturbed limbo currency (Ł), prices deviate from value. Firms do not consistently realise the entirety of their surplus value as limbo-denominated profit. These deviations are not arbitrary but the product of internal system dynamics. It is crucial to discern these patterns and their origins before introducing additional real-world noise (see earlier Graph 7), which begs the following question: What forces underlie the deviations between values and limbo-prices in the idealised model? To answer, we must first explore the mutual determination between value and price.

McDonald's holds multiple patents to protect its production and customer service methods and thereby help the company maintain its dominant position in the market.[161] That dominance would not last long if capitalism actually stuck to its proclaimed commitment to free and open competition. In capitalism's fantasy world, technological monopolies are fleeting.

Moreover, the ideal-typical capitalist system rapidly achieves equilibrium between supply and demand. When supply surpasses demand, greater amounts of value are produced than can be realised through exchange; this results in an excess of values over prices. As a result, producers divest, which theoretically drives value production back down. Conversely, a diminished supply may raise prices above values, benefiting producers of scarce commodities. However, this also incites competitors to invest in producing the same commodities, theoretically pushing prices down again.

We must, of course, recognise that technologies are guarded, that supply and demand never settle, that competition never reaches perfection, and that monopolies do endure. Nevertheless, we must also question the rationale of a model of capitalism unaffected by such 'distorting' influences (as argued in Chapter 1).

The assumed balance of supply and demand implies three so-called aggregate equalities, as posited in Marxist theory:

1. The total amount of value in society equals the total sum of prices.
2. The total amount of surplus value equals the total sum of profits.
3. Derived from 1 and 2, the total rate of profit measured in value, in society as a whole, is equal to the total rate of profit measured in money.

Starting with equality 1, it might sound inconsistent with what has been established so far. Did we not just say that prices and values diverge? The validity of the equality depends on the extent to which total value and total prices are defined. Total sum of prices refers to the total limbo-denominated revenue that all firms within a sector receive for their commodities. If total value is defined as average labour time, then this first equality makes no sense because it compares amounts of hours (or other units of labour time) with amounts of limbo. However, it makes sense when total value is defined by the average labour time equivalent of its price, i.e. by the average monetary expression of labour time ($MELT_{AV}$),[162] introduced earlier (see Chapter 2). To refresh: Suppose Bob and Mac produce a total value of 125 minutes (average labour time) which is sold for a total price of Ł125. This results in a $MELT_{AV}$ of one limbo per minute for the burger sector (Ł125 / 125V).

The question now becomes: What happens when technological advantages allow firms to price a commodity above its value? In such cases, other firms will sell commodities below their value. Consequently, when some firms realise profits exceeding their surplus value, others must realise less. Whether temporarily or long-term, the losses and gains cancel each other out. The total of all surplus values for the entire sector matches the total of all profits, as stated with equality 2. Keep in mind that MELT (the ratio of money to labour time) allows us to compare magnitudes of value and price, as well as surplus value and profit.

So, while prices and profits may deviate from values and surplus values across different firms, the aggregate equalities, if they are correct, anchor the price system in the value system, while allowing for price-to-value and profit-to-surplus deviations. This holds for a sector, and indeed for the entire economy, as I will describe.

In what follows, I will continue to assume an average monetary expression of labour time ($MELT_{AV}$) of one limbo per hour. Thus, in aggregate terms, one hour of value is worth one limbo. Strictly speaking, whenever we convert a value into a price – or vice versa, that is, whenever we move between the domains of value and money – we should multiply or divide by the MELT. However, since in this case MELT equals one, I will omit it for simplicity. When I turn to empirical data later in the book, I will reintroduce this adjustment.

But enough abstract reflections, let me demonstrate more concretely how one capitalist gains at another's expense. Take our two rival burger restaurants, Mac and Bob, both striving to increase their market share and profit margins by increasing productivity through mechanisation, automation, or robotisation. Mac, in particular, excels at replacing human work with the mechanical work of, for example, ingredient dispensers or automated frying.

This increases Mac's organic composition of capital (OC), as shown in Table 12. With organic compositions of four and 0.25 respectively, Mac is sixteen times more 'capital-intensive' than Bob (4 / 0.25).

- Mac invests in 50C = 40c + 10v, with OC = 40c / 10v = 4.
- Bob invests in 50C = 10c + 40v, with OC = 10c / 40v = 0.25.

Assuming a daily wage of Ł5 per worker (and assuming that wages correspond to the abstract value of labour power), Mac, being 'capital-intensive,' employs only two workers (10v / Ł5), while Bob, being 'labour-intensive,' employs eight (40v / Ł5). With a surplus rate (s') of fifty per cent, Mac's workers produce a surplus value of 5S (10v × 50%), while Bob's produce 20S (40v × 50%). As before, the output at the end of one production cycle (these numbers mirror my previous reproduction schemes) is as follows:

- Mac produces burgers worth 50C + 5S = 55V.
- Bob produces burgers worth 50C + 20S = 70V.

However, something seems off: Mac and Bob, despite making equal investments (their monetary capital outlay (MO) is equal to fifty limbo) and operating with identical surplus rates (fifty per cent), generate significantly different surplus values. Mac's value-based profit rate (p' = S / C), therefore, stands at a mere ten per cent, while Bob achieves forty per cent. Being more labour-intensive seems to pay off, a notion entirely at odds with the capitalist impetus for innovation and technological advancement. How should we make sense of this apparent inconsistency?

Let's first consider the scenario in which a firm's prices reflect the value of its commodities (given MELT_{AV} of one limbo per hour). The firm's money profit (P) would equal surplus value (S), and the value-based profit rate (p') would mirror the financial return that capitalists aim to maximise (m' = P / C = p' = S / C). However, we have just established an inverse relationship between organic composition and surplus value, and therefore profit. The pursuit of profit appears to clash with investments in constant capital aimed at boosting productivity – a phenomenon that is obvious in the real world. If profit aligned with surplus value, '[t]he pharmaceutical industry would disappear, and woodworking would prosper.'[163]

Of course, investing in low-wage manual-based production abroad can prove worthwhile, but that is not our focus here. Remember, we are looking at sectors within an advanced capitalist economy, not at the outsourcing of production to the Global South, which we will address later.

	Mac	Bob
Money capital (MO = C)	Ł50	Ł50
Capital invested (C = c + v):	50h	50h
Constant capital (c)	40h	10h
Variable capital (v)	10h	40h
Organic composition (OC = c / v)	4.0	0.25
Surplus rate (s')	50%	50%
Surplus value (S = v × s')	5h	20h
Value produced (V = C + S)	55h	70h
Profit rate (p' = S / C)	10%	40%
Output (o)	70	55
Breakeven price (BP = MO / o)	Ł0.7	Ł0.9
Market price (MP = ∑V / ∑o)	Ł1	
Markup (MU = MP - BP)	Ł0.3	Ł0.1
Profit (P = MU × o)	Ł20	Ł5
Revenue (R = MO + P)	Ł70	Ł55
Surplus profit (SP = P - S = R - V)	Ł15	-Ł15
MELT (R / V)	Ł1.27/h	Ł0.79/h
Average MELT ($MELT_{AV} = \sum R / \sum V$)	Ł1/h	
Monetary profit rate (m' = P / MO)	40%	10%

Table 12. Distribution Between Firms

The inconsistency stems from assuming that the firms' prices and values align. This must be abandoned: Prices and values cannot align. Monetary rates of return (m') must diverge from value-based profit rates (p') to incentivise investments in labour-saving productivity-enhancing technologies. It is clear, then, that in a developed capitalist economy, firms do not capture the entirety of the surplus value that their workers generate (if m' < > s', then P < > S). So, we must ask: What portion of surplus value do firms realise as profit?

When Mac invested in ingredient dispensers and automated frying, he increased productivity to, say, seventy burgers per turnover. Meanwhile,

Bob's labour-intensive kitchen produces, say, 55. We can now calculate the production cost per burger by dividing the money outlay (MO = C, with $MELT_{AV}$ = Ł1 per hour) by the output, as shown in Table 12. This cost represents the breakeven price (BP): the minimum price (in limbo) at which each restaurant must sell its burgers to cover costs before profit. Notably, Mac's breakeven price is lower than Bob's.

- Mac: BP = MO / o = Ł50 / 70 = Ł0.7 per burger.
- Bob: BP = MO / o = Ł50 / 55 = Ł0.9 per burger.

By contrast, a burger's market price must not only cover its production cost but also include a markup to generate a profit.[164] What determines this markup? Our answers lie in the sphere of production. As we're examining a specific sector of hamburger firms, we can assume a single market price (MP), which we calculate by dividing total value by total output. In this case: MP = ΣV / Σo = (55h + 70h) / (70 + 55) = Ł1 per burger.[165]

Let me clarify. If capitalism functions as intended, all goods are sold, supply meets demand, and the total price must equal the total value (as per the first aggregate equality). And, since total price equals the per-unit price multiplied by total output, the per-unit price (MP) is indeed equal to the total value divided by the total output. A burger's market price should thus reflect its average value (Ł1 = 1V).

Competition thus creates a tendency towards a common market price at which all producers must sell. (This price is not fixed, but changes as new innovations emerge and impact either outputs or inputs, but that it not our focus right now.) With production costs below the market price, Mac and Bob both secure a profit. However, Mac's lower cost per burger means that his markup per burger exceeds Bob's (MU = Ł1 - Ł0.7 = Ł0.3 versus Ł1 - Ł0.9 = Ł0.1).

A clever move would be for Mac to undercut Bob's breakeven price, driving him to ruin. To avoid bankruptcy, Bob would have to invest in his own technologies (or, alternatively, either intensify labour exploitation or source constant capital inputs from cheaper places, which we'll incorporate in the story soon). Temporary fluctuations around value therefore motivate and can enrich innovative capitalists, compelling others to follow suit.

Tangentially, innovation can become self-reinforcing. When Mac automates ingredient dispensing and frying, he must also modernise other kitchen processes to keep up with the faster production pace. After all, 'invention is the mother of necessity.'[166] Furthermore, capitalism glorifies change and novelty in and of itself, constantly discarding the old in favour of something new.

Key here is that innovation grants early adopters a competitive edge, if not an outright monopoly, though perhaps 'monopoly' is not the right word, given that firms aren't entirely free to set prices. Whatever we call it, their position offers significant advantages.

At the same time, individual advantages don't last in such warlike competition. As more firms reduce per-unit production costs through innovation, early adopters lose their edge and must innovate again. Transitory technological monopolies therefore constantly reemerge and refusing what Marx calls 'the coercive law of competition' generally leads to ruin. Increased productivity enables price undercutting, which, when effective, eliminates competitors (and perhaps even competition itself).[167] Unsurprisingly, then, the disciplining whip of competition has become deeply ingrained in the logic of how firms operate.

Does this imply that prices for consumers tend to decrease? Perhaps. In a highly price-competitive economy, coercive competition would compel firms to lower retail prices to match reduced costs. However, in an economy characterised by perfect monopoly, there would be no motivation to pass cost reductions on to consumers. To believe that unobstructed price mechanisms result in cheaper outcomes for consumers is to confuse the ideal-typical model with a real-life monopolistic economy.

This brings us to the final logical piece in the puzzle of how one firm gains surplus value at the expense of another. So far, we have seen that although Mac and Bob sell burgers at the same price, Mac's unit costs are relatively lower thanks to his state-of-the-art production techniques. I will now demonstrate how these differences allow Mac to realise excess profits above the surplus value that they produce, while Bob realises less.

Table 12 shows that by producing different amounts of output (o) but selling at the going market price of one limbo per burger (MP) and therefore capturing different markups (MU), Mac and Bob generate different profits, calculated as the total markup on all output, i.e. P = MU × o:

- Mac generates Ł0.3 × 70 = Ł20 in profit.
- Bob generates Ł0.1 × 55 = Ł5 in profit.

Revenue is then simply calculated as money outlay (MO), which the firms recoup in the ideal-typical situation, plus profit (P), i.e., R = MO + P (alternatively, revenue can be calculated as market price multiplied by output, i.e., R = MP × o):

- Mac generates Ł50 + Ł20= Ł70 in revenue.
- Bob generates Ł50 + Ł5 = Ł55 in revenue.

I am deliberately referring to R rather than MO', which represents the potentially greater money outlay at the start of the next turnover in the earlier MO→CO→MO' circuit shown in Diagram 4. Revenue (R) might not be reinvested in its entirety, and therefore may differ from MO', as we will see when we revisit the process of reproduction below.

What's important is this: In Mac's case, profit (P) is higher than the surplus value (S) produced by his employees; in Bob's case, it is lower. Remember, we can compare S (in hours) to P (in Ł) by using the average $MELT_{AV}$ (in this case one limbo per hour) as the conversion factor:

- For Mac: P - S = Ł20 - 5h × Ł1/h = Ł15
  (alternatively, R - V = Ł70 - 55h × Ł1/h = Ł15)
- For Bob: P - S × $MELT_{AV}$ = Ł5 - 20h × Ł1/h = - Ł15
  (alternatively, R - V × 1 = Ł55 - 70h × Ł1/h = - Ł15)

A positive profit-surplus gap (P - S), often referred to as 'surplus profit' (SP in Table 12) or 'absolute (individual) rent,'[168] denotes an excess in profits above surplus value. A negative gap implies profit shortfall. Thus, although exchange may not generate profit, it certainly moves profit around, with some gaining surplus profit at the expense of others. And remember, this occurs in the ideal-typical capitalist economy. Further excess profits can be extracted via monopoly power, in which case we refer to 'supra-profit' or 'monopoly rent,' to be discussed later.

Within a sector, we see a transfer of surplus profit from firms with a lower-than-average MELT to those with a higher one. In this case, Bob's MELT (R / V = Ł0.8/h) is below the sector average ($MELT_{AV}$ = ΣR / ΣV = Ł1/h), resulting in a transfer of surplus profit to Mac, whose MELT is higher (R / V = Ł1.3/h). By 'transfer,' I do not mean that one firm directly hands over some of its profits to another; rather, I refer to a systemic allocation of extra profit to one firm arising from another firm's inability to fully realise its own profits.

Where a firm produces commodities for final consumption, therefore, consumers may get either less or more value than what they pay for. A burger from Bob is 'better value' than one from Mac. In other words, Bob is underpaid and Mac is overpaid relative to their burgers' value. Transfers of surplus value and surplus profit also occur between firms when they purchase commodities from each other at prices either above or below value, for example when the burger sector purchases toothpicks from the toothpick sector. I will explore this further in the next section on inter-sector dynamics.

As mentioned earlier, Bob's profit rate in terms of value (p' = S / C) surpasses Mac's, standing at forty per cent compared to Mac's ten per cent. However, when we evaluate Bob's profit rate in monetary terms (m' = P / C), it lags behind Mac's, at ten per cent in contrast to Mac's forty per cent (the percentages are reversed). Innovation may not appear advantageous when looked at from the perspective of value, but from the perspective of money, it proves to be lucrative. Having abandoned the assumption that prices and values align, the earlier inconsistency is now solved. While labour-intensity pays off in terms of value, it does not in monetary terms.

Let me return to the third 'aggregate equality' from the beginning of this section. From Table 12, we can derive that total rate of profit measured in value indeed equals the total rate of profit measured in money (Σp' = Σm' = 10% + 40% = 50%). The dynamics of coercive inter-firm competition respect Marx's law of value where value regulates price, meaning that while some firms sell above value and others sell below, total profits always equal total surplus value.

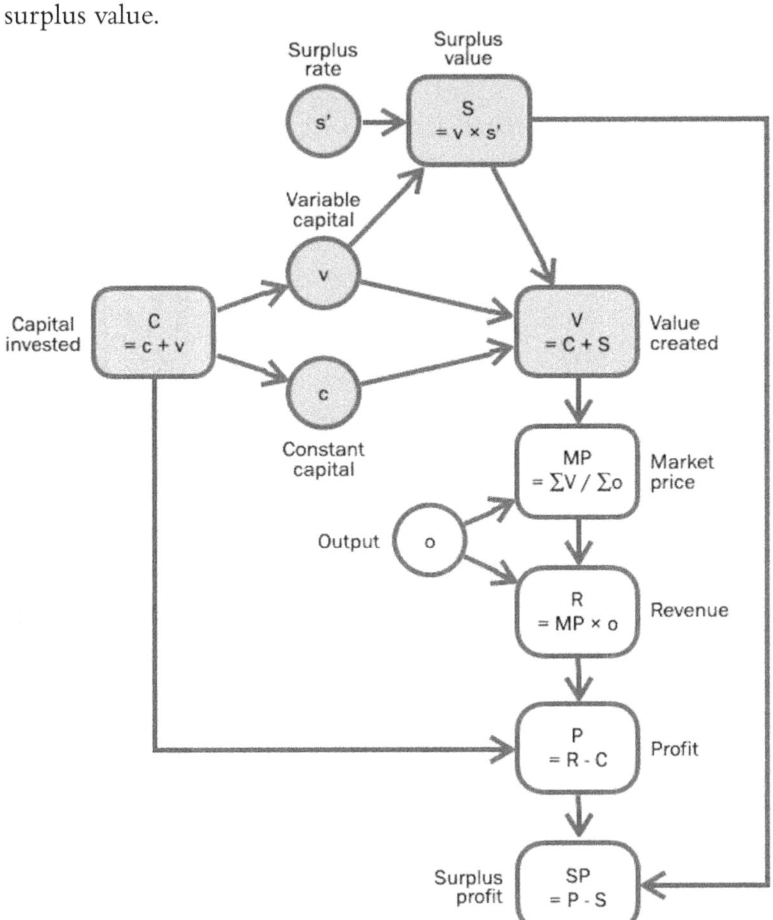

Diagram 14. Distribution Between Firms

Let's reflect on what we've covered so far. In an idealised and simplified model of capitalism – where supply meets demand and total values equal total prices – surplus value production deviates from profit realisation when competing firms operate with different organic compositions of capital. Some firms earn more profit than the surplus value that they generate, while others earn less. The difference is called surplus profit. As demonstrated, surplus profit goes to those firms that operate with above-average productivity and below-average per-unit production costs, to Mac in our example. Moreover, the surplus profit gained by Mac equals Bob's unrealised surplus value. These logical steps are summarised in Diagram 14 (building on Diagram 13). Again, since $MELT_{AV}$ is equal to one, I have removed it from the diagram's equations for visual clarity. All other variables and their initials are included in this diagram; no external lookup is required.

These excess profits are not limited to the ideal-typical model (when they take the form of surplus profit) but also occur in a more realistic context, where supply and demand are not perfectly aligned, and monopolies distort prices (when they take the form of supra-profit). However, the model enables us to analyse these deviations in isolation.

Interestingly, surplus profit arises not so much from technological innovation itself as from disparities in technological development. In fact, even if McDonald's hadn't innovated in its early days, but all other burger restaurants had regressed technologically, McDonald's would still have garnered surplus profits. Firms with comparatively limited technological capabilities cannot fully convert surplus value into profit, allowing the more technologically advanced firms in the sector to realise surplus profit above their surplus value.

If more firms are able to adopt advanced technologies, especially when innovation spreads rapidly without such hindrances as intellectual property rights, opportunities to amass surplus profit may be brief. Nevertheless, these opportunities will continue to reemerge – and they must, for capitalism to work. Indeed, instantaneous realignments of prices and values in the idealised model of competition would eliminate the incentive for firms to innovate altogether.

You might wonder, 'What's wrong with productivity? Doesn't it drive progress?' Well, first of all, our societies' material throughput intensifies, with ever more pronounced environmental impacts (more on this in Chapter 7). And there's something else going on too. Productivity rewards some firms at the expense of others, eventually leading to what we euphemistically call market consolidation: the concentration of productive capital and market power in ever fewer hands. For example, McDonald's, Burger King, and

Wendy's controlled seventy per cent of the American hamburger market in 2014.[169] Moreover, they source their inputs from other monopolistic sectors: The four largest companies' control over the American beef industry increased from 25 per cent in 1977 to 85 per cent in 2021.[170]

The ideal-typical competitive model thus coerces firms into a rat-race of endless innovation in the pursuit of increased productivity and contains the conditions for a real-life monopolistic economy.

INTER-SECTOR DYNAMICS

Time now to dive into the of value transfers between sectors across the economy as a whole. Inter-sector transfers, like inter-firm transfers, arise from deviations between prices and values, as well as between profits and surplus values. However, we cannot apply the method that we used for inter-firm transfers here. Firms from the same sector sell their goods at the same market price: Mac and Bob both sell burgers for one limbo. Hamburgers obviously sell at very different prices than, for instance, toothpicks.

Yet, both hamburger and toothpick sectors share a common trait: a tendency towards uniform profit rates. In a competitive environment, a sector's profit rate cannot significantly or persistently deviate from the average; competition equalises profit rates, generally as a result of the flow of investment into and out of different sectors, as we will see.

In turn, this equalisation gives rise to sector-specific revenues. These ideal-typical amounts of money cover production costs and secure an economy-wide average rate of profit. We will see how revenues deviate from the amounts of value that sectors produce, and how this results in transfers of value across the economy. Just as we observed with individual firms, these transfers benefit so-called capital-intensive sectors and hurt labour-intensive ones.

There's a lot to unpack here, so let's break it down step by step.

Imagine an economy consisting of two sectors. By combining Mac and Bob's capitals we form the burger sector, before then introducing a toothpick sector with a relatively higher organic composition of capital (OC). To summarise Table 13:

- The burger sector invests in: 100C = 50c + 50v, with OC = 50c / 50v = 1.
- The toothpick sector invests in: 600C = 550c + 50v, with OC = 550c / 50v = 11.

With a surplus rate of 50%, both sectors generate a surplus value of 25S (50% × 50v). The profit rates are then calculated as follows:

- Burger sector: p' = 25% (25S / 100C).
- Toothpick sector: p' = 4% (25S / 600C).

Let me reiterate that these individual profit rates (p') exist within the realm of value, and result from the extraction of surplus value from labour power. This Marxist concept of profit rate (p' = S / C) therefore differs from the conventional monetary rate of return on investment (m' = P / C). It is also useful to remember that capitalists do not actually see surplus values and value-based profit rates, only their monetary equivalents. We want to figure out how this invisible realm of value interacts with the visible realm of prices.

	Toothpicks	Burgers
Money capital (MO = C)	Ł600	Ł100
Capital invested (C = c + v):	600h	100h
Constant capital (c)	550h	50h
Variable capital (v)	50h	50h
Organic composition (OC = c / v)	11.0	1.0
Surplus rate (s')	50%	50%
Surplus value (S = v × s')	25h	25h
Value produced (V = C + S)	625h	125h
Profit rate (p' = S / C)	4%	25%
Average profit rate (P' = ∑S / ∑C)	7.1%	
Profit (P = MO × P')	Ł43	Ł7
Revenue (R = MO + P)	Ł643	Ł107
Surplus profit (SP = P - S = R - V)	Ł18	-Ł18
MELT (R / V)	Ł1.03/h	Ł0.86/h
Average MELT ($MELT_{AV}$ = ∑R / ∑V)	Ł1/h	
Monetary profit rate (m' = P / C)	7.1%	7.1%

Table 13. Distribution Between Sectors

I hope that the previous discussion of inter-firm transfers of value has clarified why a firm's monetary profit should not be derived from the surplus value generated by its workers. If it were, it would make financial sense to be less productive. McDonald's would immediately regress to earlier methods, bringing back waitresses and having chefs flip burgers to order. Productivity would wane and work would become more labour-intensive.

This is also true at the sector level. With a lower organic composition of capital, the hamburger sector achieves a higher profit rate (p') than the toothpick sector (see Table 13). The latter's higher organic composition, its greater 'capital intensity', does not seem to pay off from a value-based profit rate perspective.

If not from surplus value, where then should we derive profit? In the case of individual firms, one could determine profits using a common market price. However, as explained above, this approach cannot be applied to sectors. For Marx, a sector's profits derive from an equalised or average rate of profit across all sectors (P'), as opposed to individual rates (p').

If this strikes you as increasingly abstract, you're not alone. This part of Marx's analysis stems from the unfinished Volume 3 of *Capital* – the ultimate cliffhanger, which has sparked endless debate about the logical coherence of Marx's framework, and about which the secondary literature that I have encountered offers regrettably superficial or convoluted explanations. Here's my attempt to make sense of it.

In Volume 3, Marx states: '[C]apital withdraws from a sphere with a low rate of profit and invades others, which yield a higher profit.'[171] Two aspects of this statement initially puzzled me. First, capital cannot directly pursue higher profit rates because, intertwined with surplus value (p' = S / C), these rates are fundamentally unknowable to individual capitalists and investors. They are wholly unconscious of the transformation process in which they participate. There must, therefore, be some other factor steering the investments.

My second confusion was this: Even if investors could miraculously see and compare profit rates, it would seem illogical for them to withdraw from sectors with relatively lower ones, for this would divert capital from mechanised to manual production, thus recreating the earlier apparent inconsistency. Let me repeat: From a value perspective, it seems to pay off to be more labour-intensive, though this conflicts with capitalism's drive for productivity.

To resolve these confusions, let us imagine what might happen in reality. Productive investors spend their money capital where they see the greatest potential for profit. Importantly, they do not invest in sectors as a whole, but in firms that happen to operate in this or that sector. As explained, innovation has the potential to create temporary monopolies that generate surplus profits. This potential attracts investments – including from other sectors. The process is not, therefore, primarily about capital flowing between sectors, but involves investments that could give firms a competitive edge as early adopters, as with Mac's productivity-enhancing ingredient dispensers and automated frying.

The key insight is this: Opportunities for monetary surplus profit are more likely to be found in firms with relatively lower organic compositions and higher value-based profit rates. These firms hold the greatest potential for increasing productivity and, consequently, profits. Additionally, coercive competition forces firms with lower organic compositions to borrow and invest to stay in business. The flow of investment towards more labour-intensive firms therefore makes perfect sense from the perspective of capitalism's inherent drive for greater productivity.

To return to Marx's statement: Capital does indeed move from sectors with a low profit rate to sectors with a high one, but not because investors deliberately pursue the latter's higher profit rate. (Remember, they cannot see it.) Rather, what they are after is the prospect of surplus profit, which happens to be most promising in sectors with relatively lower organic compositions, where constant capital investments can really pay off.

Diagram 15 shows what happens next. Boosted by investment, the sought-after firms ramp up production, resulting in a surge in relative supply within their sector which exerts downward pressure on the sector's market prices and profits. Meanwhile, divestment from less profitable firms reduces their relative supply, which raises prices and profits in their sector. However, as soon as that happens, production expands again where it previously contracted, and contracts where it previously expanded.

Diagram 15. Equalising Investment Flows

Now, here's the interesting part: These investments and divestments produce a convergence of sectoral profit rates towards an economy-wide average (or general profit rate, as Marx calls it). Consider again the burger and toothpick sectors. Within each, competition drives the adoption of cutting-edge labour-saving machines, resulting in a relatively consistent organic composition for firms within those sectors. Keen investors understood the opportunity when they decided to invest in Mac's kitchen modernisation. In light of Mac's surplus profit, Bob sought investments to adopt similar technologies, gradually bringing down Mac's profit and establishing a lower average profit rate for the sector.

However, the organic composition still varies between sectors. In our example, the toothpick sector relies heavily on machines, leading to a lower (value-based) profit rate, while the burger sector's greater reliance on manual labour results in a higher profit rate. Economy-wide investment flows cause the hamburger sector's higher profit rate to fall and the toothpick sector's lower rate to rise, until both converge toward a common mean.

This does not imply, however, that sectoral profit rates stabilise on a fixed average. The endless interplay between temporary monopolies and coercive competition means that investments are also constantly changing course and speed. This salient feature of capitalism induces a tendency for an inter-sector equalisation of profit rates, with individual rates tending to move closer to an average.

How should we interpret this idea of a tendency? The ebb and flow of investments drive equalisation, but full equalisation is never reached. This is due to several factors, as barriers such as intellectual property rights, legacy equipment, and other path dependencies restrict the diffusion of technologies that would bring about equalisation.

Additionally, other forces are constantly affecting individual profit rates. For example, competing capitalists may intensify labour exploitation or cheapen their commodities, influencing their individual profit rates even as those rates converge towards an average, which thus remains a moving target. As described by Marx, this tendency to equalisation seeks an ideal mean position that does not exist in reality.

By way of analogy, consider an acrobat walking along a tightrope. To maintain balance, she must continually shift her weight to counteract the pull of gravity on either side. As she advances, she briefly experiences instability on one foot but catches herself on the other. She remains in a constant state of unstable equilibrium. In fact, her stability is contingent on being unstable.

As Ernest Mandel concludes, '[e]qualisation of the rates of profit indeed presupposes their relative inequality. It is a process which constantly realises itself by negating itself.'[172] Nevertheless, experience means that the acrobat's stability becomes more dominant than her instability. Similarly, the more advanced the capitalist system, the stronger the tendency towards equalisation relative to the counter-tendencies towards its opposite, dis-equalisation.

Let's reinforce the point via a more arithmetical approach. How do we calculate the average towards which individual profit rates tend to gravitate? If both sectors in the burger-toothpick economy were the same size, their weight would contribute equally to the average profit rate. In such cases, the arithmetic mean alone suffices: P' = (4% + 25%) / 2 = 14.5%.[173]

However, the calculation method differs in more realistic scenarios where sector sizes vary. A smaller sector with a relatively higher profit rate pulls the average up less than a larger sector with a lower profit rate pulls the average down. To determine the average profit rate here, one would combine all surplus values (S) across all sectors and divide this by the sum of all capital outlays (C). As expected, the result differs from the arithmetic mean: P' = Σ(S) / Σ(C) = 50S / 700C = 7.1%.[174]

With the average profit rate (P'), we can now finally calculate 'mass of profit [P] which falls as an average for any given period to each individual capital [C].'[175] As Table 13 shows, profit (P) equals the money outlay (MO = C) multiplied by the average profit rate (P'). In the burger-toothpick economy:

- The burger sector generates Ł100 × 7.1% = Ł7 in profit.
- The toothpick sector generates Ł600 × 7.1% = Ł43 in profit.

The currency sign means that we have left the realm of value for the realm of money. Having already distinguished between the two conceptually (see Chapter 3), we have now done so quantitatively. Profit (P) differs from each sector's surplus value (S): Ł7 < 25S × MELT in the burger sector and Ł43 > 25S × MELT in the toothpick sector (with MELT = 1).

This mismatch supports our previous deduction that profits cannot be distributed proportionally to surplus values, as otherwise there would be no incentive to invest in labour-saving technologies.

Allow me to retrace our steps: Compared to the burger sector, the toothpick sector's higher organic composition reduces its surplus value and profit rate relative to the average. However, its profit mass is based on a relatively higher economy-wide profit rate (and capital mass invested), making its larger constant capital investment worthwhile. In other words, technological development pays off because average profit rate determines returns.

Marx concludes that it is necessary for the system:

> [...] to turn profits into mere portions of surplus value. However, these are not distributed in proportion to the surplus value produced in each special sphere of production, but rather in proportion to the mass of capital employed in each sphere.[176]

Samir Amin puts it even more succinctly: 'Under the capitalist mode of production 'profit' is the specific form assumed by surplus value when it is distributed in proportion to capital invested.'[177]

We can now calculate surplus profit as the difference between a sector's profit and the surplus value that its workers produce:

- For the burger sector: SP = P - S = Ł7 - 25h = - Ł18 (a shortfall of unrealised surplus value).
- For the toothpick sector: SP = P - S = Ł43 - 25h = + Ł18 (a profit in excess of surplus value).

A quick note on terminology: In these inter-sector dynamics, surplus profit is also called 'differential (sectoral) rent.' In the previous intra-sector case discussed above (Mac versus Bob), it is also termed 'absolute (individual) rent.'[178]

What do these numbers tell us? Sectors do not transform the surplus value that their workers produce into profit. Not only does the most mechanised and automated of the two sectors realise the entirety of its surplus value (i.e., metamorphose all surplus value into profit), but it makes additional surplus profit on top of that.

Indeed, the toothpick sector's Ł43 of profit includes 25S of realised surplus value worth Ł25 plus Ł18 of surplus profit. Meanwhile, since a part of its surplus value fails to realise in profit form, the more labour-intensive burger sector suffers an equivalent loss. This sector only realises Ł7 out of 25S as profit, and so 18S is unrealised and transferred for free to whoever is purchasing burgers.

In this logic, while exchange cannot create profit, it can shuffle it around between sectors. Additional real-world disruptions can lead to further losses that may surpass even an entire sector's surplus value, preventing it from recouping production costs – as happened in many sectors during the COVID-19 pandemic.

Alternatively, we can estimate the price-value gap rather than the gap between profit and surplus value. We know that profit can be calculated as the monetary outlay of capital (MO) multiplied by average profit rate (P'). A sector's average profit is therefore weighted by the magnitude of its invested capital. Using this profit (P), we can now calculate that sector's revenue (R), referred to by Marx as 'price of production.'

Think of this revenue as the ideal-typical limbo-denominated supply price at which products should be sold to cover production costs (in our case MO invested in capital which was assumed to be fully exhausted in one turnover) and reap the sector's average profit (P). Therefore: R = MO + P, with MO = C. Table 13 shows these revenues for the burger-toothpick economy:

- The burger sector generates Ł100 + Ł7 = Ł107 in revenue.
- The toothpick sector generates Ł600 + Ł43 = Ł643 in revenue.

All sectors, Marx writes,

> [...] have the tendency, regardless of the surplus value produced by them, to realise the average profit, rather than their own surplus value in the price of their commodity, i.e., to realise the prices of production [that is, revenues].[179]

Capitalists make a profit provided that they sell above the cost of production (MO), even if they sell below value (C + S). For instance, when the burger sector earns Ł107, it may not realise the entirety of its 25S, but it still makes a seven-limbo profit above its hundred-limbo investment. So, commodities sell for prices above or below their values. The difference corresponds to the surplus profit (SP), or profit-surplus gap, mentioned previously:[180]

- For the burger sector: SP = R - V = Ł107 - 125h = - Ł18.
- For the toothpick sector: SP = R - V = Ł643 - 625h = Ł18.

Diagram 16 depicts the logical steps leading to these surplus profits. Again, I have removed MELT_{AV} from the diagram's equations for visual clarity.

As we've seen within individual sectors – where differences in the monetary expression of labour time (MELT) between firms lead to surplus profit shifting from lower-MELT to higher-MELT firms – a similar mechanism operates between sectors across economies as a whole. In this case, the burger sector's MELT (R / V = Ł0.86 per hour) is below the economy-wide average (MELT_{AV} = ΣR / ΣV = Ł1 per hour), resulting in a transfer of surplus profit to the toothpick sector, which has a higher MELT (R / V = Ł1.03 per hour).

We have already established that firms' surplus values add up to the sum of their profits. These aggregate equalities also apply to sectors. For every instance of value exceeding revenue (V > R), there is a counter instance of revenue exceeding value (R > V): 'One portion of the commodities is sold above its value in the same proportion in which the other is sold below it.'[181] In other words, the differences add up to zero: One sector's losses equal another sector's gains.

While prices and profits are not distributed evenly or proportionally between (or within) sectors, in the aggregate, total price equals total value in the burger-toothpick economy, and total profit equals total surplus value:

- $\Sigma R = \Sigma V = Ł750 = 750V$.
- $\Sigma P = \Sigma S = Ł50 = 50S$.

Our somewhat cryptic starting point should make more sense now: A sector with a higher-than-average organic composition of capital ($OC = c / v$) will tend to have a lower-than-average profit rate ($p' = S / C < P' = \Sigma S = \Sigma C$), meaning that it generates relatively less surplus value per unit of invested capital.

However, profits are not directly tied to these individual value-based profit rates (p'). Instead, they derive from the equalised monetary profit rate (P'), which determines revenue (R). As a result, profit rate equalisation in competitive markets leads monetary profits (P) that deviate from surplus value (S), and revenues (R) that deviate from values (V). All else being equal, sectors with above-average organic compositions benefit from surplus profits (P - S or R - V).

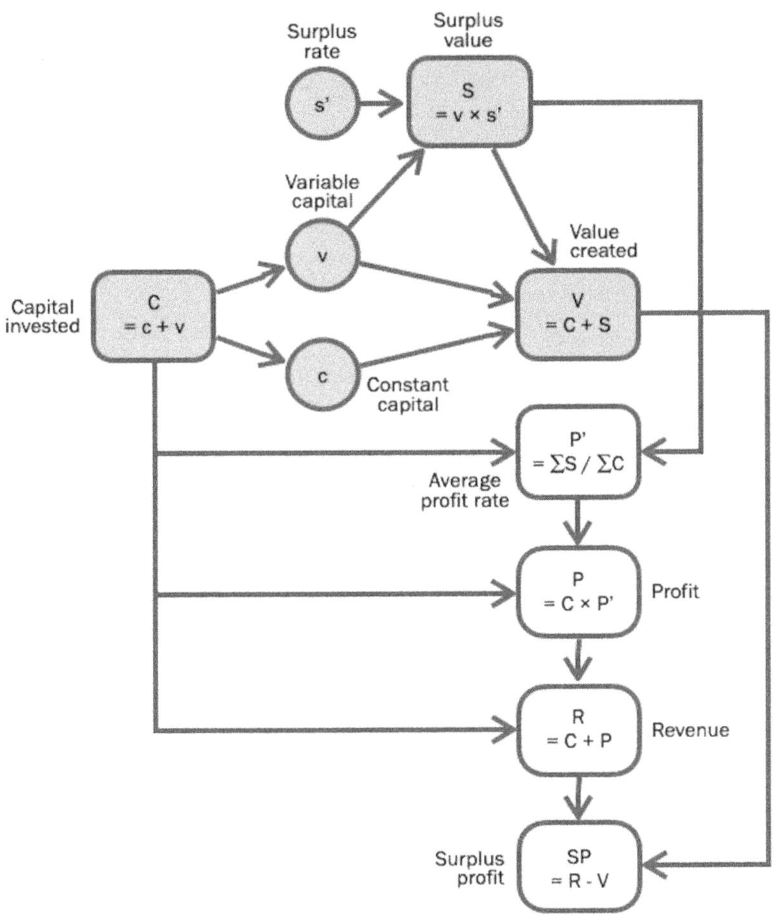

Diagram 16. Distribution Between Sectors

It is important to remember that we have assumed a uniform surplus rate (exploitation of labour) across the entire economy. In reality, this is not the case: Legal and undocumented migrant workers are paid far less than native workers, a gap sustained by racist structures and attitudes.[182] If we abandon this assumption, surplus value might not transfer from sectors with lower organic compositions to sectors with higher ones, but in the opposite direction.[183] This will be particularly relevant when we introduce global trade. In Table 14, I have increased the surplus rate of the toothpick sector (from fifty per cent to two hundred per cent) and reduced that of the burger sector (from fifty to twenty per cent). Now, the burger sector experiences a gain of surplus profit, and the toothpick sector experiences an equivalent loss of unrealised surplus value.

	Toothpicks	Burgers
Money capital (MO = C)	Ł600	Ł100
Capital invested (C = c + v):	600h	100h
Constant capital (c)	550h	50h
Variable capital (v)	50h	50h
Organic composition (OC = c / v)	11.0	1.0
Surplus rate (s')	200%	20%
Surplus value (S = v × s')	100h	10h
Value produced (V = C + S)	700h	110h
Profit rate (p' = S / C)	17%	10%
Average profit rate (P' = ∑S / ∑C)	15.7%	
Profit (P = MO × P')	Ł94	Ł16
Revenue (R = MO + P)	Ł694	Ł116
Surplus profit (SP = P - S = R - V)	-Ł6	Ł6
MELT (R / V)	Ł0.99/h	Ł1.05/h
Average MELT ($MELT_{AV}$ = ∑R / ∑V)	Ł1/h	
Monetary profit rate (m' = P / C)	15.7%	15.7%

Table 14. Deviating Surplus Rates

Here's something for robot enthusiasts, to help bring home the message that the sector's gains and losses are interconnected. Sometimes, firms almost appear to run themselves: laundromats, automatic carwashes, self-storage facilities, etc. Hypothetically, if carwashes were fully automated to remove absolutely all direct 'living' labour time, the sector would generate no surplus value. However, it would still be able to generate profits – surplus profit to be exact.[184] The services would get their value from used-up constant capital only, i.e., from indirect 'dead' labour time. Without variable capital and surplus value, the sector's profit rate would be equal to zero (p' = S / C). As long as the economy's average profit rate is above zero, however, the fully-automated sector will gain surplus profit, as shown in Table 15.

Here too, gains correspond to someone else's losses. Even with one fully-automated sector, the aggregate equalities hold: For every instance of profit exceeding surplus value, there exists a counter-instance of surplus exceeding profit.

	Carwashes	Burgers
Money capital (MO = C)	Ł600	Ł100
Capital invested (C = c + v):	600h	100h
Constant capital (c)	600h	50h
Variable capital (v)	0h	50h
Organic composition (OC = c / v)	/	1.0
Surplus rate (s')	50%	50%
Surplus value (S = v × s')	0h	25h
Value produced (V = C + S)	600h	125h
Profit rate (p' = S / C)	0%	25%
Average profit rate (P' = ΣS / ΣC)	3.6%	
Profit (P = MO × P')	Ł21	Ł4
Revenue (R = MO + P)	Ł621	Ł104
Surplus profit (SP = P - S = R - V)	Ł21	-Ł21
MELT (R / V)	Ł1.04/h	Ł0.83/h
Average MELT ($MELT_{AV}$ = ΣR / ΣV)	Ł1/h	
Monetary profit rate (m' = P / C)	3.6%	3.6%

Table 15. Profit Without Surplus

Surplus value can transfer directly between connected sectors, for example when burger restaurants purchase 'overpriced' toothpicks. Alternatively, a sector might produce 'underpriced' beef (R < V and P < S), which is then sold to the burger sector. During the production process, this beef 'cheapens' the burgers.

How about the distribution of gains and losses between sectors that do not exchange with each other? Consider again the carwash-burger economy. The carwash sector operates without any labour power, while the burger sector generates the entire economy's surplus value (25S). Marx's solution to the transformation problem explains how a fully automated sector can realise a profit without producing surplus value: as a result of other sectors' failure to convert all their surplus value into profit. In our example, the burger sector's shortfall in profit corresponds to extra profit for the carwash sector.

However, this is not a direct transfer of profits between sectors, as they don't purchase from one another. Instead, 'overpriced' carwashes are sold above their value (R > V) to consumers, who receive less value for money, while 'underpriced' burgers are sold below value (R < V), giving consumers more value.

Even though the carwash sector doesn't produce surplus value, it can still realise a profit. The profit exists because the sector sells at a price that reflects the equalisation of profit rates across the economy, not the sector's own value-based rate. Despite having zero surplus value (S), the carwash sector earns from the average profit rate (P') on its investment (C).

To conclude, surplus profit is hijacked from the economy-wide production system. While firms and sectors compete for profit, they share a common interest in the collective exploitation of labour because profit, whether above or below surplus value, ultimately comes from surplus value. The entire working class is, therefore, collectively exploited by the entire capitalist class.[185]

Falling Average Profit Rate

The structural price-value misalignments help us to examine one of Marx's stickier subjects: how – unlike the models in the previous reproduction schemes, which appeared capable of operating indefinitely (see Chapter 3) – this system tends to jam up over time. The models conveyed in those other schemes were only half-baked, so let's put them back in the oven.

By adding the transformation of value into price and surplus value into profit, we uncover a crucial dynamic: a decline in the average rate of profit. This decline signals limits on accumulation which, as many theorists argue, forces the system to expand globally, ultimately leading to unequal exchange. Before going into that, though, let me first explain the falling profit rate.

I want to bring together transformation and reproduction by integrating two of my earlier schemes. The first revealed the profit-surplus gap between sectors (in Table 13). The second detailed the accumulation and allocation of capital from one turnover to the next (in Table 9, see Chapter 3).

In that maximum reproduction scheme, the Means of Production (MOP) and Means of Consumption (MOC) sectors allocated the surplus value produced in one turnover to new investments in the next. This time, however, surplus value (S) generated in one turnover will first metamorphose into profit (P) before being reinvested in the subsequent turnover. For the sake of familiarity with the numbers, we can return to the toothpick and hamburger sectors to represent MOP and MOC. For simplicity, here too, references to the average MELT have been omitted. Since it equals one limbo per hour, all values in the tables can be expressed interchangeably in terms of currency or time.

I have already outlined the logical steps for allocating surplus value to constant and variable capital from one turnover to the next (see reproduction tables in Chapter 3). Importantly, as shown in Table 16, instead of surplus value, capitalists now allocate monetary profit. We assume that MOP reinvests all of its sales revenue: R at the end of the first turnover equals MO' at the start of the second. Specifically, the revenue at the end of t = 1 (643R) transforms into the money outlay at the start of t = 2 (643C). This means that MOP accumulates at the average profit rate (600C × [1 + 7.1%] = 643C). Both the constant and variable capital inputs of MOP grow at this average rate too (589c + 54v), thus keeping the organic composition stable (OC = c / v = 11).

As I mentioned earlier, when MOP firms acquire variable capital (i.e., pay wages), MOP workers spend their income on commodities from MOC firms. This allows MOC firms to buy an equivalent amount in constant capital from MOP firms. At t = 2, MOC's constant capital investment therefore equals MOP's variable capital investment (54c and 54v). MOC then also invests in variable capital to maintain its organic composition (54v and OC = 1.0).

There's no wage increase here (yet); the rise in variable capital from one turnover to the next comes from hiring more workers. If we were talking about a wage increase, the increase in variable capital would be offset by a reduction in surplus value, leading to a lower surplus rate (as shown in Table 10 in Chapter 3). For now, the surplus rate stays the same.

The earlier maximum reproduction scheme (Table 9 in Chapter 3), which ignored prices and profits, fixed MOP's rate of reinvestment of surplus value at one hundred per cent. However, MOP was unable to meet total demand, and this put a brake on MOC's reinvestment rate at only 25 per cent. With the transformation of values into prices, something else happens in Table 16.

	t=1		t=2	
	MOP	MOC	MOP	MOC
Capital invested (C = c + v):	600	100	643	107
Constant capital (c)	550	50	589	54
Variable capital (v)	50	50	54	54
Organic composition (OC = c / v)	11.0	1.0	11.0	1.0
Surplus rate (s')	50%	50%	50%	50%
Surplus value (S = v × s')	25	25	27	27
Value produced (V = C + S)	625	125	670	134
Profit rate (p' = S / C)	4%	25%	4%	25%
Average profit rate (P' = ∑S / ∑C)	7.1%		7.1%	
Profit (P = C × P')	43	7	46	8
Revenue (R = C + P)	643	107	689	115
Surplus profit (SP = R - V)	18	-18	19	-19

Table 16. Reproduction Revisited

Now, both sectors accumulate at the equalised profit rate (P'). MOP's relatively higher organic composition means that it earns a profit above surplus value (P > S), while the opposite is true for MOC (P < S). At t = 2, this gives MOP more money to invest, hire more workers, and increase output (and less in MOC's case). As a result, more workers buy more means of consumption from MOC. This increased demand allows MOC to earn more and purchase more from MOP, thereby boosting overall accumulation beyond what it was before the transformation of values into prices. In this ideal-typical model, supply meets demand perfectly.

I just described a single turnover in which prices are transformed into values and back again. It begins with a financial investment to cover the cost of production (C). This investment results in the production of a commodity with a certain value (V = C + S), which transforms into money when it is sold and generates revenue (R = C + P).[186] For example, McDonald's revenue (R) for hamburgers includes cost of production (C) plus average profit in the hamburger sector (P). Upstream, McDonald's cost of production includes Keystone Foods' price of production for meat, which comprises Keystone Foods' own cost of production plus the average profit in the meat sector.

You might wonder why we need the entire value structure. If prices deviate from values, why not skip values altogether and simply assert that prices equal expenditure on capital outlay and average profit? The reason is that the realm of money can only be reached through the realm of value, particularly when calculating the average rate of profit.

This rate can only be computed in value terms, as total surplus value divided by total capital. This rate of profit generates a revenue (R) by including an average mass of profit (P) above the cost of production (C). Once these profits (or losses) are realised, they influence investments in future turnovers, thereby affecting the entire accumulation process.

Focusing solely on money spent and money earned while neglecting the value of labour time is akin to theorising about snow falling and snow melting without considering temperature changes; it overlooks the fundamental factor driving the entire phenomenon.

Adam Smith and other classical economists thought equilibrium prices came from self-regulating market forces – the so-called invisible hand. But that's a shallow view. The real process is more like an 'elusive claw,'[187] guided by equalised profit rates and grabbing unrealised surpluses from workers in more 'labour intensive' firms and sectors and turning those surpluses into surplus profits for more 'capital intensive' ones.

Let's return to the issue of the declining average rate of profit. In Table 16, this rate stays at a steady 7.1 per cent and would remain so in subsequent turnovers if the table were expanded. Logically, however, one would expect it to drop over time, because when cost-cutting technologies are adopted by certain firms to boost productivity, it sparks coercive competition. As we have seen, this leads to widespread adoption of those technologies and the reduction of the need for productive labour. Assuming no other changes, less labour means less production of surplus value, which then leads to a lower rate of profit.

Concretely, when Mac gets a turbo grill, his individual value-based profit rate drops, but he doesn't care because his breakeven price for burgers is now lower than the average. This lets him temporarily increase his surplus profit. Mac's competitors feel the heat and start adopting turbo grills too, and this causes the average profit rate in the sector to drop. If this pattern holds across different sectors, the overall economy's average rate of profit will tend to fall.

Notice the reference to a tendency here. This acknowledges the fact that the average profit rate may not exhibit a continuous, empirically observable decline, as counter-tendencies come into play in reality. I will cover these later, but for now, let's attempt to simulate this decline in our reproduction scheme for a closed economy.

The scheme developed thus far does not take technical progress into

	t=1		t=2	
	MOP	MOC	MOP	MOC
Capital invested (C = c + v):	600	100	643	85
Constant capital (c)	550	50	600	43
Variable capital (v)	50	50	43	43
Organic composition (OC = c / v)	11.0	1.0	14.1	1.0
Surplus rate (s')	50%	50%	50%	50%
Surplus value (S = v × s')	25	25	21	21
Value produced (V = C + S)	625	125	664	106
Profit rate (p' = S / C)	4%	25%	3%	25%
Average profit rate (P' = ∑S / ∑C)	7.1%		5.8%	
Profit (P = C × P')	43	7	38	5
Revenue (R = C + P)	643	107	680	90
Surplus profit (SP = R - V)	18	-18	16	-16

Table 17. Technical Change and Falling Profit Rate

account. As previously mentioned, the intensive reproduction scheme proposed by Rosa Luxemburg integrates an increase in the organic composition of capital (see Chapter 3). Without getting into the extensive debate sparked by her conclusions,[188] I want to illustrate how this increase can cause a declining average profit rate.

Consider the scenario shown in Table 17. The allocation of constant capital in the MOP sector increases by two per cent with each turnover, in addition to the average profit rate. At t = 2, MOP invests 600c (550c × [1 + P' + 2%]) instead of 589c (550c × [1 + P']). Other than this adjustment, the scheme follows the same logical progression as before.

With a fixed amount of profit to allocate, MOP's greater investment in constant capital is offset by lower investment in variable capital, which decreases from 54v to 43v. The decrease in employment reduces demand for MOC's commodities, which in turn results in lower sector earnings and a corresponding decline in allocated profits for constant capital investment (43c instead of 54c), and so on.

The outcome is indeed a falling average profit rate, from 7.1 at t = 1 to 5.8 per cent at t = 2. MOP's increased productivity, driven by technological progress and coercive competition, reduces the proportion of profit reinvested in labour power. As the organic composition rises, the average profit rate tends to fall because, as we know, surplus value comes from labour. With a reduced allocation of capital to labour power, there is less surplus value to extract (assuming a steady surplus rate).

Eventually, this economy reaches zero growth and crashes (if one were to extend the table over a longer period). 'Since machines cannot produce surplus-value, [...] capital will cut off its supply of surplus value and automate itself out of existence.'[189]

A decline in average profit rate may be brought about not only by technical progress, but also by wage rises. As detailed earlier, incorporating higher wages involves a simultaneous increase in variable capital and decrease in the surplus rate. In other words, every real increase in workers' wages comes at the expense of capitalist profits.

I incorporate this in Table 18. At t = 1, MOP's 50v of variable capital generates 25S of surplus value with a surplus rate of fifty per cent. As before, variable capital increases to 54v at t = 2. However, the four-point increase now represents higher wages, not higher employment. Surplus value must therefore decrease by the same amount: from 25S at t = 1 to 21S at t = 2.

	t=1		t=2	
	MOP	MOC	MOP	MOC
Capital invested (C = c + v):	600	100	643	107
Constant capital (c)	550	50	589	54
Variable capital (v)	50	50	54	54
Organic composition (OC = c / v)	11.0	1.0	11.0	1.0
Surplus rate (s')	50%	50%	40%	40%
Surplus value (S = v × s')	25	25	21	21
Value produced (V = C + S)	625	125	664	129
Profit rate (p' = S / C)	4%	25%	3%	20%
Average profit rate (P' = ∑S / ∑C)	7.1%		5.7%	
Profit (P = C × P')	43	7	37	6
Revenue (R = C + P)	643	107	680	113
Surplus profit (SP = R - V)	18	-18	15	-15

Table 18. Wage Increases and Falling Profit Rate

This adjustment yields a decreasing surplus rate from fifty to forty per cent (21S / 54v = 40%). As both sectors' surplus values decline in this manner, the average profit rate does too.

The crisis-prone nature of the economy comes from this tendency of the average profit rate to decline. In a closed economy, such decline congests the MO→CO→MO' circuit by instilling uncertainty about future returns and prompting capitalists to withhold investment. This can lead to an accumulation of unsold and unsalable commodities by other capitalists, who may resort to layoffs and reduced hiring, resulting in further declines in aggregate demand, thereby exacerbating the initial problem.

A persistent lack of profitable investment outlets can culminate in what is known as an over-accumulation crisis:[190] The system chokes on its own success. If the circulation of capital does not resume, the over-accumulated capital faces devaluation or destruction, which manifests as underused factories, vacant shops, unused land, half-finished goods, unsold inventories, idle workers, and so on.

A crisis acts as a sort of reset button. Indeed, capital's devaluation and destruction serve to restore the rate of profit, potentially paving the way for a new round of accumulation. We operate in an economic system that regularly exposes us to its inherent and detrimental instabilities.

How might a system burdened by this tendency towards decline avoid collapsing under its own weight? As mentioned above, such a tendency does not automatically signify an infinite fall; counter-tendencies exist. For example, capitalists might turn to more speculative investments, fostering debt-fuelled growth in the short term but potentially contributing to economic instability in the long term.[191] Or, they might rely on boosted state demand for goods from the military-industrial complex (which ties into the concept of monopoly capitalism, to be examined later).

Alternatively, capital investments may flow into Global South countries, in search of higher (value-based) profit and surplus rates. The profit rate's tendency to fall (as opposed to an actual decline) is one explanation for the significant rise in global trade and investment flows over the past several decades.

The last scheme demonstrated how a wage increase in a hypothetical closed economy reduces the rate of profit. In open economies, as we shall see, unequal exchange shifts the burden of wage increases in the Global North onto the Global South. Higher wages in the capitalist economies of the North create an incentive to outsource exploitative production, thereby mitigating those economies' tendencies towards a lower average profit rate.

Essentially, the system seeks to expand in its quest for new wealth through appropriation and exploitation on a world scale, a spatial fix which underscores 'capitalism's insatiable drive to resolve its inner crisis tendencies by geographical expansion.'[192]

Closing Remarks

I began this chapter by asking: How can firms and sectors benefit at the expense of entirely different firms and sectors? By employing a Marxist framework, we gained insights into how such disequilibrium would unfold structurally in an ideal-typical capitalist economy. The root of this disequilibrium stems from a misalignment between value in production (the labour form) and value in circulation (the money form).

Our analysis differentiated between competition among firms within the same sector, and competition among sectors within the same (closed) economy. These two forms of competition give rise to two distinct laws: the 'law of one price' within a sector and the 'law of the tendential equalisation of rates of profit' across sectors.[193]

Complementing Chapter 3's reproduction models with the transformation of values into prices showed how value transfers can balance supply and demand in the ideal-typical model. Introducing technical progress and increased wages into the models showed that the average profit rate tends to decline, which can lead to an over-accumulation crisis. One potential escape from such a crisis involves the system expanding and seeking new sources of profit through exploitation on a global scale – the focus of the second part of this book.

Part 2. Value Transfers

5. Uneven Development

OPENING REMARKS

Imagine two lines of equal length: one with arrowheads pointing outwards and the other with arrowheads pointing inwards. Though they are the same length, the inwards-pointing line appears longer. Now, consider the reverse: Two lines of unequal length can appear equal (see Diagram 17).

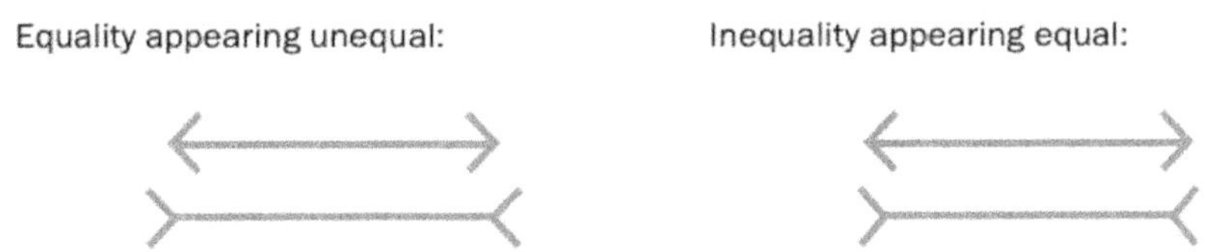

Diagram 17. The Müller-Lyer Illusion

Mainstream development narratives create just such an illusion by masking uneven development with the bogus claim, supported by bogus statistics, that all countries have an equal shot at success. These narratives generally portray development as a universal, homogenising, assimilative, and expansionist process of modernisation. 'African leaders should get serious about growth. They should embrace the self-confident spirit of modernisation', *The Economist* writes, arguing that the continent needs a 'Capitalistic Revolution'.[194]

How would I define development instead, and what makes it uneven? Development should improve the material, social, and mental conditions for life, prioritising those who struggle the most, so as to reduce substantive injustices within and between countries. It should ensure a just distribution of limited environmental resources and services, implying the adoption of sufficiency principles. To realise these conditions, development must be an endogenous, self-directed process of structural transformation, grounded in recognition and procedural justice.[195] It becomes uneven when these conditions are not met across different regions or populations.

Importantly, uneven development comes from the many connections between the regions or populations facing these divergences. Their histories and paths are intertwined: One's accumulation of wealth causes another's accumulation of misery.[196]

The present chapter explores these connections and offers some important context for the upcoming chapters on (ecological) unequal exchange. However, entire volumes have been written about uneven development, and my aim here is to present only a general outline; there will be simplifications and omissions. Importantly, this chapter focuses on uneven development's 'phenomenal' historical drivers – that is, how it appears – rather than its 'essential' underlying mechanisms, as Marx would say. The latter will be treated in subsequent chapters.

NEOCOLONIALISM

Despite all the chatter about progress, convergence, the eradication of poverty, and win-win trade, the facts tell a different story about today's world: Wealth rises while poverty deepens (see Chapter 1). However, merely pointing this out does not prove that the rich are getting richer by keeping the poor poor, let alone by making them poorer. To establish this link, we must dig deeper into the mechanisms of uneven development, leaning on Marx's value framework from Part 1. For Marx,

> [i]f the free-traders cannot understand how one nation can grow rich at the expense of another, we need not wonder, since these same gentlemen also refuse to understand how within one country one class can enrich itself at the expense of another.[197]

In Part 1, we familiarised ourselves with this process of enrichment through impoverishment in a hypothetically sealed-off national economy: Gains in the toothpick sector came with losses in the burger sector. However, both sectors ultimately relied on the extraction of surplus value from labour and the appropriation of the free gifts of (human) nature.

The goal of Part 2 is to examine this process as it plays out internationally. It will show how the capitalist class of the Global North extracts value not only from its own domestic working class, but increasingly from that of the Global South through unequal exchange.

To understand this, we should first consider the heterodox perspective of structuralist and world-system theorists, who have long reflected on uneven international development and patterns of trade as seen in measures such as 'terms of trade' or 'trade in value added' (more on this later). Their insights challenge the neoclassical myth that capitalism helps the so-called 'developing world' to catch up with the 'developed world,' showing it to lead instead to uneven development and exploitation on a world scale.

Let's sort out the terminology first. Instead of oversimplified labels such as 'rich/poor,' 'developed/developing,' or 'north/south' (which I've used so far to avoid overload), structuralist and world-system theorists prefer to differentiate nations and social strata as belonging either to the 'centre' or 'periphery.' Essentially, powerful central entities dominate profitable economic activities worldwide, to the detriment of their peripheral counterparts. This framework covers both horizontal relationships between nations and vertical relationships between social classes (see Diagram 18).[198]

The horizontal relationship isn't direct exploitation, but dependency: Dominant centre nations appropriate surplus value from dependent periphery nations; capital dominates capital. But this surplus first comes from labour, through the vertical relationship within the peripheries; capital exploits labour.[199] In population terms, the periphery is larger.

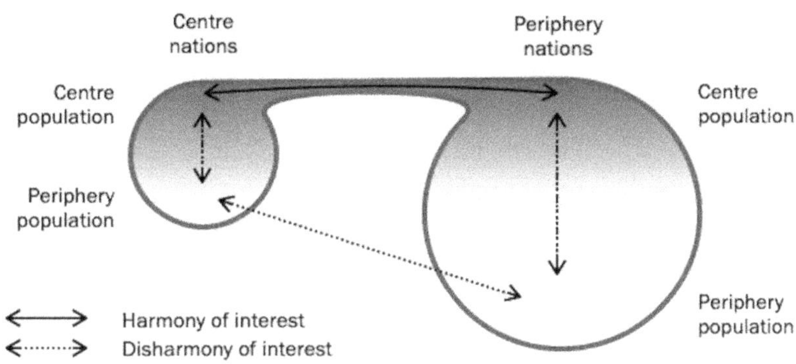

Diagram 18. Centre–Periphery Model

Like all models, this one obviously simplifies reality. For a start, the centre–periphery designation represents a spectrum rather than a strict dichotomy, as some countries act more as semi-periphery or semi-centre.[200] Also, globalisation has blurred national identities and fostered a transnational centre whose corporations enrich centre countries and classes, and exploit the peripheries, around the world.[201]

Moreover, the interactions between centres more resemble a temporary peace treaty than a true 'harmony of interest,' lasting only until one party feels strong enough to end it for their own gain.[202] The world indeed seems to be moving towards a multipolar constellation of powerful centres.

Despite these nuances, however, the model is useful for untangling the interconnected relationships of dominance and exploitation in the world system. The centres exert a gravitational pull on wealth and control; the peripheries experience a drain of both.

The prevailing mindset suggests that, rather than hinder peripheral development, centres facilitate or lead it. This idea appeared in 1940s and 1950s theories of modernisation, which posited that all societies would follow a developmental path similar to Europe's.[203] By 'modernising' – a euphemism for 'civilising' – traditional and rural economies into more advanced and urbanised ones, the peripheries were expected to boost production, savings, and investments, thereby fostering economic growth.

In 1960, economist Walt Rostow consolidated these ideas by proposing that all countries follow universal stages of growth and implying an inevitable global convergence of centres and peripheries.[204] Development scholars after Rostow continued to attribute the perceived 'backwardness' of the peripheries to a cycle of low investment, capital shortage, limited productivity, reduced income, and constrained savings. To break free, they theorised, these regions needed loans, aid, and/or foreign investment for boosting exports and rates of economic growth.[205]

With these development 'experts' essentially blaming periphery countries for a lack of openness to the world economy, the Bretton Woods institutions (see Chapter 1) moved to act on this premise. Endowed with the power to shape global economic, financial, and trade policies after World War II, these institutions began by implementing reforms in the peripheries to open up markets, regulate exchange rates, attract international capital, and foster export-oriented production – a modus operandi still in effect to this day.[206] Convergence, universalism, progress, and other similar dogmas inherent in modernisation theories continue to shape official discourses and policies of development. More generally speaking, these dogmas align with the stubborn belief that capitalism's global spread marks the pinnacle of social evolution.[207]

These discourses and policies rest on flimsy and shaky foundations. Importantly, modernisation theorists blamed the peripheries' 'backwardness' solely on internal misfortune, ignoring the huge impact of external forces from the global system orchestrated primarily by the centres.[208] This oversight misconstrued reality, as the peripheries do not exist in a vacuum, and world-system theorists, often inspired by Marxist ideas, responded by arguing that the centres accumulate wealth at the expense of the peripheries.[209]

In the mid-1960s, while discussing Latin America, economist and political activist André Gunder Frank sharply articulated how the centre develops by 'underdeveloping' the periphery.[210] Similarly, Guyanese historian and activist Walter Rodney emphatically demonstrated that Europe's capitalist development relied on the deliberate underdevelopment of Africa.[211]

Echoing these views, Brazilian economist Theotonio Dos Santos attributed the periphery's underdevelopment to the extraction of locally-generated 'surplus' (by which he meant profit, not surplus value). He argued that underdevelopment, far from a 'backwards' stage, is a process that results from 'dependent capitalism.'[212] In other words, we are dealing with a logical outcome of the system, not a correctable glitch. 'These countries are not underdeveloped, they're overexploited.'[213]

Dos Santos defined dependency as a setup in which dominant centres endowed with technological, commercial, and military advantages develop precisely by dictating and stunting the development of 'subordinate' peripheries. Their economies become dependent the more they are structured to export commodities for the centres and import commodities from them.

World-system theorists initially focused on international relationships ('horizontal' in Diagram 18), but later broadened their analysis to include internal ('vertical') structures within the peripheries, especially the dependency of traditional sectors on modern export-oriented ones.[214] This expansion led to the distinction between central and peripheral social strata within both regions.[215]

These theories traced underdevelopment and dependency to a brutal form of domination: imperialism. This conception of imperialism goes beyond the usual images of Roman legions or Mongol hordes. In Marxist theory, imperialism often represents capitalism at its highest stage, a phase marked by the dominance of monopolies and finance capital. Global capital flows become central; the world is carved up by global trusts and divided between the major capitalist powers.[216] As capital is concentrated into monopolies, these firms extend their influence over the state to create favourable conditions for their global expansion and dominance.

Accordingly, Rodney defines capitalist imperialism as a system in which capitalist development in the centres is coupled with the peripheries' underdevelopment.[217] Imperialism knows no borders, as elites in both centre and periphery countries collaborate to impose their political and economic agendas on peripheral populations, ruthlessly disregarding their conflicting interests (see Diagram 18).

Some argue that these traits have defined capitalism since its inception. Rather than representing capitalism's zenith, imperialism might in fact be its enduring and permanent form.[218] Rosa Luxemburg noted that capitalism has always relied on non-capitalist societies – such as those based on subsistence economies and simple commodity production – for expansion, often through imperialist wars.[219]

Viewed in this way, capitalist imperialism was perhaps most pronounced during its colonial phase, when it came into the world 'dripping from head to foot, from every pore, with blood and dirt,' as Marx puts it.[220]

Interconnected divergences between centres and peripheries arose with the expropriation of wealth through slavery, the enclosure of common land, destruction of communities and local markets, and the creation of a global division of labour. 'The treasures captured outside Europe by undisguised looting, enslavement, and murder, floated back to the mother-country and were there turned into capital.'[221] Smaller industrial countries in the centre that lacked colonies could nonetheless ride the wave created by the major colonial powers: Through the circulation of capital and commodities between the colonial powers and other industrial countries, each secured its share of the spoils.[222]

These blatant expropriations shaped capitalism's process of 'primitive accumulation,' with coerced dispossession laying the groundwork for capitalist relations by turning nature into constant capital and people into variable capital. This concept will be particularly important when we turn to the process of ecologically unequal exchange in Chapter 7.

While slavery clearly played a significant role in early capitalism, it ended up hindering capitalist accumulation in the centres. For one, it limited technological advancement by relying mostly on manual labour, and stifled consumption by keeping a large workforce with no money to spend. Such limitations led to the shift to colonial wage labour in the peripheries. Instead of cheap labourers, capitalists opted for cheap labour power.

As an instrument of imperialism, colonialism thus turned towards maximising the extraction of surplus value from wage labour – the source of profits. Labour power in the colonies was so cheap that workers couldn't survive on wages alone, and had to grow their own food, build their own shelter, and so on. Unlike slavery, this system was able to offload the responsibility for workers' sustenance and subsistence onto the informal sphere of social reproduction.

Meanwhile, workers in the centres had no land to produce food or gather fuel and relied solely on selling their labour power to survive. Their employers were required to provide a minimal living wage – a relative improvement compared to workers in the periphery, which saw a Scottish or German coal miner earning in an hour what a Nigerian miner made in six days.[223]

The minimal living wage that capitalists in the imperialist centres had to pay their workers could be kept low through the influx of cheap commodities from the colonies. This reduced the social reproduction costs of labour power and thus its abstract value. As a result, relative surplus value could increase even as wages rose (see Graph 6 in Chapter 3). Higher wages in the centres expanded working-class consumption, which in turn further favoured capital accumulation there.

The colonial pool of potential surplus labour incentivised such imperial powers as Britain, France, Portugal, the Netherlands, the United States, and Japan to subjugate about forty per cent of the world's land by the early twentieth century.[224] The effects were devastating. Colonialism entrenched racism, perpetuated cultural assimilation, and objectified colonised peoples within the capitalist system. It also created social divisions in the peripheries by establishing privileged classes of 'sell-outs,' who both benefited from and helped maintain colonial control.

Additionally, colonialism produced what Rodney calls 'technological regression.'[225] For instance, when the British deindustrialised textile production in India, Indian manufacturers were forced to import machine-made products from Britain; the ensuing rebellion was brutally suppressed. The British also enforced indigo cultivation, transforming the region into a supplier of raw materials. As the British empire developed, Bengal underdeveloped.[226] Even if Rostow's stages of development did exist, capitalism would surely have reversed them in the peripheries during its colonial phase.

The end of colonialism did not herald the end of imperialism. After World War II, decolonisation coincided with the establishment of the Bretton Woods system which, as described above, pushed trade liberalisation and export-oriented reforms onto newly independent countries. This thrusted these mostly agrarian nations into a harsh 'neocolonial' order.

In a short time, these countries' markets came to face intense international competition, which resulted in the further decline of local industries, increased unemployment, and entrenched exploitation. Moreover, their dependence on expensive secondary imports from industrial centres (due in part to the earlier process of colonial deindustrialisation) kept them reliant on cheap primary exports for income.[227]

By contrast, the centres industrialised, diversified, and thrived through decades of protectionism and colonial exploitation,[228] turning to liberalism only when the 'level playing field' looked sufficiently safe.[229] As Torkil Lauesen writes:

> The former colonial empires adjusted themselves to the new situation without too much grief, letting the economic laws of international trade attribute to each of them the benefits of unequal exchange.[230]

Their economic dominance also allowed them to influence global governance, as their strong GDPs granted them G8 or G20 membership as well as increased voting power in the Bretton Woods system.[231] This system enables members to impose punitive sanctions on countries deemed to be breaking free market rules, and tends to disadvantage relatively weak and undiversified economies.[232] Neocolonialism thus perpetuates colonial exploitation, with centres maintaining their advantages through strategic trade barriers and protectionist policies.[233] As Nelson Maldonado-Torres explains, 'coloniality survives colonialism'[234] – with coloniality referring to the various colonial-like power relations existing in the world today.[235]

Ghanaian revolutionary Kwame Nkrumah views neocolonialism as imperialism's final and most dangerous form. Although nominally sovereign, the economic systems and political policies of 'neocolonised' states are still controlled from abroad. Unlike traditional colonialism, however, 'neocolonising' powers do not have to justify their actions domestically and can more freely externalise various social and environmental costs to periphery countries.[236] These abuses can then conveniently be attributed to corrupt peripheral regimes or regressive cultures.

The global inequalities that I introduced in Chapter 1 have been arrived at not by the separate evolution of centres and peripheries, but through patterns of exploitation facilitated by imperialism. How imperialism perpetuated colonialist relationships into the neocolonial era is the focus of the remainder of this chapter.

THE OLD GLOBAL DIVISION OF LABOUR

As mentioned earlier, the peripheries were forced into dependency by exporting what the centres required and importing what the centres controlled. This was always going to be a win-lose relationship which, as we shall see, led to the peripheries' indebtedness, the final nail in the coffin of their dependency. But let's start from the beginning.

Simply put, international trade presents a paradox: Every country loves exports but hates imports.[237] They all seek to raise their terms of trade, that is, the ratio between the price index of exports and the price index of imports.

A country's export earnings and import expenditures depend on both the volume and prices of goods traded. If a country's export price index declines relative to its import price index, it must increase its export volume to cover its import expenses.[238] This need escalates further if the price index of essential import goods rises. In essence, a country's terms of trade are a measure of its ability to purchase imports with its exports.

When export prices rise relative to import prices, we speak of a favourable movement in that country's terms of trade: It can afford more imported goods per unit of exported goods. Conversely, if export prices decrease relative to import prices, the terms of trade are said to deteriorate (see

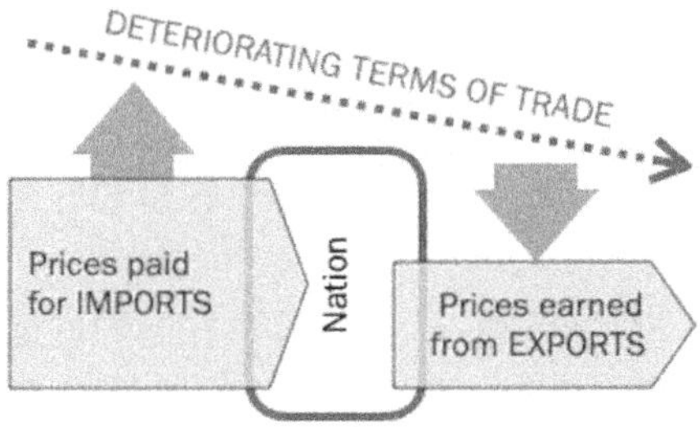

Diagram 19. Deteriorating Terms of Trade

Diagram 19). Typically, the centres experience favourable movements, while the peripheries face deterioration.

These movements were already evident during colonialism. For example, cotton grown by Ugandan farmers was shipped to English factories in Lancashire. While the Lancashire factory owner paid workers meagre wages, organised labour provided some checks on his exploitation. However, Ugandan peasants endured unchecked exploitation, forced by colonial rule to work long hours for a pittance. Some of their cotton then returned to Uganda as textiles but was priced far beyond the reach of the peasants who grew it.[239]

Such inequalities worsened over time: By 1939, African colonies could purchase only sixty per cent of the manufactured goods that they would have been able to buy with the same amount of primary goods before colonial rule (1870–80). By 1960, African purchasing power had declined even further.[240]

Neocolonialism extended this trend, as history shows that the prices of primary commodities have steadily declined relative to manufactured goods.[241] For instance, the twentieth century saw a 53 per cent drop in the terms of trade of raw materials and agricultural products.[242] Agricultural export prices fell nearly seventy per cent compared to the prices of imported manufactured goods between 1961 and 2001 in the so-called least-developed economies.[243] Despite some food price increases since 2002, the pattern of long-term decline (which ran at an average annual rate of 0.6 per cent in the twentieth century) has persisted.[244]

The overall pattern, therefore, was that monopolistic centres enjoyed increased earnings and reduced spending; while competing peripheries suffered the opposite.[245]

Who produces what and where is neither accidental nor inevitable. As Marx observes, places such as the Caribbean were not predestined to grow coffee and sugar: 'Two centuries ago, nature, which does not trouble herself about commerce, had planted neither sugar-cane nor coffee trees there.'[246] As we know, colonialism violently forced the peripheries into the extraction of raw materials for the industrial and technological benefit of imperial powers.

Neocolonialism has perpetuated this global division of labour, in which competing peripheral economies supply low-priced primary goods while monopolistic centres dominate the production of high-priced manufactured goods. We see this pattern when Ethiopia exports sesame seeds but imports sesame oil, Ghana exports cocoa beans but imports chocolate, and Nigeria exports crude oil but imports refined petroleum products.

As early as 1950, world-systems economists Hans Singer and Raúl Prebisch hypothesised that this global division of labour would lead to a continual deterioration in periphery countries' terms of trade.[247] They attributed the persistent decline in the prices of primary products relative to manufactured goods to two key dynamics.

Firstly, the peripheries' terms of trade worsen as their demand for manufactured exports from centre countries grows faster than the centre's demand for primary products. Higher incomes in the centres typically go towards luxury items rather than additional food (with some exceptions). Indeed, demand for primary goods tends to lag behind overall growth in world income.[248]

Secondly, productivity gains in the centres come with higher wages, whereas in the peripheries they translate into lower prices. Singer and Prebisch blame this on an oversupply of 'unskilled' labour in periphery countries, which limits workers' ability to negotiate higher pay,[249] while the opposite situation prevails in the centres. This makes periphery commodities cheaper and centre commodities more expensive, with both dynamics contributing to a decline in the peripheries' terms of trade relative to the centres.

In 2022, low- and lower-middle-income countries (LICs and LMICs)[250] ran a combined trade deficit, resulting in a negative balance of payments of US$433 billion.[251] By contrast, upper-middle- and high-income countries (UMICs and HICs) recorded surpluses of US$922 billion and US$162 billion, respectively. On a per capita basis, the deficit for LICs and LMICs amounted to US$109 per person, while the surplus for HICs stood at US$133 per person.[252]

As peripheries struggled to raise sufficient revenue from exports to cover imports, they resorted to borrowing, thereby setting the stage for an external debt crisis.

To grasp how this crisis unfolded, we must go back to the 1960s, when overspending in the United States led to a depreciation of the dollar.[253] This prompted major oil-producing (semi-)periphery countries to raise oil prices.[254] As they deposited their vast profits in commercial banks, interest rates fell, while the rising oil costs and declining terms of trade drove up expenses in periphery nations, which were forced to borrow from those same commercial banks.[255] Then, however, the United States started borrowing to finance its deficit, and interest rates spiked, triggering the debt trap. Mexico's default in 1982 was the first of its kind and immediately threatened the international credit system.

The threat of sovereign defaults to the international credit system led to interventions by the World Bank and International Monetary Fund (IMF), but their so-called loans of last resort came with strict conditions. To access these loans, indebted nations were forced to prioritise export-driven growth, cut social welfare, restrict local industry subsidies, reduce wages, ease foreign investment and imports, raise interest rates, and devalue their currency.[256]

Such measures were intended to fix short-term insolvency, not promote development. In fact, they worsened uneven development. In the 1970s, for example, Jamaica invested heavily in health, education, housing, and agriculture. Its population had access to well-run hospitals with skilled staff, advanced equipment, and affordable care. But then the oil shock hit, tripling import costs while profits from the country's aluminium and sugar exports plummeted. This forced Jamaica to borrow heavily and accept IMF loans with the aforementioned conditions. Fast forward forty years, and state funds today go primarily towards servicing a debt of about 160 per cent of GDP. The once-thriving hospitals now struggle with unmaintained infrastructure, undertrained staff, and unaffordable treatment.[257]

As a result of such forced structural adjustments, wealth and resources from all around periphery territories flowed to foreign investors, domestic needs were neglected, reliance on imports increased, worker rights diminished, and wages stagnated.[258] For example, although currency devaluations were supposed to improve Jamaica's international competitiveness by lowering export prices, they also raised import costs, further worsening the country's terms of trade. In this way, indebted nations found themselves ensnared in the very system that had caused their trade imbalances to begin with.

Attempts to escape the World Bank and IMF straitjacket were quickly stifled. For instance, in 2005, Ecuadorian Finance Minister Rafael Correa introduced a law to allocate eighty per cent of the country's oil revenues to welfare programs, leaving 'only' twenty per cent for debt payments. In response, the World Bank threatened to cut off all lending if the law was implemented. Correa's resignation ended the dispute, highlighting the periphery's utter loss of self-determination.[259]

This period also set the stage for the US dollar's rise as the dominant global currency – key background for understanding uneven currency exchange rates, which will be part of the analysis of unequal exchange in Chapter 6.

At the 1944 Bretton Woods conference, US Treasury official Harry Dexter White outplayed British economist John Maynard Keynes by establishing the dollar as the world's top currency. White's system pegged other currencies to the dollar, backed by gold.[260] A significant driver behind the move was the desire to break the UK's global hold, including its colonial pound-based trade preferences, which limited US market access.

Largely through its control of oil transactions, the dollar's power only continued to grow after Bretton Woods. US multinationals sold Middle Eastern oil to Europe, and Gulf states pumped oil profits into US Treasury bonds, thus embedding the dollar deep in the global financial system. The oil shocks of the 1970s further solidified global dependence on the US currency, as oil-importing and debt-ridden countries borrowed in dollars.[261]

THE NEW GLOBAL DIVISION OF LABOUR

Let me recap the key messages so far. Post-colonial global capitalism was rigged from the outset, as newly 'independent' countries entered the global trade arena at a significant disadvantage, having been deindustrialised, robbed, and weakened by their former colonial powers. The resulting international division of labour indebted the peripheries, which had no choice but to reinforce their dependence on the very system that had indebted them. To this day, these nations remain buried under mountains of debt, and struggle to repay even the interest.

This brings us to the subsequent historical phase of uneven development. From the early 1980s, the structure of international trade flows underwent a profound shift with the emergence of the 'Age of Global Value Chains.'[262]

Burdened by debt and low credit ratings, periphery nations struggled to access international capital markets for industrial development and turned instead to Foreign Direct Investment (FDI). This was further encouraged by World Bank and IMF loan conditions, specifically the removal of restrictions on investments entering the peripheries.

FDI can take multiple forms, such as horizontal integration, which involves foreign companies merging with local counterparts, and vertical integration, where a single company controls the entire supply chain. The latter describes Global Value Chains (GVCs), structures governed by large transnational corporations that disperse production across borders via outsourcing and offshoring. GVCs came to dominate global trade, with the value of intermediate goods traded within them surpassing ten trillion dollars annually since 2000,[263] and currently accounting for seventy per cent of total global trade in goods and services.[264]

Through their control over GVCs, corporations bolster accumulation for global capitalists through the exploitation of periphery labour. The existence of a large underpaid reserve army of labourers makes it highly difficult for workers to fight for decent wages and working conditions, but the problem does not stop there.

These workers' employers, the periphery firms, are unable to charge higher prices for fear of losing clients or access to distribution. This encourages exploitation in the form of forced overtime and union busting. By employing cutting-edge corporate strategies in the name of 'efficiency' and 'flexibility,' corporations can swiftly relocate production when wages, prices, or regulations threaten to rise in a given setting. This locks the peripheries into low-wage, low-profit nodes of the GVCs and consolidates the imperial dominance of the centres.[265]

These GVCs contributed to a blurring of the old agriculture-manufacturing dichotomy of the mid-1970s. The productive centres' (in this calculation defined as those whose ratio of primary to total exports is less than sixty per cent) share of world manufacturing exports fell from eighty to 54 per cent over the 1995-2023 period, reflecting both deindustrialisation and the offshoring of industrial production to the productive periphery, whose share rose from sixteen to forty per cent.[266] Some peripheries therefore 'climbed up the chain' – a little bit – and began producing (semi-)manufactured exports. However, this generally hasn't improved their terms of trade or overall position.

With the outsourcing of much heavy industry to the (semi-)peripheries, some Westerners now believe that it vanished entirely from the face of the Earth.[267] Clearly, it did not. For example, since the mid-2010s, the Democratic Republic of Congo has been refining its cobalt into cobalt hydroxide, an intermediate compound used in other cobalt products. Previously, most of its cobalt was exported to be refined elsewhere, particularly China. While this move to a local process might seem like progress, it's actually a dirty business that pollutes the environment, contaminates water, and creates toxic waste. It unburdens capital in wealthier nations that benefit from the cleaner, more profitable stages of production.[268]

To be sure, in the context of the 'new global division of labour', the centre–periphery division is no longer as clear-cut as it was in the classical dependency framework.[269] Some countries have industrialised, even if only in part. However, the 'old global division of labour' hasn't entirely vanished either. Neoliberalism has left some of that basic structure of dependency intact.

While Singer and Prebisch had warned about the long-term effects of periphery nations' dependence on cheap primary exports and costly manufactured imports, they did not anticipate that the periphery's terms of trade would remain unfavourable for (semi-)manufactured exports, and that the centre's terms of trade would remain favourable for primary exports.[270] This challenges the notion that industrialisation constitutes the primary driver of economic development in the peripheries.[271]

Singer later acknowledged that this problem did not necessarily arise from the nature of the commodities traded, but rather from deeper structural differences between centre and periphery economies. Adopting the position of 'Singer II,' he admitted that 'Singer I' had overlooked these critical issues.[272]

The traditional division of labour therefore fails to fully explain the periphery's worsening terms of trade. Development economist Arthur Lewis instead blamed the wage gap between centre and periphery,[273] and contended that when peripheral regions try to develop productive industries, they inadvertently worsen their terms of trade. As mentioned above, increased productivity under low-wage conditions drives down prices rather than boosting wages. Later, we'll see how the theory of unequal exchange can deepen our understanding of how the wage gap indeed acts as a key driver of the unequal terms of trade.

An important insight emerges here: The peripheries cannot break free from their predicament by adopting the centre's productive technologies, nor by producing its commodities.[274] Furthermore, there is no guarantee that the development of secondary and tertiary production in the peripheries will reduce uneven development. Promoting free and competitive trade between high- and low-wage nations – treating unequal partners as equals – is doomed to fail.

MONOPOLY CAPITALISM

Lewis, like Singer and Prebisch, attributed the wage gap to an excess of workers in the peripheries, leading to fierce job competition and suppressed wages. However, this explanation is incomplete and invites an overpopulation narrative that shifts the blame away from capitalism as the real culprit. As we know, (neo)colonial forces perpetuate this wage gap by exporting exploitation from centres to peripheries.

Exploitation doesn't arise from an oversupply of labour, so much as from the overwhelming concentration of corporate power in the centres – a core feature of imperialism, and the focus of neo-Marxist theories of 'monopoly capitalism' as advanced notably by Paul Baran and Paul Sweezy.[275]

Baran and Sweezy are not talking about lone monopolies, but about market-dominating giants that thrive through exclusive licenses, brand recognition, patent control, proprietary technology, (non-)tariff barriers, and so on. They argue that the growing size and influence of these monopolies reduces business risk and allows them to collude (explicitly and tacitly) to hike up prices and rake in bigger profits (or rents, to be precise).[276]

In Part 1, we examined the ideal-typical competitive model of capitalism and the distribution of surplus profit through intra- and inter-sector competition. The time has come to acknowledge monopoly, for two reasons.

First, monopoly emerges naturally from competition. Indeed, Marx wrote that 'monopoly and competition mutually devour each other [...] Monopoly produces competition, competition produces monopoly.'[277] Imagine a large number of relatively small competing firms at an earlier stage of capitalism: Some succeed, others fail. As the 'losers' go belly up, the 'winners' gain a larger market share. We all know this phenomenon. Local grocery or hardware shops disappear, out-priced and outcompeted by large chains. Advanced capitalist economies inherently evolve towards monopoly through this process of inter- and intra-sector competition.

Second, monopoly has a role to play in the rise of imperialism, as the process of wealth concentration endows the wealthy with more and more power to influence political systems.

In the 1970s, Samir Amin coined the term 'monopoly state capitalism' to expose the ways in which governments are not simply neutral referees, but active partners with big corporations.[278] State subsidies and barriers that protect industries in the centres – at the expense of those in the peripheries – are part of capitalism's neocolonial playbook. Around the time of Amin's writing, when the Bretton Woods General Agreement on Tariffs and Trade (GATT) began cracking down on direct protectionism, centre states logically turned to offshoring. For example, facing tough competition from the Japanese car industry in the early 1980s, the US government backed the offshore production of electronics and machine parts for cheap re-importation, thus cleverly shifting from direct protectionism to indirect support.[279]

After all, the capitalist state is mostly geared to protect capitalism from any social force that would oppose it. As Walter Rodney puts it, 'the government is always the servant of a particular class.'[280]

Another term, 'neoliberal monopoly capitalism,' describes capitalism's more recent phase, the pinnacle of which was the establishment of the World Trade Organisation (WTO) in 1995 (replacing the GATT). The institution became exclusively dedicated to sanctioning every infraction, no matter how minimal, of the regime of free trade.[281]

Many believed that the WTO would finally curtail the monopolistic and protectionist behaviour of the centres. However, this new era of deregulation only intensified predatory practices and price manipulations, and further concentrated capital. Today, a complex network of subsidiaries and shareholders means that less than two per cent of transnational corporations control eighty per cent of corporate revenue.[282]

Capitalism in the periphery, meanwhile, takes a diverse array of forms and the extent of its integration into economic life varies (see Chapter 1). For example, some describe rentier states in the Middle East and North Africa – where fossil fuel revenues prioritise the patronage of local autocrats over development – as examples of 'crony,' 'nepotistic,' or 'comprador capitalism.' However, these conditions have often been created by the centres, through political interventions including coups, to maintain exploitation in the service of neoliberal monopoly capitalism.

The grip of monopolies on a vast global economy drains huge profits from the peripheries, in the form of 'monopoly rents' or 'supra-profits,' to the centres. Originally, monopoly rents referred to the ground rents that landowners could make from exclusive control (Marx gives the example of wine producers with their unique vineyards).[283] But in monopoly capitalism, these rents also include profits from monopolistic control over strategic resources beyond land, such as cheap labour or mineral resources, as well as profits extracted from barriers to entry.[284] When Visa and Mastercard control eighty per cent of monetary transactions and raise transaction fees, they earn monopoly rent.[285] This all can make the concept somewhat ambiguous.[286]

That said, 'monopoly rents' or 'supra-profits' occur on top of the 'differential rents' or 'surplus profits' described in Chapter 4. You may recall that, through his advanced productive technologies, Mac generates surplus profits at Bob's expense. If Mac then uses state-sanctioned patents to monopolise these technologies, he stands to earn supra-profits. When these monopoly rents occur at a global scale, they are sometimes referred to as 'imperialist rents,' and flow to the corporations that dominate Global Value Chains (GVCs).

Given the evolution of global trade from simple bilateral exchanges to more complex network structures, traditional terms of trade no longer adequately capture who benefits. We need new methods. Intermediate goods, used as inputs for the production of exports, now constitute about two-thirds of international trade, and so export prices partially reflect the cost of these imported inputs.[287] Terms of trade analyses look at a country's ability to buy imports with export earnings, but lump together all imports and exports. They therefore miss the specific transactions within GVCs, which is where 'value added' and the 'trade in value added' (TiVA) framework come in.

Value added does not refer to the Marxist concept of value as average labour time. Rather, it refers to the money left after deducting the costs of intermediate inputs from total sales revenue. It is the difference between the market value of what was sold (price multiplied by quantity of output sold) and the market value of what was bought to produce it (price multiplied by quantity of materials, components, services, and other inputs needed for production and purchased from other firms).

Importantly, value added isn't just profit – it's the realised surplus value (in Marxist terms) that gets divided into wages for workers, rent for landlords, interest for banks, taxes for governments, and, yes, profits for capitalists. The term 'value added' is therefore misleading: It doesn't reveal anything about who adds 'value,' but rather who captures it, both domestically and internationally.[288]

In the international context, TiVA separates domestic value added (DVA) from foreign value added (FVA) in an export's total value added (EXP).[289] Gross exports (EXP) are therefore the sum of DVA and FVA. For instance, in 2020, the Netherlands reported gross exports totalling $446 billion, which included seventy per cent DVA and thirty per cent FVA.[290]

This distinction allows us to avoid double counting. Diagram 20 presents a hypothetical example. Country A imports FVA in the form of mining equipment for $10 billion and generates $20 billion in DVA during extraction. It then exports $30 billion worth of raw materials, serving as FVA when imported by Country B for further processing. Subsequently, Country B 'adds' $15 billion as its own DVA, exporting processed materials worth $45 billion. This fictional case shows how some countries can capture more value in GVCs than others. Export earnings alone fail to provide that information: Compared to Country A, Country B seems to earn more on exports, but it actually earns less in DVA terms.

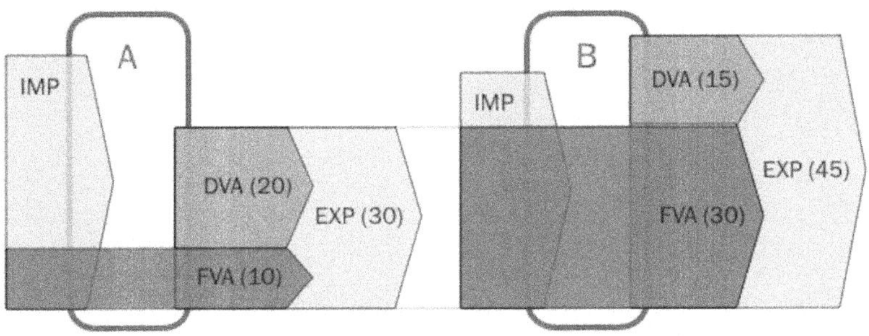

Diagram 20. Value Added

The ratios between DVA and FVA in total exports are key to understanding who captures monetary value in the global economy. For example, an increase in export revenue in peripheral economies doesn't automatically lead to a corresponding rise in value added. This can happen when those economies incorporate rising import costs (e.g., for mining equipment) into their export prices (e.g., mined resources). For example, if Country A in Diagram 20 imports FVA worth $15 billion instead of $10 billion and sells the final product to Country B for $35 billion instead of $30 billion, its DVA remains $20 billion.

However, in reality, industries in the periphery face intense competition from other peripheral economies and suffer from the neocolonial influence of global capital. As a result, they cannot easily raise their prices and can either expect reduced profit margins or resort to suppressing workers' wages. Either way, this would lead to a decline in value added. In the example above, Country A imports FVA worth $15 billion. If, however, it must still sell to Country B for $30 billion rather than passing on the increased input costs, Country A's DVA declines from $20 billion to $15 billion.

What do we see empirically? As Graph 9 shows, the periphery (defined here as low- and lower-middle-income countries) captured eighty per cent of total exports as DVA between 1990 and 1993, compared to 72 per cent for the centre (high-income countries). By 2015-2018, the periphery's share had risen to 84 per cent, while the centre's had fallen to 65 per cent. Yet these relative improvements mask the widening absolute gap. The periphery averaged just $250 in DVA per person annually between 2015 and 2018 – compared to $9,829 in the centre.[291] That's a 39:1 disparity, up from 36:1 in 1990-1993.

Low-income countries in the periphery category actually saw a reduction in yearly per capita DVA, from an average of $41 per capita in 1990-1993

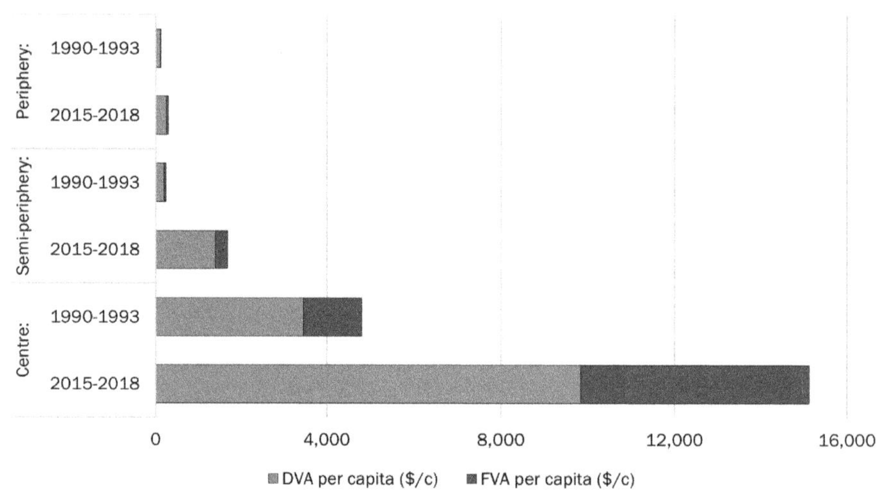

Graph 9. Trends in DVA and FVA per capita.
Graph showing per capita domestic and foreign value added in exports (DVA and FVA) across three country clusters (centre, semiperiphery, and periphery) grouped by income per capita. It compares average annual DVA and FVA per capita over two periods, 1990-1993 and 2015-2018, to smooth out year-to-year *fluctuations.*

to $35 in 2015-2018. This represents a staggering 279:1 difference with the centre. The drop in DVA as a share of exports, with FVA taking over, is especially pronounced in those periphery countries most deeply embedded in GVCs.[292]

This growing gap stems from the roles that have been systematically forced on centres and peripheries in GVCs. Typically, GVCs display a 'smile curve' of value added, with high-value activities such as engineering and design concentrated in the centres, and low-value tasks such as production and assembly relegated to the (semi-)peripheries (see Diagram 21). Take the iPhone: While China handles its assembly, the United States monopolises high-value design and marketing, capturing 58.5 per cent of the retail price, while Chinese labour accounts for just 1.8 per cent.[293]

Monopoly capitalism keeps the peripheries stuck in low value-adding segments and entrenches the centre's control over lucrative ones, where they capture ever more value added from the middle of the smile curve;[294] the smile becomes a full grin.

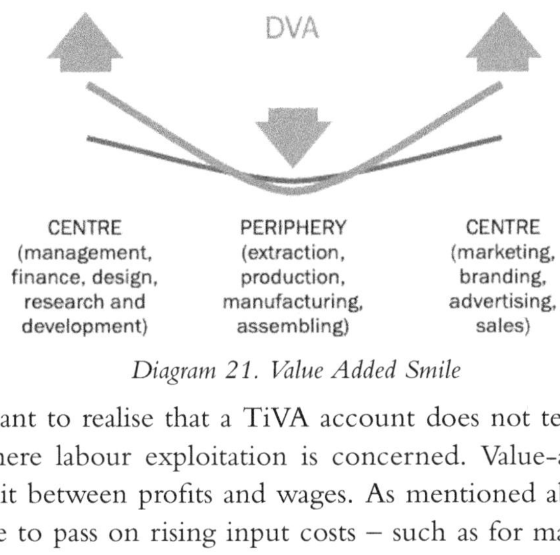

Diagram 21. Value Added Smile

It's important to realise that a TiVA account does not tell the full story, especially where labour exploitation is concerned. Value-added does not reveal the split between profits and wages. As mentioned above, periphery firms struggle to pass on rising input costs – such as for machinery, oil, or royalties – via the price of their exports. This means taking a hit to either profits or wages, with the latter far more likely to be sacrificed. Since the 1970s, mounting evidence shows a steady decline in the labour share of value added in GVCs.[295] Global capital exploits this imbalance, using its power to drive down wages, intensify worker exploitation in the periphery, and extract ever greater monopoly rents.

It's also important to realise that inequalities in DVA represent only one of many aspects of uneven development. The peripheries suffer the following annual losses: $100-650 billion to tax evasion,[296] $207-691 billion in interest payments,[297] $486 billion in profit repatriation,[298] $700 billion to trade barriers,[299] $973 billion in capital flight,[300] $875-1750 billion from trade mis-invoicing,[301] and so on. For every dollar of Official Development Assistance going to the peripheries (totalling $211 billion in 2022[302]), they lose roughly $16-25 through these various losses. We call this 'mopping with the tap on.'

Some of the periphery's losses, such as profit repatriation and interest payments, may seem justified. After all, why shouldn't investors receive rewards and debtors service their loans? However, it is essential to remember that these flows also originate from the exploitative legacies of (neo) colonialism and monopoly capitalism.

Representing the biggest loss of all, unequal exchange is responsible for draining the periphery of an estimated $6.9 trillion in 2022. We will break it down later (see Chapter 6), but the number represents an attempt to capture how much value (in the Marxist sense) is extracted by centre countries from the rest of the world. In theory, this occurs through differential rents (surplus profits) – profits siphoned between sectors in competitive markets, not through the monopoly or imperialistic rents (supra-profits) discussed in this section. Factoring in losses from unequal exchange, the aforementioned ratio of monetary losses to ODA rises from 25 to 58 times greater.

This section has sought to highlight the importance of monopolistic and imperialistic forces, and to distinguish them from competitive forces within capitalism, contrasting their roles in shaping uneven development. This distinction raises a critical question: Can the dismantling of monopolies and trade barriers mitigate uneven development? Or would such an ideal-typical form of capitalism still result in unequal gains and losses from trade? If so, the neoliberal claim that 'we need more, not less, global capitalism' falls apart.

To challenge the ideal-typical model, we will apply Marx's value framework, which differentiates monopoly rent (gained from market dominance or privileged access) and differential rent (gained from differences in productivity or exploitation). Both mechanisms drive the process of capital accumulation on a global scale, but focusing on differential rents reveals how systemic inequality persists, even under ostensibly fair, competitive, and open trade conditions.

ACCUMULATION ON A WORLD SCALE

To determine whether and how differential rents drain the periphery for the centre's benefit, we must first ask if capitalism truly dominates the global economy, especially in peripheral contexts. Differential rents arise in advanced capitalist systems; can we say the same about the world system?

Clearly, capitalists are not interested in creating competitors. From the start, metropolitan capitalists thrived on eliminating competition and forming monopolies. When imperialism took hold, they had no intention of nurturing rivals in the colonies. Despite this, however, local capitalists still emerged in the periphery.[303]

Nowadays, even the most remote places become incorporated in the capitalist production of value and extraction of surplus value, if sometimes only partially. For example, farms in remote rural Ethiopia devote considerable human and natural resources to producing cash crops destined for urban and foreign markets, through which they experience the ruthless capitalist commodification of social relations.[304]

I don't mean to suggest that capitalist relations have taken over entirely. Remember, capitalism coexists and interacts with various other ways of creating, delivering, and utilising wealth. We can call an economy capitalistic when it dominates these other systems (see Chapter 1).

Even China, despite its official communist ideology, has long embraced capitalist practices.[305] Fully integrated in global value chains, Chinese electronics workshops extract surplus value through highly efficient assembly lines and factory dormitories that facilitate flexible production, enforce overtime, and optimise labour costs. As has been well documented, these working conditions lead to loneliness, anxiety, alienation, and sometimes even suicide.[306]

For an impression of the levels of exploitation in these workshops, let us assume that values and prices align. An iPhone sold in the United States for \$999 (V) includes \$371 in constant capital (c) and \$25 in variable capital (v) – mostly wages for Chinese assembly line workers. Apple's profit of \$603 (S) reflects a surplus rate of 2,412 per cent (s' = S / v = \$603 / \$25), 25 times Marx's estimated surplus rate for nineteenth-century textile workers![307]

Compared to the centres, wages, hours, leave, health and safety, job security, and other workers' rights in the peripheries are considerably worse,[308] which is precisely why iPhones are not assembled in the United States. If they were, an iPhone would cost \$30,000.[309]

With capitalism expanding across the globe, we are both entitled and required to theorise about capitalist accumulation and exploitation on a world scale.

However, Marx was unable to develop such a theory during his lifetime. He focused primarily on closed capitalism within the advanced economies,[310] not the worldwide amalgamation of open economies, each with different shades of capitalist relations, unique (neo)colonial histories, and imperial entanglements. Nevertheless, the building blocks for such an analysis can be found in Marx.

In his examination of the national economy, Marx finds that certain sectors realise profits above surplus value, while others fall short (see Chapter

4). He suggests that this subnational discrepancy also arises globally: 'One of the nations may continually appropriate for itself a part of the surplus labour of the other, giving back nothing for it in the exchange.'[311]

Building on this observation, thinkers including Otto Bauer, Henryk Grossman, Arghiri Emmanuel, and Samir Amin examine how trade strengthens capital accumulation in centre economies by extracting surplus value from the peripheries, weakening accumulation in those economies.[312] Alongside other mechanisms, such as interest-incurring debt, capital flight, or profit repatriation, everyday trade would thus also drain the peripheries of surplus value. The theory of unequal exchange exposes this drain, hidden by the appearance of mutually beneficial trade.

Bauer, Grossman, Emmanuel, and Amin view unequal exchange as an important, if not the most important, mechanism behind the general process of uneven development and the more specific process of accumulation globally. To expose the connections between enrichment and impoverishment, they look below the surface of the circulation of exchange value (the realm of value added, balance of payment, terms of trade, etc.) and dig deeper into the underlying realm of global value production, realisation, and distribution.

The term 'unequal exchange' has also been associated with the structuralist explanations of Prebisch, Singer, and others, as well as the monopolistic explanations of Baran, Sweezy, Amin, and others.[313] However, this conceptual widening muddies the issue.[314] Concerns about capitalism's structural and monopolistic tendencies are certainly valid, and they have undeniably contributed to uneven development. However, such critiques focus on the realm of money rather than value and thus offer only a partial understanding of the situation.

The value-based approach to unequal exchange, particularly as proposed by Emmanuel, diverges from these other Marxist world-systems theories. The framework works off an ideal-typical model of global capitalism. Emmanuel therefore deliberately omits monopolistic and structuralist forces and seeks to discover those exploitative relations that arise from what he perceives to be the very core of this 'perfect' model.

To use an analogy from the realm of computers, the framework focuses on the essential kernel of global capitalism, intentionally disregarding the higher-level layers of its different operating systems.[315] Unequal exchange thus emerges as intrinsic to a competitive and unrestricted capitalist world economy.

Critics argue that the narrow focus of Emmanuel's approach diminishes its historical relevance. In the violent history of uneven development, the centres have persistently dominated shareholder networks and global financial and trade institutions, as well as monopolised lucrative markets, advanced technologies, and high-value-adding activities. Moreover, monopolies arise endogenously from competition, and then expand globally through imperialism, as discussed above. From this perspective, it makes sense to include monopoly in the ideal-typical model of capitalism.

However, Emmanuel does not dismiss monopolistic and imperialistic plunder outright but prefers to isolate unequal exchange from other forms of drainage by separating differential rent or surplus profit (gained via unequal exchange) from monopoly rent or supra-profit (gained via monopoly capitalism). Incorporating military occupation, structural divisions of labour, abuses of market power, and other forms of plunder by capitalism's 'operating systems' would only reduce logical coherence. It would obscure our understanding of the system's 'kernel' elements, specifically unequal exchange. Trade relations sustain and deepen systemic inequality even in the absence of all other forces.[316]

Here's my suggestion: Capitalism's inherently monopolistic and imperialist nature can only be excluded in mental abstractions that separate the ideal-typical model from its messy functioning in the real world. Does this mean that our limbo scenario from Part 1 deals with mere fantasy? No. For one thing, it helps explain how monopolies emerge from competition. But then, do differential rents vanish once monopoly and imperialist rents take hold? Not at all. Even under monopoly capitalism, spaces of competition persist, and with them, differential rents. Monopolies may even dominate, but they never fully extinguish competitive forces. Thus, it remains analytically useful to distinguish between them.

A theory of accumulation on a world scale, which identifies unequal exchange as its main mechanism, requires a foundational set of assumptions that reexamine and challenge mainstream notions of trade.

As mentioned, neoclassical economists consider 'unequal exchange' to be an oxymoron.[317] Since David Ricardo, the assumption has been that trade between specialised partners should benefit them both. Apologists for capitalism argue that everyone benefits when labour-rich (capital-poor) peripheries trade with labour-scarce (capital-rich) centres.

The theory of unequal exchange challenges this naive and dangerous interpretation by shedding light on the disparities that arise from centre–periphery trade. Interestingly, the theory itself emerged from an attempt to rattle the foundations of the Ricardian theory of comparative advantage and its promise of win-win outcomes,[318] restricted capital flows, and equal wages between trading partners.

First, Ricardo's assumption of international capital immobility no longer holds – if it ever did.[319] By the late nineteenth century, capital was moving much more freely, and this trend accelerated after World War II and decolonisation.[320] The increasing fluidity of global capital renders Ricardo's model obsolete: English capital would not specialise in English cloth if it could invest in the more lucrative production of Portuguese cloth or wine.[321]

As suggested earlier, the global flow of capital is a response to the long-term decline of average profit rates in capitalist centres, driven by an increasing organic composition of capital (technical progress) and/or decreasing surplus rate (higher wages) (see Chapter 4). Later, we will see how international capital mobility indeed compensates for the centre's falling average profit rate.

For now, the point is that as the economic pie grows ever more slowly, imperialist countries, like hungry wolves, not only take more from weaker prey but also increasingly turn on each other.[322] Technically speaking, this translates into hyper mobile forms of profit-seeking capital flows.

As explained for the competitive pursuit of surplus profit within closed national economies, capital abandons sectors with relatively lower average profit rates to swarm others with higher rates. This results in the equalisation of sectoral profit rates to their average, weighted by the overall size of invested capital, which is then reflected in a sector's revenue.

This logic also applies at the international level. Emmanuel suggests that a mere one or two percent lower profit rate in the centre would be sufficient to start stirring capitals towards the periphery.[323] The unhindered movement of capital across borders leads, or at least tends, towards an equalisation of the international average profit rate.

How does this global tendency lead to unequal exchange? Here's a glimpse of the next chapter. Just as within a single nation, sectors in the global economy – whether in the centre or in the periphery – sell their commodities for a revenue (R) above or below their value (V). Even though they produce surplus value (S), they realise profits (P) determined by the average profit rate (P'). This creates gaps between price and value in global trade.

Now, perfect equalisation is obviously a myth and can only exist under impossible conditions of absolute free trade, without any government interference, risk factors, monopolistic barriers, customs duties, or transport costs. In reality, such factors make global capital flows sticky. Capital 'cannot go from "England to Holland" with the same speed that it goes from "London to Yorkshire"'.[324] Although the unequal exchange model ignores these realities, it remains useful. A model that strips away barriers and stickiness brings us closer to a critique of capitalism in its ideal-typical form. What's more, as we will see, price-value gaps appear even with imperfect equalisation of profit rates, and the tendency towards equalisation outweighs opposing forces.

We have rejected Ricardo's first assumption of capital immobility. Now for his take on wages and exploitation. Ricardo assumed that wages are the same everywhere, not because labour migration equalises them (he was correct in relation to labour immobility), but because he believed that wages were fixed at subsistence levels, based on universal basic physiological and biological needs.

This is clearly wrong (see Chapter 1). Wages diverge sharply due to the historical interplay between price and abstract value of labour, spiralling upwards in the centres and downwards in the peripheries (see Chapter 3). Unlike profit rates, there's no force driving wage equalisation. For Marx, labour mobility tends to equalise the surplus rates of various sectors within national economies, not on a global scale.[325]

Given the dominant anti-immigration stance of most centre nations, a global migration of labour – and the ensuing equalisation of surplus rates – is largely blocked. This leads to workers with similar skills earning vastly different wages based on nationality. Emmanuel calls this 'the most unethical' of all monopolies, rooted in passports and birth certificates.[326]

While some firms recruit globally, such as in Qatar where 94 per cent of the workforce is foreign, such cases are exceptions to the rule: Labour mobility is nowhere near as fluid as capital flows.[327] Emmanuel noted this in the 1970s, observing that African immigration to Europe had no discernible impact on the surplus rate gap, even as capital movements started to equalise profit rates.[328]

Neoliberals might argue that assuming labour immobility fails to model a truly unimpeded capitalist system. Unequal outcomes, they would claim, are a result of barriers to the market's efficient allocation of labour, not capitalism itself.[329] 'There is no doubt that free and open immigration is the right policy in a libertarian state,' Milton Friedman argued.[330] However, very few neoliberals seem to advocate for unrestricted labour migration, supporting instead the tightening of immigration laws.

Nevertheless, let's imagine the case for the sake of argument. Labour mobility could potentially equalise surplus rates, decreasing exploitation in the peripheries (where surplus rates are higher) and intensifying it in the centres. However, capitalism depends on such disparities, for one thing, to counter the tendency of the rate of profit to fall. Borders and migration controls preserve the reserve armies of labour that suppress wages in the peripheries. Neoliberal policies of unrestricted labour mobility could never materialise, therefore, as they would quickly undermine capitalism's exploitative foundations – the very foundations the neoliberals are blind to. Some even argue that labour migration adds to unequal exchange by bringing in not just workers, but also years of training, experience, and social reproduction.[331]

To develop a more accurate exchange theory, we should therefore begin by assuming capital mobility and labour immobility at the international level, or at the very least that capital is significantly more mobile than labour. Unlike Ricardo's model, we must also assume wage disparities between nations.

On this basis, we can now start building Marxist tables of unequal exchange. Centres and peripheries sometimes compete to supply similar commodities. However, as we've discussed, they also specialise within global divisions of labour, to produce different commodities and satisfy distinct functions in value chains. Consequently, the world economy will exhibit a variation of the inter-sector dynamics that we explored at the national level (see Chapter 4).

Let us repurpose my earlier schemes for a model of a centre region, replacing the toothpick sector with the Means of Production (MOP) and burgers with the Means of Consumption (MOC). Let us keep hours as the unit of value but now assume that 700C represents 700 billion hours of value. Setting the surplus rate at one hundred per cent and assuming that these sectors cover all production, the region as a whole invests 600c + 100v = 700C and produces 700C + 100S = 800V (see Table 19) – all expressed in billion hours.

	MOP	MOC	Region
Capital invested (C = c + v, in h):	600B	100B	700B
Constant capital (c, in h)	550B	50B	600B
Variable capital (v, in h)	50B	50B	100B
Organic composition (c / v)	11.0	1.0	6.0
Surplus-rate (s')	100%	100%	100%
Surplus-value (S = v × s', in h)	50B	50B	100B
Value produced (V = C + S, in h)	650B	150B	800B
Profit rate (p' = S / C)	8.3%	50.0%	14.3%

Table 19. From Sectors to Regions

What, then, makes exchange 'unequal'? It is generally accepted that unequal exchange refers to a specific form of 'non-equivalent exchange.' Exchange is non-equivalent when values fail to trade at their equivalent exchange values, meaning that a commodity's price deviates from its value: If the average (direct and indirect) labour time required to produce a television is a hundred times greater than that of a frisbee, but its price is not a hundred times higher, then non-equivalent exchange occurs.

Such deviations lead to international transfers of surplus value, which may or may not be considered unequal depending on who you ask, and what they perceive as causing these transfers. We'll need a few more steps before we can make this assessment ourselves.

When economies engage in trade, two key variables can lead to non-equivalent exchange: productivity differences and wage differences. Otto Bauer and Henryk Grossman theorised the first form: Disparities in productivity, reflected in different organic compositions of capital, that lead to price-value deviations and surplus value transfers.[332] Arghiri Emmanuel, meanwhile, focused on the second: International transfers of surplus value that arise from wage and exploitation gaps.[333]

Emmanuel's mentor, Charles Bettelheim, referred to the two as 'broad' and 'narrow' forms of unequal exchange respectively.[334] However, as the broad form also occurs within nations (through the inter-sector dynamics discussed in Chapter 4), Emmanuel did not view it as necessarily 'unequal.'[335] He nevertheless partially adopted his mentor's terminology in some publications, but preferred to refer to the other form as 'strict' rather than 'narrow.' In the following chapters, I will use the labels 'broad unequal exchange' (from productivity differences) and 'strict unequal exchange' (from wage differences).

To assess the degree of non-equivalence, or inequality, of an exchange, we must establish a baseline of 'equivalent exchange,' i.e., when the prices of commodities paid or earned by centres and peripheries correspond to the values of those commodities. In this case, the value and price of a television are each a hundred times greater than those of a frisbee.

To be clear: Equivalent does not mean that the situation is fair. Exploitative relationships exist regardless of whether prices and values align. Even under conditions of equivalent exchange, the capitalist class retains a privileged position by appropriating the surplus value generated by the labour of workers.

It is also important to remember that we are still talking about values aligning with limbo-denominated prices: Actual dollar or rupee prices will fluctuate around these ideal-typical prices (e.g., when monopolistic forces come into play).

Table 20 introduces centre and periphery regions, each with export-oriented sectors and firms, and uses the values from Table 19. For now, we assume that both centre and periphery operate with identical organic compositions of capital (OC = c / v) and with equal surplus rates. This will change later. Additionally, we consider that the free movement of capital between centre and periphery has equalised profit rates (from p' to P').

Another reminder: Revenues encompass a monetary outlay (MO = C × $MELT_{AV}$) as well as average return on investment – specifically, a mass of profit (P) – based on an economy-wide average rate of profit (P'). This profit equals capital invested multiplied by the average profit rate of the world economy (P = MO × P'). For simplicity's sake, the models continue to assume an overall average monetary expression of labour time of one limbo per hour ($MELT_{AV}$ = ∑R / ∑V = Ł1/h). As mentioned before, conversions between value and price should involve $MELT_{AV}$, but since it equals one here, it can be omitted.

Under these conditions, individual profit rates do not deviate from the average; centre and periphery therefore generate the same revenues (R = Ł800) and trade at revenues corresponding to values (R = V = 800 Ł or h, respectively). Perfectly matching revenues and values ensures equivalent exchange and means that no uneven flows of surplus value occur between centre and periphery (SP = R - V × MELT = 0). More precisely, equivalent exchange takes place between trading partners with equal MELTs – even if those MELTs differ from one. As we will soon discover, different organic compositions and surplus rates trigger flows of unequal exchange.

	Centre	Periphery
Money capital (MO = C × $MELT_{AV}$, in Ł)	700B	700B
Capital invested (C = c + v, in h):	700B	700B
Constant capital (c, in h)	600B	600B
Variable capital (v, in h)	100B	100B
Organic composition (OC = c / v)	6.0	6.0
Surplus rate (s')	100%	100%
Surplus value (S = v × s', in h)	100B	100B
Value produced (V = C + S, in h)	800B	800B
Profit rate (p' = S / C)	14.3%	14.3%
Average profit rate (P' = ∑S / ∑C)	14.3%	
Profit (P = MO × P', in Ł)	100B	100B
Revenue (R = MO + P, in Ł)	800B	800B
Surplus profit (SP = R - V × MELT, in Ł)	0B	0B
MELT (R / V, in Ł/h)	1.0	1.0
Average MELT ($MELT_{AV}$ = ∑R / ∑V, in Ł/h)	1.0	

Table 20. Equivalent Exchange

CLOSING REMARKS

Let's wrap up this condensed overview of the extremely complex historical phenomenon of uneven development.

We know that capitalism will behave antisocially if it's profitable to do so. This is borne out by plenty of empirical evidence, not least global income disparities and levels of poverty which, in our increasingly interconnected world, are not only persistent but getting worse (see Chapter 1). Clearly, the periphery holds the short end of the stick – and that end is only getting shorter. However, these observations alone cannot establish a causal connection between the enrichment of the centres and the impoverishment of the peripheries.

Such a connection can, however, be found via an analysis of uneven development. As we have seen, uneven development involves the leveraging of mechanisms such as the division of labour, debt traps, vertical integration within value chains, and financial subjugation to perpetuate systems of dominance and subordination. As the long end of the stick grows longer, the short end becomes shorter, weakening the subjugated party yet further and making it harder for them to increase their share.

This chapter has explored the ways in which the world system drives a range of distinct but interconnected historical trajectories in centre and periphery nations. In the centres, capitalism emerged from bourgeois revolutions against feudalism; in the peripheries, it was imposed through imperialism, (neo)colonialism, monopoly capitalism, neoliberalism, foreign investment, and so on. This subjugated form of capitalism in the periphery continually feeds accumulation in the imperial centre, perpetuating uneven development.

These are the forces that maintain dominant centres and dependent peripheries, as well as perpetuating uneven trade conditions and outcomes, as partially reflected in monetary indicators such as the terms of trade and trade in value added.

Structuralist and world-system explanations such as these offer crucial insights, but leave some key questions unanswered: How unequal are the gains from trade? What makes them unequal? Can trade lead to outright losses, not just unequal gains? How are losses connected to gains? How are these outcomes a direct result of capitalism?

To answer these questions, scholars inspired by Marx developed the theory of unequal exchange – a critical mechanism of uneven development. This theory illuminates the gains and losses that result from ideal-typical capitalist forces, isolating them from those caused by monopolistic and imperialistic plunder. It rejects the idea of comparative advantage via two key assumptions

– global capital mobility and labour immobility in the context of global productivity and wage gaps.

This chapter has laid some of the groundwork for understanding unequal exchange. The following chapters will explore the theory further, focusing on Emmanuel's contributions. We won't, however, be getting bogged down in exhaustive historical accounts or in-depth critical analyses; I have attempted to stick to the basics. For deeper explorations, I would recommend the work of John Brolin, Andrea Ricci, Lefteris Tsoulfidis, Torkil Lauesen, and others.[336]

6. Unequal Exchange

OPENING REMARKS

Throughout history, empires have thrived on tribute systems, forcing conquered states to hand over wealth, resources, and skilled labour in return for military protection and access to trade. Such systems are not merely about quick wealth accumulation; they function to consolidate dominance, ensuring subordinate states remain compliant and dependent.

Those who dismiss this as ancient history should consider the vast financial flows from the periphery to the centre that persist to this day. As detailed in the previous chapter, tax evasion, interest payments, profit repatriation, trade barriers, capital flight, and trade mis-invoicing alone account for up to 25 times the Official Development Assistance (ODA) flowing to periphery nations. Clearly, the peripheries develop the centres. And trade offers little remedy, with low-income countries capturing just 1/279 as much domestic value-added per capita as high-income countries (see Chapter 5).

But there's more; the greatest loss of all is hidden. Unequal exchange represents a significant yet concealed drain of value – in the Marxist sense – from poorest regions to richest. To give a sense of its scale, it is often expressed in monetary terms. As mentioned, my own estimate puts the monetary losses at roughly 58 times the amount of ODA flowing in the opposite direction. (This chapter will present the underlying method.)

Unequal exchange is therefore one of several mechanisms driving uneven development, alongside the more evident divisions of labour, debt traps, vertical integration in value chains, and financial subjugation (some of which are connected to unequal exchange, as we will explore). In chapter 5, we saw how these further shorten the periphery's already short end of the stick. Unequal exchange uncovers something different: It exposes the paradox that products requiring greater human effort to produce tend to be cheaper. Returning to the metaphor, rather than comparing the lengths of the stick's ends, unequal exchange captures the disproportionate human effort when the sticks are used to carry a load. Due to the dynamics of leverage, the bearer at the short end must exert more effort.

I've made this point before, but so far, we've approached uneven development through its surface expressions: historical forms and secondary phenomena such as terms of trade or trade in value-added. As Marx warned, we must not confuse appearance with essence. What I've offered in Chapter 5 is not a theory, but a descriptive account of how underdevelopment unfolds across space and time through centre–periphery dependencies.

To grasp the essence of uneven development, we need theory, for which we can adopt key Marxist concepts such as value, organic composition of capital, surplus profit, surplus value transfer, etc. Largely missing from the world-systems analyses discussed in the previous chapter, these concepts allow us to see uneven development as a deeply rooted mechanism for the transfer of surplus value from a dependent capitalist economy to a more dominant one.[337]

This unequal exchange represents the modern equivalent of a labour tribute from periphery to centre, and it manifests in two ways: broad and strict. Both contribute to the ongoing drain of value, reinforcing and sustaining uneven development.

BROAD UNEQUAL EXCHANGE

The 'broad' manifestation of unequal exchange originates from productivity gaps between centre and periphery regions. These reflect a global division of labour in which the peripheries operate 'labour-intensive' industries, leaving (constant) 'capital-intensive' production to the centres. Despite some industrialisation in select periphery countries, productivity gaps remain largely unbridged.

From a Marxist perspective, two factors can increase the quantity of goods produced per unit of time: productivity of technology and intensity of labour power (see Chapter 2). Broad unequal exchange describes differences in technical progress, as reflected in capital's organic compositions ($OC = c / v$, the ratio of constant to variable capital, i.e., of machinery to labour power). These differences, as we shall see, result in a net flow of value to the most technologically advanced regions. To spotlight this effect, broad unequal exchange ignores likely differences in the intensity of labour power.

Allow me to recapitulate the ways in which value flows within closed advanced capitalist economies, since this is the basic logic behind broad unequal exchange. Chapter 4 explained how these flows result from discrepancies between the value embodied in produced commodities and the prices they fetch, as well as between surplus value and profit.

Sectors with a lower-than-average organic composition of capital benefit from those with a higher composition. All else being equal, sectors with a higher organic composition generate relatively less surplus value (S) and experience a comparatively lower individual profit rate (p' = S / C, where total invested capital C = c + v), which is a value-based variable. However, sectors do not make profits (P) based on these individual rates. Rather, the distribution of profits across sectors is dictated by the economy-wide rate of profit (P'). A sector's profit is given by P = MO × P', where MO denotes the initial capital advanced, and P' is the total sum of all surplus value divided by total invested capital (P' = ΣS / ΣC). P' is a money-based variable established through competition and investment flows (see Chapter 4).

Commodities are consequently sold at what Marx calls 'production prices' adjusted by this average profit rate. I refer to this simply as revenue (R = MO + P). 'Capital-intensive' sectors below the average profit rate sell above their value (R > V), resulting in profits exceeding surplus value (P > S). Conversely, 'labour-intensive' sectors with an above-average individual profit rate sell below their value (R < V), with surplus value exceeding profits (P < S).

To interpret these expressions, remember that magnitudes related to capital and value (C, c, v, S, V) are measured in average labour time (e.g., hours), whereas revenue and profit (R, P) are denominated in limbo (Ł) – the imaginary currency of an ideal-typical, competitive, market-clearing capitalist economy (see Chapter 3). These two sets of magnitudes are linked through the average monetary expression of labour time ($MELT_{AV}$, defined as total R divided by total V). For simplicity, I have assumed $MELT_{AV}$ equals one limbo per hour, allowing direct comparison between the two sets, for instance, between a profit of Ł90 and a surplus value of one hundred hours (Ł90 < 100h × $MELT_{AV}$, with $MELT_{AV}$ = Ł1/h).

The difference between revenue and value (or between profit and surplus value) is called surplus profit (SP). It results in a transfer of value from sectors with below-average organic composition to those above average, as the former cannot fully convert surplus value into profit, while the latter gains an equivalent of the lost portion.

Let us extend this logic of domestic value transfers to the international level. The tendency for profit rates to equalise among trading countries leads to the emergence of international 'prices of production,' and the generation of revenue on that basis. This, in turn, leads to broad unequal exchange, characterised by international net transfers of average labour time from periphery to centre countries engaged in trade. These transfers arise from variations in the magnitudes, compositions, and rates of the capital components used in trading countries' production processes.

Note that the schemes of unequal exchange presented here make no assumptions about structural divisions regarding the nature of the commodities exported by the centres and peripheries, only in the way they are produced. Structuralist world-systems theorists linked the periphery's declining terms of trade to their specialisation in primary production, and the centre's monopolisation of secondary production, but more recent studies question this (see Chapter 5). The schemes therefore clarify how the peripheries' terms of trade can decline irrespective of what they export.

In the 1920s, the Austrian leftist thinker and politician Otto Bauer and the Polish Marxist economist Henryk Grossman took important steps in applying Marx's framework beyond the national context.[338] Bauer and Grossman pointed to a transfer of surplus value from regions with a lower to those with a higher organic composition of capital.

Grossman added that a higher composition alone does not guarantee increased productivity: The composition (c / v) can increase even if constant capital (c) remains constant, as long as variable capital (v) decreases. Moreover, reduced variable capital does not necessarily mean fewer workers operating the same instruments of production; it may signify lower wages, leaving productivity unaffected. To accurately portray and isolate non-equivalent exchange due to productivity gaps, therefore, Grossman deduced that only the amounts of constant capital between centre and periphery must differ.[339]

Arghiri Emmanuel acknowledged broad unequal exchange that stems from variations in productivity and the magnitudes of constant capital.[340] However, his scheme differs from Grossman's in how they integrate surplus rate differentials, something I will return to in the next section. In the interests of maintaining a focus on productivity differentials and to align with my previous schemes, I have adapted Emmanuel's scheme, though my adjustments in no way deviate from Emmanuel's underlying logic.

In Table 21, I assume no wage or exploitation differences (100v and s' = 100% in both countries). This also means that the number of people employed in both countries must necessarily be equal. For reference, I've copied the previous equivalent exchange scheme from Table 20 in the left columns of Table 21. The right columns, meanwhile, illustrate the consequences of enhanced productivity in centre regions, achieved by increasing constant capital from 600c to 800c (the change is underlined in the table). This simple alteration results in a drop in the centre's profit rate. However, profit rates equalise to an international average, giving rise to different masses of profit (P) and revenues (R).

Commodities from the centre generate a revenue of Ł1013 billion, covering production costs (or money outlay, MO = Ł900 billion) and yielding a 12.5 per cent monetary profit on investment (Ł1013 / Ł900 - 1, which logically amounts to the equalised rate P'). However, capitalists in the centre are unaware that their revenue exceeds the 1000 billion hours of value produced (1000V × $MELT_{AV}$ = Ł1000 billion), which includes only an 11.1 per cent value-based profit on a Ł900 billion investment. Conversely, commodities from the periphery yield a 14.3 per cent value-based profit rate, but only a 12.5 per cent monetary profit rate. The periphery's commodities therefore generate a revenue of Ł788 billion, while they embody 800 billion hours of value (800V × $MELT_{AV}$ = Ł800 billion). The centre earns above value, the periphery, below.

	Equivalent		Broad	
	Cen.	Per.	Cen.	Per.
Money capital (MO = C × $MELT_{AV}$, in Ł)	700B	700B	900B	700B
Capital invested (C = c + v, in h):	700B	700B	900B	700B
Constant capital (c, in h)	600B	600B	800B	600B
Variable capital (v, in h)	100B	100B	100B	100B
Organic composition (OC = c / v)	6.0	6.0	8.0	6.0
Surplus rate (s')	100%	100%	100%	100%
Surplus value (S = v × s', in h)	100B	100B	100B	100B
Value produced (V = C + S, in h)	800B	800B	1000B	800B
Profit rate (p' = S / C)	14.3%	14.3%	11.1%	14.3%
Average profit rate (P' = ∑S / ∑C)	14.3%		12.5%	
Profit (P = MO × P', in Ł)	100B	100B	113B	88B
Revenue (R = MO + P, in Ł)	800B	800B	1013B	788B
Surplus profit (SP = R - V × MELT, in Ł)	0B	0B	13B	-13B
MELT (R / V, in Ł/h)	1.00	1.00	1.01	0.98
Average MELT ($MELT_{AV}$ = ∑R / ∑V, in Ł/h)	1.00		1.00	

Table 21. Broad Unequal Exchange

The price-value gap results in a transfer of surplus value from the periphery to the centre. Together, centre and periphery produce 1800 billion hours of value (ΣV), which Emmanuel terms 'total labour.' This includes embodied living or direct labour (variable capital and surplus value) and dead or indirect labour (constant capital). The centre imports 800 billion hours (V) of this total labour from the periphery for Ł788 billion (R) while the periphery imports 1000 billion hours from the centre for Ł1013 billion.

Each region produces 100 billion hours of surplus value, yet neither realises Ł100 billion in profit. The centre realises Ł13 billion above what it would have received under conditions of equivalent exchange; for the periphery, the amount is Ł13 billion below. In short, trade transfers a 'tribute' of Ł13 billion, in the form of surplus profit, from periphery to centre. As Bauer puts it, surplus value from both regions effectively goes into a single pile and is then shared out among capitalists in proportion to their capital.[341] It's like the buffet analogy: Everyone pays the same cover charge, but some plates are fuller than others. Marx summarises these logical steps as follows:

> The favoured country recovers more labour in exchange for less labour, although this difference, this excess is pocketed, as in any exchange between labour and capital, by a certain class. Since the rate of profit is higher, therefore, because it is generally higher in a colonial country, it may, provided natural conditions are favourable, go hand in hand with low commodity-prices.[342]

Let's take stock. Assuming equal wages and surplus rates, commodities from the more productive centre generate revenue above value, while those from the periphery generate revenue below value. This results in broad unequal exchange: a drain of surplus value from periphery to centre, which would also occur if I decreased productivity in the periphery instead of increasing it in the centre in Table 21. Unequal exchange arises from the mismatch between value in production (or labour form) and value in circulation (or money form).

We can also summarise Table 21 with the following equations:

- Value in production:
  - With 900C (800c + 100v) and s' = 100%, the centre produces 1000V (900C + 100S).
  - With 700C (600c + 100v) and s' = 100%, the periphery produces 800V (700C + 100S).
- Value in circulation:
  - With a profit of P = Ł113 billion (Ł900 billion × 12.5%), the centre sells for R = Ł1013 billion (Ł900 billion + Ł113 billion) and therefore gains Ł13 billion through trade with the periphery.
  - With a profit of P = Ł88 billion (Ł700 billion × 12.5%), the periphery sells for R = Ł788 billion (Ł700 billion + Ł88 billion) and therefore loses Ł13 billion through trade with the centre.

Marxist theorists sometimes express non-equivalent exchange as the disparity between a hypothetical exchange at values and the actual exchange on the basis of revenues: $1000V_{centre} / 800V_{periphery} < 1013R_{centre} / 788R_{periphery}$, or $1.25 < 1.29$. The broad unequal exchange explanation basically attributes international transfers of value to the concentration of more technically advanced sectors in global centres.[343]

The average monetary expression of labour time ($MELT_{AV}$) will play an important role later when we empirically measure unequal exchange. During exchange, each region's value (V) is realised as revenue (R) according to that region's MELT. For example, with a regional MELT of Ł0.98 per hour, the periphery produces a value of eight hundred billion hours but realises only Ł788 billion. Hypothetically, had the periphery been remunerated at the $MELT_{AV}$ of Ł1 per hour, it would have realised the entirety of its value and earned Ł800 billion (R_{EQ}) – a difference of Ł13 billion with the actual exchange ($R - R_{EQ}$, rounded off), as shown in Table 22. I will explain this later, but it is worth noting that comparing actual MELT-based earnings with hypothetical $MELT_{AV}$-based earnings also reveals how differences in currency strength contribute to unequal exchange.

	Centre	Periphery
Value produced (V = C + S, in h)	1,000B	800B
Revenue (R = MO + P, in Ł)	1,013B	788B
MELT (R / V, in Ł/h)	1.01	0.98
Average MELT ($MELT_{AV} = \sum R / \sum V$, in Ł/h)	1.00	
Equalised Revenue ($R_{EQ} = V \times MELT_{AV}$)	1,000B	800B
Unequal Exchange ($UE = R - R_{EQ}$, in Ł)	13B	-13B

Table 22. Unequal Exchange revealed through the equalised MELT

Marx refers to profit generated through the appropriation of surplus value produced by others, rather than one's own productive activity, as differential rent (see Chapter 4). He emphasises that this type of rent is not generated via the process of exchange; exchange merely distributes the total. In fact, these transfers of surplus value occur through the regular operation of the price-formation mechanism in a competitive capitalist economy, including the global economy. 'All the destructive phenomena which unlimited competition gives rise to within one country are reproduced in more gigantic proportions on the world market.'[344]

Table 21 shows that Emmanuel's model of broad unequal exchange incorporates temporary forms of monopolies for the early adopters of technology. In a world without barriers such as patents, copyrights, and trademarks, technology would spread quickly, reducing productivity gaps. In reality, however, these barriers enable monopolies to tighten their grip on technology, adding monopoly rents on top of differential rents; this is especially true on a global scale. Emmanuel's model disregards how these more persistent forms of monopoly, as well as those that arise from imperialism and monopoly capitalism, disrupt the equalisation of profit rates.

Emmanuel faced criticism for assuming fully equalised global profit rates, particularly given his lack of empirical support for the stance.[345] I can see two responses to this critique. First, the absence of empirical evidence is

	Full equal.		Partial equal.	
	Cen.	Per.	Cen.	Per.
Money capital (MO = C × $MELT_{AV}$, in Ł)	900B	700B	900B	700B
Capital invested (C = c + v, in h):	900B	700B	900B	700B
Constant capital (c, in h)	800B	600B	800B	600B
Variable capital (v, in h)	100B	100B	100B	100B
Organic composition (OC = c / v)	8.0	6.0	8.0	6.0
Surplus rate (s')	100%	100%	100%	100%
Surplus value (S = v × s', in h)	100B	100B	100B	100B
Value produced (V = C + S, in h)	1,000B	800B	1,000B	800B
Profit rate (p' = S / C)	11.1%	14.3%	11.1%	14.3%
Average profit rate (P' = ΣS / ΣC)	12.5%		12.5%	
Partially equalised rate ([p' + P'] / 2)	/	/	11.8%	13.4%
Profit (P = MO × P', in Ł)	113B	88B	106B	94B
Revenue (R = MO + P, in Ł)	1,013B	788B	1,006B	794B
Surplus profit (SP = R - V × MELT, in Ł)	13B	-13B	6B	-6B
MELT (R / V, in Ł/h)	1.013	0.984	1.006	0.992
Average MELT ($MELT_{AV}$ = ΣR / ΣV, in Ł/h)	1.00		1.00	

Table 23. Broad Unequal Exchange with Partial Equalisation

obvious as we operate within an ideal-typical limbo currency model that imagines the perfect mobility of international capital. Second, broad unequal exchange occurs regardless of whether profit rates achieve total equalisation, as demonstrated in Table 23.

To show this, I propose a scenario in which individual profit rates do not equalise to the average; instead, they gravitate toward the midpoint between individual and average profit rates (expressed as [(p' + P') / 2]). Broad unequal exchange already occurs under such partial equalisation, albeit to a lesser extent than under full equalisation: $1006R_{centre} / 794R_{periphery} < 1013R_{centre} / 788R_{periphery}$, or 1.27 < 1.29.

Sometimes, the periphery's organic composition can surpass the centre's. For example, Swiss watchmaking might involve more manual labour than timber production in Papua New Guinea, transferring value in favour of the latter. Emmanuel illustrates this via a comparison of Katangese copper mines and Belgian shoe factories.[346] However, he emphasises that Katanga still loses out to Belgium in terms of trade due to the wage gap, which drives strict unequal exchange, as explored in the next section.

His point is that even if broad unequal exchange were to transfer value from the centre to the periphery, strict unequal exchange could easily cancel out these gains and cause a net drain of value from periphery to centre. This lends theoretical support to the earlier insight from Chapter 5 that the periphery cannot escape its subjugated position simply by adopting the centre's production techniques.

To conclude, broad unequal exchange essentially replicates the closed-economy inter-sector dynamics discussed above at a global scale. However, in those dynamics, the absence of inter-sector gaps in wages and exploitation was facilitated by labour's domestic mobility. By contrast, labour's international immobility sustains global wage gaps. We must therefore move beyond broad unequal exchange and consider the strict form.

STRICT UNEQUAL EXCHANGE

Like the broad form, strict unequal exchange stems from an idealised model of capitalism in which capital's international mobility equalises profit rates. Unlike the broad form, however, the strict form assumes equal productivity between centre and periphery due to the global diffusion of technology.[347] The extent of this diffusion is debatable, but it undeniably represents a driving force in the idealised model that we aim to challenge.

More importantly, assuming equal productivities and ignoring broad unequal exchange allows us to spotlight the strict form. This reveals another factor underlying the drain of value from the peripheries: unequal wages.

In reality, both forms coexist but given the increasing deployment of modern technology in production worldwide, global wage gaps will only become more significant as the primary driver of value transfers from periphery to centre.

Earlier, we explored the ways in which imperialistic and (neo)colonial forces drove wage cuts in the peripheries and played a part in shaping stronger labour movements in the centres (see Chapter 5). These forces contributed to a global wage gap, which Emmanuel considered exogenous – that is, originating from factors outside the purely economic realms of labour markets or productivity.[348] The perspective ignited significant debate, as we shall see.

What is not open to debate, though, is the sheer size of the gap. In 2022, average nominal hourly wages in high-income countries were 26.3 times higher than those in low-income countries (see calculations later in this chapter). Some attribute this discrepancy to skills differences, although high-skilled workers in 'emerging and developing economies' still earn 68 per cent less than low-skilled workers in 'advanced economies.' Even with similar skills, wages in the former are 87-95 per cent lower than in the latter. Moreover, the gap affects every sector and is only getting worse. Between 1995 and 2021, hourly wage increases in wealthy nations were eleven times higher than in poorer countries.[349]

Once established, the international wage gap becomes self-perpetuating, driven by the feedback loop between real income and the abstract value of labour: Rising wages increase the consumption of value-embodying commodities, thereby augmenting labour's abstract value (see Chapter 3). The loop operates more intensely in the centres, where it fuels larger wage increases and widens the gap with the peripheries. It means that even if we could put an end to the forces of monopoly capitalism and imperialism, the gap would continue to widen within the imagined competitive model of capitalism.

Now let's incorporate a wage gap into the baseline model of equivalent exchange from Table 20. The initial step involves augmenting variable capital in the centre (and/or diminishing it in the peripheries). However, an increase in variable capital (v) can signify two things: a rise in the number of employed workers and/or a rise in their average wages.

For example, in the first case, if Bob hires a burger chef who works forty hours a week at Ł10 per hour, he spends Ł400 on variable capital. If he hires a second chef at the same rate, the cost doubles to Ł800. With constant capital unchanged, this implies a decline in the organic composition of capital, making the industry more labour-intensive and reducing productivity, as more workers operate with the same means of production.

Alternatively, variable capital can also rise if wages increase while the number of workers stays the same; if Bob doubles his chef's wage to Ł20 per hour, his variable capital investment also doubles to Ł800. As before, the organic composition of capital decreases (assuming constant capital is unchanged), but in this case, productivity remains the same because the number of workers has not changed.[350]

How do we make sure that our model captures an increase in wages and not in workers? Basically, we must ensure an increase in 'necessary labour' and an equivalent decrease in 'surplus labour' (see Chapter 3). Marx defines necessary labour as time spent producing the commodities needed for reproduction. Workers tend to be paid accordingly (v). Surplus labour represents time spent producing surplus value (S). Surplus rate (s') is then defined as the ratio of surplus labour to necessary labour (s' = S / v). You might recall the example: When I give a lecture, I perform sixty minutes of unpaid surplus labour on top of every sixty minutes of paid necessary labour, resulting in a surplus rate of one hundred per cent (s' = 60 / 60 = 100%). If my wage increases, I might carry out, say, only forty minutes of unpaid surplus labour on top of every eighty minutes of paid necessary labour, yielding a new surplus rate of fifty per cent (s' = 40 / 80 = 50%). To paraphrase Marx, a fall or rise in wages (reflected in v), other things being equal, effects an opposite change in the surplus rate (s').[351]

In short, to signify a wage increase, we must therefore increase variable capital and reduce the surplus rate. This deducts labour's greater value from capital's surplus value. Simply put, capital covers the higher wage bill.

Let's implement the logic outlined above. I have adjusted Emmanuel's table to align with my earlier schemes and address minor misconceptions, without straying from his guiding logic.[352] Table 24 adapts the equivalent exchange scenario from Table 20 by doubling the centre's variable capital (from 100v to 200v) and halving its surplus rate (from one hundred to fifty per cent). Centre workers therefore earn twice the wages of periphery workers (though this is an underestimation, as indicated earlier).

Emmanuel goes on to describe the effect of this wage gap:

> If the wage is exogenous (institutional, independent variable), and if a tendency exists for the formation of a general international rate of profit, then any autonomous variation in the wage-rate in one branch or in one country will entail a variation in the same direction of the respective price of production [revenue] and a variation in the opposite direction of the general rate of profit.[353]

	Equivalent		Strict	
	Cen.	Per.	Cen.	Per.
Money capital ($MO = C \times MELT_{AV}$, in Ł)	700B	700B	800B	700B
Capital invested (C = c + v, in h):	700B	700B	800B	700B
Constant capital (c, in h)	600B	600B	600B	600B
Variable capital (v, in h)	100B	100B	200B	100B
Organic composition (OC = c / v)	6.0	6.0	3.0	6.0
Surplus rate (s')	100%	100%	50%	100%
Surplus value (S = v × s', in h)	100B	100B	100B	100B
Value produced (V = C + S, in h)	800B	800B	900B	800B
Profit rate (p' = S / C)	14.3%	14.3%	12.5%	14.3%
Average profit rate (P' = ∑S / ∑C)	14.3%		13.3%	
Profit (P = MO × P', in Ł)	100B	100B	107B	93B
Revenue (R = MO + P, in Ł)	800B	800B	907B	793B
Surplus profit (SP = R - V × MELT, in Ł)	0B	0B	7B	-7B
MELT (R / V, in Ł/h)	1.00	1.00	1.01	0.99
Average MELT ($MELT_{AV} = \sum R / \sum V$, in Ł/h)	1.00		1.00	

Table 24. Strict Unequal Exchange

Essentially, higher wages in one country increase its revenue while lowering the global average profit rate. We can see this at work in Table 24. Relatively higher wages reduce the profit rate (12.5 per cent in the centre versus 14.3 per cent in the periphery) and increase revenue (R = Ł907 billion in the centre versus Ł793 billion in the periphery). The centre therefore purchases commodities from the periphery for below-value prices (Ł793 billion against 800 billion hours), while the periphery purchases commodities for above-value prices (Ł907 billion against 900 billion hours). These price-value gaps give rise to strict unequal exchange: a +Ł7 billion deviation of revenue from value in the centre and a -Ł7 billion deviation in the periphery.

To summarise Table 24:

- Value in production:
    - With 800C (600c + 200v) and s' = 50%, the centre produces 900V (800C + 100S).

  - With 700C (600c + 100v) and s’ = 100%, the periphery produces 800V (700C + 100S).
- Value in circulation:
  - With a profit of P = Ł107 billion (Ł800 billion × 13.3%), the centre sells for R = Ł907 billion (Ł800 billion + Ł107 billion) and therefore gains Ł7 billion through trade with the periphery.
  - With a profit of P = Ł93 billion (Ł700 billion × 13.3%), the periphery sells for R = Ł793 billion (Ł700 billion + Ł93 billion) and therefore loses Ł7 billion through trade with the centre.

We can now compare exchange at values with strict unequal exchange as follows: $900V_{centre} / 800V_{periphery} < 907R_{centre} / 793R_{periphery}$, or 1.12 < 1.14. In this case, it is not an exogenously determined productivity gap that causes unequal exchange (in the broad form), but an exogenously determined wage gap in the presence of an internationally equalised profit rate.

In summary, any rise in nominal wages in the centre exacerbates the terms of trade for the periphery, as reflected in a decline in the periphery’s revenue and an increase in the centre’s. The centre’s decline in its value-based profit rate doesn’t matter because it gets a return based on a higher monetary-based global profit rate. A nominal wage decrease in the periphery would have the same effect on the terms of trade.

Moreover, this dynamic operates irrespective of the type of commodity. Thus, unequal exchange persists, with or without enduring specialisations in the global division of labour.

You might be wondering what this means for real wages and actual consumption, especially given variations in purchasing power. We will address this in detail later. For now, it is important to emphasise that we’ve been examining wage differences in nominal terms, comparing wages and prices based on market exchange rates, an approach which befits assessments of purchasing power within the global economy.

Emmanuel’s strict unequal exchange has attracted much criticism, particularly for neglecting the impacts of monopoly capitalism and treating the wage gap as exogenous. These critiques will be explored shortly but first let’s look at reactions to Emmanuel’s assumptions of complete equalisation through perfect capital mobility, and of a lower surplus rate in the centre.

On complete equalisation, I have already demonstrated that even with partial equalisation of profit rates, broad unequal exchange still takes place (see earlier Table 23). I haven’t included the table, but this also applies to strict unequal exchange. Moreover, Emmanuel justified his decision to overlook imperfect equalisation by asserting that as long as the wage gap (v) is greater than the profit rate gap (p’), unequal exchange occurs:

> [P]ossible disparities in the rates of profit, even if they move in the right direction, are of another order of magnitude than the disparities of wages, so that it is excluded that the one offsets or diminishes the others.[354]

Indeed, unequal exchange already appears with a minute difference:

$v_{centre} / v_{periphery} > p'_{centre} / p'_{periphery}$, or 1.01 > 0.99, as shown in Table 25.

	Equivalent			Strict		
	Cent.	Peri.	Ratio	Cent.	Peri.	Ratio
Money capital ($MO = C \times MELT_{AV}$)	700B	700B		701B	700B	
Capital invested ($C = c + v$):	700B	700B		701B	700B	
Constant capital (c)	600B	600B		600B	600B	
Variable capital (v)	100B	100B	1.00	101B	100B	1.01
Organic composition ($OC = c / v$)	6.0	6.0		5.9	6.0	
Surplus rate (s')	100%	100%		98%	100%	
Surplus value ($S = v \times s'$)	100B	100B		99B	100B	
Value produced ($V = C + S$)	800B	800B		800B	800B	
Profit rate ($p' = S / C$)	14.3%	14.3%	1.00	14.1%	14.3%	0.99
Average profit rate ($P' = \sum S / \sum C$)	14.3%			14.2%		
Profit ($P = MO \times P'$)	100B	100B		100B	99B	
Revenue ($R = MO + P$)	800B	800B		801B	799B	
Surplus profit ($SP = R - V \times MELT$)	0B	0B		1B	-1B	
MELT (R / V)	1.000	1.000		1.001	0.999	
Average MELT ($MELT_{AV} = \sum R / \sum V$)	1.000			1.000		

Table 25. Emmanuel's Condition

The second critique refuted Emmanuel's assertion of a lower surplus rate in the centre and originated from Emmanuel's mentor, Charles Bettelheim, who suggested that the surplus rate was, in fact, 'paradoxically' higher in the centres.[355] Was Bettelheim right to suggest this adjustment? And would such an adjustment indeed flip the direction of unequal exchange in favour of the periphery? I would say no on both accounts.

The argument posits that a higher surplus rate (s') in the centre arises from higher worker productivity, ostensibly reducing the necessary labour time needed to produce the means of consumption (relative to surplus labour time). Bettelheim therefore combines broad unequal exchange (higher productivity in the centre) and an odd form of strict unequal exchange (higher 'exploitation' in the centre).

Without going into excessive detail, the argument suffers from two important flaws. First, necessary labour denotes the labour time required to reproduce labour power, that is, to produce value equivalent to variable capital (see Chapter 3). Bettelheim reduces the centre's surplus rate but not its variable capital. Yet if variable capital were also reduced, consistent with his contention that necessary labour is lower in the centre, the balance could in fact shift back in favour of the centre.

Second, the argument incorrectly assumes that centre labour consumes only commodities produced by centre labour power. Bettelheim was correct to note that a productivity gap reduces the labour time embodied in commodities produced in the centre while increasing it for those produced in the periphery (see also Chapter 2). In an integrated economy, however, this implies that the centre appropriates value from the periphery. Once this appropriation is taken into account, necessary labour in the centre increases, contrary to Bettelheim's reasoning. This, in turn, implies a relatively lower surplus, taking us back to strict unequal exchange as formulated by Emmanuel.[356]

For the final part of this section, let's explore how strict unequal exchange might evolve over time, by incorporating the logic of expanded reproduction into the scheme.

Earlier, we hypothesised that unequal exchange may mitigate the centre's looming over-accumulation crisis, a product of its falling national average profit rate (see Chapter 4). Following Emmanuel, we can test this hypothesis by contrasting two extended reproduction tables – one before and one after profit rate equalisation (i.e., capital immobility and mobility).[357]

We start with the closed economy of the centre from Table 18 in Chapter 4, which accounts for an increase in wages over time by offsetting rises in variable capital (v) with a decrease in surplus value (S), which implies a reduction in the rate of surplus value (s´). As explained, this ensures that the increase in v reflects higher wages rather than an expansion of the workforce.

As before, the Means of Production (MOP) and Consumption (MOC) sectors reinvest profits in additional constant (c) and variable capital (v), and in proportions consistent with their organic compositions. To remind you, the tables perform this calculation first for the MOP sector. Any portion of c not absorbed by MOP is then purchased by MOC, which invests a

	t = 1				t = 2			
	Cent.		Peri.		Cent.		Peri.	
	MOP	MOC	MOP	MOC	MOP	MOC	MOP	MOC
$MO = C \times MELT_{AV}$	600B	200B	600B	100B	675B	225B	686B	114B
	800B		700B		900B		800B	
$C = c + v$	600B	200B	600B	100B	675B	225B	686B	114B
	800B		700B		900B		800B	
c	500B	100B	550B	50B	563B	113B	629B	57B
	600B		600B		675B		686B	
v	100B	100B	50B	50B	113B	113B	57B	57B
	200B		100B		225B		114B	
$OC = c / v$	5.0	1.0	11.0	1.0	5.0	1.0	11.0	1.0
	3.0		6.0		3.0		6.0	
s’	50%	50%	100%	100%	33%	33%	75%	75%
	50%		100%		33%		75%	
$S = v \times s'$	50B	50B	50B	50B	38B	38B	43B	43B
	100B		100B		75B		86B	
$V = C + S$	650B	250B	650B	150B	713B	263B	729B	157B
	900B		800B		975B		886B	
$p' = S / C$	8.3%	25.0%	8.3%	50.0%	5.6%	16.7%	6.3%	37.5%
$P' = \sum S / \sum C$	12.5%		14.3%		8.3%		10.7%	
$P = MO \times P'$	75B	25B	86B	14B	56B	19B	73B	12B
	100B		100B		75B		86B	
$R = MO + P$	675B	225B	686B	114B	731B	244B	759B	127B
	900B		800B		975B		886B	
$SP = R - V \times MELT$	25B	-25B	36B	-36B	19B	-19B	31B	-31B
	0B		0B		0B		0B	
$MELT = R / V$	1.04	0.90	1.05	0.76	1.03	0.93	1.04	0.81
$MELT_{AV} = \sum R / \sum V$	1.00		1.00		1.00		1.00	

Table 26. Reproduction of Unequal Exchange, Pre-Equalisation

corresponding amount of v in accordance with its own organic composition. In this way, the scheme assumes constant productivity.

To that, I add a closed periphery economy consisting of the same two sectors, with sizes and compositions identical to those utilised for the periphery thus far but otherwise following the same logic of reproduction as the centre economy.

In the absence of trade and capital flows, there is no international equalisation of profit rates as shown in Table 26. In both economies, rising wages prompt rapid reductions in average profit rates. From t = 1 to t = 2, the profit rate (P') in the centre plummets from 12.5 to 8.3 per cent, and from 14.3 to 10.7 per cent in the periphery; this downward trend persists after that. Since there is no trade, the wage disparity does not result in any drain of surplus value (SP = R - V) between countries.

Let's now introduce global trade, capital flows, and profit rate equalisation. Table 27 shows increasing unequal exchange, as the surplus profits (R - V) gap widens from +/- Ł7 billion (t = 1) to +/- Ł12 billion (t = 2). After equalisation, the centre's accumulation accelerates, benefiting from a 13.3 per cent global profit rate at t = 1, compared to 12.5 per cent before equalisation. Meanwhile, the periphery's profit rate suffers, dropping from 14.3 to 13.3 per cent. Although the global rate drops to 9.4 per cent at t = 2, this is still higher than the 8.3 per cent that it would have been in the centre without equalisation (see Table 26).

Back to the question: Does unequal exchange mitigate the centre's looming over-accumulation crisis? Yes. By expanding into the periphery, the centre can bypass the limits of exploitation within its own borders. This unequal exchange functions as a counter-tendency tempering the decline of the centre's profit rate, at the cost of stifling capitalist accumulation in the periphery.[358]

Looking at this last reproduction scheme, the terms of trade (ToT) seem to widen no further. Estimating the periphery's ToT by dividing its export revenue with that of the centre, using the numbers from Table 27, reveals a stable deficit (793R / 907R at t = 1 equals 868R / 992R at t = 2, and so on).

However, the schemes do reveal a widening gap in domestic value added (DVA). In the simplified Marxist model used so far, where R = C + P = c + v + P, and wages (equal to v, since we assume that MELT equals one) and profits are the only two shares of total value added (excluding taxes, rents, dividends, and other components, and assuming all capital invested is consumed in one circulation), DVA is expressed as the remainder of the revenue (R) after deducting the costs of constant capital (c). This leaves us with wages (v) and profit (P): R = c + DVA, where DVA = v + P.[359]

	t = 1				t = 2			
	Cent.		Peri.		Cent.		Peri.	
	MOP	MOC	MOP	MOC	MOP	MOC	MOP	MOC
$MO = C \times MELT_{AV}$	600B	200B	600B	100B	680B	227B	680B	113B
	800B		700B		907B		793B	
$C = c + v$	600B	200B	600B	100B	680B	227B	680B	113B
	800B		700B		907B		793B	
c	500B	100B	550B	50B	567B	113B	623B	57B
	600B		600B		680B		680B	
v	100B	100B	50B	50B	113B	113B	57B	57B
	200B		100B		227B		113B	
$OC = c / v$	5.0	1.0	11.0	1.0	5.0	1.0	11.0	1.0
	3.0		6.0		3.0		6.0	
s'	50%	50%	100%	100%	32%	32%	76%	76%
	50%		100%		32%		76%	
$S = v \times s'$	50B	50B	50B	50B	37B	37B	43B	43B
	100B		100B		73B		87B	
$V = C + S$	650B	250B	650B	150B	717B	263B	723B	157B
	900B		800B		980B		880B	
$p' = S / C$	8.3%	25.0%	8.3%	50.0%	5.4%	16.2%	6.4%	38.2%
$P' = \sum S / \sum C$	12.5%		14.3%		8.1%		10.9%	
	13.3%				9.4%			
$P = MO \times P'$	80B	27B	80B	13B	64B	21B	64B	11B
	107B		93B		85B		75B	
$R = MO + P$	680B	227B	680B	113B	744B	248B	744B	124B
	907B		793B		992B		868B	
$SP = R - V \times MELT$	30B	-23B	30B	-37B	27B	-15B	21B	-33B
	7B		-7B		12B		-12B	
$MELT = R / V$	1.05	0.91	1.05	0.76	1.04	0.94	1.03	0.79
$MELT_{AV} = \sum R / \sum V$	1.007		0.992		1.012		0.986	

Table 27. Reproduction of Unequal Exchange, Post-Equalisation

The ratio of the periphery's value added to that of the centre decreases over time, as evidenced by the magnitudes in Table 27), meaning that the periphery's share of value added also decreases (in billion hours and limbo). This supports the deepening of the DVA smile curve into a full grin (see Diagram 21 in Chapter 5):

- At t = 1: (100v + 93P) / (200v + 107P) = 63%.
- At t = 2: (113v + 75P) / (227v + 85P) = 60%.

There is also a widening gap if we focus on wages alone. The variable capital ratio between centre and periphery grows over time: 200v / 100v = 2 at t = 1, and 227v / 113v = 2.01 at t = 2. This rise is not due to an increase in the number of workers, but rather to increasingly unequal levels of exploitation, indicated by the surplus rate ratio between centre and periphery: 100% / 50% = 2 at t = 1, and 76% / 32% = 2.4 at t = 2. This indicates that the system not only perpetuates but actually intensifies unequal exchange, as it is driven by wage disparities.

Let's reflect briefly on some real-world implications. In the words of Walter Rodney, 'colonialism gave capitalism an added lease on life.'[360] Surplus profits extracted from the colonies acted as something of a bribe, dampening revolutionary tendencies in the imperial centres. This bribe took the form of cheaper goods, higher wages, better working conditions, and expanded social services.

While monopoly/imperialist rents (supra-profit) indeed palliate the impacts of exploitation in the centre, differential rents (surplus profits) extracted through the competitive model of unequal exchange achieve similar palliative effects. It should be added that unequal exchange not only brings higher wages and cheaper goods to centre workers, but also provides cheaper constant capital for centre firms, boosting profits and reducing wage pressures. As the schemes show, unequal exchange constitutes a major safety valve for capitalist over-accumulation.[361]

Let me repeat Marx's claim that the privileged country exchanges more labour for less, and that this difference 'is pocketed by a particular class.'[362] First and foremost, this class includes the national bourgeoisie of the centre country, but also a better-paid and cared-for 'labour aristocracy,'[363] which is a term that Emmanuel adopted to describe the entire labour force of centre countries: '[The] working classes of today's advanced countries constitute the labour aristocracy of the Earth.'[364] However, it seems disingenuous to include delivery drivers, street sweepers, baggage handlers, and those in other similar occupations in this category, merely for being located in the centre. Whether a centre worker belongs to the so-called 'labour aristocracy' depends on the balance between the surplus value extracted from them and the surplus value they appropriate through consumption from peripheral workers.

Ultimately, though, the label is less important than the recognition that colonialism, imperialism, and unequal exchange benefit all centre workers materially, albeit unequally, and at the expense of the peripheries. These systems favour upper-strata workers and leave crumbs for the rest – crumbs that potentially still form part of a bribery system. I return to this question later in the chapter in the context of empirically measuring unequal exchange.

Emmanuel therefore comes to the logical conclusion that class solidarity does not extend globally. Nationalism and right-wing populism exacerbate this divide, conditioning workers to align with national interests over those of workers elsewhere. This is the subject of significant controversy, as I will discuss later.

CRITIQUES OF UNEQUAL EXCHANGE

Let's pause to consider the essence of what the models of unequal exchange reveal. In an ideal-typical global capitalist economy, commodities sell above or below value (given an average MELT). This divergence comes from variations in the amounts of constant and variable capital employed in production, and in surplus rates, while competition drives the equalisation of profit rates across countries. As a result, surplus value is siphoned away from low-productivity, low-wage peripheries and transferred to high-productivity, high-wage centres. There, it is realised as surplus profit and helps to offset the centre's falling rate of profit. This is the fundamental dynamic revealed by the models.

If you find these models simplistic, that's because they are. I've intentionally reduced complexity to distil Emmanuel's work to its core logic, focusing on the basic mechanisms of unequal exchange, though this incurs a risk of missing key elements or overemphasising minor ones.

We've already covered the lack of empirical evidence for a global equalisation of profit rates and the supposed paradox that workers in the centre might be more exploited than those in the periphery. Let's now dive into two additional critiques of Emmanuel: his neglect of monopolistic tendencies, and his view of wage differentials as external.

Let me first flag that these critiques seem to stem more from a reluctance to accept the implications of Emmanuel's theory than actual flaws in the theory itself.[365] As explored above, a logical outcome of Emmanuel's thought is limited solidarity between international workers – a conclusion that many Marxists struggle to accept. As we tackle these critiques, we'll also shed light on this issue of solidarity, but what follows should be read as an open-ended exploration, nothing more.

Earlier, I mentioned how the Marxist schools of monopoly capitalism and unequal exchange attribute the draining of value from the periphery to different causes. First, though, what do they share? Both propose theories of how value is drained from where it is produced, and both see this as an inevitable outcome of capitalism. Both also describe zero-sum processes in which the rich and powerful exacerbate uneven patterns of development and assert their global dominance.[366]

However, these perspectives also diverge considerably, at least according to their champions. Paul Sweezy and Paul Baran, in their analysis of monopoly capitalism, dismiss the idea of unequal exchange, or attribute it to imperialism and monopolistic power rather than competition. They argue that the centres can't drain value from the peripheries through trade, but that this happens through foreign investment, the ownership of capital, and profit repatriation.[367] In other words, unequal exchange would belong to the superstructure of the capitalist mode of distribution rather than the structural base of the capitalist mode of production.[368]

For his part, Emmanuel saw monopoly as wholly irrelevant for understanding accumulation on a world scale, comparing it to other forms of direct plunder. Viewing it as a surface manifestation rather than a root cause, he left monopoly out of his analysis altogether and focused instead on differential rents, particularly those driven by wage disparities.[369] His findings imply that even without monopolistic tactics, so-called free trade between high-wage centres and low-wage peripheries reflects the old saying that 'there is nothing more unequal than the equal treatment of unequals.'

Unfortunately, neither tradition clearly articulated why its approach should be considered superior.[370] Here are a few brief thoughts.

Sweezy acknowledges that labour immobility hinders the equalisation of the surplus rate but dismisses the idea that capital mobility would equalise profit rates. He argues that Otto Bauer's unequal exchange theory only holds if capital mobility is a given, with capitalists moving their capital from low- to high-profit-rate regions, which would drive these rates towards convergence.[371] While thus conceding that unequal exchange occurs with mobile capital, Sweezy rejects the idea of international capital flows,[372] and argues against extending Marx's model of competitive sectors within a specific economy to the world economy.[373]

However, the deregulation of global capital flows under the Bretton Woods system is undeniable (see Chapter 5), and it's reasonable to imagine that capital has always been far more mobile than labour.[374] This is theoretically sufficient to cause unequal exchange (see Table 25). Moreover, while unequal exchange operates at full capacity when profit rates have completely equalised, it already occurs with partial equalisation, as demonstrated earlier (see Table 23).

Ultimately, both monopoly and competition deserve attention, as both perpetuate uneven development through the extraction of rents, albeit of different kinds. They are also interconnected: As Marx notes, competition breeds monopoly when price wars push firms to merge for greater market power. Monopolistic tendencies are therefore systemic. Monopoly also breeds competition. Historically, less advanced capitalist economies have protected themselves by rejecting international competition and building national monopolies (see Chapter 5). This would also be the natural response of the peripheries, were it not for the centres using institutions such as the World Bank, IMF, and WTO to bulldoze trade barriers and impose market competition.

Though monopoly and competition may coexist and interact, they must nevertheless be analysed as distinct processes. Unequal exchange theory reveals how surplus profits (differential rents) arise from competition. Monopoly capitalism, meanwhile, reveals a different kind of rent: supra-profit (monopoly rent), from (non-)tariff barriers, intellectual property, price gouging, domestic subsidies, imposed standards, etc.

Given this difference, each phenomenon reveals and conceals something else. For instance, while my reproduction model of unequal exchange simulates an increasingly unequal capture of (monetary) domestic value added (DVA), it makes sense to assume that DVA is further skewed through additional monopoly rents. It might even be the case that the distribution of DVA is more closely linked to the forces of monopoly capitalism than to unequal exchange. This shall remain an open question, but I'll add that it doesn't actually matter whether supra-profits from monopoly capitalism are empirically larger than super profits from unequal exchange; what matters is that unequal exchange provides an essential foundation for interpreting monopoly capitalism.[375] Let's explore this.

With a focus on the distribution of monetary gains, monopoly capitalism alone cannot explain uneven development. To grasp the systemic basis of this unevenness, we must consider the mismatch between prices and values, and profit versus surplus value. Metrics such as DVA reveal some of the unevenness, but don't expose how 'underpriced' or 'overpriced' commodities are relative to the total labour invested in them.

Unequal exchange occurs when privileged buyers acquire underpriced commodities ($R < V$) produced under exploitative conditions, instead of sourcing them domestically at higher costs. Meanwhile, impoverished buyers struggle with overpriced commodities (R > V) produced under more favourable conditions, rather than sourcing them cheaply domestically.

As we've seen within capitalist economies, variations in the monetary expression of labour time (MELT = R / V) between sectors result in surplus profit transfers from those with a lower MELT to those with a higher one. This logic also applies at the global level, where even a small gap triggers a transfer. In Emmanuel's strict unequal exchange scheme (Table 24), the periphery's MELT (Ł0.99 per hour) is below the global average (ΣR / ΣV = Ł1 per hour), leading to a transfer of surplus profit to the centre with an above-average MELT (Ł1.01 per hour).

One way to illustrate this is by contrasting the neoclassical and Marxist views of value added, as in Diagram 22. This builds on the earlier value-added smile from Diagram 21, which highlighted how the peripheries remain stuck in low value-added middle segments of the chain, often involving low-wage, labour-intensive forms of production, while the centres dominate the high value added, high-wage, capital-intensive segments. This new 'frowning curve,' meanwhile, shows that the periphery adds most of the labour value during the middle stages of production, and thus demonstrates how under- or overpriced commodities are relative to their value.[376] This systemic mismatch leads to non-equivalent value transfers, as Torkil Lauesen explains:

> [T]he basis of the value transfer is the difference between the exchange-value expressed by the market price of the commodity and the exchange-value of the commodity, calculated by the socially necessary labour time remunerated at average global wage.[377]

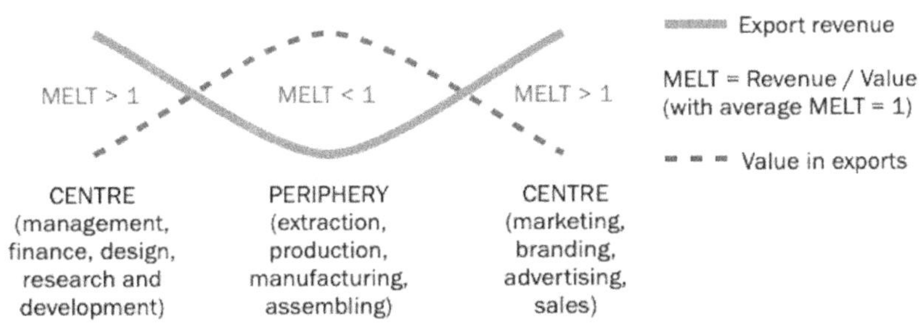

Diagram 22. Value Added Frown

To be clear, I'm not claiming that there's a 'correct' monetary compensation for labour time (or, indeed, for any resource).[378] Labour time isn't 'underpaid' because it falls short of some imagined 'true price';[379] it's underpaid when a country's average Monetary Expression of Labour Time (MELT) is below the global average, and overpaid when it's above. I'm also not suggesting that there's a right or wrong MELT; only that when countries with different MELTs trade, one inevitably ends up over- or underpaying the other.

Differences in MELT in the ideal-typical model, therefore, produce unequal exchange: a transfer of surplus value from the periphery realised as surplus profit (differential rent) in the centre. While these rents emerge during the 'realisation phase,' supra-profits (monopoly rents) are generated during the 'distribution phase,' after value has taken its monetary form.

For example, Nestlé and other cocoa importers in the centre generate surplus profit by sourcing cocoa produced with the cheap labour of farmers in Ghana and other periphery exporters. As a brand-owning firm, Nestlé also captures supra-profits on final sales, since its monopoly over consumer demand allows it to charge a premium for chocolate products. In this case, surplus profit comes from cocoa producers earning less, while supra-profit comes from chocolate consumers paying more.

By linking money and labour time, unequal exchange provides the foundation for interpreting monopoly capitalism. Without super profit, defined as the gap between price and value in the idealised model, the further real-world impact of supra-profit on commodity mispricing relative to value cannot be assessed – even if this contribution were empirically larger than that of super profit.

Analytically separating unequal exchange from monopoly capitalism also serves as a potent critique of the neoliberal doctrine. This doctrine cunningly deflects critiques of capitalism by blaming uneven development on trade barriers, market imperfections, government interventions, monopolistic behaviour, and other interferences in the system's efficient operations.

Milton Friedman famously remarked that giving bureaucrats control over the Sahara Desert would soon lead to a sand shortage, encapsulating the belief that capitalism could resolve all problems if fully unleashed. Such rhetoric preserves capitalism's cultural hegemony and absolves it of all responsibility.

To be most effective, critics should therefore target capitalism at its purest, free of alleged distortions. Though such a form is unrealistic, its implications are worth considering. The earlier unequal exchange schemes reveal that those who produce most value receive the least reward (Table 21 and Table 24). Privileged regions amass more value at the expense of impoverished ones – even after conceptually eliminating imperfections in the model.

This strikes at the core of capitalism and is a charge that proponents of neoliberalism are unable to deflect without advocating for global labour mobility to equalise wage rates – unlikely, as previously discussed. Unequal exchange challenges the notion that uneven outcomes result from a lack of capitalism, and points to the need for a radical post-capitalist transformation.

Let's move on to the second point of critique. Emmanuel faced pushback not only for disregarding monopoly capitalism but also for assuming that wages are set exogenously and therefore act as an independent variable in the model. He argued that the wage gap is historically shaped, particularly by successful union campaigns in centre nations – to which we could also add unsuccessful ones in colonised peripheries.[380] Emmanuel's model takes the wage gap as a starting point; it doesn't address how it came about.

Is this a problem? The theory of unequal exchange aims to debunk the myth of convergence through trade, which in my view justifies starting the model with a gap at t = 1, to then see whether or not it closes. Furthermore, setting an initial wage gap here doesn't mean that it necessarily remains independent from then on. Indeed, Emmanuel's model allows for internal recalculations of variable capital and surplus rates. This implies that wages are not actually independent and that the wage gap can evolve endogenously within the model.[381]

Beyond t = 1, the wage gap between centre and periphery does widen endogenously, as demonstrated in Table 27. This outcome reflects Marx's prediction of 'relative immiseration' and aligns with the empirical trend of rising income inequality, as noted in Chapter 1.

Emmanuel's critics seem to ignore this internal mechanism driving the wage gap, often arguing that differences in productivity are the main cause of it. As Walter Rodney points out, the hourly earnings of an early twentieth-century cotton peasant in Chad were insufficient to purchase even a centimetre of the cloth woven from his cotton in France. Meanwhile, a French textile worker could spin out several metres in minutes using modern machines.[382] One may infer from this that the French worker earns more because they're more productive, that is, more 'skilled.'

This argument is flawed. French textile factories invested in spinning machines to boost profits, not increase wages. Take our earlier hamburger example: If Mac invests in a turbo-grill that can double burger production to maximise his profits, surely his chef's piece rate would halve, not double. Increased productivity does not lead to higher wages; instead, capitalists will tend to pocket or reinvest the profits from productivity gains.

If anything, the relationship between productivity and wages works in the opposite direction: Wages influence productivity. Historically, the goal of mechanisation was often to counter union demands for higher wages.[383] Indeed, Marx notes that many inventions were created specifically to arm capital against worker revolts.[384] If burger chefs strike for higher wages, Mac and others in the industry may try to cut the need for chefs by upgrading their kitchens.

If higher wages drive productivity-boosting technological developments, lower wages are likely to result in lower productivity. In the peripheries, firms have little incentive to modernise, as profits can be maintained through cheap labour.[385]

There's also sufficient evidence to disprove the claim that centre wages are higher because productivity there is higher (or vice versa for the periphery) – especially when we move beyond conventional monetary metrics of productivity such as GDP per worker and focus on actual material productivity. Wage gaps persist between centre and periphery, even when actual productivity is comparable, and wage gaps often far exceed productivity gaps.[386] In many cases, production in the periphery uses modern techniques, with workers matching or even surpassing the hourly output of better paid workers in the centre.[387] Nonetheless, average wages for workers in the periphery – whether low-skilled cleaners, medium-skilled machine operators, or high-skilled technicians – are between 87 and 95 per cent lower than their counterparts in the centre (see Chapter 1).[388]

There is one noteworthy situation where productivity does influence wages, but not in a way that aligns with the claims made by Emmanuel's critics.[389] If productivity does increase, it tends to enlarge the industrial reserve army, increase competition among workers, and decrease, not increase, wages – a phenomenon Marx describes as 'the absolute general law of capitalist accumulation.'[390]

With high wages in the centres driving productivity, and low wages in the peripheries deprioritising it, one can argue that broad unequal exchange emerges from strict unequal exchange. It also implies that the peripheries cannot effectively improve their terms of trade by boosting productivity as long as wage gaps persist, i.e. by tackling broad unequal exchange but neglecting strict unequal exchange.

John Brolin argues that these critiques, motivated by frustration with Emmanuel's conclusions, serve as a diversion.[391] Unequal exchange highlights an exploitative division between workers in centre and periphery, and hinders international worker solidarity. Opposition to Emmanuel's theory is more about this political implication than genuine flaws in its logic. Allow me to explain.

Through unequal exchange, the centre trades its overpriced exports ($R > V$) for underpriced imports from the periphery ($R < V$). This enables centre capitalists to offset higher wages by importing cheaper constant capital produced by underpaid, overexploited periphery labour. These capitalists also benefit from higher domestic wages and demand. As accumulation advances, growing employment opportunities further drive up domestic demand. Instead of trying to expand markets and sell to impoverished consumers in the periphery's so-called bottom of the pyramid, centre firms profit by exploiting them as low-wage workers.

Such trade practices also benefit centre consumers, who avoid the higher prices and reduced consumption that would accompany those commodities had they been produced in the centre. Conversely, periphery workers would have enjoyed lower prices and increased consumption if the overpriced imports from the centre had been produced locally.

This dynamic implicates the working classes of the centres in exploitation elsewhere, and aligns their interests with global capital.[392] Workers in the centres, who labour under conditions of lower surplus rates, end up benefiting by appropriating surplus value from those in the periphery, where surplus rates are higher.[393] It bears repeating that not all centre workers benefit equally, and some may not benefit at all where their own exploitation is high.

In traditional class struggle, wealth accumulation by the capitalist class leads to an accumulation of misery among the working class. This struggle is universal: 'The working men have no country,' wrote Marx and Engels in their manifesto. However, by globalising this 'zero-sum game,' unequal exchange can create a 'positive-sum game' within the centres (to some extent).

Unequal exchange reduces the disharmony of interest between centre workers and capitalists and exposes the conflict of interest between centre and periphery workers (see Diagram 18 in Chapter 5). Unequal exchange makes the supposedly inescapable antagonism between capitalist and working class escapable, precisely by outsourcing exploitation.

Clashing with the call 'Proletarians of all countries, unite!', Emmanuel's conclusions remain unacceptable for many traditional Marxists committed to international worker solidarity in the fight against imperialism, neocolonialism, and monopoly capitalism.

Bettelheim, for instance, argues that higher productivity in the centre increases exploitation, as discussed earlier. Based on this flawed logic, he then proposes that by organising for higher pay, centre workers inadvertently support peripheral workers by boosting the competitiveness of periphery firms, thus improving the conditions for class struggle in those countries.[394]

Let's end with a limitation of the unequal exchange model, one tied to the wage gap, though not part of the original critique of Emmanuel's approach. As noted, the above reproduction table simulates a widening wage gap but fails to capture a wage fall in absolute terms. We know from Chapter 1 that peripheral populations increasingly struggle to afford basic commodities, yet our unequal exchange table shows that wages do rise in the periphery, just not as quickly as in the centre.

One explanation for this weakness is again the idealised nature of the model. Surplus value is reinvested in variable and constant capital (proportionally to organic composition), and this leads to wage rises by introducing falling surplus rates – even in the periphery. The result is growing inequality but not increasing poverty. By focusing on an ideal-typical form of capitalism, the model excludes the monopolistic or imperialistic factors that could cause an absolute reduction of wages in the periphery.

For example, due to their disempowered position in global value chains, periphery firms intensify exploitation, extracting more absolute surplus value from workers by extending working hours and reducing wages below the value necessary to reproduce the capacity to work. As mentioned earlier, Marini refers to such pressure as 'super-exploitation.'[395] Periphery firms compete by lowering wages, neglecting working conditions, and violating labour rights. In turn, periphery states often tolerate this due to the threat of capital relocating to other low-wage countries and taking vital foreign currency with it.

Strictly speaking, however, centre countries do not exploit so much as 'appropriate from' periphery countries. Looking back at the centre–periphery model in Diagram 18, labour in the 'vertical' relationship is violently coerced to sell itself; in the 'horizontal' relationship, periphery capital is violently coerced into global competition (as discussed in Chapter 5). The systemic horizontal drain of differential rent in the competitive model makes it necessary for the peripheries to super-exploit wage labour;[396] a race to the bottom of which super-exploitation is a predictable consequence. We could account for this in the unequal exchange model by making further reductions to variable capital (and increasing surplus rates) beyond the forces already included. Emmanuel does this in one of his schemes.[397] This would reveal increasing poverty in the periphery.

Another reason that the model fails to show increasing poverty is its use of nominal rather than real wages, which would reflect changes in social reproduction costs. Marx notes absolute declines in real wages in British colonies, where workers' purchasing power dropped below subsistence levels. Persistently low pay in the periphery lowers reproduction costs, which in turn reduces the abstract value of labour power and drives wages down further, assuming wages adjust to abstract value (see Chapter 3).

To conclude, the unequal exchange model may start with a wage gap set externally, but this gap reproduces and grows naturally over time, as revealed in Table 27. Additional forces would have to be included to simulate not just growing inequality but also deepening poverty.

MEASURING UNEQUAL EXCHANGE

Money and wealth flow from the peripheries to the centres through various mechanisms, with unequal exchange likely the most significant. How can we back this up? While Marx helps us understand value qualitatively, he doesn't provide a way to measure it quantitatively – in fact, he may have even dismissed the idea of doing so.[398] Similarly, Emmanuel's definition of unequal exchange is theoretical, not operational.[399]

The impracticality becomes obvious when we consider complicated products such as cars or computers, whose value comes from a mix of materials, components, and machines sourced from regions with varying levels of technological advancement and working conditions. Even a toothpick, simple though it appears, embodies an unknowable amount of (in)direct human effort.[400]

Far from undermining the theory, this unknowability underscores the idea that much of what is real exists beneath the surface of empirical perception.[401] For instance, if total human effort embodied in goods consumed equals total effort exerted to produce them (a fair assumption), and if some contribute less than they consume (another fair assumption), then others must contribute more than they consume. That we can't measure the imbalance empirically doesn't make it any less real.

Despite this challenge, recent improvements in economic data, especially input-output tables,[402] breathe new life into empirical research on unequal exchange. At the same time, attempts to quantify the phenomenon do not help to explain it, nor do they seem to measure it fully or directly. Empirical work, therefore, is no substitute for strong conceptual foundations. With that groundwork established in the previous chapters, let's move on to some of the measurement approaches.

In the following calculations, I categorised countries using the World Bank's GDP-based classifications: low- and lower-middle-income countries form the periphery; upper-middle-income countries form the semi-periphery; and high-income countries form the centre.[403] The income gap alone cannot capture centre–periphery relations, and other ways of drawing that distinction should also be considered (see Chapter 5), but for a general calculation of unequal exchange, this division suffices. The final dataset covers almost one hundred per cent of the world population, across 74 periphery, 45 semi-periphery, and 68 centre countries. In the sample, fifty per cent of the population lives in the periphery, 35 per cent in the semi-periphery, and fifteen per cent in the centre. All results reflect annual values for 2022.

In that year, periphery labour worked 3.4 trillion hours; semi-periphery labour worked 2.8 trillion hours; and centre labour worked 1.1 trillion hours (see Table 28). These numbers reflect total direct labour force expressed in full-time equivalent multiplied by the average annual hours per worker (averaging 2,220 in the periphery, 1,972 in the semi-periphery, and 1,726 in the centre).[404] The regions contributed an average of 46 per cent, 39 per cent, and fifteen per cent of the global total, roughly matching their shares of world population.

It is important to realise that these amounts of labour time don't capture value in its true theoretical form. Value deals with homogenous labour time – labour averaged across differences in skill, intensity, and productivity. The estimates above reflect direct labour time, which accounts for all these differences. More intensive work (e.g., fewer breaks) produces more value, while more productive work (e.g., through automation) reduces value per unit of output but increases total value produced per unit of time. These, along with many other factors, contribute to the difference between an hour of direct labour and an hour of homogenous labour (value).

Work intensity, for instance, may be also higher where employers use monitoring tools, restrict phone use, or impose strict time limits on customer interactions. The above estimates of direct labour time already partially consider differences in intensity by accounting for annual hours per worker, but we could go a step further. If a typical centre worker takes a five-minute break per hour of work, and periphery workers don't, the ratio of total direct labour in the periphery to that in the centre increases from 3.2 to 3.4.

Some studies propose using 'homogenous labour time' – labour time adjusted to the world's average levels of intensity and productivity.[405] Homogenous labour is logically greater than direct labour in more productive regions, and less than direct labour in less productive regions. Globally, however, total direct labour logically equals total homogenous labour (see Table 28).[406] This distinction between direct and homogenous labour will be important when we calculate value transfers through trade. Working with homogenous labour time essentially filters out broad unequal exchange, which arises precisely because of international productivity gaps.

To estimate a region's homogenous labour, I take global direct labour (defined as the sum of all regions' direct labour inputs in production, and equal to global homogenous labour), and scale it by the ratio of the region's Gross Domestic Product (GDP) to world GDP (see Table 28).[407] Essentially, I allocate global labour based on a region's share in total output. Expressing GDP in PPP$, that is, controlling for differences in price levels (see Chapter 1), allows for a more accurate comparison of real economic output.

In 2022, the centre's 1.1 trillion hours of direct labour convert to 3.3 trillion hours of homogenous labour, reflecting higher productivity ('cen.'

in Table 28). In contrast, the periphery's 3.4 trillion hours equal only 1.3 trillion hours of homogenous labour ('per.'). The semi-periphery's direct and homogeneous labour inputs are similar in scale, at 2.8 and 2.7 trillion hours respectively ('sem.'). As expected, total homogenous labour equals total direct labour: 7.3 trillion hours.

	Per.	Sem.	Cen.
Direct Labour Input (DLI, in h)	3.4T	2.8T	1.1T
World DLI (ΣDLI, in h)		7.3T	
Gross Domestic Product ($GDP_{PPP\$}$, in PPP$)	30.7T	63.9T	76.9T
World GDP ($\Sigma GDP_{PPP\$}$, in PPP$)		171.4T	
Share in total output ($O = GDP_{PPP\$} / \Sigma GDP_{PPP\$}$)	18%	37%	45%
Homogenous Labour Input ($HLI = \Sigma DLI \times O$, in h)	1.3T	2.7T	3.3T
World HLI ($\Sigma HLI = \Sigma DLI$, in h)		7.3T	
Gross Domestic Product ($GDP_{US\$}$, in US$)	8.7T	30.4T	61.9T
World GDP ($\Sigma GDP_{US\$}$, in US$)		101.0T	
Direct labour MELT ($GDP_{US\$} / DLI$, in US$/h)	2.6	10.7	57.6
Homogenous labour MELT ($GDP_{US\$} / HLI$, in US$/h)	6.7	11.2	18.9
Average MELT ($MELT_{AV} = \Sigma GDP_{US\$} / \Sigma HLI$, in US$/h)		13.8	

Table 28. Combined Labour and Monetary Imbalances

However, even homogeneous labour time does not fully capture value, since it represents only a redistribution of total 'living labour' expended in commodity production (i.e., variable capital, v), as we shall see. This ignores the transfer of 'dead labour' inputs contributed by the machines and materials used and consumed in production (constant capital, c).

I lack direct data, but rough estimates can help. For example, we could posit organic compositions (OC = c / v) of 1:1, 2:1, and 3:1 for periphery, semi-periphery, and centre respectively. This would mean 1, 2, and 3 hours of 'dead labour' per hour of homogenous 'living labour,' reflecting more capital-intensive production in the centre and more labour-intensive production in the periphery. We could then assume a ten per cent yearly depreciation of constant capital to reflect the gradual transfer of value as 'dead labour' to the commodities produced. The value of the periphery's invested capital, or 'cost price' in Marxist terms, rises from 1.3 trillion hours

(v) to 1.4 trillion hours (c + v), while the centre's rises from 3.3 to 4.3 trillion hours. Applying this adjustment reduces the ratio of total periphery to total centre labour from 0.4 to 0.3.

In what follows, I won't apply this rather arbitrary mental exercise as it would need to be further tested to draw proper conclusions and improve quantitative estimations of value. With this limitation in mind, let's proceed to the next step in quantifying unequal exchange.

As shown in Diagram 23, I can now divide a region's GDP (in US$) by its labour (in hours) to calculate its Monetary Expression of Labour Time (MELT, in US$ per hour). Similarly, world MELT equals world GDP in US$ divided by world labour. From the theory, we know that MELT captures how much money corresponds to the net product of one unit of value (see Chapter 2). We also know that unequal exchange occurs when trading partners have differing MELTs – differences that result from productivity and/or wage gaps (broad and strict unequal exchange). As mentioned, using homogenous labour in MELT would remove the broad form.

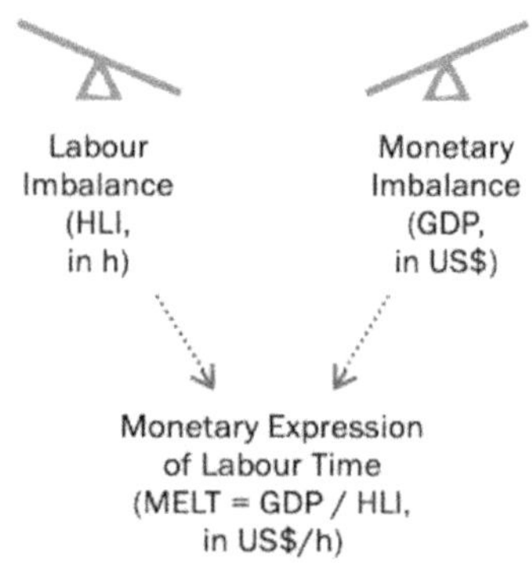

Diagram 23. Combined Labour and Monetary Imbalances

As shown in Table 28, MELT amounted to US$2.6 per hour of direct labour in the periphery and US$57.6 per hour in the centre in 2022. An hour of direct labour in the centre therefore generates 22.2 times more money than in the periphery. The gap is narrower when estimated using homogenous rather than direct labour. The centre's MELT falls to US$18.9 per hour, 2.8 times that of the periphery's (US$6.7 per hour). Still, even after eliminating productivity differences, a MELT gap remains. Either way, with an above average MELT (the global $MELT_{AV}$ is US$13.8 per hour), the centre drains a certain amount of value from the other two regions with below average MELT.

The theory holds that MELT gaps have both historical and systemic origins. Historically, they arise from relatively stronger labour struggles in the centres and from competitive pressures among peripheral capitals that intensify super-exploitation. Systemically, MELT gaps are reproduced and amplified within the schemes themselves (as shown earlier in Table 27). These divergences in MELT thus correspond directly to differences in the exploitation of labour. In the periphery, higher labour intensity – achieved through more annual working hours and more minutes of work packed into each hour – increases the total labour extracted and decreases the MELT. The wider the resulting gap with the centre, the more severe the unequal exchange, as we will demonstrate.

Perhaps the most straightforward approach calculates unequal exchange as a net-transfer of direct working hours from periphery to centre. The reasoning goes as follows: Imagine Bangladesh exports T-shirts to the Netherlands, requiring one hundred hours of work at €0.8 per hour, while importing chemicals from the Netherlands, representing one hour of work at €80 per hour. Although the nominal trade value is the same (€80), the Netherlands effectively net drains 99 hours of work from Bangladesh.

To explore this empirically, I calculated each region's direct labour time embodied in imports (IMP_{EL}) and in exports (EXP_{EL}). I did so by dividing the import and export flows between the regions (in US$) by their MELT (in US$ per hour of direct labour), assuming MELT applies equally across domestic and export-oriented production.[408] The approach therefore overlooks a potential gap in the productivity of tradable goods sectors versus non-tradable goods sectors. However, studies find that this introduces only modest errors.[409]

I then derived the following indicators, as illustrated in Diagram 24: labour trade balance, defined as the difference between imports and exports ($LTB = IMP_{EL} - EXP_{EL}$); total labour input, defined as the sum of direct (i.e., domestic) and imported labour inputs ($TLI = DLI + IMP_{EL}$); and domestic labour consumption, defined as the sum of direct labour input and the labour trade balance ($DLC = DLI + LTB$). This can also be calculated as the difference between total labour input and exported labour ($DLC = TLI - EXP_{EL}$).

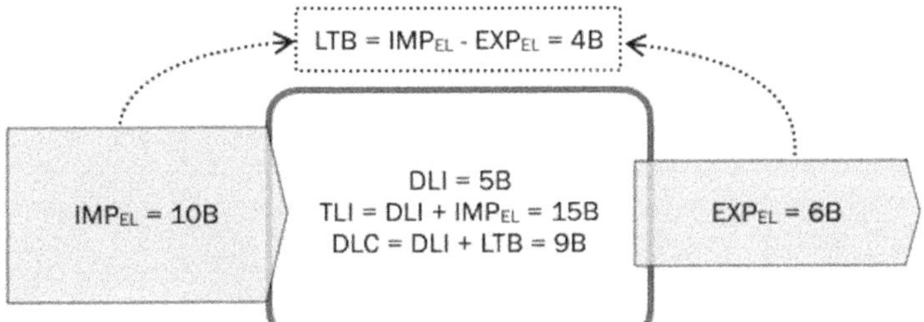

Diagram 24. Labour Flows and Balance

As shown in Table 29, the periphery imported 141 billion hours of embodied labour (IMP_{EL}) and exported 476 billion hours in 2022 (EXP_{EL}). Meanwhile, the centre imported 1,086 billion hours and exported only 233 billion hours. Together, these flows resulted in a net annual drain of 335 billion hours from the periphery, and a net annual gain of 853 billion hours by the centre (LTB). This equals the full-time efforts (FTE) of 495 million centre workers,[410] far exceeding the combined workforce of the EU and US in 2022 (219 and 169 million FTE).[411] These flows can also be interpreted in relative terms. For instance, imported embodied labour constitutes fifty per cent of the centre's total labour input,[412] compared with just four per cent in the periphery. An estimated 79 per cent of the centre's direct labour inputs are imported, while ten per cent of the periphery's direct labour inputs are exported. In other words, the periphery exports six minutes for every domestic hour of work, and the centre imports 47 minutes for every domestic hour worked.

	Per.	Sem.	Cen.
Imported embodied labour (IMP_{EL}, in h)	141B	387B	1,086B
Exported embodied labour (EXP_{EL}, in h)	476B	575B	233B
Labour Trade Balance (LTB = IMP_{EL} - EXP_{EL}, in h)	-335B	-187B	853B
Ratio of exported to imported labour (EXP_{EL} / IMP_{EL})	3.38	1.48	0.21
Direct Labour Input (DLI, in h)	3,396B	2,836B	1,074B
Total Labour Input (TLI = DLI + IMP_{EL}, in h)	3,536B	3,224B	2,160B
Percentage of Total Labour Input Imported (IMP_{EL} / TLI)	4%	12%	50%
Percentage of Domestic Labour Input Traded (LTB / DLI)	-10%	-7%	79%

Table 29. Unequal Exchange of Labour

Billions of hours of embodied labour time transfer from the (semi-) periphery to the centre through trade. Several other studies confirm this pattern and, in some cases, suggest it to be even more severe than my estimates, depending on the country clusters and time periods analysed.[413] Furthermore, these and other studies indicate that the labour imbalance increases over time.[414]

The labour and monetary imbalances underlying the MELT values used to estimate unequal exchange in labour hours must now be complemented by an analysis of currency imbalances.

In domestic markets, locally-produced values are exchanged at prices denominated in a single national currency. In international markets, however, nationally produced values encounter different national currencies. The realisation of these values into market prices therefore involves an extra step: currency exchange.[415] This brings me to a second quantification of unequal exchange that works on the basis of a currency imbalance, as proposed by political scientist and peace researcher Gernot Köhler. Let's explore this in a series of small, logical steps.

Money's purchasing power changes not only over time (through inflation) but also across currencies (via exchange rates).[416] An exchange rate indicates the price of one country's currency in another's. International payments are mediated by market exchange rates, which convert national currencies into a common reference currency (e.g., dollar, euro, yen). So, if India wants to buy commodities from the United States, it must acquire dollars – either through export earnings, foreign investment, selling real assets abroad, or currency exchange markets.

In this global context, a nation's purchasing power is influenced by the nominal exchange rate between its national currency and the US dollar. Essentially, the stronger the national currency (i.e., the more dollars it can buy), the more goods and services it can afford on the international market. However, this nominal measure is only part of the story. Real purchasing power adjusts for domestic price levels and reveals the amount of goods and services that money can buy at home. When we account for these differences in domestic price levels, we discover that the disparity between international and domestic purchasing power is larger than the nominal exchange rate suggests.

Gernot Köhler illustrates the point as follows: Imagine I'm a barber from Canada visiting Cuba. I meet Gerardo, a Cuban barber, and we agree to give each other haircuts. Gerardo cuts my hair, I cut his – a fair exchange of use value, haircut for haircut. Now, let's introduce money. I buy a haircut from him for the equivalent of one Canadian dollar. When he asks what a haircut costs in Canada, I tell him 26 dollars. So, with the dollar he earned, he couldn't afford a haircut from me in Canada. Unequal exchange occurs when, instead of trading use values directly, we exchange money with very different purchasing powers.[417]

Köhler argues that currency imbalances cause unequal exchange. As currencies have unequal purchasing power, wages and profits stretch further when disbursed in 'stronger' currencies, those of the centres. In global trade, centres therefore buy more labour value (and use value) with a dollar than they sell for a dollar, while the peripheries face the reverse.[418]

Let's jump to some calculations. Köhler's method first contrasts 'nominal' market exchange (ME) rates and 'real' Purchasing Power Parity (PPP) exchange rates. Suppose you walk into an exchange office in Delhi to exchange dollars (US$) for Indian rupees (₹). The office quotes a ME rate of US$1 = ₹74, the 2021 exchange value of a dollar in rupees.[419] PPP rates, meanwhile, compare currencies based on living costs. You can buy less with one dollar in the United States than with ₹74 in India. As Diagram 25 shows, while the ME rate was 74 rupees per dollar in 2021, the PPP rate was closer to 23 rupees per so-called international dollar (PPP$).[420]

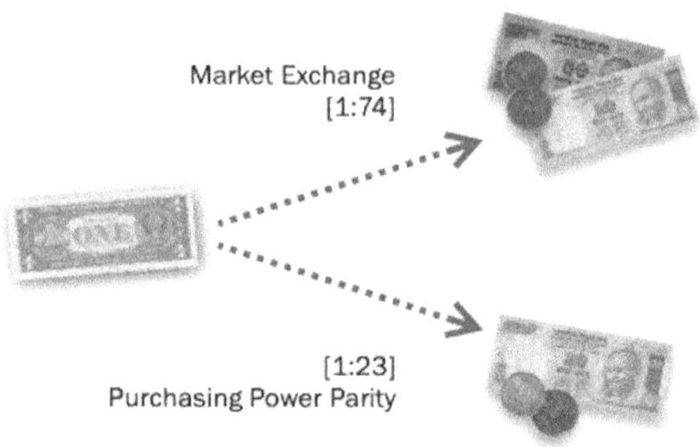

Diagram 25. ME and PPP Rates

We can then calculate a country's relative price level as the ratio between ME and PPP rates, expressed in US$ per PPP$. Here, India's 2021 price level was 1:74 / 1:23 = 23 / 74 = 0.31,[421] meaning that local prices were about a third of those in the United States. Köhler refers to it as the Exchange Rate Deviation Index (ERDI).[422] For the United States, the price level is always one US$ per PPP$. The lower it is, the more 'undervalued' a country's currency is compared to the ME rate.

Neoclassical economists believe that, in a competitive market, PPP and ME rates would eventually align; assuming there are no major distortions such as high transportation costs, tariffs, or taxes, over time, the price levels between different countries should converge. In theory, an identical Big Mac should one day cost the same in New York as in Delhi, but as any traveller knows, this gap is remarkably persistent.[423] Evidence shows consistently lower price levels in countries with lower GDP per capita. This phenomenon is known as the 'Penn effect.'[424]

The reasons for this deviation remain a puzzle for mainstream and unorthodox economists alike.[425] Lower wages reduce price levels in the peripheries relative to the centres, but this hardly explains anything since low price levels also suppress wages. The question remains: Why the deviation? Another possible explanation is that a currency's ME rate is influenced by its overall demand, particularly in relation to other currencies. International currencies – or 'world money' as Marx calls it – such as the US dollar (predominantly), euro, and yen are in high demand globally as they are commonly used for cross-border transactions, with most other domestic currencies used primarily for local payments. Among other influences, this heightened demand for international currencies tends to drive their ME rate above their PPP rate.

But why, then, is there greater demand for some currencies than others? This is a complex question with multiple explanations.[426] Factors include the limited monetary sovereignty of peripheral nations and, more broadly, the influence of US imperialism, as previously discussed (see Chapter 5). But let's get back to how high-ERDI centres extract value from low-ERDI peripheries.

With a ME rate of 1:74 between dollars and rupees, trade between India and the United States would appear balanced if India exports goods worth ₹74 and imports goods worth US$1. However, using the PPP rate of 1:23, ₹74 equates to approximately US$3.2 in domestic purchasing power. This means that for every dollar the United States spends on imports from India, it would have to spend 3.2 dollars if those goods were sourced from countries with US price levels. In other words, if the United States paid India its domestic prices, India would earn ₹238 instead of ₹74. This currency imbalance effectively creates a discount on Indian exports to the United States.

Meanwhile, India faces a surcharge on imports from the United States. For every ₹74 India spends on US imports, it would spend only ₹23 if those goods came from countries with Indian price levels. So, if India paid domestic prices for US goods, the United States would earn just 0.3 instead of one dollar on its exports to India. India therefore earns less on exports and spends more on imports, while for the United States, the situation is reversed.

Following Köhler, we can therefore calculate these discounts and surcharges as the difference between 'nominal' and 'real' Domestic Value Added (DVA and DVA_{EQ}) – a measure of how much money countries take home from global trade (see Chapter 5): $UE = DVA - DVA_{EQ} = DVA - [DVA \times d] = DVA \times [1 - d]$,[427] where:

- UE: unequal exchange expressed as a monetary drain;
- DVA: Nominal Domestic Value Added in exports;
- DVA_{EQ}: Real Domestic Value Added in exports, calculated as: $DVA \times d$;
- d: ERDI ratio, calculated as: $ERDI_{IMPORTER} / ERDI_{EXPORTER}$.

As mentioned earlier, ERDI was one for the United States and 0.31 for India in 2021. Using the formula, if India earns ₹74 on exports to the United States (nominal DVA), it should have earned ₹239 (real DVA_{EQ}, calculated as: $74 \times [1 / 0.31]$). India therefore misses out on an additional ₹165 (UE), or US$2.2 ($165 \times$ ME rate).

What global patterns are we observing? As mentioned, studies of the Penn effect reveal that ERDI values are not random but align with the division of the world into centre and periphery nations:[428] The ERDI of centre countries is typically close to one, and that of periphery countries well below it (see average ERDI values for periphery, semi-periphery, and centre countries in Table 30).

This is not a recent phenomenon, as Marx already observed that '[t]he relative value of money will [...] be less in the nation with more developed capitalist mode of production than in the nation with less developed.'[429] It follows that while centre countries trade with 'fairly valued' currencies (where ME rate is relatively close to PPP rate), periphery countries use undervalued currencies and lose in every international transaction with the centre.[430]

I'll back this up with empirical evidence shortly, but first, a quick summary of what Köhler's method sets out to do. It is built on a straightforward idea: Gernot can't get a haircut for one Canadian dollar at home, but in Cuba, Gerardo can offer him one for that price. Recognising the arbitrary privilege of being born in a country with a stronger currency, they could agree to split the difference and pay each other the average price. Köhler's approach simply scales up this logic to the global economy, aiming to equalise price levels across countries. Comparing this hypothetical balance with money's actual flows gives us a sense of the scale of unequal exchange.

Here's how it's done. I first gathered each region's nominal DVA in exports (DVA),[431] and calculated their ERDI as the ratio of GDP at ME rates and GDP at PPP rates.[432] Then, using ERDI, I calculated the real DVA in exports (DVA_{EQ}) by multiplying the actual DVA by the ratio between the importer's ERDI and that of the exporter, as explained above. This equalises price levels across regions. Following Gernot and Gerardo's example of splitting the difference, I use the average global price level ($ERDI_{AV}$) to represent the importer's price level in the ERDI ratio formula. With this, I can calculate the real DVA_{EQ} in exports: $DVA_{EQ} = DVA \times d$, with $d = ERDI_{AV} / ERDI$ (see Table 30).

Unequal exchange then equals the difference between nominal and real DVA ($UE = DVA - DVA_{EQ}$). Table 30 shows that the periphery captured of US$1.6 trillion in DVA in 2022. Had it been paid according to average price levels, this would have been US$3.3 trillion – US$1.7 trillion more, or 108 per cent of its actual earnings. Meanwhile, the centre saved US$3.1 trillion (27 per cent of its earnings) simply because of differences in price levels.

Köhler's approach has recently been applied by Andrea Ricci and Jason Hickel, whose studies confirm the above pattern, and reveal a worsening trend over time.[433] Unequal exchange appears as a double gain for the centre: (1) In savings made sourcing goods from the (semi-)periphery at lower prices rather than producing them domestically at higher costs, and (2) in earnings made selling goods to the (semi-)periphery at prices exceeding what it would

	Per.	Sem.	Cen.
Domestic Value Added in Exports (DVA in $)	1.6T	5.7T	11.6T
Gross Domestic Product ($GDP_{US\$}$, in US$)	8.7T	30.4T	61.9T
Gross Domestic Product ($GDP_{PPP\$}$, in PPP$)	30.7T	63.9T	76.9T
Exchange Rate Deviation Index (ERDI = $GDP_{US\$}$ / $GDP_{PPP\$}$, in US$/PPP$)	0.3	0.5	0.8
Average ERDI ($ERDI_{AV}$ = $\sum GDP_{US\$}$ / $\sum GDP_{PPP\$}$, in US$/PPP$)	0.6		
ERDI ratio (d = $ERDI_{AV}$ / ERDI)	2.1	1.2	0.7
Equalised DVA (DVA_{EQ} = DVA × d, in US$)	3.3T	7.1T	8.5T
Unequal Exchange (UE = DVA - DVA_{EQ}, in US$)	-1.7T	-1.4T	3.1T
Unequal Exchange as % of DVA	-108%	-24%	27%

Table 30. Combined Monetary and Currency Imbalances

have cost to produce those goods there. These double gains correspond to double losses for the (semi-)periphery – the money it could have earned on exports and saved on imports under fair conditions.

Let's take a moment to examine the equal currencies approach through the theoretical lens of unequal exchange. Some critics dismiss it as a mere stand-in for unequal exchange, with no real explanatory power of its own.[434] Because it does not deal directly with labour time, let alone value, it does indeed seem like something of a shortcut. However, as mentioned, Köhler argues that currency imbalances actually cause unequal exchange of value.[435] But he issues the following disclaimer: '[T]he exchange rate system is one of the mechanisms by which high-wage countries extract value from low-wage countries,'[436] acknowledging the existence of other mechanisms of unequal exchange.

Andrea Ricci goes a step further by asserting that this currency imbalance, i.e., the gap between ME and PPP rates, represents 'the visible manifestation of the systematic transfer of value from poorer to richer countries hidden under the apparently equivalent exchange of commodities in the capitalist global market.'[437] He argues that ME rates distort the relationship between value produced and value realised as prices, while PPP rates correct these distortions. Thus, we can say that PPP acts as an equaliser, revealing value drains in international trade. If Ricci is right, Köhler's approach actually exposes the price-value discrepancies responsible for unequal exchange. We can shed light on this question by combining the currency imbalance with the monetary and labour imbalances discussed so far.

As explained, MELT combines the monetary and labour imbalances, measuring the amount of money earned per unit of labour time in different countries (see Table 28). However, it doesn't adjust for price level differences. How do we approach this?

You may recall the international comparison of Big Mac affordability in minimum-wage hours from Chapter 3. For example, a Big Mac requires 42 minutes of minimum-wage work in the United States, compared with 404 minutes in India.[438] We now extend this logic to the economy as a whole. For example, if India's MELT is ₹74 per hour and, using ME rates (1:74), this converts to US$1 per hour, while the United States' MELT is, say, US$10 per hour, the US economy enjoys a price-to-value ratio ten times higher – more than enough to drive unequal exchange between the two countries. However, it gets worse when using a MELT adjusted for differences in purchasing power. In this case, India's MELT drops to just US$0.31 per hour based on PPP rates (1:23). As the ME and PPP rates for the United States are both logically equal to one, its MELT remains US$10 per hour. This adjustment reveals that while the US economy earns enough to purchase US$1 worth of goods with just six minutes of labour time (1h / US$10), the Indian economy requires over three hours (1h / US$0.31) to buy the exact same goods.

In other words, MELT within a national economy is tied to the currency's local purchasing power, reflecting domestic wage levels and prices. However, in global trade, we must somehow account for differences in the international purchasing power of a given country's currency.

In a hypothetical price-level equilibrium, the MELT must be recalculated to represent a hypothetical scenario in which it takes the same amount of labour time everywhere to generate a unit of money with the same purchasing power, i.e., the ability to buy the same goods.[439] How do we get there? We already established the following relationships (see Table 28):

1. Homogenous Labour Input: $HLI = \Sigma DLI \times O$, with O representing the share in total output and calculated as $GDP_{PPP\$} / \Sigma GDP_{PPP\$}$
2. Homogenous labour MELT: $MELT = GDP_{US\$} / HLI$
3. Exchange Rate Deviation Index: $ERDI = GDP_{US\$} / GDP_{PPP\$}$

Equation 4 then reformulates equation 2 by substituting equation 1 into the denominator. After some algebraic simplifications, the regional MELT equals global average MELT – only now in PPP$ per hour ($MELT_{AV(PPP\$)}$) – multiplied by the regional ERDI from equation 3, as shown in equation 4:

4. Homogenous labour: $MELT = GDP_{US\$} / HLI$ (equation 2)
$= GDP_{US\$} / (\Sigma DLI \times GDP_{PPP\$} / \Sigma GDP_{PPP\$})$
$= GDP_{US\$} / (GDP_{PPP\$} / MELT_{AV(PPP\$)})$
$= MELT_{AV(PPP\$)} \times ERDI$

Essentially, a region's MELT (in US$ per hour of homogenous labour) is equal to the global average MELT (in PPP$ per hour) multiplied by the region's ERDI (in US$ per PPP$). From this, it follows that the hypothetical ERDI-adjusted MELT for all regions ($MELT_{AV}$, in US$ per hour) equals the global average MELT (in PPP$ per hour) multiplied by the global average ERDI instead of the regional ERDI, or more simply, world GDP in US$ divided by total homogenous work. These last algebraic steps are developed in equation 5:[440]

5. ERDI-adjusted MELT: $MELT_{AV} = MELT_{AV(PPP\$)} \times ERDI_{AV}$ (adjusted equation 4)
$= (\Sigma GDP_{PPP\$} / \Sigma HLI) \times (\Sigma GDP_{US\$} / \Sigma GDP_{PPP\$})$
$= \Sigma GDP_{US\$} / \Sigma HLI$

On a side note, and consistent with Köhler's approach, we can also calculate the global average $MELT_{AV}$ by multiplying a region's MELT by its ERDI ratio: $MELT_{AV} = MELT \times d$, with $d = ERDI_{AV} / ERDI$ (from Table 30). Either way, this averaging should logically pull above-mean centres down and below-mean peripheries up toward the average MELT.

In short, if all regions had the same MELT, it would be equal to the global average $MELT_{AV}$, which can be calculated as World GDP divided by total labour (see Table 28). As I have just shown mathematically, the difference between the actual and the average MELT reveals the triple imbalance depicted in Diagram 26 (which integrates the currency imbalance into the

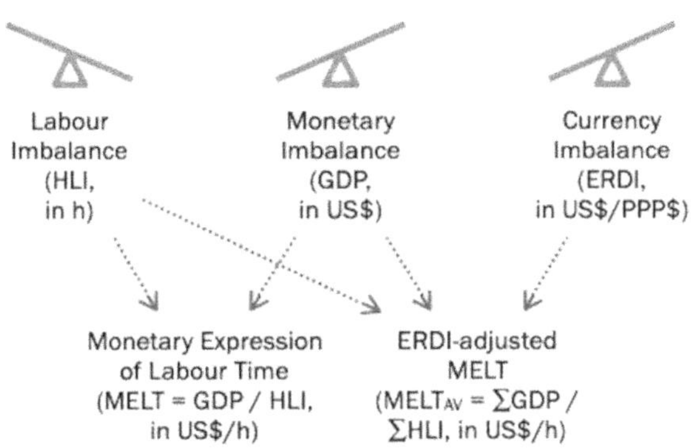

Diagram 26. Combined Labour, Monetary and Currency Imbalances

earlier Diagram 23). Let me repeat it here: With $MELT_{AV}$, it takes the same amount of labour time everywhere to generate a unit of money with the same purchasing power.

The last step is easier. It involves recalculating what each region would hypothetically have earned (DVA_{EQ}) had MELT been equalised ($MELT_{AV}$). Unequal exchange is then the difference between actual and hypothetical earnings ($UE = DVA - DVA_{EQ}$). In Table 31, I calculate the homogenous labour (HLI) embodied in each region's exports as the ratio of actual DVA to MELT: $HLI_{DVA} = DVA / MELT$ (assuming MELT applies to their export sectors). I then multiply this embodied labour by the average MELT ($MELT_{AV}$) to get the hypothetical or equalised DVA ($DVA_{EQ} = HLI_{DVA} \times MELT_{AV}$).

Finally, I calculate the resulting drain in through unequal exchange as the difference between actual and hypothetical DVA. The results match those from Table 30 which combined monetary and currency imbalances. Table 31 adds to it by integrating the labour imbalance. I explained this logic earlier when I theoretically compared a region's MELT-based earnings with $MELT_{AV}$-based earnings in Table 22. I'll come back to the theoretical connections at the end of this section.

Table 31 shows that instead of earning US$13.8 in domestic value added (DVA) per hour of labour time embodied in exports ($MELT_{AV}$), the periphery earned only US$6.7 per hour (MELT), simply because its takes

	Per.	Sem.	Cen.
MELT ($GDP_{US\$}$ / HLI, in US$/hour)	6.7	11.2	18.9
Average MELT ($MELT_{AV} = \sum GDP_{US\$} / \sum HLI$, in US$/h)		13.8	
Domestic Value Added in Exports (DVA, in US$)	1.6T	5.7T	11.6T
Embodied labour in DVA (HLI_{DVA} = DVA / MELT, in h)	235B	513B	613B
Equalised DVA ($DVA_{EQ} = HLI_{DVA} \times MELT_{AV}$, in US$)	3.3T	7.1T	8.5T
Unequal Exchange ($UE = DVA - DVA_{EQ}$, in US$)	-1.7T	-1.4T	3.1T
Unequal Exchange as % of DVA	-108%	-24%	27%
Gross Domestic Product (GDP, in US$)	8.7T	30.4T	61.9T
Unequal Exchange as % of GDP	-19%	-4%	5%
Population (People)	4.0B	2.8B	1.2B
Unequal Exchange per Capita (in US$)	-426	-484	2,554

Table 31. Combined Labour, Monetary and Currency Imbalances

less of a stronger currency to buy from places where price levels are relatively lower (remember Gernot getting a haircut in Cuba). The opposite is true for the centre, where $MELT_{AV}$ is below MELT. Indeed, the centre captured US$18.9 instead of US$13.8 per hour simply because it takes more of a weak currency to buy from places with higher price levels (remember Gerardo getting a haircut in Canada).

Because of these imbalances, the periphery captured US$1.6 trillion DVA in 2022, but would have captured US$1.7 trillion more, or 108 per cent of its actual earnings, in a world without MELT gaps. Essentially, the periphery lost that amount as a discount on its exports. Meanwhile, the centre enjoyed a surcharge on its exports of US$3.1 trillion, or 27 per cent of its actual earnings.

Here's the bottom line: In 2022, unequal exchange effectively drained nineteen per cent of the periphery's GDP and contributed five per cent of the centre's GDP. The average person in the economies of the centre saved US$2,554 thanks to unequal exchange, or US$231 per person per month, children and retirees included![441] The average person in the periphery missed out on an additional US$35 per month – a considerable amount considering the dollar's purchasing power in the periphery.

But there's more. Remember that we filtered out the productivity gap by calculating unequal exchange on the basis of homogenous labour. As mentioned, Gernot gets a haircut in Cuba for just one twenty-sixth of the price of a haircut in Canada. In addition to this price difference, however, there's also a productivity difference, as a Canadian hairdresser can complete a haircut much faster by using electric trimmers, washing stations, dryers, and vacuum systems. Let's see what happens when we factor this back in, that is, when we account for broad unequal exchange.

Replacing the homogenous labour-based MELT in Table 31 with the direct labour-based MELT from Table 28, the unequal exchange is considerably worse as shown in Table 32. This makes sense, as it now accounts for the broad form too. In 2022, unequal exchange drained 79 per cent of the periphery's GDP and boosted the centre's GDP by fourteen per cent. That means the average person in the periphery lost out on US$145 each month, while someone in the centre effectively pocketed US$603 on average. For my family of four living in the Netherlands, that translates into a hidden subsidy of US$2,412 every single month from unequal exchange!

Of course, as an average measure, this per capita subsidy rises for higher-consuming groups in the centres, who appropriate a larger share of the total gains from unequal exchange. It also decreases for the working class as a whole, since a substantial portion of DVA accrues to capitalists as profit rather than to labour as wages. I'll come back to this point shortly.

	Per.	Sem.	Cen.
MELT ($GDP_{US\$}$ / DLI, in US$/hour)	2.6	10.7	57.6
Average MELT ($MELT_{AV} = \sum GDP_{US\$} / \sum HLI$, in US$/h)		13.8	
Domestic Value Added in Exports (DVA, in US$)	1.6T	5.7T	11.6T
Embodied labour in DVA (DLI_{DVA} = DVA / MELT, in h)	612B	534B	201B
Equalised DVA ($DVA_{EQ} = DLI_{DVA} \times MELT_{AV}$, in US$)	8.5T	7.4T	2.8T
Unequal Exchange (UE = DVA - DVA_{EQ}, in US$)	-6.9T	-1.7T	8.8T
Unequal Exchange as % of DVA	-440%	-29%	76%
Gross Domestic Product (GDP, in US$)	8.7T	30.4T	61.9T
Unequal Exchange as % of GDP	-79%	-5%	14%
Population (People)	4.0B	2.8B	1.2B
Unequal Exchange per Capita (in US$)	-1,737	-589	7,239

Table 32. Combined Imbalances with Direct Labour

Let me first return to whether Köhler's currency imbalance (with ERDI as key variable) fully explains unequal exchange or captures only one of its mechanisms. As said, Köhler himself argues for the latter, while Ricci treats it as foundational. How should we reconcile these views? Greater clarity emerges by considering one final approach to measuring unequal exchange – one that locates its basis in national wage differentials.[442]

To illustrate this wage-based approach, let's revisit the earlier Bangladesh–Netherlands trade example. Although the nominal exchange is equal (€80 each way), the embodied labour is not: One hundred hours of low-wage labour are exchanged for one hour of high-wage labour. If wages were globally equalised at €40.4 per hour ([€0.8 + €80] / 2), Bangladesh's one hundred hours would be worth €4,040 rather than €80, while the Dutch hour would cost €40.4 rather than €80. The result is a net loss of €3,999.6 for Bangladesh, including €3,960 from underpaid domestic labour and €39.6 from overpriced imports.

In Table 33, I apply this logic to the empirical data. Using GDP, labour's share of income,[443] and direct labour inputs, I calculate average regional wage rates (w') and the global average (W'). Although it simplifies some details, this method still gives a useful big-picture comparison. I then apply these rates to the embodied labour time in exports (DLI_{DVA}, as calculated in Table 32) to estimate and compare the actual and equalised labour shares of DVA.

This difference constitutes unequal exchange: a US$3.4 trillion loss for the periphery and a US$4.4 trillion gain for the centre. Calculated this way, the average person in the periphery forfeited about US$71 per month, while the average person in the centre pocketed US$303. These amounts are about half as large as the flows reported in Table 32, reflecting that labour captures only around half of the income redistributed through unequal exchange.

	Per.	Sem.	Cen.
Gross Domestic Product ($GDP_{US\$}$, in US$)	8.7T	30.4T	61.9T
Labour Share of Income (LASH, %)	42%	46%	50%
Wage Bill (WB = $GDP_{US\$}$ × LASH, in US$)	3.7T	13.9T	30.7T
Direct Labour Input (DLI, in h)	3.4T	2.8T	1.1T
Wage Rate (w' = WB / DLI, in US$/h)	1.1	4.9	28.6
Average Wage Rate (W' = ∑WB / ∑DLI, in US$/h)		6.6	
MELT ($GDP_{US\$}$ / DLI, in US$/hour)	2.6	10.7	57.6
Domestic Value Added in Exports (DVA, in US$)	1.6T	5.7T	11.6T
Embodied labour in DVA (DLI_{DVA} = DVA / MELT, in h)	612B	534B	201B
Labour Share of DVA (DVA_{LAB} = DLI_{DVA} × w', in US$)	0.7T	2.6T	5.7T
Equalised DVA_{LAB} (DVA_{LABEQ} = DLI_{DVA} × W', in US$)	4.0T	3.5T	1.3T
Unequal Exchange (UE = DVA_{LAB} - DVA_{LABEQ}, in US$)	-3.4T	-0.9T	4.4T
Population (People)	4.0B	2.8B	1.2B
Unequal Exchange per Capita (in US$)	-852	-326	3,636

Table 33. Combined Labour and Wage Imbalances

Unequal exchange calculated by equalising wage rates is larger than when calculated by equalising ERDI alone: For example, the periphery losses are US$3.4 trillion in Table 33 versus US$1.7 trillion in Table 30. I would therefore agree with Torkil Lauesen's conclusion:

> It seems to me that the under-valuation of the local currencies in the Global South, compared to the 'strong' dollar, euro, or yen – measured in PPP (consumption power) – is an unequal exchange which comes on top of the unequal exchange generated by the difference in national wage compared to the global average wage (global value).[444]

Unequal exchange is even larger when calculated on the basis of combined imbalances, e.g., amounting to a US$6.9 trillion loss for the periphery (Table 32). As discussed, Ricci's approach incorporates a labour imbalance into Köhler's currency imbalance and equalises the MELT rather than wages. This allows Ricci to capture gains and losses not only for labour (through wages) but also for capital and the state (through profits and taxes). By contrast, the wage-based approach captures only the labour share. Indeed, if the labour shares in Table 33 are all set to a hundred per cent, the resulting estimate coincides with the US$6.9 trillion loss for the periphery. Ricci's approach thus offers a more comprehensive account of unequal exchange, though at the cost of obscuring the specific wage-based mechanism.

Focusing on the wage-based mechanism helps to put the earlier per capita estimate of unequal exchange into perspective. In the centre, capital can employ high-wage labour and nonetheless realise a profit, even as those workers consume more value than they individually generate. This is made possible through the consumption of goods produced by low-wage labour (a possibility already flagged in Chapter 3). Remember: For every sixty minutes of work, the periphery net-exports six minutes of embodied labour, while the centre net-imports 47 minutes (Table 29).

Does this mean that the centre worker ceases to be exploited and instead becomes an exploiter in a global context? The answer depends on how one defines exploitation. If it is understood as the extraction of surplus value from labour by capital, then it is more accurate, I would argue, to say that workers can simultaneously endure exploitation and gain from the exploitation of others. Sometimes, these gains may even outweigh their own exploitation. Such a situation logically implies a negative rate of surplus value in places where workers can buy with their wages more value than they themselves contribute.[445]

The question then becomes: Where do we draw the line? Lauesen argues that the global average wage determines 'the threshold above which workers begin to appropriate more value by consumption than they produce.'[446] I've estimated this at US$6.6 per hour in Table 33, which roughly amounts to US$1,121 per month for an average full-time worker.[447] About thirteen per cent of Americans earn below that threshold and are therefore exploited more than they themselves benefit from the exploitation of others.[448] Above the threshold, whether someone earns US$10 or US$100 per hour changes the extent of the value transfer but not its nature, Lauesen adds.

I believe the threshold wage diverges from the average wage. The threshold is a theoretical benchmark where the value generated by labour equals the value received through consumption. For (global) capitalism to extract surplus value, the threshold wage must be above the actual average wage. A more precise calculation would therefore multiply the average annual hours (2,035) by the global average $MELT_{AV}$ (US$13.8 per hour), resulting in a threshold wage of US$2,344 per month below which roughly 29 per cent of Americans fall. The threshold isn't a strict cut-off. Those earning moderately above it may benefit. from cheapened imports like food and clothing but still lack access to affordable healthcare, housing, or energy.

Let's end with a reflection on how this empirical evidence relates to the theory. In Table 34, I have fitted the data from Table 32 into the conceptualisations of broad and strict unequal exchange (from Table 21, Table 22 and Table 24), by matching the key variables between these empirical and theoretical interpretations.

The DLI variable measures only living labour; It doesn't represent value which also includes dead labour, the value transferred from constant capital. Essentially, with value including constant capital, variable capital and surplus value ($V = c + v + S$), DLI represents only the latter two, i.e., 'total labour' in Marxist terms ($DLI = v + S$).[449] DLI therefore groups together necessary and surplus labour time in proportion to the surplus rate (s'). It therefore does not distinguish between variable capital and surplus value embodied in the final value of commodities. DLI_{DVA} applies the same logic, but only to commodities produced for export. The share of DLI devoted to production for export is denoted by DLI_{DVA}. During the realisation phase, value (V, in h) is transformed into revenue (R, in Ł), and DLI_{DVA} into DVA. Accordingly, R in Table 34 corresponds to the DVA in Table 32, and V to DLI_{DVA}.

In Table 34, only DVA and DLI_{DVA} are entered directly; the remaining variables are derived. Let's discuss those, starting with MELT. The regional MELT in Table 34 (R / V) logically aligns with that in Table 32 (DVA / DLI_{DVA}). The average MELT, however, shows a slight discrepancy between the two tables (US$14.0 versus US$13.8 per hour), because Table 34 recalculates it as total DVA divided by total DLI_{DVA}, rather than as world GDP divided by world DLI in Table 32.

As noted, $V = DLI_{DVA}$. Since the data exclude constant capital ($c = 0$), DLI_{DVA} represents only the realisation of variable capital and surplus value. Consequently, the organic composition must also be zero: With $c = v \times OC$, if $c = 0$ and $v \neq 0$, it follows that $OC = 0$. In value terms, only v and S remain, and DLI_{DVA} must be distributed between them. Assuming a uniform surplus rate (s') of one hundred per cent across all regions, $v = S$, and DLI_{DVA} is therefore divided equally between the two. This logic is implemented in Table 34, where v is calculated as: $DLI_{DVA} / (1 + s')$. The remaining variables are derived from the original equations.

		Per.	Sem.	Cen.
Money capital ($MO = C \times MELT_{AV}$)	derived	783B	2,861B	5,788B
Capital invested ($C = c + v$)	derived	306B	267B	100B
Constant capital (c)	unaccounted	0B	0B	0B
Variable capital (v)	$v = V / (1 + s')$	306B	267B	100B
Organic composition ($OC = c / v$)	derived	0.0	0.0	0.0
Surplus rate (s')	assumed	100%	100%	100%
Surplus value ($S = v \times s'$)	derived	306B	267B	100B
Value produced ($V = C + S$)	$V = DLI_{DVA}$	612B	534B	201B
Profit rate ($p' = S / C$)	derived	100%	100%	100%
Average profit rate ($P' = \sum S / \sum C$)	derived		100%	
Profit ($P = MO \times P'$)	derived	783B	2,867B	5,788B
Monetary profit rate ($m' = P / C$)	derived	100%	100%	100%
Revenue ($R = MO + P$)	$R = DVA$	1.6T	5.7T	11.6T
MELT (R / V)	derived	2.6	10.7	57.6
Average MELT ($MELT_{AV} = \sum R / \sum V$)	derived		14.0	
Surplus profit ($SP = R - V \times MELT_{AV}$)	derived	-7.0T	-1.8T	8.8T

Table 34. Matching Empirical and Theoretical Tables

Although the model is too crude to serve as a simulation tool, it remains useful for demonstrating how the theory operates. As shown in Table 35, increasing productivity in the centre (raising OC from 0 to 0.1) intensifies unequal exchange in the broad form, while lowering wages in the periphery (raising the surplus rate from 100% to 110%) does so in the strict form.

CLOSING REMARKS

We began with a model of equivalent exchange and introduced modifications to reveal two forms of unequal exchange, each driven by a different imbalance: For the broad form, we introduced a productivity gap by increasing constant capital in the centre; for the strict form, we introduced a wage gap by increasing variable capital and reducing the surplus rate in the centre. In both cases, the centre exchanges less value for more with the periphery. This value imbalance is not reflected in commodity prices, though, as high prices coincide with low value and vice versa.

		Per.	Sem.	Cen.
Money capital ($MO = C \times MELT_{AV}$)	derived	746B	2,921B	6,367B
Capital invested ($C = c + v$)	derived	291B	272B	111B
Constant capital (c)	unaccounted	0B	5B	10B
Variable capital (v)	$v = V / (1 + s')$	291B	267B	100B
Organic composition ($OC = c / v$)	derived	0.0	0.0	0.1
Surplus rate (s')	assumed	110%	100%	100%
Surplus value ($S = v \times s'$)	derived	320B	267B	100B
Value produced ($V = C + S$)	$V = DLI_{DVA}$	612B	539B	211B
Profit rate ($p' = S / C$)	derived	110%	98%	91%
Average profit rate ($P' = \sum S / \sum C$)	derived	102%		
Profit ($P = MO \times P'$)	derived	761B	2,981B	6,499B
Monetary profit rate ($m' = P / C$)	derived	102%	102%	102%
Revenue ($R = MO + P$)	$R = DVA$	1.5T	5.9T	12.9T
MELT (R / V)	derived	2.5	10.9	61.0
Average MELT ($MELT_{AV} = \sum R / \sum V$)	derived	14.9		
Surplus profit ($SP = R - V \times MELT_{AV}$)	derived	-7.6T	-2.1T	9.7T

Table 35. Additional Broad and Strict Unequal Exchange

As a consequence, unequal exchange reinforces capital accumulation in the centres, by mitigating their falling profit rates: 'wealth begets wealth,' Arghiri Emmanuel reminds us.[450] At the same time, unequal exchange hinders accumulation in the peripheries, by transferring a large portion of their surplus value to the centres for free: 'poverty begets poverty,' we should add. In the absence of unequal exchange, accumulation would fall in the centre and rise in the periphery.

If there's one key takeaway to be had from this chapter on measuring unequal exchange, it's the US$145 per capita monthly 'discount' on the periphery's exports and the US$603 per capita 'surcharge' on the centre's – a snapshot of a trend that has only worsened over time.[451] These 'tributes,' as Andrea Ricci aptly puts it, underscore how labour exploitation in the periphery offers a counter-tendency to falling rates of profit and partially defuses class conflict in the centre, weakening (not entirely preventing) notions of international solidarity.

7. Ecologically Unequal Exchange

OPENING REMARKS

After wandering through the world of value, this chapter draws attention to the material world and the distribution of its resources through the process of ecologically unequal exchange. This process describes a reality that, given the environmental and planetary crises of the present moment, cannot be ignored.

As you read this, you might be holding in your hands the product of a particular value chain that started with felling a tree: a book, which might one day be recycled as toilet paper. We flush the equivalent of 27,000 trees per day this way.[452] Nature obviously means more to us humans than a mere resource tap and waste bin, but capitalism nevertheless treats it in this way. And trade enables the abuse.

We usually think of trade as a simple two-way exchange: Money flows one way, commodities the other. But market prices hide many other flows. As we have seen, unequal exchange emerges as asymmetrical transfers of value, defined within a Marxist framework as the average labour time embodied in traded commodities. However, commodities also embody energy, matter, land, and so on, and this realisation has given rise to research on so-called ecologically unequal exchange.[453] These studies attempt to measure trade's asymmetrical transfers of embodied biophysical resources. Simply put, if unequal exchange means trading more labour for less, ecologically unequal exchange means trading more resources for less.[454]

We will now explore this, as both a theoretical concept and real-world phenomenon, as well as its connections with unequal exchange in its original form. These connections underline the shared origins of today's environmental and social crises.[455] As Walter Rodney explains,

> Man has always exploited his natural environment in order to make a living. At a certain point in time, there also arose the exploitation of man by man, in that a few people grew rich and lived well through the labour of others. Then a stage was reached by which people in one community called a nation exploited the natural resources and the labour of another nation and its people.[456]

SOCIAL METABOLISM

First, let's consider the flows of matter and energy into, through, and out of an economy as its social metabolism. Analogous to the physiological processes of organisms and ecosystems, we can say that the economy resembles a metabolic system that lives off the environment by absorbing raw material and energy and returning waste material and energy. Nicholas Georgescu-Roegen, the pioneer of ecological economics, calls this the 'metabolic flow,'[457] while Marx refers to it as a material exchange ('stoffwechsel') between humans and nature.[458]

Global capitalism is a voracious beast that devours an entire Mount Everest's worth of resources every eighteen months. Moreover, its metabolism is always accelerating, with this level of consumption expected to take just ten months in two decades' time.[459] As it fills its belly, the beast exhausts and burdens its environment, disrupting nature's capacity to regenerate resources and recover wastes.

Sooner or later, the beast will hit hard biophysical limits, such as depleted natural resources and overloaded environmental sinks – spaces that soak up and process waste and pollutants.[460] It will, ultimately, annihilate its own habitat. However, harms are felt long before these limits are reached:[461] Climate change will cook the planet before the oil runs out;[462] biodiversity will collapse before we run out of forests to chop down.

The environmental crisis stems not only from a quantitative imbalance between available resources and their consumption by global capitalism, but also from the qualitative deterioration of matter and energy coursing through the economy. To fully comprehend this, we need a crash course in thermodynamics, a branch of physical science that examines how energy transforms from one form to another. These transformations follow a few fundamental laws.

There's been much debate about whether Marx understood thermodynamics, and many attempts to expand his framework around it.[463] I side with those who argue that Marx did incorporate basic thermodynamic principles, though it ultimately matters little whether he did. More importantly, his framework does not need overhauling – it can easily accommodate an updated understanding of the thermodynamics of capital accumulation. Let me explain.[464]

In my garden, I find concentrated chemical energy in the form of an apple. I eat it and that energy is converted into something I can use. The initial chemical energy held within the apple is transformed into chemical energy that regenerates cells in my body, kinetic energy fuelling physical activities, and thermal energy radiating as body heat. The first law of thermodynamics states that while energy can change forms, it can neither be created nor destroyed.

The same principle applies to natural gas: When one measures the energy contained in a cubic meter of natural gas and burns it to run a generator, the energy stored in the natural gas equals the energy consumed in electricity generation, plus the heat released by the generator. In short: Energy changes form but never disappears.

Why, then, are we facing an energy crisis if energy cannot be destroyed? The answer lies in the second law of thermodynamics, or the Entropy Law, which states that energy flows naturally from areas of higher to lower concentration. For example, when a warm radiator is turned off, the thermal energy it contains spreads out into the cooler room, and eventually through the walls, until a state of thermal equilibrium is reached. At this point, entropy, which measures energy dispersion, reaches its maximum. The Entropy Law therefore explains our need to constantly consume new energy to stay warm when it is cold (one factor contributing to the energy crisis).

Entropy relates to the idea that energy possesses a certain quality: its potential to perform useful work, such as heating a house. Stating that I used a lot of energy this winter is ambiguous: The energy didn't vanish; it simply transformed. Intuitively, however, we feel that something did vanish. The energy's useful form, known as exergy, is what is consumed and dissipated. Natural gas, for instance, contains abundant exergy – energy available for use – whereas warm water in a radiator system has considerably less. Entropy increases in direct proportion to exergy losses.

Energy dispersion also affects matter, leading to phenomena such as food spoilage, metal corrosion, and general wear and tear. Such degradation occurs because the energy that holds atoms and molecules together is released spontaneously. As a consequence, the Entropy Law implies that both energy and matter tend to disperse, resulting in an overall increase in entropy. Entropy is also the principle behind the gradual breakdown of the body's cells and our inevitable ageing. 'Entropy carries a rather ominous connotation,' my partner once remarked.

Fortunately, entropy's rise can be reversed so that we can heat up radiators, grow fresh apples, and regenerate cells, by concentrating energy. This reversal follows a sub-law of the Entropy Law: Energy moves from dispersed to concentrated states by performing work, which requires additional energy. For example, a heating system uses gas to concentrate thermal energy, and I consume apples to replenish lost chemical energy in my body. In short: Energy concentration requires supplementary energy.

But there's a catch: This work comes at a cost, for while it reduces local entropy, it increases entropy elsewhere. By eating the apple, I reduce body entropy, but raise entropy in my surroundings through discarded peel, body heat, and faeces. Gas heaters reduce radiator entropy but heighten biosphere entropy as a result of the extraction, purification, and burning of low-entropy natural gas.

Moreover, total entropy always increases. A second sub-law of the Entropy Law states that no energy transfer for useful work is one hundred per cent efficient. Energy losses occur as food waste and perspiration during the transfer from the apple to my body. As I reduce my entropy at the expense of an increase in my surroundings, inefficiencies make the reduction smaller than the increase. In short: Energy conversions are never fully efficient.

What do these laws mean for capitalism? In the 1970s, Georgescu-Roegen predicted its inevitable downfall as a result of its inherent tendency to increase entropy.[465] Capitalism operates not only as a circulation system, but as a digestion system directly connected to the environment at both ends.[466] Essentially, capitalist accumulation represents the rate at which we convert low-entropy resources into high-entropy waste. Fossil fuels enter the economy as organised matter and energy but leave as dispersed heat, chemicals, carbon dioxide, and microplastics.

Worse still, capitalism's metabolism expands too fast for the biosphere to keep up. Ecosystems have evolved over millions of years to optimise energy consumption in ecological food webs and delay or reduce entropy through biodiversity. Indeed, a healthy and functioning biosphere is the only force on Earth capable of counterbalancing rises in entropy through, for example, photosynthesis, ecological succession, or cellular regeneration. Tragically, by disrupting this balance and overwhelming natural processes of entropy reduction, capitalist economies are doing the precise opposite at an alarming rate.

The biosphere can harness solar power to perform useful work that concentrates dispersed energy and matter in accordance with the Entropy Law's first sub-law. However, the rate at which recovery and regeneration occur is limited. For me to be able to consume an apple to decrease my body's entropy, the tree must first consume energy to produce the apple through the gradual processes of photosynthesis, nutrient uptake, growth, and fruiting. This natural pace restricts my rate of apple consumption.

Furthermore, by actively seeking to bypass such natural limits, capitalism creates new environmental disruptions, which ultimately lead to new limits. The capitalist mode of production, Marx writes, 'is based on the dominion of man over nature.'[467] For example, we create monocultures to facilitate mechanical agriculture, but these result in soil dehydration. To combat this, we introduce irrigation, but this depletes groundwater, and so we invent drought-resistant crops. When those crops harm soil life, we invent something else. 'Control breeds its own necessity.'[468]

Unfortunately, such problem-solving zeal contributes significantly to the climate and biodiversity crises. 'Every innovation leads to the extinction of a species,' a colleague once stated for dramatic effect.[469] Capitalism, in its relentless pursuit of growth, undermines the very biosphere that it needs to mitigate its entropy-amplifying activities. For example, noting that 71 per cent of Bhutan is forested but the forestry sector contributes only two per cent to GDP, the World Bank wonders how the country might unlock this underutilised resource.[470]

To be clear, capitalism can't help it; it crashes when its accumulation is hindered. A typical response to the ecological crisis is, therefore, to pin all hopes on efficiency, circularity, dematerialisation, decarbonisation, and other profit-driven green innovations within capitalism, rather than restrict accumulation. However, such hopes are false, as entropy always looms.

Wasteful economies must obviously strive to become more circular, but this has limits. No economy can sustain itself, let alone grow, by only reusing its own waste and by-products. Like organisms that cannot survive on their own faeces or trees that cannot survive on falling leaves, economies require new inputs of low-entropy matter and energy to function. As discussed above, the concentration of dispersed materials requires energy investments, and comes with inevitable transmission losses that increase overall entropy. Additionally, energy consumption increases as recycling rates increase, and energy itself cannot be recycled.

To conclude this crash course in thermodynamics, the economy requires a continuous inflow of new, low-entropy matter and energy to counteract inevitable losses and inefficiencies. This applies equally to so-called green capitalism. While the biosphere can convert certain types and quantities of waste back into raw materials, we cannot expect it to match the accelerating rate at which capitalist accumulation drives entropy.

NATURAL USE VALUES

As social metabolism speeds up, it causes what some Marxists refer to as 'metabolic rifts.'[471] These rifts manifest as biophysical imbalances between over-extracted and over-polluted places, as well as between under- and over-consuming populations. Marx provides an early example in the form of a nutrient rift that connects depleted soil in the countryside with towns overwhelmed by sewage. Countless other rifts exist, of course, such as the rerouting of entire river systems or the clearing of vast ecosystems to support either industrial agriculture or urban development elsewhere.

As a result of colonial plunder, these rifts spread far and wide, and they continue to expand through neocolonial trade relations. For example, phosphorus mining in Morocco and nitrogen fixing in the United States contribute to the proliferation of eutrophic dead zones in the Arabian Sea and the Gulf of Mexico. The further expansion of such rifts will eventually breach safe planetary boundaries, with the nutrient rift now representing a dangerous disruption of the Earth's biogeochemical cycles.[472]

However, other Marxists find the concept of rifts simplistic. They take a more interconnected view, emphasising that environmental disruptions arise not only from spatial rifts but also fundamental 'metabolic shifts,' or transformations of 'nature.'[473] Such a shift can be observed in the alteration of soils and devastation of soil life caused by industrial agriculture – a far more profound change than the mere depletion of soil nutrients.

Global capitalism not only circulates and degrades natural resources but fundamentally alters the environments that (re)generate them. Apprehending the soil nutrient problem as a mere rift means that we solve it by simply applying fertiliser and thus fail to fix the shift. In fact, we make it worse, as fertilisers disturb the intricate symbiosis between plants and essential microbes.[474]

That said, the shift school's rejection of the idea of a separate nature overlooks nature's evolution of its own endogenous functions and adherence to its own laws (such as thermodynamics), regardless of human influence. For example, certain fungi beneath the soil extract minerals from decaying matter and trade them for sugars from plants. Such natural functions must be recognised in order to understand their anthropogenic degradation.

The historical practice of exploiting and transforming nature overseas deepens both rifts and shifts. Known as ecological imperialism, it was crucial for capitalism's emergence and expansion, and brought environmental benefits to the centres while offloading environmental costs to the peripheries.[475] As a result, the centres steadily accumulated an 'ecological debt' owed to the periphery.[476]

Sociologist Stephen Bunker introduced the term 'ecologically unequal exchange' (EUE) to refer to the modern form of ecological imperialism.[477] Instead of describing the unequal distribution of environmental costs and benefits caused by colonial and military ransacking, EUE focuses on their distribution through the more ordinary process of trade under capitalism. EUE is thus a perennial driving force behind today's global metabolic rifts and shifts, and the environmental injustices and conflicts associated with them.

We already know that unequal exchange, as Emmanuel conceptualised it, plays a key role in determining the distribution of accumulation's costs and benefits on a world scale. However, with its focus on value (as average labour time), unequal exchange does not directly expose the material flows and entropic transformations propelled by trade. Two countries could export unequal amounts of grain embodying equal amounts of value if their production processes differ in their organic composition of capital. Since labour is the source of value, a ton of manually harvested grain may embody as much value as a hundred tons harvested mechanically.

To fill this gap, Bunker's EUE emphasises the uneven transfer of what he calls 'natural values.'[478] He argues that extractive industries – such as mining, quarrying, fishing, logging, and farming – prevail in the peripheries. Global trade thus siphons off vast amounts of 'natural value' from these regions.

While some argue that EUE is based on Emmanuel's theory of unequal exchange,[479] I find this claim questionable. Bunker deviated from the Marxist value framework by combining labour value with his loosely defined notion of natural value to determine a commodity's total value. According to him, the peripheries primarily export natural value, and labour value is added later by productive centres further along the supply chain. He contends that by focusing solely on labour value, the original theory of unequal exchange overlooked the appropriation of natural value – the extraction and depletion of natural resources.

> The use of labour as a standard of value for unequal exchange thus ignores the exchange inequalities inherent in extractive economies, where value in nature is appropriated in one region and labour value incorporated in another [...] Additional value is created when extracted materials are transformed by labour. The important point, however, is that this additional value is generally realized in the industrial centre, rather than at the periphery.[480]

However, Arghiri Emmanuel himself suggests that an explanation of unequal exchange based solely on wage and exploitation differentials may be 'too abstract and illusory.' He therefore points to another comparison in physical terms, considering the 'exhaustion of deposits and reserves,' and other burdens placed on 'ecological limits.'[481] So, too, does Samir Amin, when he refers to 'a whole series of cases of "unequal exchanges"' related to ecological factors existing side by side with the unequal exchange of labour.[482] Clearly, the environmental dimension was acknowledged by the original theorists of unequal exchange, but it was never integrated into their theories.

One might think that their theories are meaningless because labour is only one of several inputs for material production. Although this is true to an extent, it does not negate the relevance of unequal exchange with periphery countries that rely primarily on the extraction of natural resources. Extractive industries which, like all other capitalist sectors, appropriate surplus value from labour, can be engaging in unequal exchange. For instance, due to lower wages, Ethiopia may export raw sesame to Dutch food processing firms at a price below value.

We must of course recognise the substantial disparities in natural resource allocation through trade, but by combining natural and labour value, we conflate human labour time with natural substance, and consequently the exploitation of labour with the destructive appropriation of nature.[483] In a capitalist agricultural context, for example, farmhands, microorganisms, and aquifers would all suffer the same type of abuse if we were to generalise the concept of value.

The challenge lies in distinguishing drains of value through unequal exchange from drains of resources through EUE. Like other commentators, I therefore advocate for disentangling unequal exchange from its environmental variant.[484] Bunker's is an important step towards this goal, but he unfortunately blurs processes that should be analytically separated (before being reconnected, as we will see).

Let's look at how Marx's value framework engages with environmental issues. He argues that both human and non-human labour contribute to the creation of use values: 'Labour is not the source of all wealth. Nature is just as much the source of use-values […] as labour.'[485] This is true of all economic systems, including capitalism. Specific to capitalism is the transformation, through production, of natural use values into values (and exchange values). They acquire value from both living and dead labour – variable and constant capital used during the extraction of resources, be that the harvesting of soy, the mining of coal, or the felling of trees.

In certain extractive industries, inputs of living labour power may be very low compared to inputs of natural resources (measured in energy contributions), but the Marxist framework still applies. For example, Australian copper mining companies have higher organic compositions of capital and lower surplus rates than their Zambian counterparts. As a result, they benefit from the mechanisms of broad and strict unequal exchange: Australian copper exports will be overpriced (Revenue surpasses Value at a given Monetary Expression of Labour Time), and Zambian exports underpriced ($R < V \times$ MELT).

Under capitalism, processed natural use values gain both value and exchange value. As we know, exchange value represents the value ratio between traded commodities and sets the foundation for market prices. The key is that while natural use values are crucial for production, they don't affect exchange value. Let me explain.

The book you hold in your hands derives its value from components such as printing paper, ink, and other materials of production, along with instruments of production and labour power. As previously explained, the infusion of value into commodities resembles tributaries converging within a watershed (Diagram 1 in Chapter 2). The value of the printing paper includes that of wood pulp, which, in turn, includes the value of woody biomass. Biomass harvested from an unmanaged forest gains value solely from the logger and their tools. Trees, created by ecosystems and not waged labour, have no value.

Similarly, the value of the logger's chainsaw traces back through a supply chain to someone mining ore for chainsaw components. It inherits no value from the ore, only from the miner and their tools. At the origin of all supply chains lies labour power, extracting, harvesting, and capturing the raw material use values provided by nature. Through processing, these resources become materials of production that embody value.

Under capitalism, nature's contributions are therefore not reflected in prices but treated as free gifts that capital exploits without compensation (see the 'free gifts of nature' in Diagram 8, Chapter 2). There's no such thing as 'natural capital,' as Marx points out:

> In the extractive industries, mines, etc., the raw materials form no part of the capital advanced. The subject of labour is in this case not a product of previous labour, but is furnished by Nature gratis, as in the case of metals, minerals, coal, stone, etc.[486]

To be precise, trees in plantations differ from trees in unmanaged forests because they embody value after pruning, fertilisation, and other tasks involving human labour. However, plantation trees also depend on such free natural elements as atmospheric carbon dioxide, photosynthesis, and transpiration, which contribute to their use value but not their value. One can argue about where exactly labour begins to add value to nature, but nature itself has no value under capitalism; it only holds potential value until human intervention imparts value to it.[487] This notion of a valueless nature obviously vexes people. In *Small is Beautiful*, Ernst Schumacher writes:

> [W]e are estranged from reality and inclined to treat as valueless everything that we have not made ourselves. Even the great Dr Marx fell into this devastating error when he formulated the so-called 'labour theory of value.'[488]

Ecological economist Herman Daly makes the same point in starker terms:

> Marx, with his theory that labour was the source of all value, was even more eager than standard economists to deny any important role to nature in the functioning of the economy and creation of value.[489]

I understand where they are coming from, but these critiques should be directed at capitalism, not Marx.[490] Capitalism treats nature like a cornucopia, simply slapping price tags on its (perceived) endless gifts. 'When they assume this money-shape,' Marx explains, 'commodities strip off every trace of their natural use-value.'[491] This separation allows capitalism to exploit nature without replenishing or restoring it. The price of a hamburger doesn't reflect the loss of a rainforest to a cattle ranch; the carbon offset of an airfare doesn't undo its climate impact. Capitalism's systemic blind spot results in ongoing harms to nature, reflecting not an undervaluation or cheapening but a complete denial of 'value' to the natural world.

Still, the idea that only human labour imbues value continues to bug people. Why doesn't non-human work also contribute to a commodity's value? This seems like a significant oversight when the energy potential of a barrel of oil, for example, is equivalent to almost twelve years of human muscle power.[492] Given nature's undeniable role, what is the main Marxist argument against accepting and acknowledging its contribution to the creation of commodity value? Commodities not only embody paid labour time, but also energy, matter, and unpaid work. Are these factors not just as crucial to capital in generating value and surplus value?[493]

For example, if Bob hand-forms one hundred hamburger patties in one hour, his labour time for a single patty is 36 seconds (3600 / 100). However, when Bob starts producing 600 patties in the same length of time after purchasing an automatic burger patty press, his labour time is only six seconds per patty (3600 / 600). Shouldn't we conclude that the difference between 36 and six seconds is an increase in surplus value, and the result of relying less on human labour and more on energy from natural sources?

It appears so, but Marxists present a different story. They emphasise that the energy consumed by Bob's patty press is not purely a natural substance, but a result of the human labour involved in extracting, transporting, and refining fossil energy into electricity, thus creating value.[494] Bob purchases the electricity as constant capital and transfers its value to burgers.

More importantly, though, Marxists would argue that the patty press does not create additional surplus value but instead transfers its value – along with that of the electricity – to the patties. Even if the press ran on a purely natural substance with no value, the logic would still hold: Per-unit production costs would fall below the average, generating surplus profit rather than additional surplus value (see Chapter 4). Meanwhile, producers who fail to mechanise struggle to fully realise their surplus value as profit.

Despite constituting only one per cent of total global energy expenditure,[495] human labour remains the sole source of surplus value. Marx does not overlook non-human work but acknowledges nature's significance as a source of natural use values, including the fossil fuels that run the machines responsible for generating surplus profit.

What, then, makes a use value 'natural'? As mentioned above, producing commodities involves using nature's free gifts, such as raw materials, groundwater, soil microbes, and sunlight. These natural use values play a role in the supply chains that eventually lead to someone eating a burger. Human-made use values such as tractors, packages, and refrigerators also contribute, and their production also relies on natural use values. In this way, the burger embodies various amounts of natural use values from the different supply chains that helped to create it. This is similar to how we can think of the direct and indirect labour time embodied in a commodity's value.

If both human labour and nature contributed to creating value, the definition of value would shift from average labour time to a common factor shared by human and non-human work, possibly energy expenditure. This would reduce the complexity and unique significance of each contribution, blurring the distinction between the exploitation of workers and the destruction of natural use values, as mentioned earlier.

Let's now revisit our earlier insights on metabolism and thermodynamics, this time through the lens of value and use-value.

First, it is conceptually helpful to associate unequal exchange with a net appropriation of labour value, and EUE with a net appropriation of natural use value. However, this association comes with a warning. In the realm of abstract labour, you may recall that, in ten minutes, Bob prepares one burger while Rick produces one hundred toothpicks (see Chapter 2). While value represents a one-dimensional magnitude (labour time), natural use values differ in substance, quality, and function. For example, a forest provides natural use values such as firewood, carbon sinks, cultural services, and genetic resources. Hence Joan Martinez-Alier's caution against measuring EUE solely in terms of, say, energy, as this would be reductionist: 'Can "biopiracy" be reduced to energy calculations?'[496] Use value, which relates to what people find useful, should not be confused with biophysical metrics such as joules, tons, or hectares. However, these are the only tools available to us to demonstrate EUE.[497]

At the same time, the diversity of natural use values does not necessarily mean that they have nothing in common. For ecological economist Nicholas Georgescu-Roegen, '[...] every object of economic value [in the colloquial sense] – be it a fruit just picked from a tree, or a piece of clothing, or furniture, etc. – has a highly ordered structure, hence, a low entropy.'[498]

As we have seen, lower entropy refers, broadly speaking, to forms of matter and energy that are more useful from an instrumental perspective, in contrast with high-entropy waste matter and energy. He therefore ascribes greater use value to relatively low-entropy resources and commodities.[499]

Georgescu-Roegen adds that 'this is only the material side of the process. The true product of the economic process is an immaterial flux, the enjoyment of life.'[500] In Marxist terms, this end-user benefit could also be referred to as an 'immaterial use value' – one that cannot be measured in biophysical units.[501] While it is immaterial, this flux nevertheless feeds on the transformation of usable natural use values into unusable waste.[502]

Thus far, we have discussed the rapid acceleration of social metabolism, which entails transforming low-entropy natural use values such as raw materials and energy into commodities that possess both value and use value. These commodities' entropy may initially be lower than the resources used to produce them. For example, the purification of iron ore into usable metal may reduce entropy within the material itself. However, the purification process requires external energy sources and generates high-entropy waste in the form of heat, pollution, and emissions.[503]

Over time, however, the commodities degrade into high-entropy waste, losing their original use value, and so capitalism contributes to a net increase in entropy on planet Earth. As explained, the pace of this increase exceeds natural systems' ability to counteract it, thereby compromising the regeneration of low-entropy natural use values.

Low-entropy natural use values do not hold value (as socially necessary labour time!). The first step in all capitalist production chains involves wage labour acting upon those natural resources to create value: A fisherman transforms wild fish (natural use value) into seafood (value and processed use value); an engineer transforms a water flow (natural use value) into electricity (value and processed use value); a logger transforms a tree (natural use value) into timber (value and processed use value). These materials of production then provide essential use values for labour to produce further (surplus) values and, in the case of energy, to run the machines that lead to surplus profit.

To better understand this last point, we can integrate natural use values into the Marxist schemes applied earlier. This will clarify how surplus profit is generated through two key functions of natural use values: reducing costs and increasing productivity. Let's start with the first.

Firms maintain a competitive edge by lowering their cost per unit of output below that of their competitors, as denoted by the ratio C / o (capital invested divided by output, see Intra-Sector Dynamics). Mac did this to Bob, if you recall. Lowering this cost requires either the ratio's numerator (C) to decrease, or its denominator (o) to increase. To begin, we will look at how natural use values achieve the former.

To paraphrase Marx, envision a toothpick sector comprising two firms, where Rick employs a steam engine and Mick a waterfall. Thanks to the waterfall, Mick requires less constant capital than Rick (285c and 265c, respectively). In Table 36, the capital outlay is expressed as follows:

- 285c + 25v = 310C for Rick.
- 265c + 25v = 290C for Mick.

Assuming a surplus rate of fifty per cent for both firms, and considering production cost equals invested capital (i.e., all investment is consumed in a single circulation), the total values produced are:

- 310C + 25v × 50% = 323V for Rick.
- 290C + 25v × 50% = 303V for Mick.

	Rick (Steam engine)	Mick (Waterfall)
Capital invested (C = c + v):	310	290
Constant capital (c)	285	265
Variable capital (v)	25	25
Organic composition (OC = c / v)	11.4	10.6
Surplus rate (s')	50%	50%
Surplus value (S = v × s')	13	13
Value produced (V = C + S)	323	303
Profit rate (p' = S / C)	4%	4%
Output (o)	30,000	30,000
Breakeven price (BP = MO / o)	0.0103	0.0097
Market price (MP = ΣV / Σo)	0.0104	
Markup (MU = MP - BP)	0.0001	0.0007
Revenue (R = MP × o)	313	313
Profit (P = R - C = MU × o)	3	23
Surplus profit (SP = P - S = R - V)	-10	10

Table 36. Cost Reductions

With equal output (30,000 toothpicks each) and a single market price of Ł0.01 per toothpick, this leads to revenue of Ł313 for both. Profits then amount to:

- 313R - 310C = Ł3 for Rick.
- 313R - 290C = Ł23 for Mick.

Rick manages to realise only a Ł3 profit from a ~13S surplus value. In contrast, with a Ł23 profit, Mick achieves a Ł10 surplus profit on top of his ~13S surplus value. Mick owes this advantage to the waterfall and its associated cost reduction.

Natural use values can therefore function to lower the per-unit cost of production (or breakeven price, BP = C / o) by reducing C. Much like the waterfall, for instance, gravity-fed irrigation systems harness the natural flow of water, eliminating the need for mechanical pumps. These natural use values serve as substitutes for instruments of production. Diverse natural use values can also substitute for materials of production: A beekeeper extracting honey from hives incurs lower production costs than artificial honey producers. Similarly, access to pollinators and healthy soil lowers farmers' production costs by allowing them to circumvent inputs such as hybrid seeds and artificial fertilisers.

If natural use values can reduce capital investment, why does capital continue to substitute nature's free contributions with technology – plants with air purifiers, bees with pollinator robots, soil with hydroponics, and so on? One reason, of course, is the ongoing destruction of nature and its services. The collapse of bee colonies, for instance, led to the development of technological alternatives to natural pollination. However, another reason relates to the denominator 'o' in per unit production cost (C / o), which brings me to the second key function of natural use values: enhancing productivity.

The waterfall lowers Mick's production costs, generating surplus profit. In response, Rick accelerates his steam engine, increasing coal consumption (from 285c to 300c) and output (from 30,000 to 35,000). Rick's profits jump to Ł20 (from Ł3), while Mick's fall to Ł5 (from Ł23), as shown in Table 37.

The introduction of the coal-fired steam engine marked a dramatic leap in productivity, providing a reliable and powerful energy source. Unlike water power, steam engines could be installed virtually anywhere and operated independently of water supply.[504] Hence, a second role for natural use values is to boost output. Marx notes:

> [T]he natural force [coal in this case] is not the source of surplus profit, but only its natural basis, because this natural basis permits an exceptional increase in the productiveness of labour.[505]

	Rick	Mick
	(Steam engine)	(Waterfall)
Capital invested (C = c + v):	325	290
Constant capital (c)	300	265
Variable capital (v)	25	25
Organic composition (OC = c / v)	12.0	10.6
Surplus rate (s')	50%	50%
Surplus value (S = v × s')	13	13
Value produced (V = C + S)	338	303
Profit rate (p' = S / C)	4%	4%
Output (o)	35,000	30,000
Breakeven price (BP = MO / o)	0.0093	0.0097
Market price (MP = ∑V / ∑o)	0.0098	
Markup (MU = MP - BP)	0.0006	0.0002
Revenue (R = MP × o)	345	295
Profit (P = R - C = MU × o)	20	5
Surplus profit (SP = P - S = R - V)	7	-7

Table 37. Productivity Boosts

Rick and Mick's story illustrates how productivity is locked in a self-reinforcing feedback loop with competition: One firm's increase in productivity triggers its competitors to follow suit. As the cycle persists, technological innovation advances through mechanisation, automation, and robotisation, all driving the consumption of matter and energy.[506] Clearly, the more productive toothpick producer will also consume production materials faster. With greater productivity, each hour of abstract labour is supported by a greater quantity of natural use values.[507]

How do capitalists get access to the natural use values that will serve them or their buyers to reduce costs and increase productivity? By paying someone ground rents (not monopoly or differential rents, discussed earlier in the chapter). Consider again Mick's waterfall: The surplus profit that it generated doesn't stem from Mick's capital, but from the monopolisation of a 'natural force.'[508] If Mick doesn't own the waterfall himself, he can purchase access from some who does. If he has to pay Ⱡ10 rent for this access, Mick would still retain a Ⱡ13 from his original Ⱡ23 profit and would still outcompete Rick.

Unless they control the resources themselves, capitalists claim natural use values through the rent system. These payments are part of the revenue that capitalists must distribute among various factions of the ruling class, in this case landholders who control the resources.

How did this rent system arise? Marx's investigation into the 'hidden abode of production' reveals a grim reality: Accumulation relies on exploitation. Beyond this lies an even grimmer reality of violence and theft,[509] known as primitive accumulation, which Marx describes as follows:

> [A] process that transforms, on the one hand, the social means of subsistence and of production into capital, on the other, the immediate producers into wage labourers. The so-called primitive accumulation, therefore, is nothing else than the historical process of divorcing the producer from the means of production.[510]

The accumulation is termed 'primitive,' meaning 'original,' because the genesis of capitalism cannot be explained by the accumulation process outlined in the reproduction tables of Chapters 3, 4, and 6.[511] In those tables, commodities – including labour power – are assumed to exist already at $t = 1$, and thus cannot account for their own original emergence.

The clearest example of primitive accumulation comes from eighteenth and nineteenth century England, where commons lands were seized from subsistence producers to remedy labour shortages in the factory system. This paved the way for a parasitical class of rent-seeking landlords who accumulated wealth without directly contributing to production. Today, less than one per cent of the population owns half of England's land.[512] This 'original sin' of capitalism quickly spread to the colonies,[513] and at its peak, the British Empire controlled a quarter of all land on Earth.[514] Similar transformations occurred across Europe, as feudal rights were dismantled and common lands privatised.

Following formal decolonisation, landownership in the peripheries was transferred to local comprador elites – a class that continues to facilitate global capitalist resource expropriation today. Their ownership of farmland, fishing grounds, and mineral reserves allows these elites to extract ground rents, license fees, property rights payments, and other charges from firms seeking access to biomass, food, and ore.

On a side note, ground rents also represent an inflow of international currency needed to pay for essential imports in a deeply uneven global system (see Chapter 5), not just a tool for the enrichment of local elites.

This directly ties to EUE, where centre countries and corporations assert massive global claims on peripheral resources, profiting even after paying ground rents in the peripheries. At the same time, the lure of these rents drives the expansion of resource frontiers and the privatisation of more communal lands, forests, and waterways. These turn into zones of commodity production that favour exports over less lucrative domestic requirements. Consequently, local populations lose access to their own resources – a process that David Harvey calls 'accumulation by dispossession.'[515]

Peripheral elites may benefit from ground rents, but the real winners are centre corporations, which snap up cheap access to resources. This was especially clear during the colonial era: In 1926, Firestone Rubber secured a million acres of Liberian forest for just six cents an acre and one per cent of the exported rubber's value.[516] The same story plays out today. In 2008, the Luxembourg-based Socfin group favourably acquired 12,000 hectares in Cambodia's Mondulkiri province for rubber plantations.[517]

As Walter Rodney notes, while imperial powers no longer use armies to dominate peripheral lands and mines, foreign control remains entrenched.[518] This allows centre firms higher up the global value chain to secure cheap resources, easing pressures on their profit rates ($p' = S / C$, see Chapter 4) by lowering the costs of constant capital (part of C).

In summary, we have so far reflected on the following functions of nature in the context of capitalist production: It provides the raw material basis for production materials, the energetic basis for performing work along a supply chain, and the capacity to process waste and absorb pollution from production and consumption.

Marx's framework has allowed us to highlight three critical functions of natural use values. First, capitalists aim to acquire natural use values to cut costs. Rivers, trees, and bees 'work' (for free) to provide the power, wood, and honey that could lower production expenses. Second, natural use values raise output. Geological processes 'work' to produce crude oil and natural gas, which we refine into gasoline (petrol) and liquefied natural gas to power tools that boost productivity.

Third, natural use values can result in ground rents for those who own or control the spaces where these resources are mined, fished, and harvested, etc. This rent varies depending on the ease of extraction, which is itself influenced by labour and capital efficiencies, but the raw materials in situ remain fundamentally free.[519] This mix of extraction, productivity, and competition fuels capitalism's ever-expanding metabolism.

MEASURING ECOLOGICALLY UNEQUAL EXCHANGE

Capitalism's growing metabolism leads to rifts and shifts, as well as an uneven global distribution of gains and losses. The political logic behind this dynamic is known as ecological imperialism, which unfolds in unjust patterns of global trade known as 'ecologically unequal exchange' (EUE). EUE commonly refers to the trade of more natural use values for less within a capitalist system. More specifically, it involves the appropriation of environmental sources of useful low-entropy matter and energy, and the overloading of environmental sinks with high-entropy waste matter and energy. In the literature, EUE is associated with the trade-related transfer of three impacts from centres to peripheries:

1. Drains: the depletion of environmental resources.
2. Strains: the displacement of environmental burdens, either through:
   a. Local strains: environmental harms directly related to the extraction of the traded resource or to other harmful industrial processes, including waste disposal, involved in global supply chains;
   b. Global strains: environmental harms indirectly related to trade and associated with disproportionate use of the global commons.

To clarify, while EUE refers to the draining and straining of other territories, the third environmental injustice arises from the centre's disproportionate use (or disruption) of the global commons, such as the atmosphere, oceans, and biogeochemical cycles.[520] These global strains often affect the peripheries the most, but differ from the local strains inflicted upon the peripheries' ecosystems directly through trade. I am referring here to the difference between, say, the carbon dioxide released into the atmosphere by an Indian cement factory versus the mercury it releases into local waterways.

EUE research hypothesises that powerful centres control these drains and strains, allowing them to maintain material trade surpluses (i.e., to disproportionately appropriate resources) and to avoid domestic environmental harm (i.e., to disproportionately appropriate environmental sinks). As a result, EUE strengthens the accumulation of wealth in the centre at the expense of the periphery.

The old question related to unequal exchange was: Does international trade contribute to uneven development through disproportionate levels of exploitation or productivity? In the context of EUE, however, it becomes: Does international trade contribute to uneven environmental conditions through disproportionate appropriation of the environmental space (its sources and sinks)?[521]

EUE studies break from traditional trade analysis by recognising that market prices ignore the biophysical drains and strains imposed by trade. Some argue that these biophysical impacts alone already make the exchange unequal. For Alf Hornborg, 'ten tons of iron embodied in a product exchanged for a hundred tons of iron, is unequal.'[522] Along with his colleagues, he defines EUE as an 'asymmetric net flow' of biophysical resources (including labour),[523] thus primarily treating inequality as a quantitative imbalance (see Chapter 1).[524]

With a broader take on inequality, EUE becomes socially unfair and systematically unjust when we incorporate other factors. For Jennifer Givens, 'the inequality in unequal ecological exchange arises from how we value things in the current economic system.'[525] A branch of EUE scholarship therefore argues that for an exchange to be considered unequal in the sense of unfair, it must incorporate a monetary imbalance. The central claim here is that exchange becomes socially unfair when monetary exchange fails to reflect 'real' material exchange.

This seems absurd if, like neoclassical economists, one assumes that prices reflect a commodity's 'real value,' whatever that means (see Chapter 2). As we avoid this trap, we'll need another way to measure 'real value' across heterogeneous commodities. Marxist theories of unequal exchange use average labour time as the common measure (which indeed deviates from price); for EUE, we need something else.

Let's first look at how to measure EUE as a drain. All commodities are born from natural resources which, unlike derived materials, are not produced by capitalism. The total biophysical quantity of original resources consumed in production, that is, embodied in traded commodities, forms the basis for measuring EUE. The EUE thesis argues that even if international trade were balanced in monetary terms, there would be a biophysical imbalance, with embodied natural resources systematically transferred from one region to another.[526]

When the centres trade with the peripheries, they net import natural use values in the form of embodied raw materials, energy, water, and land, alongside labour. With a focus on 'net' transfers, the centres import more embodied resources in exchange for less. Over time, a global imbalance in the material preconditions for development accrues. Regions with abundant resources tend to be economically poor, while resource-poor regions are often economically rich.[527] 'The Third World is not poor,' in Michael Parenti's stirring words. 'You don't go to poor countries to make money.'[528] Only their people are poor, as a result of the pillage they have endured.

How did this situation come about? Capitalist narratives call it coincidental or natural, but it began with colonialism, when imperial powers deliberately deindustrialised and forced resource extraction from the peripheries for their own industrial development. Resources were drained via direct political and military control by the imperial centres, and this global division of labour carried on well into the postcolonial era (see Chapter 5).

Associating EUE with this division, many scholars are aligned with the structuralist perspective of uneven development.[529] However, that division began to blur. For example, several centre countries such as Australia and Canada thrive as net exporters of natural resources, and many semi-peripheries in Asia have undergone significant industrialisation.[530] In fact, seventy per cent of contemporary periphery exports consist of (semi-)manufactured goods – a shift largely driven by the rise of global value chains.[531] Such processes complicate and reshape the global division of labour, and mean that the structuralist version of EUE is no longer adequate; we are not dealing with a simple story of industrial centres draining resources from extractive peripheries.

How might EUE account for this reality? Trade in monetary terms obfuscates what is happening in material terms.[532] Balanced terms of trade could hide asymmetric transfers of embodied resources. However, ignoring monetary terms altogether prevents us from seeing the inequality in ecological exchange between peripheral secondary/tertiary industries and primary industries in the centres.

I will return to this point later with empirical evidence. To get there, we'll first focus on how to track the origins and destinations of embodied resource flows. Think back to the watershed analogy from Diagram 1, but this time, instead of value, consider the material inputs used in all the supply chains involved in grain production. Diagram 27 includes equipment and material inputs such as tractors and fertilisers for cultivation, as well as those required for stages further upstream, such as steel for tractors and natural gas for fertiliser production. Grain may then be traded internationally. For example, if grain from the United States is processed into bread in Denmark and biofuel in Germany, we must allocate the consumption of steel, grain, etc., in these products.

Studies of EUE sometimes use life-cycle analysis for individual products.[533] This approach tells us, for example, that a standard AA alkaline battery stores less than one percent of the energy required to produce it.[534] Other studies adopt more systemic approaches that zoom out to sectors and/or nations according to, for example, environmental footprints or the global human appropriation of net primary production (which essentially measures the direct and indirect human use of biomass).[535] In what follows, I will focus on two other systemic approaches: Material Flow Analysis (MFA) and Environmentally-Extended Multi-Regional Input-Output Analysis

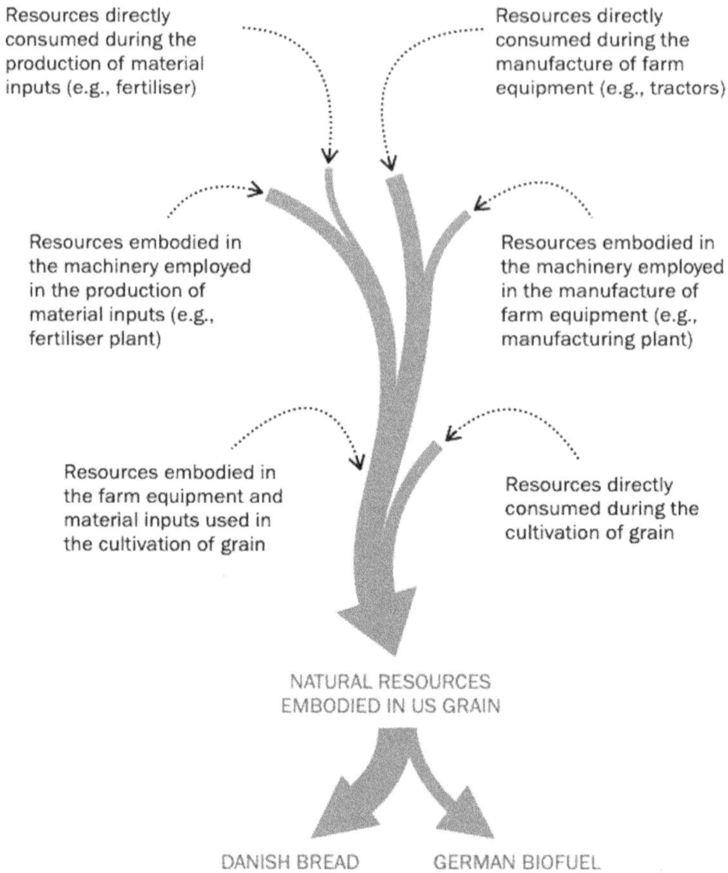

Diagram 27. Embodied Resources Through Production

(EEMRIO) – not because I believe they are necessarily better, but because I find them intuitively useful.

MFA monitors the movements of biophysical resources in order to determine who is ultimately responsible for their extraction and the accompanying environmental impacts. Unsurprisingly, a substantial portion of these movements can be attributed to trade. In 2023, the global economy extracted 104.2 gigatons (Gt) of raw materials, with over thirty per cent (31.4 Gt) used for producing traded commodities.[536] These raw materials include biomass, fossil fuels, metal ore, and non-metallic minerals.

MFA employs two approaches: domestic and footprint. The domestic approach tallies the materials used in domestic production, adding the weight of imports and subtracting that of exports. The footprint method assigns all materials used throughout a supply chain to the territory of final consumption, no matter where production took place.[537] This captures embodied inputs not visible in the final product's weight, as traded goods' actual weight is always less than the raw materials needed to make them:[538] In 2023, the global totals were 15.1 Gt and 31.4 Gt respectively.[539]

To be clear, the material footprint approach isn't a straightforward tonnage comparison, such as France exporting twenty tons of cheese to Spain for tens tons of almonds. Instead, it looks at the natural use values involved in producing those goods. Even if France exports more cheese by weight than it imports in almonds, the natural resources required for Spanish almond production may exceed those required for France's cheese production; it is like comparing a single cup of coffee and the 130 litres of water it took the entire production chain to make it.[540]

The following diagrams depict the various indicators and their relationships. They illustrate trade in biomass (e.g. grain) and biomass products (e.g. bread) between a country and the rest of the world, not for a single bilateral trade relationship. What do domestic versus footprint approaches reveal?

In Diagram 28, the Domestic Material Consumption (DMC = 9 million tons, Mt) of bread is supported by both Imports (IMP = 10 Mt) of bread and Domestic Extraction (DE = 5 Mt) of grain for domestic bread production. If the country in question also imported grain, IMP would then add the weight of imported grain and bread. Similarly, direct exports (EXP = 6 Mt) encompass all commodities exported. The Physical Trade Balance (PTB) is simply imports minus exports (PTB = IMP - EXP = 10 - 6 = 4 Mt). I have used a similar conceptualisation of flows of embodied labour time to measure unequal exchange in the previous chapter (Diagram 24).

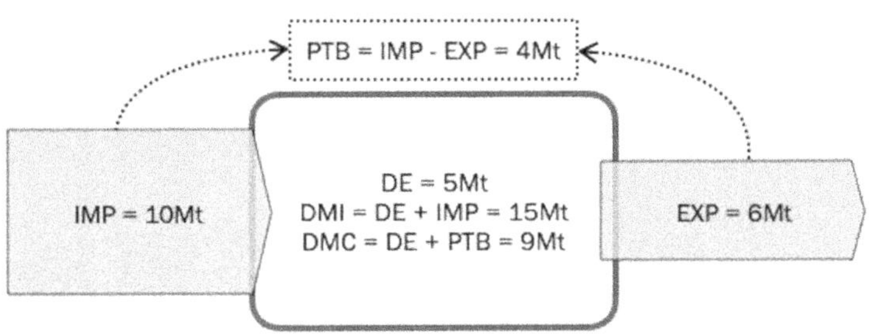

Diagram 28. Material Flows and Balance, Domestic Approach

As shown in Diagram 28, the sum of DE and IMP yields what is called the Domestic Material Input (DMI). DMI indicates the total materials available within the domestic economy (DMI = DE + IMP = 5 + 10 = 15 Mt). Domestic Material Consumption (DMC) is then derived by subtracting EXP from DMI, to produce the total quantity of materials used and consumed domestically (DMC = DMI - EXP = DE + IMP - EXP = DE + PTB = 5 + 4 = 9 Mt).

The picture sharpens when we turn to consumption. Diagram 29 considers the original resources required throughout a supply chain, measured in Raw Material Equivalents (RME). These estimates reveal indirect trade flows, encompassing trade flows not accounted for in final product weights. The Raw Material Equivalent of Imports (IMP_{RME}) reflects the total amount of primary materials extracted abroad to produce imports. Therefore, while the country imports ten million tons of bread, the actual import volume in RME might be twenty million tons. Similarly, the Raw Material Equivalent of Exports (EXP_{RME}) represents the primary materials extracted to produce exports. For example, although the country exports six million tons of bread, this translates to twelve million tons in RME. RMI indicates the total RME available within the domestic economy ($DMI = DE + IMP_{RME} = 5 + 20 = 25$ Mt).

The Raw Material Trade Balance (RTB) is then calculated as imports minus exports in RME ($RTB = IMP_{RME} - EXP_{RME}$), amounting to eight million tons in our example. RTB thus provides a RME version of the earlier PTB (IMP - EXP), which was only four million tons. In other words, net imports embody eight million tons, though they weigh only four million tons.

Finally, including DE yields Raw Material Consumption (RMC), capturing total domestic and foreign extraction required for final domestic consumption ($RMC = DE + IMP_{RME} - EXP_{RME} = DE + RTB = RMI - EXP_{RME}$). In our example, RMC totals thirteen million tons, surpassing DMC's nine million tons. Concretely, the country consumes nine million tons directly, but thirteen million tons when accounting for what's also consumed in the supply chains.

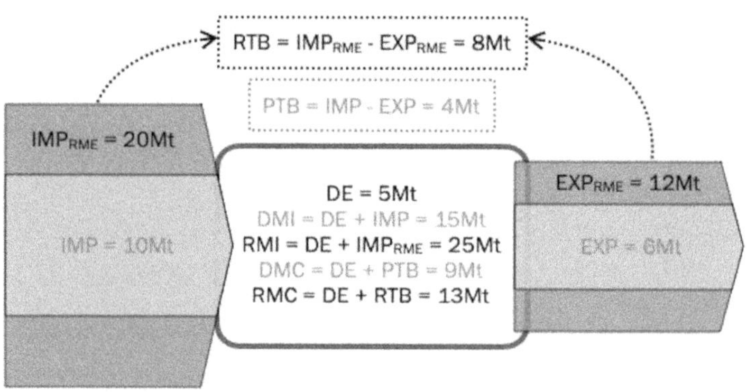

Diagram 29. Material Flows and Balance, Footprint Approach

Unlike the Domestic Material Consumption (DMC) and Physical Trade Balance (PTB) indicators, which reflect only direct physical imports and exports, Raw Material Consumption (RMC) and Raw Material Trade Balance (RTB) more accurately capture a given country's claim on the world's material resources. These indicators assign the upstream material requirements of traded goods and services to the country where they are ultimately consumed. Table 38 summarises the various indicators.[541]

Variable	Initials / Formula	Description
Domestic Extraction	DE	Primary materials extracted within domestic territory
Imports	IMP	Direct physical imports at various processing stages into domestic territory
Domestic Material Input	DMI = DE + IMP	Direct physical inputs from domestic and foreign sources into domestic production system
Exports	EXP	Direct physical exports at various processing stages from domestic territory
Physical Trade Balance	PTB = IMP - EXP	Difference between the direct physical imports and exports of a territory
Domestic Material Consumption	DMC = DE + PTB	Direct physical inputs from domestic and foreign sources to meet final domestic consumption
Raw Material Equivalents	RME	Primary material requirements of upstream supply chains
Raw Material Equivalents of Imports	IMP_{RME}	RME requirements of foreign supply chains to produce the imports into domestic territory
Raw Material Input	$RMI = DE + IMP_{RME}$	RME requirements of foreign and domestic supply chains into domestic production system
Raw Material Equivalents of Exports	EXP_{RME}	RME requirements of foreign and domestic supply chains to produce the exports from domestic territory
Raw Material Trade Balance	$RTB = IMP_{RME} - EXP_{RME}$	Difference between the RME imports and exports of a domestic territory
Raw Material Footprint of Consumption	RMC = DE + RTB	RME requirements of foreign and domestic supply chains to meet final domestic consumption

Table 38. Summary MFA Indicators

How to quantify these material flows? With limited physical inter-sectoral trade data, we must take a roundabout approach based on Environmentally-Extended Multi-Regional Input-Output Analysis (EEMRIO), which first matches material needs to sectors within the national economy using monetary data from input-output tables. Bilateral trade data then links those material needs to exports and imports, allocating domestic extraction to wherever final consumption occurs.[542] For example, EEMRIO can allocate Indian steel used to produce German tractors to the American grain sector, and then German biofuels, and finally cloud computing services for US markets based on the monetary trade flows between these countries.

However, the results of EEMRIO analyses must be interpreted with caution. First, they should not be mistaken for actual physical trade data. Other weaknesses include the assumption that sectors produce uniform products, which makes it harder to track specific environmental impacts; the lack of data on unpaid and non-market activities; and inconsistent and sometimes outdated data collection across countries.[543] Additionally, both use countries as the unit of analysis, overlooking possible intra-national EUE.[544] The approach has most to offer when the data is aggregated at the regional or global level to dilute local inaccuracies.

How does MFA relate to EUE? Both physical and raw material trade balances (PTB and RTB) indicate the ecological burden that a country either internalises (negative trade balance) or externalises (positive trade balance). While both indicators can therefore estimate a material drain, the more comprehensive RTB method better approximates global imbalances.[545]

What empirical evidence can be found for EUE as a raw material drain? Based on a global dataset,[546] I calculated regional-level totals of Imported and Exported Raw Material Equivalents (IMP_{RME} and EXP_{RME}), as well as Domestic Extraction (DE), for 2022, and with that the Raw Material Trade Balance (RTB). As with the previous chapter's estimates of unequal exchange, I categorised countries into three regions based on World Bank income classifications: low- and lower-middle-income countries form the periphery; upper-middle-income countries form the semi-periphery, and high-income countries form the centre.

The results in Table 39 show that the centre net imported six gigatons (Gt) of embodied resources in 2022. Meanwhile, the semi-periphery and periphery net exported 3.3 Gt and 2.7 Gt respectively. This gap has been growing over time, particularly if we take a longer historical view.[547] Dividing these figures by population size, we find that the average person in the centre net appropriated 4,949 kilograms per capita (RTB/c) in 2022, thus draining 1,183 and 675 kilograms per capita per year from the semi-periphery and periphery.

These flows can also be interpreted in relative terms. For example, eighteen per cent of the Raw Material Inputs (RMI) in a typical periphery country is imported, compared to forty per cent in the centre. The centre is the only region where IMP_{RME} exceeds EXP_{RME}; both periphery and semi-periphery export more embodied resources than they import. The periphery net exports ten per cent of its RMI, while the centre net imports fifteen per cent of its RMI.

	Per.	Sem.	Cen.
Imported embodied resources (IMP_{RME}, in t)	4.7Gt	9.6Gt	16.5Gt
Exported embodied resources (EXP_{RME}, in t)	7.4Gt	12.9Gt	10.5Gt
Raw Material Trade Balance (RTB = IMP_{RME} - EXP_{RME}, in t)	-2.7Gt	-3.3Gt	6.Gt
Ratio of exported to imported labour (EXP_{RME} / IMP_{RME})	1.6	1.3	0.6
Domestic Extraction (DE, in t)	22.1Gt	55.1Gt	24.8Gt
Raw Material Input (RMI = DE + IMP_{RME}, in t)	26.8Gt	64.6Gt	41.3Gt
Percentage of Raw Material Input Imported (IMP_{RME} / RMI)	18%	15%	40%
Percentage of Raw Material Input Traded (RTB / RMI)	-10%	-5%	15%

Table 39. Ecologically Unequal Exchange Through RME Imbalances

While many countries fit the pattern of centres draining resources from the peripheries, many others don't, as shown in Table 40. In 2022, most centre nations (covering 85 per cent of the centre's population) were net importers (RTB ≥ 0) with a combined RTB of ten gigatons, with the remainder (covering fifteen per cent of the centre's population) left as net exporters (RTB < 0) with a combined RTB of -4 Gt. Most periphery countries (covering 75 per cent of the periphery's population) followed the expected pattern of net exporting, and accounted for a combined RTB of -3.6 Gt, leaving the remainder as net importers with a combined RTB of 0.9 Gt. EUE research often fails to acknowledge these 'exceptions.' Unlike typical periphery net exporters, centre net exporters are not in a dependent relationship – they maintain high returns alongside their net exports, as I will show later.

Furthermore, while the periphery as a whole net exports less than the semi-periphery (2.7 Gt and 3.3 Gt, respectively), the drain is more pronounced when compared to domestic extraction (DE). This can be calculated as: 100

Region (% pop.)	Per. (50%)		Sem. (35%)		Cen. (15%)	
Sub-region (% pop.)	Net imp. (25%)	Net exp. (75%)	Net imp. (57%)	Net exp. (43%)	Net imp. (85%)	Net exp. (15%)
RTB (in t)	-2.7Gt		-3.3Gt		6.0Gt	
	0.9Gt	-3.6Gt	2.0Gt	-5.3Gt	10.0Gt	-4.0Gt
DE (in t)	22.1Gt		55.1Gt		24.8Gt	
	4.1Gt	18.0Gt	35.4Gt	19.7Gt	15.5Gt	9.3Gt
RTB / DE (in %)	-12%		-6%		24%	
	22%	-20%	6%	-27%	64%	-43%

Table 40. RTB and DE by Net Importers and Net Exporters

× RTB / DE. As shown in Table 40, the semi-periphery consumed six per cent less embodied resources than they extracted, with the rest going to global markets. For the periphery, this relative drain amounts to twelve per cent. For net exporter peripheries, the relative drain was even higher, at twenty per cent. Meanwhile, the centre group used 24 per cent more than they extracted, relying on imports to cover the gap, although this rose to 65 per cent for the net importer centres. Such a relative measure is important in discussions about the possible implications of EUE on local access to resources.

Many studies confirm this pattern on bilateral, regional, and global scales,[548] with a few (less convincing) exceptions.[549] However, a negative trade balance in RMEs does not automatically imply a problem, as positive balances may exist for other resources. One strategy has therefore been to expand the range of indicators beyond raw materials.[550] Again, these findings reveal that EUE tends to benefit centre countries at the expense of the periphery.[551]

For example, the World Bank's high-income countries net appropriated embodied land totalling close to 31 per cent of global land in 2015,[552] while countries in the IMF's 'advanced economies' category appropriated 822 million hectares – roughly the size of Brazil. They also appropriated 21 exajoules of energy from the rest of the world – approximately a third of the European Union's annual primary energy consumption.[553] These imbalances have worsened since 1990.[554]

These studies all strongly suggest that EUE is a salient feature of global capitalism. Their findings also clearly reject a typical 'green capitalism' claim, according to which centre nations have reduced resource use while maintaining economic growth (or 'decoupled'). In fact, as their wealth grows, these nations shift from domestic resource extraction to consuming more through global trade. Their per capita Raw Material Consumption (RMC) surpasses their Domestic Material Consumption (DMC), because imports of (semi-)finished goods indirectly embody more resources than they directly contain. Producing a single computer weighing just two kilograms requires about 1.8 tonnes of raw materials, including 240 kilograms of fossil fuels.[555] Meanwhile, periphery nations consume less of those goods and instead supply the raw materials for their production. The findings also highlight China's complex semi-peripheral/central role in both draining and being drained,[556] suggesting a possible global shift in the forces of (ecological) imperialism.

The persistence of these biophysical imbalances has given rise to the idea of a so-called ecological debt;[557] drains accumulate over time as a debt owed by the centre to the rest of the world. Between 1970 and 2024, the centre accumulated 290 Gt of RMEs – almost twice the mass of Mount Everest.[558] Between 1990 and 2015, it also accumulated an ecological debt of 550-650 exajoules of embodied energy and 30-33 billion hectares of embodied land.[559]

So far, we have seen evidence of EUE as a drain; let's now turn to the strains. Despite their utility, material trade balances fail to specify specific damages caused and therefore offer only a partial picture of EUE. Neither PTB nor RTB reveals changes in entropy along supply chains, such as the higher levels of entropy associated with traded textile waste compared to completed items.[560]

Many scholars have therefore highlighted EUE's role in destroying the ecological basis that normally provides and regenerates natural use values.[561] As mentioned at the start of this section, we can distinguish between several strains: (1) those directly related to the extraction of traded resources; (2) those directly related to the disposal of traded waste; and (3) those indirectly related to trade and associated with disproportionate use of the global commons.

Starting with the first type, increased forest loss and other environmental impacts in the peripheries correlate with agricultural and mining exports to China, India, and the EU.[562] Such strains impact not only forests and land use, but also air, water, and biodiversity.[563] Indeed, global trade threatens an estimated thirty per cent of global species,[564] with centre economies in Europe, North America, and East Asia essentially net importing extinction-risk footprints.[565]

Several other studies tackle EUE by examining the second type of strain: waste disposal, including plastics and e-waste, along with associated air and water pollutants.[566] With some exceptions,[567] they support the claim that EUE causes environmental strains through waste disposal.

Now to the third type of EUE. The environmental strains imposed by wealthy centres on poorer peripheries create a specific type of ecological debt: unequal sink appropriation.[568] This affects both local and global sinks. For example, the extraction, processing, and consumption of fossil fuels trigger two major pressures: direct strains at extraction sites (such as deforestation and chemical runoff – the first type of strain), and climate change, catalysed by the accumulation of greenhouse gas emissions in the atmosphere.

Global climate impacts are unevenly distributed: There's no straightforward spatial correlation between where extraction happens, emissions occur, and harm strikes. However, the connection between wealth and emissions is straightforward: It's the wealthy centres that drive this climate debt.[569] The real injustice lies in their appropriation of the atmospheric commons, not just local resources. A similar pattern is evident with microplastics, which overwhelm ocean commons worldwide. Like carbon dioxide emitted from fossil fuel combustion, microplastics (and nanoplastics) released from the degradation of polymers are a harmful form of high-entropy waste. These contaminants find their way back to us through the food we eat, the water we drink, and the air we breathe. Welcome to the 'plastisphere.'[570]

How, though, does unequal sink appropriation constitute a form of EUE? As with raw materials, the allocation of emissions should be consumption-based, that is, attribute emissions from production to the consuming country. Studies show that emissions embodied in trade from centre to periphery countries are lower than in the opposite direction, thereby facilitating the centres' reliance on emissions-intensive production abroad.[571] More generally, the net difference between production-based and consumption-based emissions in 2015 was minus sixty million metric tons (Mt) of CO_2 for high-income countries and +31 Mt for low- and lower-middle-income countries. This disparity has grown since 1990.[572] Trade, therefore, enables the centres to offset direct emissions by shifting production – and its associated emissions – to the peripheries.

Capitalism consistently disregards these various, interconnected strains: By overwhelming the sinks, high-entropy waste undermines the regeneration of low-entropy resources. For instance, microplastics severely impair the global photosynthesis rate.[573] In general, persistent organic pollutants bioaccumulate in the environment, while organic waste does not biodegrade fast enough relative to the processing capacity of ecosystems. 'Internalising' this harm would raise clean-up costs and impede accumulation, which is exactly why capital externalises.[574]

This dynamic recurs globally, with peripheral nations and sectors accepting harmful forms of production and waste as they compete with each other in desperate attempts to attract capital. Global financial institutions exacerbate this 'race to the bottom' by enforcing short-term debt servicing and export-led growth strategies (see Chapter 5),[575] perpetuating drains and strains in indebted peripheries.

I'd like to end this section by returning to something raised earlier. Uneven resource flows between countries do not always indicate inequality, as counter-flows may also occur. As discussed, researchers have therefore broadened the range of resources under study, and their work reveals a general pattern of appropriation of peripheral resources and sinks. However, this introduces a new problem. We cannot compare specific exchanges across different biophysical metrics; it is pointless to ask whether exchanging a million hectares of land for a gigaton of raw materials is unequal.

Others, therefore, propose standardising the measurement of biophysical flows with a unified unit of measurement, usually related to energy. This differs from traditional calculations of embodied energy by converting other resources into a common energetic metric, either emergy (with an 'm') or exergy (with an 'x').[576] While still experimental, these methods are worth discussing briefly.

Ecologist Howard Odum's approach converts all productive inputs – such as labour, materials, energy, and information – into a single unit called emergy.[577] To avoid confusion with the energy within the product itself, emergy is measured in emjoules, though it uses the same unit as energy (Joule).[578] Emergy traces energy flows in ecosystems and supply chains back to their ultimate source, sunlight, which powers all life and processes on Earth. A product's total emergy is measured in 'solar equivalent joules,' still in the same unit (Joule). For instance, it takes about one thousand joules of sunlight to produce one joule of organic matter, forty thousand joules for one joule of coal, and even more for one joule of electricity.[579]

Odum's EUE theory builds on an 'emergy exchange ratio,' which resembles the raw material footprint approach from before. This ratio is calculated by dividing imported emergy by exported emergy.[580] Periphery ratios tend to be higher than those of the centres, indicating a net emergy transfer to the latter.[581] For example, in the 1980s and 1990s, countries including the Netherlands, Germany, and Japan imported four times more emergy than they exported, while Ecuador exported 8.4 times more than it imported.[582]

Critics of the emergy method argue that it ignores the second law of thermodynamics, which deals with exergy. Exergy is useful energy, such as the burnable calories in a burger. As we have seen, when energy changes form, output is always less than input due to energy losses. These losses depend on technology, but even at peak efficiency, some energy is lost because of the second law. The remaining useful output is exergy.[583]

Capitalism uses and partially exhausts exergy, which is more present in some resources than others. A kilogram of dry wood contains eighteen million joules (MJ) of exergy, while a kilogram of coal has 27 MJ.[584] In another example, a steam engine running at 80°C with an ambient temperature of 40°C converts one joule of heat into 0.1 joules of work. Since exergy applies to both matter (such as coal) and energy (such as heat), it offers a unified metric.[585]

Tracking exergy flows helps to reveal the exergy content of products throughout the supply chain and the exergy lost as heat, emissions, and waste.[586] An exergy analysis of EUE might show how centres extract exergy from the peripheries, while outsourcing entropy.[587] One study comparing trade data between China, Japan, and the EU found that the EU has an exergy trade surplus, as it imports more exergy than it exports (900 GJ versus 137 GJ per billion dollars), while China and Japan face deficits (96 GJ and 834 GJ, respectively).[588] Despite some country- and product-level studies, however, no global research consistently tracks exergy flows from extraction to disposal, as far as I know.[589]

The two modes of analysis might appear similar, but their goals and methods differ. Emergy evaluation traces the accumulated solar energy embodied in a product, while exergy measures the energy used and lost in its supply chain. Indeed, there has been an ongoing debate between 'Emergists,' who argue that emergy is embodied exergy, and 'Exergists,' who disagree.[590] I'll leave that alone, and simply conclude that EUE could indicate that emergy gains are net imported, cumulative exergy content is net imported, and/or exergy destruction is net exported. This last point might reveal who bears the most responsibility for humanity's increasing entropy relative to the Earth's capacity to mitigate it. Clearly, more work and debate are needed here.

To conclude this section, it is beyond doubt that capitalism's relentless drain on natural resources and strain on natural systems is driving it towards self-destruction. Over time, damage inflicted on ecosystems leads to their collapse, depriving the economy of the vital services that they once provided. For example, declining bee populations are forcing farmers to either adopt costly processes of manual pollination or transport bees over long distances.[591] Meanwhile, industrial agriculture depletes soil health, reducing its fertility and water retention capacity, and necessitating increased investments in fertilisation, irrigation, and crop modification. As natural use values enhance productivity, their depletion has the opposite effect. The end of cheap fossil fuels marks a transition to significantly lower energy availability and reduced productivity.[592]

From an uneven development perspective, we should also be concerned about the imbalances that mark capitalism's ecologically (self-)destructive path. These include the allocation of resource drains, the distribution of environmental strains, and the attribution of responsibility for them. EUE research shows these imbalances empirically.

Given humanity's dependence on natural resources and their limited regenerative capacity, a systemic extraction of resources to satisfy the centres' escalating material demands deprives the rest of the world. Essentially, EUE is often deemed unequal because it functions as an environmental zero-sum game, and due to the uneven distribution of localised environmental strains that often accompany resource extraction.

TOWARDS A COMMON THEORY

Empirical research on ecologically unequal exchange (EUE) is valuable and revealing, but must be paired with a clear theoretical understanding of its causes and effects in the context of global capitalist accumulation.[593] Although there have been attempts to link EUE with theories such as metabolic rift, emergy, and exergy, they tend to describe rather than actually explain it. EUE scholarship is yet to find solid theoretical roots.[594] In this final section, I will highlight recent theoretical developments that can deepen our understanding of EUE, particularly what makes it unequal in the fullest sense of the term: quantitatively unbalanced, socially unfair, and systemically unjust.

First, let's recall what we mean by unequal in the context of exchange. The 'original' theory of unequal exchange (UE) combines a quantitative imbalance in the exchange of value with a monetary imbalance. Relative to each region's value contribution, the centre underpays the periphery, and the periphery overpays the centre. These discounts and surcharges are largely due to the currency imbalance (see Chapter 6). UE therefore represents a socially unfair push-pull dynamic between values and prices among trading nations.

It is also structurally unjust. Scholars such as Grossman, Emmanuel, and Amin demonstrate how UE both arises from and exacerbates productivity and wage gaps. In turn, these feedback loops reproduce ever deeper inequalities and perpetuate UE still further, thus making it a structural injustice.

What, then, makes ecological exchange unequal? The previous section revealed EUE as a quantitative material imbalance. This section will argue that the full extent of the inequality can only be seen by combining material with other imbalances (labour, monetary and currency). Combining EUE with UE may seem unlikely given the theoretical disagreements between scholars representing the two schools of thought. However, these disagreements amount to a dialogue of the deaf;[595] and in reality, the integration is quite seamless.

To begin, I want to reiterate a basic commonality between EUE and UE. We have discussed UE as a drain of value, and EUE as both a drain of natural use values and a strain on their regeneration. As a drain, EUE adds up the indirect and direct inputs of natural use values throughout supply chains, paralleling Marx's distinction between indirect (dead) and direct (living) inputs of labour time. The peripheries exchange more value for less in the case of UE, and more natural use value for less in the case of EUE.

Beyond acknowledging this similarity, EUE scholarship has typically remained disconnected from Marxist UE theory – and even that similarity is complicated by the fundamental difference between value and use value. Value represents an abstract, homogenised quantity; an hour of average labour time in the hamburger sector equals an hour of average labour time in the toothpick sector. Use value is concrete and specific. Use values denote tangible, practical, sensory, or symbolic qualities. A ton of biomass and a hectare of land represent very different natural use values, not least because neither is homogeneous.

Emergy and exergy researchers aim to establish their own homogeneous measures, but these arise from very specific energetic perspectives on use value. Emergy represents the claim a commodity has made on the sun's use value, while exergy reflects another specific use value: the capacity to do work. However, neither addresses other important properties such as electrical conductivity, nutritional value, or toxicity. The fact that a kilogram of potatoes contains 4.2 million joules of exergy and a kilogram of iron ore only 0.5 does not mean that the potatoes have 8.4 times more use value;[596] it obviously depends on the intended use.

This is a caveat in any assessment of EUE as an exchange of more natural use value for less, including the Raw Material Equivalents (RME) method that I have relied on. As explained above, measuring an import or export flow in terms of RME represents an attempt to homogenise by accounting not only for raw materials but also the products derived from them, such as grain and bread, or iron and nails. However, a country might actually benefit from exporting grain amounting to a thousand tons of RME, while importing only half a thousand tons of RME in the form of nails.

At the same time, a long-term, persistent, and growing drain of RMEs from the periphery to the centre undoubtedly increases uneven development. I don't deny this. Rather, I am referring to specific exchanges and pointing to the fact that some countries with negative Raw Material Trade Balances (RTBs) thrive economically while others with positive RTBs do not. How, then, can we objectively ascertain that a drain of RMEs is unequal? In other words, when can we truly speak of EUE?

To answer this, we should consider that the periphery is not just drained of resources but also underpaid, reinforcing long-term patterns of uneven development. In the context of UE, underpayment means prices below value. It happens when trading nations have divergent price-to-value ratios, or monetary expressions of labour time (conceptually, MELT = R / V; empirically,

GDP / HLI, see Chapter 6). Through trade, value flows from peripheries with below-average MELT to centres with above-average MELT (see Chapter 6).

Earlier, I compared Zambia's copper extraction, which relies on low-wage, labour-intensive methods, with Australia's, which uses high-wage, capital-intensive methods. Consequently, Australian copper exports are overpriced ($R > V \times MELT_{AV}$), whereas Zambian exports are underpriced ($R < V \times MELT_{AV}$).

In the context of EUE, underpayment becomes evident when we juxtapose a material imbalance with a monetary one, such as by dividing a country's monetary export earnings by the biophysical resources embodied in those exports. This gives us the monetary expression of a unit of biophysical resources – measured in dollars per embodied ton, joule, or hectare exported – across countries.[597] I'll refer to this as the 'monetary expression of nature' (MEN) – EUE's version of UE's MELT. Not only do Zambian and Australian copper exports embody different amounts of value (with unequal monetary returns), but they may also embody different amounts of material resources, for example, if Australia uses more resources in production.

As shown in Diagram 30, I can now divide a region's GDP (in US$) by its domestic extraction (DE, in tons) to calculate its MEN (in US$ per ton). Alternatively, MEN could be based on other biophysical resources, such as emergy.[598] MEN should not be confused with a price on resources, as we are reflecting on embodied amounts (similarly, MELT does not refer to a wage). For my calculations, I rely on the earlier regional categorisations, monetary data (GDP data and DVA), currency data (ERDI), and material data (DE).

In 2022, the periphery extracted 22.1 gigatons (Gt) of raw material equivalents (DE), while the semi-periphery extracted 55.1 Gt, and the centre extracted 24.8 Gt. This means a GDP per ton (MEN = GDP / DE) of US$394 for the periphery, US$552 for the semi-periphery, and US$2,494 for the centre (see Table 41). On average, centre countries earned 6.3 times more per unit of domestically-extracted raw materials than periphery countries.[599] The global MEN equals US$990 per ton.

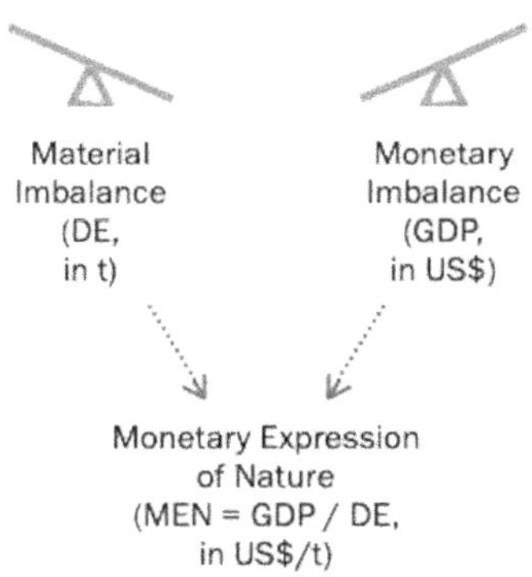

Diagram 30. Combined Monetary and Material Imbalances

The basic assumption is this: Through trade, natural use value flows from peripheries with below-average MEN to centres with above-average MEN. In the context of trade, MEN is the average monetary compensation that a country receives for each unit of natural use value embodied in their exports. To explore this, we need the amount of Domestic Extraction (DE) embodied in the Domestic Value-Added (DVA) in exports, calculated as follows: $DE_{DVA} = DVA / MEN$.

Importantly, these calculations presume that MEN applies equally to both domestic and export-oriented production, as we assumed for MELT in Chapter 6. It is also important to note that DE_{DVA} differs from the earlier Raw Material Equivalent of Exports (EXP_{RME}), which accounts for all the primary materials extracted along the global supply chains to produce a country's exports – not just those extracted domestically (see Table 39).

Table 41 shows that in 2022, the periphery captured US$1.6 trillion in domestic value-added (DVA), compared to US$5.7 trillion for the semi-periphery and US$11.6 trillion for the centre. After dividing DVA by MEN, we find that the periphery's exports 4 gigatons (Gt) of embodied domestically-extracted raw materials (DE_{DVA}). This amounted to 10.4 Gt for the semi-periphery's exports and 4.6 Gt for those of the centre.

	Per.	Sem.	Cen.
Gross Domestic Product (GDP, in US$)	8.7T	30.4T	61.9T
Domestic Extraction (DE, in t)	22.1Gt	55.1Gt	24.8Gt
Monetary Expression of Nature (MEN = GDP / DE, in US$/t)	394	552	2,494
Domestic Value Added in Exports (DVA in US$)	1.6T	5.7T	11.6T
DE Embodied in DVA (DE_{DVA} = DVA / MEN, in t)	4.0Gt	10.4Gt	4.6Gt

Table 41. Monetary Expression of Nature and Exported Domestic Resources

Given that MEN is the ratio of DVA to DE_{DVA}, we can analyse the extent to which the MEN gap arises from imbalances in DVA versus DE_{DVA}. The 6.3-1 MEN gap between centre and periphery countries results from a 7.4-1 monetary imbalance and a 1.2-1 material imbalance. In other words, the centre's export earnings are 640 per cent higher than those of the periphery, while its exports in material terms are only twenty per cent higher.

While revealing, this regional division also hide certain information. As pointed out before, the classic EUE argument posits that the centres benefit by draining resources from the rest of the world, but this pattern is not universal.[600] Table 42 shows other patterns emerging: Net importers (RTB ≥

0) systematically capture higher MEN than net exporters (RTB < 0) within their respective regions. When comparing regions, net importing (semi-) peripheries capture significantly less than net importing centres. All sub-regions except the net-importing centre earn below the global average MEN of US$990 per ton. All, including net exporting centres, may therefore be subject to unequal exchange when the average MEN for imports surpasses that of their exports. Let's explore this in more depth.

Region (% pop.)	Per. (50%)		Sem. (35%)		Cen. (15%)	
Sub-region (% pop.)	**Net imp. (25%)**	**Net exp. (75%)**	**Net imp. (57%)**	**Net exp. (43%)**	**Net imp. (85%)**	**Net exp. (15%)**
GDP (in US$)	8.7T		30.4T		61.9T	
	2.0T	6.7T	19.6T	10.8T	54.0T	7.9T
DE (in t)	22.1Gt		55.1Gt		24.8Gt	
	4.1Gt	18.0Gt	35.4Gt	19.7Gt	15.5Gt	9.3Gt
MEN (in US$/t)	394		552		2,494	
	478	374	555	549	3,483	846
DVA (in US$)	1.6T		5.7T		11.6T	
	0.3T	1.3T	3.8T	1.9T	9.9T	1.7T
DE_{DVA} (in t)	4.0Gt		10.4Gt		4.6Gt	
	0.7Gt	3.2Gt	6.9Gt	3.4Gt	4.0Gt	0.7Gt

Table 42. MEN and DE_{DVA} by Net Importers/Exporters

Most periphery nations are net exporters, yet they are typically underpaid, with an average MEN of just US$374 per ton – well below the US$990 global average and below that of net exporters in the semi-periphery and centre: US$549 and US$846 per ton, respectively. A smaller group of periphery countries net imports, and overpays for imports, as the global average surpasses their MEN of US$478 per ton (assuming import-related MEN reflect the global average MEN). For example, despite having positive raw material trade balances (RTB ≥ 0, meaning that they import more RMEs than they export), Cambodia, El Salvador, Uganda, Bangladesh, Kenya, and many other low-income countries face a monetary imbalance: They pay more per unit of RME for imports than they receive for their exports, making trade disadvantageous and suggesting that they forego potentially cheaper domestic production.

By contrast, most of the centre economies are net importers who underpay for imports, as their MEN far exceeds the global average (US$3,483 compared to US$990) – allowing them to avoid more expensive domestic alternatives. However, some centre economies net export, and although they receive higher monetary compensation per ton than all other sub-regions in the (semi-)periphery, they still overpay for imports (as the global average exceeds their MEN of US$846). We must, therefore, look elsewhere to understand why they don't suffer from unequal exchange.

By studying EUE as a combined material and monetary phenomenon, we can begin to capture both the expected cases of centres draining peripheries and the so-called exceptions to the rule – net exporting centres and net importing peripheries. The global division of labour has blurred, and we must free a theory of EUE from a mistaken view that strictly segments the world into extractive peripheries and industrialised centres – even if that division remains dominant.

I agree with those who say that a persistent material imbalance is already unequal in its own right, but when you add the monetary imbalance, the inequality appears more clearly, deepening on both fronts. Moreover, it will become even clearer after incorporating a third critical imbalance: the value, or labour imbalance of UE.

How do we combine these three imbalances? By beginning with Marx's assertion that nature and labour represent the source of all wealth.[601] Building on this, Italian economist Andrea Ricci argues that EUE and UE each focus on a different source:[602] EUE deals with embodied matter or energy, tracing them back to their origins such as raw materials in mineral deposits or emergy in biomass. UE, meanwhile, deals with embodied average labour time, which also extends upstream throughout the supply chain.

However, in the case of EUE, natural use values are freely available, meaning that the material imbalance does not perfectly square up or overlap with the monetary imbalance. This is because the latter doesn't start at the source, as nature is part of no monetary exchange, as explained before. By contrast, labour – the other fundamental input – receives monetary compensation from the outset. The ocean isn't paid for its fish; fishermen are.

Ricci therefore argues that the relationship between the material and monetary realms (MEN), as previously depicted in Diagram 30, is fundamentally social, and that labour should be interposed between the two: The first part of the relationship is between biophysical resources and labour in production, the second between labour and money in circulation,[603] as depicted in Diagram 31.[604] Let's go through this step by step.

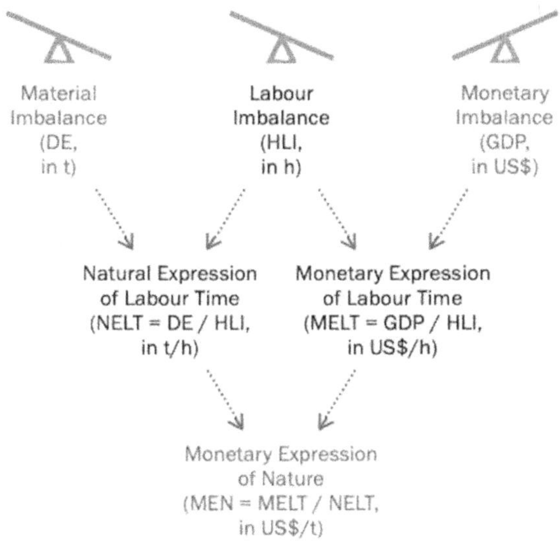

Diagram 31. Relationships Between MELT, NELT and MEN

To characterise the first part of the relationship, Ricci introduces the 'natural expression of labour time' (NELT). NELT quantifies the biophysical resources embodied in the net product of one unit of labour, measured in units such as joules, tons, or hectares per year, week, or hour of labour. In what follows, I will calculate NELT as domestic extraction (DE, in tons) divided by homogenous labour (HLI, in hours) and expressed in tons per hour.[605]

NELT is not to be confused with conventional measures of productivity, such as number of commodities produced per hour. Rather, it captures some of the social metabolism underlying production. While higher physical productivity (through higher organic compositions of capital) logically increases metabolism, they are not the same. Other factors, such as more intensive production, or producing larger rather than more numerous goods, can also increase metabolism.

To characterise the second part of the relationship – the link between labour and money in circulation – we can simply bring back the 'monetary expression of labour time' (MELT). As before, I will rely only on GDP and homogenous labour input (HLI). Replacing this with direct labour input (DLI) would increase the degree of unequal exchange as discussed earlier (see Chapter 6).

As we know, UE manifests in two directions. First, when centre countries obtain underpriced commodities from the peripheries where revenue falls below value – that is, where MELT is relatively low, which may be due to lower wages and/or productivity. Second, when peripheries obtain overpriced commodities from centres where revenue exceeds value – where MELT is relatively high.

By introducing NELT alongside MELT, Ricci offers the missing link for getting to the monetary expression of nature (MEN). As shown in Table 43, with NELT defined as DE divided by HLI (in tons per hour), and MELT defined as GDP divided by HLI (in US$ per hour), we then calculate MEN (in US$ per ton) as MELT divided NELT.[606] Earlier, we calculated MEN directly by dividing monetary value (GDP) by resources (DE). Ricci's approach reveals the essential intermediate step that allows us to incorporate a value imbalance (in HLI).

Now that we've broken down MEN into its MELT and NELT components, we can better understand how these imbalances interact. Table 43 shows that a higher MELT and a lower NELT in the centre both contribute to a higher MEN, while a lower MELT and a higher NELT in the periphery both contribute to a lower MEN. Compared to the periphery, the semi-periphery's higher NELT pushes down its MEN, but a much higher MELT more than compensates, and ultimately raises its MEN above the periphery's.

It's worth noting that the centre's NELT is lower than the periphery's because it is calculated using homogeneous labour (HLI). The centre's higher productivity increases the amount of homogeneous labour in NELT's denominator. Measured in terms of direct labour (DLI), however, the centre's NELT would exceed that of the periphery. Moreover, NELT here is based solely on domestic extraction; the centre's far greater metabolism becomes evident only when traded raw materials are included.

Breaking down MELT and NELT within MEN clarifies which factor dominates the per ton returns, with MELT emerging as the stronger determinant because its gap is wider than for NELT. By way of an econometric test, Ricci confirms that (his version of) MEN correlates with per capita income, as MELT in the numerator grows faster than NELT in the denominator.[607]

	Per.	Sem.	Cen.
Domestic Extraction (DE, in t)	22.1Gt	55.1Gt	24.8Gt
Homogenous Labour Input (HLI, in h)	1.3T	2.7T	3.3T
Natural Expression of Labour Time (DE / HLI, in t/h)	0.017	0.020	0.008
Gross Domestic Product (GDP, in US$)	8.7T	30.4T	61.9T
Monetary Expression of Labour Time (GDP / HLI, in US$/h)	6.7	11.2	18.9
Monetary Expression of Nature (MELT / NELT, in US$/t)	394	552	2,494

Table 43. Relationships Between MELT, NELT and MEN

To summarise:

- The natural expression of labour time (NELT, in tons per hour) represents the connection between nature and labour in production, indicating a metabolic rate that tends to be lower in the centres when calculated on the basis of domestic extraction and homogenous labour.
- The monetary expression of labour time (MELT, in US$ per hour) represents the connection between labour and money in circulation, indicating monetary productivity, which tends to be higher in the centres (due to higher wages).
- The monetary expression of nature (MEN, in US$ per ton) represents the connection between nature and money, conceptualised (and calculated) as MELT divided by NELT.

In this way, we correct Bunker's problematic separation of natural value extraction in the periphery from labour value added later in supply chains. The critique, as we saw, was that extractive sectors in the periphery both appropriate nature and exploit labour (while extractive sectors in the centres don't exploit labour as much). With NELT and MELT, we can analyse appropriation and exploitation within a unified framework that combines material, monetary, and labour imbalances.

This is where we incorporate a fourth imbalance: the gaps in price levels around the world. Global trade involves the use of certain dominant currencies (dollar, euro, yen), which the peripheries must acquire to purchase goods from the centre. Earlier, we saw how centre currencies buy more in the periphery than at home, while the opposite is true of peripheral currencies. This imbalance could indicate or even explain (some of the) unequal exchange (see Chapter 6). Let's explore how it applies in the context of EUE and how it interacts with the other imbalances introduced so far.

In Chapter 6, I explained how the currency imbalance creates a discount on the periphery's exports and a surcharge on the centre's. This creates a double loss for the periphery: First, through exporting goods at prices below what they would fetch if produced in the centre. Second, through importing goods from the centre at prices above what it would cost to produce them domestically.

I also explained the calculations in Chapter 6 but allow me to briefly run through them again. First, we calculated each region's average price level, or Exchange Rate Deviation Index (ERDI), as the ratio of GDP at ME rates and GDP at PPP rates. The second step involved using ERDI to recalculate what a region would earn in a world without such imbalances – and comparing that to what it actually earns.

The quickest way to do this was to make this comparison on the basis of domestic value-added in exports (DVA). We estimated a hypothetical, equalised DVA by multiplying the actual value-added by the ratio of the global ERDI to the region's: $DVA_{EQ} = DVA \times d$, with $d = ERDI_{AV} / ERDI$. Unequal exchange was then calculated as the difference between 'nominal' and 'real' value added: $UE = DVA - DVA_{EQ} = DVA \times [1 - d]$ (see earlier Table 30).

Instead of correcting the monetary imbalance with the currency imbalance, a more elaborate approach in Chapter 6 adjusted the monetary expression of labour time (MELT). First, we used MELT to calculate the homogenous labour input (HLI) embodied in each region's exports ($HLI_{DVA} = DVA / MELT$). MELT shows how much money is earned per hour of labour but doesn't account for international price differences. Within a national economy, where MELT reflects domestic wages and prices, which is perfectly fine, but not for global trade. At that scale, different national currencies have different purchasing powers.

The second step was therefore to equalise to an average MELT ($MELT_{AV}$) – a hypothetical scenario in which it takes the same length of time anywhere to earn a unit of money with the same purchasing power. This $MELT_{AV}$ was calculated as world GDP divided by total global labour (see Chapter 6). We then multiplied $MELT_{AV}$ by the labour embodied in each region's exports to get the equalised DVA ($DVA_{EQ} = HLI_{DVA} \times MELT_{AV}$). As before, unequal exchange equals nominal minus real value-added (see earlier Table 31).

For a more comprehensive approach that integrates UE with EUE, we can connect the currency imbalance to the material imbalance. Earlier, we

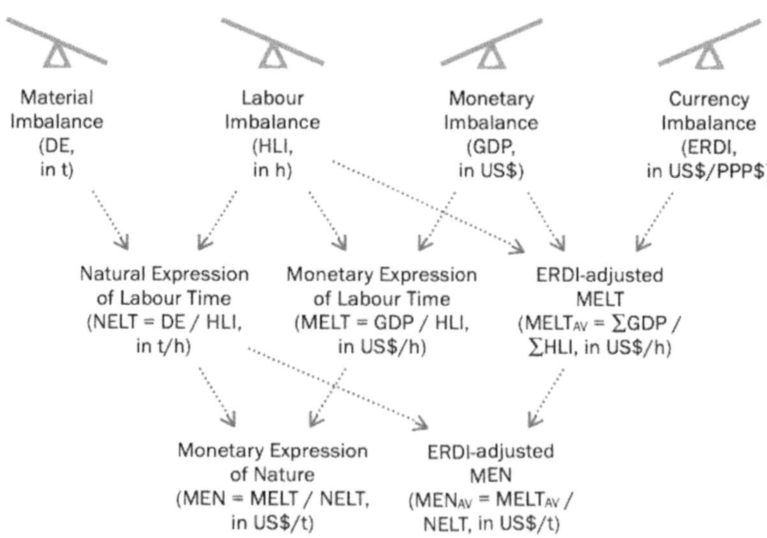

Diagram 32. Integrated Imbalances

calculated the nominal monetary expression of a ton of RME as follows: MEN = GDP / DE. We then conceptualised the link between nature and money as mediated by labour. In this framing, MEN became the ratio of MELT to NELT (Diagram 31).

Armed with $MELT_{AV}$, we can now calculate an equalised 'real' monetary expression of nature as: $MEN_{AV} = MELT_{AV} / NELT$. This represents the hypothetical monetary compensation per unit of raw material equivalent if price level differences did not exist. Diagram 32 summarises how the currency imbalance was integrated with the other imbalances to reveal the full magnitude of (ecological) unequal exchange.[608]

Table 44 extends Table 41 from before by adding the regions' homogenous labour (HLI) to calculate their NELT, and by adding $MELT_{AV}$ to calculate their MEN_{AV}. I used this information to calculate the equalised DVA (DVA_{EQ}). Previously, I derived it through labour, multiplying the labour embodied in each region's exports (HLI_{DVA}) by $MELT_{AV}$. Now, I arrive at the same measure by multiplying the embodied raw materials (DE_{DVA}) by MEN_{AV}. With DVA_{EQ}, I estimate unequal exchange both in absolute terms as difference between nominal and real DVA, as well as a percentage of nominal DVA.

The end result is the same as it was when we estimated unequal exchange as a combination of the three imbalances: labour (HLI), monetary (DVA),

	Per.	Sem.	Cen.
Gross Domestic Product (GDP, in US$)	8.7T	30.4T	61.9T
Domestic Extraction (DE, in t)	22.1Gt	55.1Gt	24.8Gt
Monetary Expression of Nature (GDP / DE, in US$/t)	394	552	2,494
Domestic Value Added in Exports (DVA in US$)	1.6T	5.7T	11.6T
DE Embodied in DVA (DE_{DVA} = DVA / MEN, in t)	4.0Gt	10.4Gt	4.6Gt
Homogenous Labour Input (HLI, in h)	1.3T	2.7T	3.3T
Natural Expression of Labour Time (DE / HLI, in t/h)	0.017	0.020	0.008
Average MELT ($MELT_{AV} = \sum GDP_{US\$} / \sum HLI$, in $/h)		13.8	
Average MEN ($MEN_{AV} = MELT_{AV}$ / NELT, in US$/t)	818	684	1,825
Equalised DVA ($DVA_{EQ} = DE_{DVA} \times MEN_{AV}$, in US$)	3.3T	7.1T	8.5T
Unequal Exchange (DVA - DVA_{EQ}, in US$)	-1.7T	-1.4T	3.1T
Unequal Exchange as % of DVA	-108%	-24%	27%

Table 44. Integrated Imbalances

and currency (ERDI) (see Table 30 and Table 31 in Chapter 6). Here, we have merely interposed the material imbalance. This doesn't change the monetary magnitude of the drain, with the periphery suffering a forgone amount of US$1.7 trillion (108 per cent of DVA), for example. However, it does reveal the interaction between the unequal exchange of value and natural use value.

If Table 44 were redone using direct instead of homogeneous labour, we would arrive at the same earlier, but higher, estimate of unequal exchange (see Table 32 in Chapter 6). For example, the periphery's forgone DVA totals US$6.9 trillion based on direct labour. Either way, the peripheries miss out on a considerable amount of revenue due to unequal resource pricing in global trade. This loss is hidden; it does not appear in mainstream measures of terms of trade and trade in value added.

Let us revisit the question of why net exporting centre countries do not appear to suffer from unequal exchange. As mentioned, although this sub-region receives higher monetary compensation per ton than all other sub-regions in the (semi-)periphery, on average, it still overpays for imports from the world: the global MEN is US$990 per ton compared to US$846 for the net exporting centre (see Table 42). For this sub-region, MELT really tilts the balance in its favour. Its MELT of US$16.8 per hour of homogenous labour not only exceeds all other sub-regions in the (semi-)periphery but also exceeds the global $MELT_{AV}$ of US$13.8 (see Table 45). This means that the net exporting centres, which should have earned US$0.5 trillion in 2022 ($DVA_{EQ}$) instead of US$1.7 trillion (DVA), enjoyed a staggering 258 per cent surcharge over what should have been earned (calculated as: $[DVA - DVA_{EQ}] / DVA_{EQ}$). Though effectively depleted of resources, net exporting centre countries clearly do not suffer from unequal exchange – quite the opposite, in fact.

By what mechanisms does this ruinous combination of imbalances persist? Answers can be sought in either actually existing capitalism, or the ideal model of capitalism.

Regarding the former, one can explain the situation through a structuralist, monopolist, or imperialist perspective. As Jennifer Givens notes, 'inequality comes into play not only in the pricing, but in the power of negotiating the pricing.'[609] For example, raw cocoa beans from countries such as Côte d'Ivoire and Ghana can enter the EU duty-free under preferential trade agreements. However, when these countries try to process the cocoa into paste, butter, or powder, the EU imposes taxes and tariffs. Meanwhile, various patents on cocoa processing technologies are controlled from within the EU.

This inequality in negotiating power is the product of a long history of colonial and postcolonial imperialism which has led to global supply chains

Region (% pop.)	Per. (50%)		Sem. (35%)		Cen. (15%)	
Sub-region (% pop.)	Net imp. (25%)	Net exp. (75%)	Net imp. (57%)	Net exp. (43%)	Net imp. (85%)	Net exp. (15%)
ERDI (in US$/PPP$)	0.283		0.476		0.805	
	0.312	0.276	0.541	0.391	0.820	0.714
MEN_{AV} (in US$/t)	818		684		1,825	
	902	798	604	827	2,502	698
HLI (in h)	1.3T		2.7T		3.3T	
	0.3T	1.0T	1.5T	1.2T	2.8T	0.5T
MELT (in US$/h)	6.7		11.2		18.9	
	7.3	6.5	12.7	9.2	19.2	16.8
DE_{DVA} (in t)	4.0Gt		10.4Gt		4.6Gt	
	0.7Gt	3.2Gt	6.9Gt	3.4Gt	4.0Gt	0.7Gt
DVA_{EQ} (in US$)	3.3T		7.1T		8.5T	
	0.7T	2.6T	4.2T	2.8T	9.9T	0.5T
DVA (in US$)	1.6T		5.7T		11.6T	
	0.3T	1.3T	3.8T	1.9T	9.9T	1.7T
UE (in US$)	-1.7T		-1.4T		3.1T	
	-0.4T	-1.3T	-0.4T	-0.9T	0.0T	1.2T
UE (% of DVA)	-108%		-24%		27%	
	-129%	-103%	-9%	-50%	0%	72%

Table 45. MELT and DVA_{EQ} by Net Importers/Exporters

that typically start in the periphery with labour-intensive and low (monetary) value-added processes, and end in the centres with capital-intensive and high value-added processes. Competitive peripheries import at high prices and export at low ones, while monopolistic centres do the opposite. This monetary imbalance is self-perpetuating, as the centres reinvest in high-return production, and the peripheries remain trapped by low returns.

Moreover, the monetary imbalance drives the material imbalance.

Periphery industries, particularly extractive ones, face unfavourable terms of trade and low domestic value-added. Persistently worse than in the centres, these conditions have forced the peripheries into borrowing, debt accumulation, and perpetual interest payments. Indebtedness itself further shores up the capitalist logic through the imposition of economic policies that intensify resource extraction and labour exploitation.[610]

Many periphery countries turn to extractivism to pay off debt, only to end up deeper in the red. For example, Mozambique saw its debt double in 2013 on the promise of vast returns from gas mining. When prices crashed two years later, the country spiralled into crisis – only to be bailed out with more loans tied to future gas revenues.[611] The combination of monetary and material imbalances results in cheap resource drains and an ever-widening material imbalance. In technical terms, it reduces the periphery's monetary compensation per unit of exported embodied resources – expressed as the monetary expression of nature (MEN).

This dynamic becomes clearer through MEN's two components: the monetary and natural expressions of labour time (MEN = MELT / NELT). Revisiting Arthur Lewis's insight from Chapter 5, peripheries that develop productive industries may inadvertently worsen their terms of trade. Under low-wage conditions, increased physical productivity lowers prices; it does not raise wages. Higher productivity likely increases metabolic rate (NELT), thus reducing MEN. Furthermore, greater productivity expands the industrial reserve army, intensifies labour competition, and suppresses wages (see Chapter 6), again reducing MEN by driving down MELT.

While productivity gains in the peripheries tend to push prices down, they raise wages in the centres, where workers are better positioned to negotiate higher pay. Various (neo)colonial forces have entrenched this imbalance in labour's bargaining power by shifting exploitation from centre to periphery.

The currency imbalance acts as a major culprit in the centre–periphery MELT and MEN gaps. As explained above, weaker periphery currencies lead to lower ERDI values (i.e., price levels below the global average) and below average MELT for the periphery. Consequently, the equalised MEN (MEN_{AV}) for the periphery is higher than before the adjustment. The opposite is true for the centre: In a hypothetical price-level equilibrium, the MEN_{AV} is lower than before the adjustment. The difference between MEN and MEN_{AV} represents the effect of the currency imbalance.

The currency imbalance also stems from monopolistic forces within capitalism. While multiple paths exist to access global money, periphery economies are constrained by a so-called monetary hierarchy in which more expensive, dominant centre currencies dominate international transactions.

This grants a few powerful nations a money-spinning monopoly and leaves the peripheries dependent. To obtain these currencies, periphery countries primarily sell real assets or run trade surpluses, both of which deplete natural resources, either by ceding land, minerals, water, and forests or by over-extracting and exporting raw materials.[612]

Actual capitalism, therefore, drives the interconnected material, labour, monetary, and currency imbalances that trap extractive, labour-intensive, low-wage, and weak-currency economies. The discounts that they grant centre economies and the surcharges that they endure lock the peripheries into debt cycles, stifle their development, and force greater resource extraction, cheapened through suppressed wages. This unfolds under the guise of neoliberal trade and investment, though direct control – via bribery, coercion, and political destabilisation – remains a key tool for the domination of industrial production by centre nations. The various imbalances are structurally embedded in global power imbalances, shaped by the above structuralist, monopolist, and imperialist forces.

These forces are undeniable, but are they enough to fully explain the imbalances? Would they disappear in an imagined ideal-typical model of capitalism free of structuralist, monopolist, and imperialist 'distortions'? Answering this requires a second inquiry, this time into capitalism's ideal-typical model, to see how deeply rooted the causes of these imbalances really are. We need a strong theoretical foundation that not only accounts for but integrates the imbalances into a more complete theory of unequal exchange, such as the one developed earlier in this chapter.

As discussed previously, we should distinguish between the drains generated through monopoly/imperialist rents from the differential rents that arise from strict and broad unequal exchange. Now, we know that unequal exchange occurs under hypothetical, ostensibly idealised conditions where there are no supply and demand gaps, structural divisions of labour, price-setting monopolies, and oppressive corporate control over supply chains. Furthermore, even if broad unequal exchange from productivity gaps were eliminated by the hypothetical, unrestricted diffusion of technology, strict unequal exchange from wage gaps would still persist.

Theoretically, if unequal exchange exists in the ideal-typical model, ecologically unequal exchange will too. For Ricci, 'the unequal exchange of value also entails the unequal exchange of biophysical resources.'[613] The latter can only come from the former, in which differences between MELTs more than compensate for differences in NELTs. The higher MELT of the centres causes both dimensions of unequal exchange, the economic and the biophysical. Ecologically unequal exchange is a part of unequal exchange.

CLOSING REMARKS

I began this chapter with the statistic that 'we' flush the equivalent of 27,000 trees down the toilet every day.[614] I trust that the above has deepened your appreciation of this simple fact by: (1) exploring broader thermodynamic implications, that is, the qualitative difference between trees and toilet paper; (2) highlighting the system's failure to regenerate or restore, that is, the rapid rate at which we produce and consume toilet paper relative to tree regeneration (not to mention deforestation); (3) exposing the unequal costs and benefits of resource extraction and environmental burdens activated by trade, that is, who grows the trees, who flushes the toilet paper, and who profits from these activities; and (4) revealing capitalism's trajectory towards self-destruction, that is, how the system will ultimately flush itself down the toilet.

It's paradoxical, to say the least, that a system so deeply reliant on natural use values undermines the very sources and sinks at both ends of the social metabolism on which it depends. Indeed, accumulation and the environment are caught in an 'enduring conflict.'[615] James O'Connor, an ecological Marxist, identifies this as capitalism's 'second contradiction of capital,' where accumulation inevitably damages and depletes these essential resources.[616] This may lead to a crisis of under-production, which both contrasts and echoes Marx's original contradiction related to over-production (see Chapter 4).[617]

Consider the production and disposal of toilet paper again: Capitalism responds to the soil exhaustion and deforestation that it causes by substituting synthetic fertilisers and timber plantations for natural ecosystems, artificially producing what was once natural. Elsewhere, it responds to municipal waste through expansive sewerage infrastructure, as natural wetlands vanish or fail to cope with pollution. However, these technological fixes increase financial burdens and disrupt natural cycles, thereby exposing capitalism's undeniable dependence on nature – a reality often obscured or downplayed in capitalist narratives.

Unequal exchange – including in its ecological form, as discussed here – enhances O'Connor's concept of capitalism's second contradiction by introducing the crucial dimension of distributional justice. As environmental constraints restrict accumulation, the distribution of resources becomes increasingly critical, transforming it into a zero-sum scenario. The more biophysical resources are allocated to mitigating the centre's second contradiction, the less they are available for the peripheries.

International trade volume has multiplied by a factor of 45 over the past seventy years.[618] Despite the claim that it reduces inequalities between countries, however, trade in fact connects overconsumption in one place with underconsumption in another. The centres import goods that require more material, energy, land, and labour inputs than those needed for their exports.

Meanwhile, high-entropy waste and its associated impacts accumulate in the peripheries. Global metabolism, therefore, has grave justice implications: Outflows of low-entropy resources and inflows of high-entropy waste deprive the world's poor of vital resources and damage local ecosystems.

Moreover, this exchange is also economically unequal: Given the periphery's relatively low prices and wages, every unit imported from the centre can only be paid for with many more units exported. The losses sustained by the periphery would have been enough to end extreme poverty many times over.[619] While this is admittedly a simplistic monetary perspective on poverty, it nonetheless speaks volumes. The resulting lack of access to basic resources in the periphery follows from worsening (ecologically) unequal exchange, which enables net appropriation and overconsumption in the centre. Growing worldwide income inequality is symptomatic of this deeper material reality. Next time a defender of capitalism claims 'But the system brought so much wealth!' ask them where it was extracted from.

7. General Conclusions

OPENING REMARKS

Let's remind ourselves of what we set out to understand. Capitalism generates contradictions; its exploitation of labour to the point of undermining consumption and depletion of nature to the point of undermining production are just two examples. These contradictions give rise to struggles for social and environmental justice, which have the potential to bring about change. But the system has long found ways to wriggle free from such demands – by expanding into new territories, forcing more people into waged labour, and converting ever greater swathes of nature into commodities. As a result, capitalism steers vast flows of human effort and natural resources from one region to another and from one group to another, while passing off these injustices as legitimate forms of economic cooperation and mutual benefit. In this way, capitalism hides in plain sight; we're as oblivious of it as fish are of the water in which they swim.[620] This is just as true in the peripheries, as Paulo Freire wrote: 'Submerged in reality, the oppressed cannot perceive clearly the 'order' which serves the interests of the oppressors.'[621] And if we don't see it, we can't fight it.

This is why Marx matters. Invoking his name, as with the notorious Beetlejuice, threatens chaos and disruption until he is banished back to the afterlife. However, unlike the fictional ghoul, banishing Marx's ideas will not bring comfort. In fact, the disruption that they cause serves as a powerful force for rethinking and challenging the status quo. When people start talking about capitalism, you know it is in trouble. It means that the system is no longer as natural as the air we breathe.[622]

This book deconstructs the Marxist value-based model of unequal exchange to better understand the global production and allocation of commodities within the social and material system known as capitalism. It simplifies, as all models do, but it also reveals dynamics of uneven development that are generally overlooked, lost in all the noise. The model makes the invisible visible and even suggests ways to measure the unmeasurable. In this final chapter, I'll summarise the book's key theoretical arguments and offer some perspectives on how to resist and even escape the logic of unequal exchange.

SUMMARY OF THE BOOK

Once thought to be a bygone concern, imperialism has re-emerged in protest slogans and academic debates alike. I've tried to intervene in this revival by offering an accessible interpretation of imperialism in its modern form: unequal exchange. This manifestation of imperialism no longer needs military occupation or monopoly capital; it can transfer wealth from the periphery to the centre through seemingly ordinary market exchanges – by 'commodifying plunder.'

Developed by economist Arghiri Emmanuel in the 1960s and 1970s, unequal exchange theory sparked intense debate in both mainstream and Marxist circles. Interest faded for a time, but has recently returned, fuelled by new data and rising concerns about the very problem it tries to explain.

Through this book, I aim to provide an accessible, theoretically rigorous, and up-to-date account of how unequal exchange operates. The account includes the periphery's role as a supplier not only of underpaid labour but also of underpriced material resources – through what is known as ecologically unequal exchange.

Marxist and ecological approaches to unequal exchange are often treated separately, and at times even positioned in opposition. I attempt to bring them into conversation, showing how both forms of commodified plunder stem from the same systemic logic and mutually reinforce one another.

Unequal exchange has never mattered more. As global social and environmental injustices, conflicts, and crises intensify, the theory offers a powerful lens on how they intersect, and how the exploitation of labour and appropriation of nature spring from the same system. Yet the theory has long been buried in jargon-laden academic debates that alienate activists and strategists alike. I attempt to cut through that noise and unite the unequal exchange critiques of capitalism.

Let's go through some of the book's main messages.

Chapter 1 opens with a straightforward question: How does a rich country get richer off a poorer one without war or conquest? The answer: trade. Disguised as cooperation and mutual benefit, trade becomes a tool of exploitation and appropriation. It is inherently violent, not the win-win fantasy we're sold. Drawing on fifty years of global data, this chapter shows deepening inequalities among nations, within them, between classes, in resource sovereignty, wealth accumulation, and pollution burdens. And poverty, far from falling, rises when measured against more realistic poverty lines.

However, these observations alone do not prove that enrichment requires impoverishment. Chapter 1 proposes that the relationship happens, above all, through unequal exchange. To discover this mechanism, we must first establish the required Marxist theoretical backbone.

Part 1. Chapter 2 starts by defining Marxist value as socially necessary labour time, not price. It presents how value is produced, realised as money, and reinvested in an ever-expanding cycle of accumulation, turbocharged by finance. It unpacks Marx's core categories: constant capital (materials and machinery), variable capital (labour), the organic composition of capital (their ratio), and the rate of exploitation. The chapter also makes the crucial distinction between value and use value. Finally, it introduces the Monetary Expression of Labour Time (MELT): total price divided by total value.

In Chapter 3, we see how labour-power itself also carries value, which workers transfer into the commodities they produce, along with some of the value of the tools and materials they deploy in the process. Capital accumulation hinges on labour producing an extra boost of value called surplus value, whose magnitude is determined by the rate of exploitation: the ratio between necessary labour (the paid working time required to reproduce labour power) and surplus labour (the unpaid working time that generates profit). Finally, Chapter 3 explains simple, expanded, and maximum reproduction, with the latter two revealing what drives endless accumulation and as discussed in Chapter 6, how they deepen unequal exchange over time.

While Chapters 2 and 3 mention that prices diverge from values, Chapter 4 explores exactly how this divergence occurs. Here, we crack one of Marxism's toughest nuts, and an often overlooked, yet essential step in the third volume of *Capital*: the transformation problem. This pulls the whole system into view, showing not only how and why price strays from value, but also profit from surplus value.

As opposed to all sorts of extra-economic influences on prices and profits, these divergences stem from capitalism's inner dynamics. While some sectors capture more than the surplus value they generate, others capture less. Why? Because commodities tend to sell at production prices – that is, cost plus a profit determined by a rate equalised across the economy, thanks to the free flow of capital. Labour-saving industries, whose goods embody less (surplus) value as a result, still reap average profits, creating systematic price-value gaps.

Finally, Chapter 4 also confronts the hot button issue of the falling average profit rate. Since profits stem from surplus value, and surplus value from labour, widespread automation erodes the overall profit rate over time. Revisiting the earlier reproduction schemes, Chapter 4 incorporates the realisation of values into prices to show how technical progress squeezes long-term profitability. This tendency, Marxists argue, propels capital's expansion beyond national borders (and therefore underpins the emergence of unequal exchange).

Equipped with this framework, the second part of the book turns to unequal exchange, with Chapter 5 mapping the historical roots of uneven development and paving the way for more theoretical roots in Chapter 6.

Calling to mind the book's opening data, Chapter 5 upends the myth of trade as a win-win and shows how capitalism has long split the world into dominant centres and dependent peripheries. In its colonial phase, capitalism forged this hierarchy through slavery, enclosures, theft, and forced deindustrialisation. Formal decolonisation hardly changed the situation, as peripheries stayed locked into low return, extractive, labour-intensive roles, while the centres developed high return, productive, capital-intensive industries. That structural divide triggered peripheral debt crises, structural adjustment programs, and the growing reliance on foreign capital, leading to today's monopoly capitalism and corporate-controlled global value chains. And even where periphery nations did industrialise, most of the gains still flowed back to the centres.

Chapter 5 closes by discarding Ricardian free trade myths and anchoring unequal exchange in three more realistic assumptions: mobile capital, immobile labour, and global wage gaps.

Based on these assumptions, Chapter 6 unpacks how unequal exchange siphons value from periphery to centre, not because of what's produced, but how it's produced. It comes in two forms. Broad unequal exchange stems from productivity gaps: Centre countries deploy more machines and materials (greater constant capital). Strict unequal exchange arises from wage gaps: Centre countries enjoy relatively higher wages (more variable capital combined with a lower exploitation rate). In both cases, the periphery exports more value at lower prices compared to the centre. Value flows from low-wage, low-productivity economies to high-wage, high-productivity ones. Historically, as technology spreads and productivity gaps narrow, wage gaps may take the lead. Unequal exchange wanes in its broad form but waxes in its strict form.

Finally, Chapter 6 outlines an accessible method to estimate unequal exchange using labour trade balances, value added gaps, and price-level differentials. It reveals a hidden monthly loss of US$145 per capita for the periphery and a gain of US$603 for the centre because of unequal exchange. In Chapter 7, the analysis turns to the transfer of embodied natural resources through trade, drawing on eco-Marxism and ecological economics. For Marx, capitalism boosts productivity and profits by transforming nature's free use-values into constant capital. This potential drives the expansion of resource frontiers and extractivism. Capitalist centres disproportionately appropriate these natural use-values through a process known as ecologically unequal exchange. From an eco-Marxist perspective, this process distorts the global social metabolism and triggers metabolic rifts and shifts.

I conclude this chapter with a theoretical integration of economic and ecological approaches to unequal exchange. This integration informs an approach to measure unequal exchange as the interplay of material, labour, monetary, and currency imbalances. The findings are stark: Centre countries received 6.3 times more compensation per unit of raw materials embodied in exports than peripheral countries (US$2,494 versus US$394 per ton). Currency imbalances alone account for much of this disparity. Without them, the centre's compensation would have been 2.2 times greater than that of the periphery.

REFLECTIONS ON THEORY

We make sense of the world through abstractions – simplified mental representations of reality. Nothing wrong with that. It gets problematic when these abstractions become opaque black boxes, understood only by specialists, which the rest of us are expected to trust blindly. Mainstream economic models are a prime example. No wonder they provoke hostility: They're seen as rigid dogmas imposed by technocrats who mistake their models for reality.

Marxist frameworks, including the theory of unequal exchange, are not immune to this weakness, their insights often obscured by insular academic debates, far from Marx's intention to make them accessible. In response, some Marxists have worked to extend his ideas to broader audiences.[623] This book aims to bring the theory of unequal exchange into the open too, where it can illuminate social and environmental injustices in ways that mainstream models cannot.

However, even if the framework of unequal exchange succeeds in explaining these phenomena, it remains an abstraction. That's not a flaw – it's a feature, and a good thing. Mental models are deliberate caricatures that capture only certain essential features.[624] The mistake isn't simplification, then, but over-complication.[625] While the act of simplification ignores much real-life complexity, there is another side to it: By isolating certain parts of the system, such as the ideal-typical capitalist model discussed in this book, we can investigate how those parts would behave if we really could ignore everything that we are ignoring. This only sounds absurd until one recognises that we ignore things all the time.[626] The real question is whether we've ignored critical elements or overemphasised trivial ones; the challenge is to simplify without oversimplifying.

Where to draw the line? Evidently, like a caricature of Cyrano de Bergerac that leaves out his monumental nose, a model will fail if it omits the essential. More vexing are those salient features that do not stand out as prominently as Cyrano's nose. Many forces that shape our social, political, and economic world are subtle, gradual, hidden, and indistinct. This is certainly the case with unequal exchange.

I therefore hope that the theory presented here speaks to those on the front lines of social and environmental struggles against capitalism and its global expression, imperialism; those who experience its violent manifestations firsthand; and those who stand in solidarity with them. While their goals and tactics frequently diverge and occasionally clash, these struggles respond to the same underlying system. Furthermore, I hope that the theory can help us to expose this common enemy and build a more united anti-capitalist and anti-imperialist movement as a result.

To be genuinely revolutionary, such movements need theoretical frameworks that lay bare the system's internal mechanisms. One of these mechanisms is unequal exchange, which acts as a major force for uneven development, despite mainstream claims that trade is win-win, and that capitalism will save the planet, reduce inequality, and eradicate poverty. We must come to a profound understanding that this is all fantasy, and it is here that the theoretical framework comes in. It can equip activists, scholars, policymakers, and organisers with useful analytical tools to dismantle the myths of capitalist trade and to confront modern imperialism head on.

Two challenges arise. First, unequal exchange remains a subject of academic disagreement. Scholars from various ecological and economic strands of unequal exchange studies often talk over each other.[627] This dialogue of the deaf stifles theoretical development and limits our ability to grasp the system as a whole. The previous chapter demonstrated how such differences might be reconciled by conceptualising unequal exchange as the convergence of material, labour, monetary, and currency imbalances. Hopefully, this was more than just an academic puzzle and can mend the rift between fragmented and antagonistic viewpoints.

I believe that doing so could help deepen alliances between movements and sharpen strategies for resistance. However, even if we do manage to reconcile those distinct theoretical approaches to unequal exchange, a second challenge lies in the tendency to dismiss theory as academic navel-gazing, detached from action. On the other hand, throughout history, labour, feminist, and liberation movements have drawn on theory to examine and expose their struggles and oppressions, guide radical action, and tackle root causes instead of symptoms. Theory does not replace action; it sharpens and channels it towards more effective strategies and tactics.

While plenty of answers to the problem of uneven development are being proposed, few are guided by its root causes. Unequal exchange, in my opinion, is one of the most significant of these overlooked causes, and my primary goal has been to figure out what it is, not how to escape it – that's a whole other project. I do, however, want to end with some reflections on that.

The classification that I'll use is subjective. I'll differentiate between three types of approach: Reformist approaches aim to gradually improve existing systems; structural approaches address deeper systemic issues; and radical approaches advocate for complete system change. It is important to mention that this list is far from exhaustive and definitely not a blueprint, and that different situations will call for different strategies.

It is also important to emphasise that even reformist strategies can advance more radical aims when aligned with transformative goals. That said, we must be wary of temporary solutions that relieve symptoms without addressing underlying causes – like a nasal spray that offers instant relief but fosters dependency and neglects the body's natural healing capacity.

Finally, the more structural or radical the strategy, the greater the retaliation from powerful interests. Radical approaches, by definition, target the root of systemic problems. Yet it's precisely this depth of change that's needed to disrupt and dismantle the systems responsible for unequal exchange.

RESISTING AND ESCAPING UNEQUAL EXCHANGE

To begin, let's address one of the more obvious critiques of the prevailing economic system: Neoliberal capitalism has failed to eradicate poverty, reduce global socioeconomic inequalities, or solve environmental crises. Those who argue that, because of protectionist policies, state intervention, corruption, cronyism, rent-seeking, or other structural barriers, true neoliberal capitalism has never been fully realised, must contend with the ideal-typical model from which unequal exchange emerges. It is abundantly clear that more free markets, further deregulation, increased privatisation, deeper financialisation and an even greater dismantling of public services, safety nets, labour protections, and ecological safeguards can never be the solution.

For example, one of the mainstream's go-to mechanisms is currency depreciation, which it uses to lower prices and boost exports. This supposed fix keeps the exploitative system intact by ignoring and concealing the real reasons for low prices, such as cheap labour, weak protections, soft currencies, and lax environmental standards. It won't get rid of strict unequal exchange; it will increase it. Second, currency depreciation often backfires: While it may boost exports, it also raises import costs, fuels inflation, squeezes household budgets, and makes foreign debt harder to repay. Third, and in connection to the empirical part of Chapters 6 and 7, it contributes to (ecological) unequal exchange via currency imbalances.

A variety of other instruments, including minimum wage laws, fair trade certification, corporate codes of conduct, and bans on forced labour, claim to ensure fair pay and decent working conditions in global supply chains. However, they are riddled with flaws, such as poor traceability, impossible burdens of proof, evasion loopholes, and weak enforcement. Worse, they lack ambitions beyond marginally increased wages. As Marx warns,

> [a]n enforced increase of wages [...] would therefore be nothing but better payment for the slave and would not win either for the worker or for labour their human status and dignity.[628]

Most importantly, though, is that these instruments face far stronger opposing forces. Drawn into a brutal race to the bottom, dependent economies must slash wages and labour rights to stay competitive. The instruments fail because they operate within a system designed to maximise profit, which cannot help but maximise exploitation. By promising ethical capitalism, they convey the illusion of progress while disregarding and obscuring unequal exchange's systemic roots.

The same flaws plague mainstream instruments designed to combat ecological harm, such as carbon pricing, environmental due diligence laws, and voluntary green standards. Like their labour-focused counterparts, they suffer from loopholes, poor traceability, and weak enforcement. Green capitalism, much like ethical capitalism, cannot succeed in a system that demands relentless accumulation – where accumulation correlates with a growing social metabolism through ecologically unequal exchange.

Rather than reinforcing extractivism in the peripheries and disguising it as comparative advantage, a more structural approach would prioritise the peripheries' economic diversification and sovereign development. To escape its extractivist trap, Nigeria has recently banned shea nut exports, aiming to turn its forty per cent share of global production into more than one per cent of the US$6.5 billion market for shea-based products.[629] Similarly, Zimbabwe plans a ban on lithium concentrate exports, effective 2027, to boost local refining and battery manufacturing.[630] But such shifts are no small tasks, and would require peripheral countries to break from structural adjustment programs, invest in domestic industrial capacity, and cut their dependence on capital from the global centres – all the while cushioning vulnerable groups during the transition.

One path forward is for peripheral nations to form regional trading blocs that bypass the global centres, such as the Bolivarian Alliance for the Peoples of Our America (ALBA). Grounded in social welfare, ALBA fosters integration through barter, knowledge sharing, and mutual aid. Trade among economies with similar wage and price levels could, in theory, make exchange more equivalent, and although inequalities may still emerge, they're likely to be far less severe than in centre–periphery trade, significantly softening the impact of unequal exchange.[631]

However, resistance is fierce. The Word Trade Organisation (WTO), for instance, enforces 'most-favoured nation' rules which restrict such solidarity-based blocs, and pressure nations into trade liberalisation, tariff cuts, and privatisation – directly clashing with protectionist, state-led welfare policies. ALBA's success hinges on its ability to resist such pressures.

Few realise that the WTO's predecessor, the General Agreement on Tariffs and Trade (GATT), was initially a temporary postwar measure. When the GATT was designed, John Maynard Keynes proposed a more durable and potentially equitable alternative: the International Clearing Union (ICU), which had its own dedicated trade currency. By charging interest on both deficits and surpluses, it was intended to prevent trade imbalances and encourage surplus nations to reinvest in deficit countries.

Speculatively speaking, the ICU could have curbed inequalities in terms of trade, reduced overall trade and capital mobility, shifted production towards domestic needs, tempered overconsumption in the centres, and thus mitigated unequal exchange. Under pressure from the United States, determined to remain the world's biggest creditor and motivated by the interests of its corporations, Keynes' proposal was never ratified.[632]

The forces working against formations like the ALBA or the ICU reveal how centre states, and the actors they represent, dominate decision-making in the institutions that govern global trade. This underscores the urgent need for radical democratisation – or the outright dismantling of such institutions in favour of alternatives that empower the periphery. Some express optimism that the decline of US hegemony and the rise of a multipolar world system will open up a window of opportunity for progressive actors to resist imperialist exploitation through unequal exchange.[633] However, swapping one emperor for several won't end imperialism. The challenge, therefore, goes beyond merely aiming for less unequal exchange.

Structural approaches are more ambitious than reformist ones but still fall short of tackling the systemic roots of unequal exchange, hence Samir Amin's advocacy of a more radical strategy of 'delinking,' or 'disengagement' following Water Rodney:[634] a full economic and political break from a world system dominated by capitalist centres and their corporations. 'The choice is between unequal exchange and autarky,' Arghiri Emmanuel warned.[635] However, delinking does not reject foreign technology, knowledge, or cultural exchange outright, but prioritise import substitution to protect, develop, and diversify domestic industry based on resource sovereignty. These strategies require measures to limit and, where necessary, expropriate private ownership of the means of production in favour of a common management of national economic resources.[636] At the same time, delinking need not be confined to a single nation; it could occur through alliances within the global periphery.

For resource sovereignty, import substitution must be paired with other delinking strategies, particularly the cutting of extractive foreign investment, which entails losses in both revenue and control. In theory, unequal exchange declines when international capital flows are immobilised, thus halting the equalisation of profit rates. In practice, this might mean banning foreign ownership of essential industries and assets, dismantling export-promotion zones, and enforcing strict capital controls to block profit repatriation. Peripheral states could also nationalise key sectors to retain and reinvest surplus domestically, and shift subsidies from export-oriented firms to the development of local industries that meet domestic needs.

Some key questions to revisit later: First, how would these strategies be financed? Second, can peripheral economies develop domestic industries without replicating the logic of capital accumulation, deepening class divisions, and draining value from less productive rural and agricultural sectors? These inter-sector dynamics risk critical deficits, including food shortages.

Countries depend on exports to pay for imports, making import substitution a key step towards delinking. But exports also service debt, which heralds a second essential step: default, ideally collectively, as proposed by revolutionary Burkinabé president Thomas Sankara. After all, debt locks the peripheries into extractive practices as their primary short-term revenue source, deepening rather than resolving their debt crises.

So-called debt relief offers no real solution; it's a paternalistic gesture in which 'benevolent' lenders 'forgive' debtors without ceding control. What's actually needed is a reckoning with odious debt, that is, loans forced on populations by despotic regimes but enabled by complicit institutions such as the IMF, World Bank, and private banks. There is nothing to forgive; such debt should simply be cancelled and the interest reimbursed with interest.

However, the problem runs much deeper than despotism and corruption. (Neo)colonialism, monopoly capitalism, neoliberalism, currency hierarchy, socio-ecological unequal exchange, and other systemic injustices rig the terms of trade and brought about the external debt crisis. This debt may be technically legitimate, but it is no less odious.

Finally, default alone isn't enough if the system that breeds debt remains. This returns us to the urgency of delinking, import substitution, and other structural changes. Though delinking brings challenges such as isolation, limited resources, and potential inefficiencies, it is vital for dismantling the foundations of unequal exchange.

Without taking on more debt – especially the kind laced with neoliberal conditions – or selling off assets to foreign capital, and refusing foreign investment, how are these nations supposed to fund the productive capacity needed to break free from export-oriented, exploitative, and extractive revenue sources?

History is clear: The centres built their industrial capacity behind tariff walls and through public investment, including nationalisation. This road was then blocked for the peripheries by the Bretton Woods system after WWII and torn up entirely by neoliberal monopoly capitalism. Periphery nations are, therefore, stuck in low-value-adding, low-wage, and labour-intensive (usually) primary production. This directs a massive drain of surplus value flows to the centres, leaving little to reinvest locally. The system isn't broken; it's working exactly as intended – to maintain imperial access to cheap labour, resources, and markets.

Again, how can periphery countries break free? The mainstream development narrative insists that economic growth must come first to fire up investment in productive capacity and, through taxes, fund social welfare. Its proponents relentlessly push more globalisation, more markets, more financialisation, more modern technologies, and more foreign loans and investment – the precise opposite of delinking. When all you have is a hammer, everything looks like a nail![637]

Modern Monetary Theory (MMT) reveals this to be an unnecessary detour – governments can achieve their goals directly. They are not households, and don't need to earn money before spending it, but can create money by issuing currency and running deficits.[638] Sovereign nations can't go bankrupt in their own currency, which allows them to invest in industry and public services without obsessing over balanced budgets.[639] As Keynes said, 'whatever we can do, we can afford.'[640]

Yes, money creation has limits. Overspending risks inflation if demand exceeds capacity. The solution? Expand the production of essential goods and services and tax the rich to rein in excess demand. Taxation's real function isn't to fund the government: It's to control inflation and inequality.[641]

Most periphery states, except those tied to foreign currencies, have the power to use sovereign money and mobilise domestic resources for self-development. However, external debt forces them to continue seeking foreign currency through extractive and exploitative production.[642] This again underscores the potential of debt default, which, along with other policies, has been advocated by MMT scholars to advance monetary sovereignty.[643] National currencies reduce reliance on foreign credit, enabling investment in domestic industries, cutting dependence on costly imports, and weakening unequal exchange.

Achieving all this requires a political struggle for economic sovereignty that, in some ways, echoes twentieth century anti-colonial movements. While the first wave of decolonisation physically removed colonial rulers, their economic and political presence remains. Delinking, then, isn't simply a domestic issue; it hinges on favourable external conditions to complete the process of national liberation. Building an international anti-imperialist coalition is therefore fundamental.[644]

It is important to recognise this: Anti-colonial struggles did not dispose coloniality (see Chapter 5). For that, we must turn to 'de-' rather than 'anti-' colonial movements. These seek to expose coloniality as an integral part of the contemporary world system and that decolonisation therefore remains an ongoing project.[645]

Decoloniality challenges not only power in its racialised, hierarchical, patriarchal, capitalist, or imperial forms and structures. Additionally, as Nelson Maldonado-Torres argued,

> [coloniality is] maintained alive in books, in the criteria for academic performance, in cultural patterns, in common sense, in the self-image of peoples, in aspirations of self, and so many other aspects of our modern experience.[646]

Decoloniality is therefore not informed by a single theoretical school, such as Marxism, but by a constellation of diverse positions united by the conviction that coloniality is a defining problem in the modern age.[647] I want to be clear: This book engages with just one of those positions and does not claim to be decolonial scholarship. My intent is simply to acknowledge the importance of decolonial thought for resistance against unequal exchange.

Let's turn to the related matter of escaping ecologically unequal exchange. We have seen that more material wealth in the centres means more misery in the peripheries. The centres must therefore curb – whether by choice or by force – their social metabolism to free up ecological space for the peripheries. As Stephen Bunker argues, we must 'slow the flow of energy to the world centre.'[648] With planetary systems overstretched, this is more urgent than ever.

The degrowth movement demands exactly that – a scaling back of the centre's social metabolism to respect ecological limits and promote well-being. Unlike today's unplanned economic decline, this downscaling would be intentional, and could include such concrete measures as pollution caps, advertising restrictions, extended product warranties, regenerative alternatives, wealth taxes, labour protections, decommodification, and commoning.[649]

Importantly, proponents argue that this planned downscaling is no sacrifice for centre populations: Through a just allocation of resources and responsibilities, more people can enjoy more free time, fulfilling work, stronger social ties, healthy environments, and so on. If the aforementioned degrowth measures were to gain sufficient traction in the global centre, they could reduce labour's material dependence on (ecological) unequal exchange. This shift might, in turn, improve the prospects for international worker solidarity.

But these measures reflect only the 'polite' side of degrowth; there is a more disruptive side to it too. Taking redistribution in the centre seriously means targeting wealth, and capital must not be allowed to flee to tax havens or hide behind shell companies. This requires bold measures: asset appropriation through strong wealth taxes, closing tax loopholes, imposing strong exit taxes, and cracking down on offshore tax havens. In this way, degrowth should worry less about appearing attractive or constructive – it must be disruptive. The key questions are: Do these movements have the radical vision, courage, and motivation to take that leap? And will they across all centre countries?

This last question is important. Curbing growth in only some centres won't automatically free up eco-space for the peripheries but may lead to a rebound effect: Downscaling in Spain could lower prices, fuelling demand in France.[650] Currently, a collective move towards degrowth across global centres feels like a distant prospect, despite signs of increased popular appeal.[651] After all, why would powerful vested interests abandon a system from which they profit so handsomely?! As the centres aren't proactively planning for degrowth, and instead continue to contribute to environmental collapse, they will need a push. 'If you can't comfort the afflicted, you can at least afflict the comfortable.'[652]

Such a push may need to come from the periphery. Indeed, degrowth should be framed as a project led by the periphery – not because these regions need to consume less (an absurd misinterpretation of degrowth principles), but because of the leverage that they hold. Delinking from exploitative trade networks, defaulting on illegitimate debts, and asserting monetary sovereignty could force centre economies to scale back by cutting off their access to cheap labour and raw materials. As Magdoff and Foster put it, 'The real degrowth problem in the periphery is overcoming imperial linkages.'[653] Of course, such a course of action is unlikely to go without retaliation – and that is a truly scary prospect.

To be clear, a managed metabolic downscaling of the centres would be immensely preferable to one imposed by crisis. The global market contraction that would follow from a widespread delinking agenda in the peripheries might worsen inequality and environmental harm in the centres, as unregulated market forces and entrenched power imbalances exacerbate neoliberalism's failures.[654] Though the initial trigger would come from the peripheries, a deliberate degrowth process would have to follow swiftly in the centres (and preferably prepared for beforehand).

Likewise, if the peripheries move to intentionally downscale their extractive sectors, they would avoid the economic crises caused by a scenario in which the centres transition first (less likely, in my opinion).[655] Downscaling in the centre, essential for just ecological redistribution, seems to me more likely to result from an anti-imperialist self-liberation of the peripheries. A degrowth agenda in the peripheries would therefore mean dismantling exploitative, extractivist sectors while supporting affected workers, expanding domestic productive capacity, and strengthening public services.

If such transformations are to succeed, long-term material throughputs in the former peripheries will also need to be curbed. After all, delinking is not meant as a route to accelerating the global majority's access to the capitalist centre's 'imperial mode of living.'[656]

The peripheries' direct material interest in ending unequal exchange makes it likely, therefore, that they will be the main drivers of transformative struggle. However, although much of the working class in the centres still identifies with their respective nation-states, signs of change are emerging. In 2025-26, for example, the anti-imperialist protests against the genocide in Gaza were the largest since Vietnam. Besides student walkouts and mass marches in major cities, the protests included union-organised actions. Solidarity with Palestine was prompting urgent work in organising and understanding how the system worked.[657]

Whether imposed or deliberate, a downscaling in the global centres will almost certainly provoke resistance from powerful vested interests, as well as from the system's inherent growth imperative: 'No-growth capitalism is an oxymoron: when accumulation ceases, the system is in a state of crisis.'[658] Clearly, downscaling demands a systemic post-capitalist transformation, both in the centres and the peripheries.

By post-capitalist, I don't automatically mean socialism. Emmanuel warns that a 'socialist' revolution in privileged nations could lead to its own form of imperialism, thereby preserving unequal exchange. This would be akin to pirates overthrowing their captain and redistributing their loot equally – the loot was still acquired through piracy.[659] Moreover, actually-existing socialist states also follow environmentally destructive development models.[660] Post-capitalism must be more imaginative.

To return to the question flagged earlier: Can the peripheries delink without deepening national class divisions or draining value from less productive yet essential sectors? Let's not lose ourselves in naive nationalism, as class and other conflicts remain. Import substitution and resource sovereignty won't automatically dismantle surplus value extraction, coercive competition, or monopoly capitalism – they would just replicate them within closed capitalist economies. If, instead of delinking individually, periphery nations were to form regional blocks, they might be able to address unequal exchange by closing productivity and wage gaps between them, but this would not put an end to capitalism. Those countries would be engaged in equivalent exchange of commodities, but these would still be produced by exploited labour.

Neither delinking nor equivalent exchange will end exploitation, but they will shake things up – for better or worse. They might push the world closer to transcending capitalism by accelerating the decline of domestic profit rates. Globalisation, as we know, has long served as a safety valve for such crises. However, and precisely for this reason, the peripheries' self-liberation might lead to a resurgence of violent resource plundering by military powers.

To conclude, these various radical strategies for challenging unequal exchange cannot be pursued by individual countries in isolation. They demand a broad, coordinated social and political coalition, one that unites national liberation movements in the peripheries with social and ecological struggles globally. The simultaneous convergence and divergence that we see today within messy, contested alliances is precisely why we must continue to work towards a unified theory of unequal exchange.

CLOSING REMARKS

If we don't end capitalism, other forces will do it for us. Capital won't stop accumulating pre-emptively, but it will eventually be forced to. The profit rate's tendency within capitalism to fall fuels crises that no strategy – be it commodification, dispossession, debt-fuelled growth, or globalisation – can stave off indefinitely. Furthermore, accumulation must eventually collide with immutable biophysical realities. As Walter Rodney puts it, 'all phases of development are temporary or transient and are destined sooner or later to give way to something else.'[661]

Marx famously argues that capitalism contains contradictions that will lead to its downfall and create the conditions for socialism. However, this is by no means inevitable.[662] With fascist and techno-feudalist tendencies currently rising as the elite's desperate final attempts to maintain power and wealth in a collapsing system,[663] the key question is whether these spasms – like those of a dying beast – will successfully stabilise a new form of hierarchy or mark the emergence of something radically different. We cannot afford to sit back and hope for the best.

Four core propositions from the Marxist tradition remain vital for transformation.[664] First, capitalism obstructs human flourishing, fuelling resistance and demands for alternatives. Second, another world is possible – one in which radical economic democracy replaces capitalist control over investment and production. Third, capitalism's contradictions breed crises, creating openings for transformative struggle that can and must be seized. We find interesting clues in Marxist and anarchist writings on how such struggles might occur.[665] When the system crumbles, what was once 'radical becomes common sense,'[666] and there are a good many radical proposals already out there.[667] Finally, emancipatory transformation depends on popular mobilisation; collective action from below is essential because the struggle for power is confrontational.[668]

This is how capitalism, and its commodified plunder around the world, will be resisted and from where something radically different will begin to emerge. Some say it is easier to imagine the end of the world than the end of capitalism. Yet, if we do not resist the apparently inevitable, we will never know how inevitable the inevitable actually was.[669]

ENDNOTES

1 Amitav Ghosh, *The Nutmeg's Curse: Parables for a Planet in Crisis*, Chicago: University of Chicago Press, 2022, p. 51.

2 Dierk Walter, *Colonial Violence: European Empires and the Use of Force*, Oxford: Oxford University Press, 2017.

3 https://www.theguardian.com/world/2025/feb/22/its-blackmail-ukrainians-react-to-trump-demand-for-500bn-share-of-minerals

4 https://www.theguardian.com/global-development/2022/aug/26/peru-land-invaders-gold-fields-miners

5 https://www.wsj.com/politics/policy/trump-foreign-policy-expansion-canada-greenland-panama-canal-b1cbe478

6 Adam Hanieh, *Framing Palestine: Israel, the Gulf States, and American Power in the Middle East*, Amsterdam: Transnational Institute, 2024a.

7 http://www.cleanclothes.org/news-archive.htm

8 Charles Eisenstein, *The More Beautiful World Our Hearts Know Is Possible*, Berkeley, California: North Atlantic Books, 2013, p. 18.

9 Arghiri Emmanuel, *Unequal Exchange: A Study of the Imperialism of Trade*. London and New York: Monthly Review Press, 1972, new edition 2025.

10 Carl Nordlund, 'Preceding and Governing Measurements: An Emmanuelian Conceptualization of Ecological Unequal Exchange' in *Structures of the World Political Economy and the Future of Global Conflict and Cooperation*, Münster: LIT Verlag, 2014.

11 Milton Friedman, *Commanding Heights: An Interview with Milton Friedman: America's Best Known Libertarian Economist*. Arlington, Virginia: Public Broadcasting Service, 2000.

12 David Ricardo, *On the Principles of Political Economy and Taxation*. London: John Murray, 1817.

13 The Ricardian model, which treated labour as the only factor of production, was later superseded by the Heckscher–Ohlin model, which incorporates multiple factors of production. Bertil Ohlin, *Interregional and International Trade*. Cambridge: Harvard University Press, 1933.

14 Eric Sheppard, 'Trade, Globalization and Uneven Development: Entanglements of Geographical Political Economy' in *Progress in Human Geography*, No. 36, 2012.

15 https://blogs.worldbank.org/developmenttalk/economic-development-in-resource-rich-labor-abundant-economies

16 Peter Korotayev, 'Why is the world divided into poor and rich countries?' in *Commons*, No. 07/04, 2021.

17 Jeffrey Sachs, *The End of Poverty: Economic Possibilities for Our Time*, New York: Penguin, 2005, p. 7.

18 The 1944 UN Monetary and Financial Conference at Bretton Woods created three institutions: (1) the World Bank (WB), or International Bank for Reconstruction and Development, to deal with structural issues, what a country spends money on, financial institutions, labour markets, infrastructures; (2) the International Monetary Fund (IMF) to deal with monetary problems, stability of global financial system (budget deficits, monetary policies, inflation, borrowing, etc.); and (3) the General Agreement on Tariffs and Trade (GATT) to stimulate world production and trade. Originally a temporary measure, GATT became part of World Trade Organisation (WTO) in 1994.

19 John Bellamy Foster and Hannah Holleman, 'The Theory of Unequal Ecological Exchange: a Marx-Odum Dialectic' in *Journal of Peasant Studies*, No. 41, 2014; Andrea Ricci, *Value and Unequal Exchange in International Trade: The Geography of Global Capitalist Exploitation*, London: Routledge, 2021.

20 International Monetary Fund, *World Economic Outlook, April 2007, Spillovers and Cycles in the Global Economy*, New York: IMF, 2007, p. 163.

21 Jason Hickel et al., 'Unequal Exchange of Labour in the World Economy' in *Nature Communications*, No. 15, 2024.

22 Trade (% of GDP), at https://data.worldbank.org/indicator/NE.TRD.GNFS.ZS GDP (constant 2015 US$), at https://data.worldbank.org/indicator/NY.GDP.MKTP.KD

23 From the source data used in the graphs, in 2022: Trade Volume: T_2022 = US$ 56,485 T; World GDP: G_2022 = US$ 90,369 T. With average annual growth rates of 5.093 per cent for trade volume and 3.138 per cent for world GDP (1970–2022), the growth functions are: T(t) = T_2022 x $(1 + 0.05093)^{t-2022}$; G(t) = G_2022 x $(1 + 0.03138)^{t-2022}$. A simple extrapolation then reveals that T(t) = G(t) when t = 2048.

24 GVC-related trade/output (% trade or output), at https://wits.worldbank.org

25 Pol Antràs and Davin Chor, 'Global Value Chains' in *Handbook of International Economics: International Trade, Volume 5*. Elsevier, 2022.

26 Serge Latouche, 'La Déraison de la Croissance des Transports' in *À bâbord!* No. 011, 2005.

27 Foreign direct investment (Inward and outward flows and stock, annual), at https://unctadstat.unctad.org/datacentre/dataviewer/US.FdiFlowsStock External debt stocks, total (DOD, current US$), at https://databank.worldbank.org/reports.aspx?source=2&series=DT.DOD.DECT.CD Personal remittances, received (current US$), at https://databank.worldbank.org/reports.aspx?source=2&series=BX.TRF.PWKR.CD.DT

28 Purchasing Power Parity (PPP) allows currencies to be compared based on differences in the costs of living. With an 'international' PPP dollar, one can in principle buy the same amount of goods and services in any country. PPP rates are updated once every few years and tracked over the years using the Consumer Price Index (CPI) – essentially to account for inflation.

29 Income share of percentile, at https://doi.org/10.35188/UNU-WIDER/WIIDcomp-281123

30 Average hourly earnings of employees by sex and economic activity (Annual), at https://rshiny.ilo.org/dataexplorer71/?lang=en&segment=indicator&id=EAR_4HRL_SEX_ECO_CUR_NB_A

31 https://finance.yahoo.com/news/jeff-bezos-made-over-7-172628289.html

32 Global income gaps narrow when using PPP rates primarily because lower wages in the Global South reduce the real cost of low-skill services. Source: Michael Todaro and Stephen Smith, *Economic Development*, London: Pearson, 2020 [2014].

33 Income share of percentile, at https://doi.org/10.35188/UNU-WIDER/WIIDcomp-281123

34 Domestic Value-Added data from Bruno Casella et al., 'Improving the Analysis of Global Value Chains: the UNCTAD-Eora Database' in *Transnational Corporations*, No. 26, 2019 Income Classification (World Development Indicators), at https://datatopics.worldbank.org/world-development-indicators/stories/the-classification-of-countries-by-income.html

35 United Nations Conference on Trade and Development, *Global Value Chains and South-South Trade: Economic Cooperation and Integration Among Developing Countries*, Geneva: UNCTAD, 2015.

36 Jason Hickel et al., (2024).

37 Oxfam International, *Survival of the Richest, How We Must Tax the Super-rich Now to Fight Inequality*, Nairobi: Oxfam International, 2023a.

38 Oxfam International, 'An Economy for the 99 Percent' in *Oxfam Briefing Paper*, No. 16/01, 2017.

39 Primary Energy, Raw Material Use and Climate Change, at https://scp-hat.org/data-download/ Income Classification (World Development Indicators), at https://datatopics.worldbank.org/world-development-indicators/stories/the-classification-of-countries-by-income.html

40 Crelis Rammelt and Raimon Cardelus Ylla-Català, 'Ecological Unequal Exchange: Winners and Losers in Global Raw Material Trade and Consumption' in *Journal of World-Systems Research*, No. 31, 2025.

41 Oxfam International, *Climate Equality: A Planet for the 99%*, Nairobi: Oxfam International, 2023b.

42 Shaohua Chen and Martin Ravallion, *An Update to the World Bank's Estimates of Consumption Poverty in the Developing World*, Washington DC: World Bank, 2012; https://www.un.org/sustainabledevelopment/poverty/

43 Population Living in Poverty, at pip.worldbank.org

44 According to the Food and Agriculture Organization of the United Nations (FAO), the average minimum cost of a healthy diet amounts to $3.75 per day (2011 PPP) on average (between $3.27 and $4.57). With inflation this increases to $4.36 in 2017 (2017 PPP). The FAO defines

food affordability as a situation where the cost of the diet does not exceed 63 per cent of total expenditures, meaning that to cover a healthy diet, the IPL should at the very least be $6.9 (2017 PPP). Sources: Food and Agriculture Organization of the United Nations, 'Cost and Affordability of Healthy Diets Across and Within Countries' in *FAO Agricultural Development Economics Technical Study*, No. 9., 2020; 'Inflation, Consumer Prices (Annual %)', at https://data.worldbank.org/indicator/FP.CPI.TOTL.ZG

45 In the original calculations, the threshold occurred between $2.90 and $4.20 (1993 PPP), which increases with inflation to $8.14 and $11.78 in 2017 (2017 PPP), or a median of $9.96. Sources: Angus Deaton, 'Health, Inequality, and Economic Development' in *Journal of Economic Literature*, No. 41, 2003; Peter Edward, 'The Ethical Poverty Line: A Moral Quantification of Absolute Poverty' in *Third World Quarterly*, No. 27, 2006; David Woodward and Saamah Abdallah, *Redefining Poverty: A Rights Based Approach*, London: New Economics Foundation, 2010; 'Inflation, Consumer Prices (Annual %)', at https://data.worldbank.org/indicator/FP.CPI.TOTL.ZG

46 Original calculations estimate the income level at $10 (2005 PPP), which rises to $15.38 in 2017. Sources: Luis López-Calva and Eduardo Ortiz-Juarez, 'A Vulnerability Approach to the Definition of the Middle Class' in *The Journal of Economic Inequality*, No. 12, 2014; Andy Sumner et al., 'The Prospects of the Poor: A Set of Poverty Measures Based on the Probability of Remaining Poor (or Not) in Indonesia' in *Working Papers in Economics and Development Studies*, No. 10, 2014; 'Inflation, Consumer Prices (Annual %)', at https://data.worldbank.org/indicator/FP.CPI.TOTL.ZG

47 John Kenneth Galbraith, *The Essential Galbraith*, New York: Harper Business, 2001, p. 153.

48 Erik Olin Wright, 'The Continuing Relevance of the Marxist Tradition for Transcending Capitalism' in *tripleC*, No. 16, 2018.

49 Ayn Rand, *Capitalism: The Unknown Ideal*, New York: New American Library, 1966.

50 Diego Andreucci and Terrence McDonough, 'Capitalism' in *Degrowth: A Vocabulary for a New Era*, London: Routledge, 2014; Ellen Wood, *The Origin of Capitalism: A Longer View*, London: Verso, 2002.

51 Harold Walsby, *Walsby Answers Walsby*, London: George Walford International Essay Prize, 1950.

52 https://www.theguardian.com/commentisfree/2019/apr/25/capitalism-economic-system-survival-earth

53 Robert Reich, *Saving Capitalism*, London: Icon Books, 2016; Joseph Stiglitz, *People, Power, and Profits: Progressive Capitalism for an Age of Discontent*, London: Penguin, 2019.

54 Marx, *Capital*, Vol 1, Part VII, Chapter 24, Section 4.

55 Charles Eisenstein, (2013), p. 24.

56 Stanislav Andreski, *Max Weber on Capitalism, Bureaucracy and Religion*, London: Routledge, 2013.

57 Murray Bookchin, *Remaking Society: Pathways to a Green Future*, Boston: South End Press, 1990, p. 94.

58 Terry Eagleton. *Why Marx Was Right*, New Haven: Yale University Press, 2018

59 In a market for lemons, buyers can't tell good products from bad ones, so they pay only an average price. This pushes high-quality goods out of the market, leaving mostly low-quality ones. George Akerlof, 'The Market for "Lemons": Quality Uncertainty and the Market Mechanism' in *The Quarterly Journal of Economics*, No. 3, 1970.

60 https://www.monbiot.com/2014/10/14/falling-apart/

61 David Graeber, *Debt: The First 5,000 Years*, Hoboken: Melville House, 2011, p. 430.

62 Otto Bauer, *The Question of Nationalities and Social Democracy*, Minneapolis: University of Minnesota Press, 2000 [1924]; Henryk Grossman, *The Law of Accumulation and Breakdown of the Capitalist System*, London: Pluto Press, 1992 [1929]; Arghiri Emmanuel, (1972).

63 Marx, *Capital*, Vol 3, Part III, Chapter 14

64 'Social metabolism' is a metaphor borrowed by eco-Marxists from biology, where metabolism denotes the set of life-sustaining chemical reactions in organisms, including the conversion of food into bodily structures, the transformation of energy to power cellular activity, and the elimination of waste. Ecological economists apply a comparable perspective to economies, referring to their metabolism as throughput.

65 GDP (constant 2015 US$), at https://data.worldbank.org/indicator/NY.GDP.MKTP.KD Domestic Extraction (gigatons), at https://www.resourcepanel.org/global-material-flows-database Primary Energy Consumption (terawatt-hours), at https://ourworldindata.org/grapher/primary-energy-cons CO_2 Emissions from Fossil Fuels and Land-Use Change (tons), at https://ourworldindata.org/grapher/co2-fossil-plus-land-use

66 Jefim Vogel and Jason Hickel, 'Is green growth happening? An empirical analysis of achieved versus Paris-compliant CO_2-GDP decoupling in high-income countries in *The Lancet Planetary Health*, No. 9, 2023.

67 Fridolin Krausmann et al., 'From resource extraction to outflows of wastes and emissions: The socioeconomic metabolism of the global economy, 1900–2015' in *Global Environmental Change*, No. 52, 2018; Heinz Schandl et al., 'Global Material Flows and Resource Productivity: Forty Years of Evidence' in *Journal of Industrial Ecology*, No. 22, 2018.

68 Steve Keen, 'The Appallingly Bad Neoclassical Economics of Climate Change' in *Globalizations*, No. 18, 2021.

69 Brian Czech et al., 'Effects of Economic Growth on Biodiversity in the United States' in *Natural Resource Forum*, No. 36, 2012; Joeri Sol, 'Economics in the Anthropocene: Species Extinction or Steady State Economics' in *Ecological Economics*, No. 165, 2019; Chen Liu et al., 'Socioeconomic Driving Factors of Nitrogen Load from Food Consumption and Preventive Measures' in *Ambio*, No. 43, 2013; Judith Krauss et al., 'Mapping Sustainable Development Goals 8, 9, 12, 13 and 15 through a decolonial lens: falling short of "transforming our world"' in *Sustainability Science*, No. 17, 2022; Gergely Toth and Cecília Szigeti, 'The historical ecological footprint: From over-population to over-consumption' in *Ecological Indicators*, No. 60, 2016.

70 Nate Hagens, 'Economics for the future–Beyond the superorganism' in *Ecological Economics*, No. 169, 2020.

71 Johan Rockström et al., 'A Safe Operating Space for Humanity' in *Nature*, No. 461, 2009.

72 Dennis Meadows et al., *The Limits to Growth*, London: Earth Island, 1972; Gaya Herrington, 'Update to Limits to Growth: Comparing the World3 Model with Empirical Data' in *Journal of Industrial Ecology*, No. 25, 2021.

73 Jason Moore and Raj Patel, 'Unearthing the Capitalocene: Towards a Reparations Ecology' in *Reflections on a Revolution (ROAR) Magazine*, No. 7, 2018.

74 Christian Dorninger et al., 'Global Patterns of Ecologically Unequal Exchange: Implications for Sustainability in the 21st Century' in *Ecological economics*, No. 179, 2021; Crelis Rammelt and Raimon Cardelus Ylla-Català, (2025).

75 Alf Hornborg, 'Zero-Sum World: Challenges in Conceptualizing Environmental Load Displacement and Ecologically Unequal Exchange in the World-System' in *International Journal of Comparative Sociology*, No. 50, 2009.

76 https://www.marxists.org

77 https://www.climatechangenews.com/2019/03/20/ecologists-capitalists-gilets-jaunes-climate-justice/

78 https://paxvoorvrede.nl/nieuws/nieuwe-wet-tegen-verheerlijking-terrorisme-zet-deur-open-voor-politieke-vervolging/; https://www.theguardian.com/world/article/2024/may/20/uk-review-of-protest-tactics-expected-to-stop-short-of-banning-groups

79 Joseph Jacobs and John Batten, *More English Fairy Tales*, London: David Nutt, 1894.

80 Marx quoted in Torkil Lauesen, *Unequal Exchange: Past, Present, and Future*, London: Iskra Books, 2025.

81 Jason Hickel et al., (2024).

82 David Graeber, (2011).

83 André Gorz, *Critique of Economic Reason*, London: Verso, 1989, p. 22.

84 Ellen Meiksins Wood, *The Origin of Capitalism: A Longer View*, London: Verso, 2002.

85 Marx, *Capital*, Vol 1, Part VII.

86 Steve Keen, 'A monetary Minsky model of the Great Moderation and the Great Recession' in *Journal of Economic Behavior & Organization*, No. 86, 2013.

87 Paul Baran and Paul Sweezy, *Monopoly Capital: An Essay on the American Economic and Social Order*, New York: Monthly Review Press, 1966.
88 Hadas Thier, *A People's Guide to Capitalism: An Introduction to Marxist Economics*, Chicago: Haymarket Books, 2018.
89 Marx, *Capital*, Vol 3, Part VII, Chapter 48.
90 Marx, *Capital*, Vol 1, Part VII.
91 David Harvey, *Marx, Capital, and the Madness of Economic Reason*, London: Profile Books, 2017, p. 3.
92 David Harvey, (2017), p. 3.
93 Marx, *Grundrisse*, Notebook VII.
94 https://www.workstream.us/blog/mcdonalds-pay-hourly-workers
95 David Harvey, (2017).
96 Adapted from 'Figure 2: The paths of value in motion as derived from the study of Marx's writings on political economy,' David Harvey, (2017), p. 6.
97 Frederick Soddy, *Wealth, Virtual Wealth and Debt*, London: Britons Publishing Company, 1933.
98 Lefteris Tsoulfidis and Persefoni Tsaliki, *Classical Political Economics and Modern Capitalism: Theories of Value, Competition, Trade and Long Cycles*, Cham: Springer, 2019.
99 Lefteris Tsoulfidis and Persefoni Tsaliki, (2019).
100 Jason Hickel, *less is More*, New York: Random House, 2020.
101 Herman Daly and Joshua Farley, *Ecological Economics: Principles and Applications*, Washington, DC: Island Press, 2011.
102 A one-carat diamond costs about US$12,000. In the United States, the average cost of water is US$1.50 per thousand gallons. The price of eight million gallons of water is therefore equal to the price of one diamond. An Olympic swimming pool holds about 660,000 gallons. A one-carat diamond is therefore equivalent to more than twelve pools of freshwater. Sources: https://www.diamondse.info/diamonds-price-index.asp; https://mcmua.com/story_of_water/html/costs.htm; https://en.wikipedia.org/wiki/Olympic-size_swimming_pool
103 Steve Keen, *Debunking Economics: The Naked Emperor Dethroned?* London: Zed Books, 2011.
104 Giorgos Kallis, *Degrowth*, Newcastle upon Tyne: Agenda Publishing, 2018.
105 Thorstein Veblen, *The Theory of the Leisure Class: An Economic Study of Institutions*, London: Macmillan, 1899.
106 Amartya Sen, *Poverty and Famines: An Essay on Entitlement and Deprivation*, Oxford: Oxford University Press, 1983, p. 161.
107 Marx, *Capital*, Vol 1, Part II, Chapter 5.
108 Later, I will rely on Andrea Ricci's concept of 'homogenous labour.' This is explicitly aimed at quantification, whereas Marx's 'abstract labour' serves a broader analytical role in explaining value under capitalism, but both ultimately designate the same underlying process. Source: Andrea Ricci, 'Ecologically Unequal Exchange and the Value of Money' in *Capitalism Nature Socialism*, No. 34, 2023.
109 A piece rate refers to a system where an employee gets paid based on the number of units they produce or tasks they complete. In our example, a hired burger chef on a piece rate system earns one dollar for each burger prepared and packed.
110 https://morningstaronline.co.uk/article/f/whats-difference-between-absolute-and-relative-surplus-value
111 Arghiri Emmanuel, (1972), p. 100.
112 Marx, *Capital*, Vol 1, Part VII, Chapter 24, Section 4.
113 Aristotle quoted in Alf Hornborg, *Nature, Society, and Justice in the Anthropocene*, Cambridge: Cambridge University Press, 2019.
114 https://www.thestreet.com/markets/history-of-mcdonalds-15128096
115 Edward Yardeni, *In Praise of Profits!* Brookville: Yardeni Research, 2021, p. 2.
116 https://www.theguardian.com/us-news/2023/sep/28/california-fast-food-workers-minimum-wages-victory

117 Walter Rodney, *How Europe underdeveloped Africa*, Baltimore: Black Classics Press, 1981 [1972].
118 Marx, *Capital*, Vol 1, Part VIII, Chapter 31.
119 https://www.ilo.org/topics/forced-labour-modern-slavery-and-trafficking-persons
120 Richard Wolff, 'On the Meaning of Capitalism, We Don't Agree' in *Truthout*, No. 13/02, 2016.
121 Marx, *Capital*, Vol 1, Part VII, Chapter 23.
122 Nela Richardson and Sara Klein, *People at Work 2021: A Global Workforce View*, ADP Research Institute, 2021.
123 Torkil Lauesen, (2025).
124 Minimum Wage by Country ($), at https://worldpopulationreview.com/country-rankings/minimum-wage-by-country
125 Average Workweek by Country (hours), at https://worldpopulationreview.com/country-rankings/average-work-week-by-country
126 Torkil Lauesen, (2025).
127 Richard Wolff, (2016).
128 Ian Gough, 'Marx's Theory of Productive and Unproductive Labour' in *New Left Review*, No. 1/76, 1972.
129 Catherine Liu, *Virtue Hoarders: The Case Against the Professional Managerial Class*, Minneapolis: University of Minnesota Press, 2021.
130 Tomás Rotta, 'Value capture and value production in the world economy' in *Environment and Planning A: Economy and Space*, No. 57, 2024.
131 David Graeber, *Bullshit Jobs: A Theory*, New York: Simon and Schuster, 2018.
132 Marx, *Capital*, Vol 1, Part II, Chapter 6.
133 Arghiri Emmanuel, (1972).
134 https://www.rabobank.nl/kennis/d011308097-besteedbaar-inkomen-van-huishoudens-staat-al-bijna-veertig-jaar-vrijwel-stil
135 https://www.cbs.nl/nl-nl/publicatie/2023/51/armoede-sociale-uitsluiting-2023
136 https://www.fao.org/prices/en/
137 Ruy Mauro Marini, *The Dialectics of Dependency*, London and New York: Monthly Review Press, 2021 [1973].
138 Torkil Lauesen, (2025).
139 Jason Hickel et al., (2024).
140 Organisation for Economic Co-operation and Development, *Employment Outlook 2025: Can We Get Through the Demographic Crunch?*, Paris: OECD Publishing, 2025.
141 https://ourworldindata.org/rich-poor-working-hours
142 https://www.economist.com/big-mac-index
143 https://wageindicator.org/about/overview-wageindicator-newsletters/news/2017/buying-one-big-mac-with-your-minimum-wage-7-hours-of-work-for-indian-workers-30-minutes-for-dutch-employees
144 https://ourworldindata.org/poverty
145 Silvia Federici, *Revolution at Point Zero: Housework, Reproduction, and Feminist Struggle*, Oakland: PM Press, 2012.
146 Nancy Fraser, *Cannibal Capitalism: How Our System Is Devouring Democracy, Care, and the Planet - and What We Can Do about It*. London: Verso, 2022.
147 Nancy Fraser, (2022).
148 Giorgos Kallis and Erik Swyngedouw, 'Do Bees Produce Value? A Conversation Between an Ecological Economist and a Marxist Geographer' in *Capitalism Nature Socialism*, No. 29, 2018.
149 Nancy Fraser, 'Behind Marx's Hidden Abode: For an Expanded Conception of Capitalism' in *Critical Theory in Critical Times*, New York: Columbia University Press, 2017.
150 Marx, *Capital*, Vol 1, Part VII, Chapter 25, Section 4.
151 Torkil Lauesen, (2025).

152 Michael Perelman, 'An Application of Marxian Theory to Environmental Economics' in *Review of Radical Political Economics*, No. 6, 1974; Alf Hornborg, 'The World-System and the Earth System' in *Journal of World-Systems Research*, No. 26, 2020.
153 Communist Working Group, *Unequal Exchange and the Prospects of Socialism*, London: Iskra Books, 2025 [1986].
154 Ian Gough, (1972).
155 Marx, *Capital*, Vol 1, Part VII, Chapter 24, Section 4.
156 Table 10 in John Brolin, *The Bias of the World: Theories of Unequal Exchange in History*, Lund: Lund University, 2007, p. 182.
157 Crelis Rammelt, 'The Dynamics of Financial Instability: Simplifying Keen's Goodwin–Minsky Model' in *System Dynamics Review*, No. 35, 2019.
158 Samir Amin, 'The Surplus in Monopoly Capitalism and the Imperialist Rent' in *Monthly Review*, No. 64, 2012.
159 Rosa Luxemburg, *The Accumulation of Capital*, London and New York: Routledge & Kegan Paul, 1951 [2013].
160 John Brolin, (2007).
161 https://oatuu.org/mcdonalds-intellectual-property-protecting-the-golden-arches-and-more/
162 https://heteconomist.com/marx-mmt-part-3-finer-points-of-marxs-conception-of-labor-and-his-aggregate-equalities/
163 Torkil Lauesen, (2025), p. 41.
164 The markup is the amount added to the cost-price of goods to cover overheads and profit.
165 Marxists also calculate this market price using the 'market value,' or average value: V_{AV} = (55V + 70V) / 2 = 62.5V. By dividing this market value by the average output, o_{AV} = (70 + 55) / 2 = 62.5 burgers per firm, we also arrive at a market price of MP = V_{AV} / o_{AV} = 62.5V / 62.5 = Ł1 per burger.
166 Melvin Kranzberg, 'Technology and History: "Kranzberg's Laws"' in *Technology and Culture*, No. 27, 1986, p. 548.
167 Lefteris Tsoulfidis and Persefoni Tsaliki, (2019).
168 Other terms include 'extra surplus value' and 'super-profit.'
169 https://bambooinnovator.com/2014/06/09/mcdonalds-has-been-eating-burger-kings-lunch-for-more-than-a-decade/
170 https://www.reuters.com/business/how-four-big-companies-control-us-beef-industry-2021-06-17/
171 Marx, *Capital*, Vol 3, Part II, Chapter 10.
172 Ernest Mandel, 'Introduction' in *Capital, A Critique of Political Economy, Volume Three*, Harmondsworth: Penguin Books, 1981, p. 20.
173 The arithmetic mean is calculated as the sum of values in a data set divided by number of values in the set.
174 Another way to calculate it is by dividing the average surplus values by the average capital invested: 25 / 350 = 7.1%.
175 Marx, *Capital*, Vol 3, Part II, Chapter 9.
176 Marx, *Capital*, Vol 3, Part II, Chapter 10.
177 Samir Amin, *Unequal Development: An Essay on the Social Formations of Peripheral Capitalism*, New York: Monthly Review Press, 1976, p. 18.
178 Andrea Ricci, (2021).
179 Marx, *Capital*, Vol 3, Part II, Chapter 10.
180 This also makes sense purely mathematically: If V = C + S and R = C + P, it follows that R - V = (C + P) - (C + S) = P - S.
181 Marx, *Capital*, Vol 3, Part II, Chapter 9.
182 Torkil Lauesen, (2025).
183 Mathematically, we can understand why changes in the surplus rate messes up the profit rate and therefore the transfers of surplus value between sectors. The rate of profit (p') depends on the

rate of surplus (s'), and on the composition of capital ($OC = c / v$): (a) $p' = S / C = S / (c + v)$; (b) $S = v \times s'$; (b) From (a) and (b) it follows that $p' = (v \times s') / (c + v) = s' \times (1 + v / c) = s' \times (1 + 1 / OC)$.

184 Ernest Mandel, *Late Capitalism*, London: Verso, 1999; James Steinhoff, *Automation and Autonomy: Labour, Capital and Machines in the Artificial Intelligence Industry*, Cham: Palgrave Macmillan, 2021.

185 Ernest Mandel, (1981).

186 Marx was accused of a logical inconsistency for deriving revenues (that is, prices of production) from inputs expressed in values rather than prices. However, given that the aggregate sum of prices equals the aggregate sum of values – multiplied by the economy-wide MELT – treating inputs as values is analytically justified. See further explanations in: Alfredo Saad-Filho, *Value and Crisis: Essays on Labour, Money and Contemporary Capitalism*, Leiden: Brill, 2019.

187 https://www.econlib.org/library/Columns/y2004/PrychitkoMarx.html

188 John Brolin, (2007).

189 James Steinhoff, (2021), p. 46.

190 David Harvey, 'Exploring the Logic of Capital' in *Socialist Worker*, No. 33, 2009.

191 David Harvey, (2009).

192 David Harvey, 'Globalization and the "Spatial Fix"' in *Geographische Revue*, No. 2, 2001, p. 24.

193 Lefteris Tsoulfidis and Persefoni Tsaliki, (2019).

194 https://www.economist.com/leaders/2025/01/09/the-capitalist-revolution-africa-needs

195 Based on Marc Nerfin and Fernando Henrique Cardoso, *Another Development: Approaches and Strategies*, Uppsala: Dag Hammarskjöld Foundation, 1977; Joyeeta Gupta et al., 'Earth System Boundaries and Earth System Justice: Sharing the Ecospace' in *Environmental Politics*, No. 33, 2024.

196 Marx, *Capital*, Vol 1, Part VII, Chapter 25, Section 4.

197 Marx, *Works of Karl Marx 1848*, On the Question of Free Trade.

198 Crelis Rammelt and Jan Boes, 'Galtung meets Daly: A Framework for Addressing Inequity in Ecological Economics' in *Ecological Economics*, No. 93, 2013.

199 Enrique Dussel and Aníbal Yáñez, 'Marx's Economic Manuscripts of 1861-63 and the "Concept" of Dependency' in *Latin American Perspectives*, No. 17, 1990.

200 Terence Hopkins and Immanuel Wallerstein, *The Age of Transition: Trajectory of the World-System 1945-2025*, London: Zed Books, 1996.

201 Jan Boes, *De Maat van de Economie (The Measure of the Economy)*. Rotterdam: Erasmus University, 1990; Crelis Rammelt and Jan Boes, (2013).

202 Paul Sweezy, *The Theory of Capitalist Development*. London and New York: Monthly Review Press, 1942.

203 Michael Todaro and Stephen Smith, (2020) [2014].

204 Walt Rostow, *The Stages of Economic Growth: A Non-Communist Manifesto*, Cambridge: Cambridge University Press, 1960.

205 Jan Boes, (1990); Michael Todaro and Stephen Smith, (2020) [2014].

206 Joseph Stiglitz, *Globalization and its Discontents*, New York: W.W. Norton, 2002; Maggie Black, *The No-Nonsense Guide to International Development*, Oxford: New Internationalist Publications, 2007; Jason Hickel, *The Divide: A Brief Guide to Global Inequality and Its Solutions*. New York: Random House, 2017.

207 https://www.theatlantic.com/ideas/archive/2022/10/francis-fukuyama-still-end-history/671761/

208 Andre Gunder Frank, *The Development of Underdevelopment*, Boston: New England Free Press, 1966.

209 Raúl Prebisch, *The Economic Development of Latin America and Its Principal Problems*, New York: Economic Commission for Latin America, 1950; Hans Singer, 'The Distribution of Gains between Investing and Borrowing Countries' in *The American Economic Review*, No. 2, 1950; Andre Gunder Frank, *Capitalism and Underdevelopment in Latin America: Historical Studies of Chile and Brazil*, London and New York: Monthly Review Press, 1967; Theotônio Dos Santos, 'The Crisis of Development Theory and the Problem of Dependence in Latin America' in *Underdevelopment and Development: The Third World Today*, Baltimore: Penguin Books, 1969.

210 Andre Gunder Frank, (1966).
211 Walter Rodney, (1981) [1972].
212 Theotônio Dos Santos, (1969).
213 https://archive.org/details/michael-parenti-lecture-1986-yellow-parenti
214 Gunnar Myrdal, *Economic Theory and Under-Developed Regions*, London: Duckworth, 1957; Raúl Prebisch, 'The Role of Commercial Policies in Underdeveloped Countries' in *American Economic Review*, No. 49, 1959.
215 Johan Galtung, 'Structural Theory of Imperialism' in *Journal of Peace Research*, No. 8, 1971.
216 Vladimir Lenin, *Imperialism, the Highest Stage of Capitalism*. London: Penguin, 2010 [1917].
217 Walter Rodney, (1981) [1972].
218 Zak Cope, *The Wealth of (Some) Nations: Imperialism and the Mechanics of Value Transfer*, London: Pluto Press, 2019.
219 Rosa Luxemburg, (1951) [2013].
220 Marx, *Capital*, Vol 1, Part VIII, Chapter 31.
221 Marx, *Capital*, Vol 1, Part VIII, Chapter 31.
222 Torkil Lauesen, (2025).
223 Walter Rodney, (1981) [1972].
224 Jan Hansen et al., *The European Experience: A Multi-Perspective History of Modern Europe, 1500–2000*, Cambridge: Open Book Publishers, 2023.
225 Walter Rodney, (1981) [1972].
226 William Brian Arthur and Geoffrey McNicoll, 'An Analytical Survey of Population and Development in Bangladesh' in *Population and Development Review*, No. 4, 1978 Betsy Hartmann and James Boyce, *A Quiet Violence: View from a Bangladesh Village*, Dhaka: Dhaka University Press, 1983.
227 Primary industries involve the direct extraction or cultivation of raw materials from natural resources, such as agriculture, mining, and forestry. Secondary industries transform these raw materials into finished products using manufacturing and processing methods. Tertiary industries provide various services such as retail, finance, education, and healthcare.
228 Raúl Prebisch, (1959).
229 Raúl Prebisch, (1959).
230 Torkil Lauesen, (2025), pp. 53–54.
231 Lorenzo Fioramonti, *Gross Domestic Problem: The Politics Behind the World's Most Powerful Number*, London: Zed Books, 2013.
232 Peter Wilkin, 'Solidarity in a Global Age - Seattle and Beyond' in *World Systems Research*, No. 6, 2000.
233 Joseph Stiglitz, (2002); Lefteris Tsoulfidis and Persefoni Tsaliki, (2019).
234 Nelson Maldonado-Torres, 'On the Coloniality of Being: Contributions to the Development of a Concept' in *Cultural Studies*, No. 21, 2007, p. 243.
235 Sabelo Ndlovu-Gatsheni, 'Decoloniality as the Future of Africa' in *History Compass*, No. 13, 2015.
236 Kwame Nkrumah, *Neo-Colonialism, the Last Stage of Imperialism*. London: Thomas Nelson & Sons, 1965.
237 Kenneth Hermele, *Ecologically Unequal Exchange*, Lund: Lund University, 2010.
238 Michael Todaro and Stephen Smith, (2020) [2014].
239 Walter Rodney, (1981) [1972].
240 Walter Rodney, (1981) [1972].
241 Michael Todaro and Stephen Smith, (2020) [2014]; World Bank, *World Development Report 2000/2001: Attacking Poverty*, Washington, DC: World Bank, 2000.
242 Jose Antonio Ocampo and Mariángela Parra-Lancourt, 'The Terms of Trade for Commodities Since the mid-19th Century' in *Revista de Historia Económica-Journal of Iberian and Latin American Economic History*, No. 28, 2010.
243 Food and Agriculture Organization of the United Nations, *The State of Agricultural Commodity Markets*, Rome: FAO, 2004.

244 Michael Todaro and Stephen Smith, (2020) [2014].
245 Eric Sheppard, (2012); Michael Todaro and Stephen Smith, (2020) [2014]
246 Marx, Works of Karl Marx 1848, On the Question of Free Trade.
247 Hans Singer, (1950); Raúl Prebisch, (1950).
248 Shashi Shaw, *A Revisit to the Prebisch-Singer Hypothesis*, Kazi Nazrul University, West Bengal, 2020.
249 Arthur Lewis, The Theory of Economic Growth, London: Routledge, 1955.
250 Income Classification (World Development Indicators), at https://datatopics.worldbank.org/world-development-indicators/stories/the-classification-of-countries-by-income.html
251 A country's balance of payments records all international economic transactions, including remittances, interest and dividends, while its terms of trade focuses solely on imports and exports. By excluding those other international flows, the terms of trade capture how much a country can afford to import on the basis of its own exports.
252 Balance of Payment (current US$), at https://data.worldbank.org/indicator/BN.GSR.GNFS.CD
253 The dollar depreciated due to a range of factors, including: (1) an increase in the money supply to fund social programs and the Vietnam War; and (2) strong domestic demand leading to higher imports than exports, which resulted in an outflow of dollars to pay for imports, putting downward pressure on the dollar's value.
254 In 1970s, the Organisation of Petroleum Exporting Countries (OPEC), supplying 85 per cent of the world's oil raises its prices: the 1980 oil price is ten time higher than in 1970. Source: World Bank, (2000).
255 Adam Hanieh, *Crude Capitalism: Oil, Corporate Power, and the Making of the World Market*, London: Verso, 2024b.
256 Sharon Beder, 'Debt and the International Monetary System' in *The Nature of Sustainable Development*, Newham: Scribe Publications, 1993; Maggie Black, (2002); George Monbiot, *The Age of Consent: A Manifesto for a New World Order*, London: Flamingo, 2003.
257 Stephanie Black, *Life and debt [Film]*, Kingston: Tuff Gong Pictures, 2001.
258 Sharon Beder, (1993); Maggie Black, (2002); George Monbiot, (2003)
259 http://www.cadtm.org/Video-The-Ecuador-debt-audit-a
260 Benn Steil, *The Battle of Bretton Woods: John Maynard Keynes, Harry Dexter White, and the Making of a New World Order*, Princeton: Princeton University Press, 2013.
261 Adam Hanieh, (2024b).
262 Pol Antràs and Davin Chor, (2022).
263 https://www.mckinsey.com/featured-insights/innovation-and-growth/globalization-in-transition-the-future-of-trade-and-value-chains
264 https://www.oecd.org/en/topics/policy-issues/global-value-and-supply-chains.html
265 Intan Suwandi, *Value Chains: The New Economic Imperialism*, London and New York: Monthly Review Press, 2019.
266 Andrea Ricci, 'Global Structure of Dependency and Socio-Ecological Crisis: Intersecting Delinking and Degrowth for an Ecosocialist Transition' in *Capitalism, Nature, Socialism*, No. 36, 2025.
267 Terry Eagleton, (2018).
268 Marijn Moes, *Implications of the Lithium-ion Battery Supply Chain Between the Democratic Republic of Congo, China and the European Union*, Amsterdam: University of Amsterdam, 2024.
269 Andrea Ricci, (2025).
270 John Smith, *Imperialism in the Twenty-First Century: Globalization, Super-Exploitation, and Capitalism's Final Crisis*, London and New York: Monthly Review Press, 2016; Andrea Ricci, (2021).
271 Andrea Ricci, (2025).
272 Hans Singer, 'The Distribution of Gains from Trade and Investment – Revisited' in *Journal of Development Studies*, No. 11, 1975; John Brolin, 'Unequal Exchange' in *The Palgrave Encyclopaedia of Imperialism and Anti-Imperialism*, Cham: Palgrave Macmillan, 2021.
273 John Brolin, (2007)

274 Samir Amin, *Accumulation on a World Scale: A Critique of the Theory of Underdevelopment*, London and New York: Monthly Review Press, 1974; Arghiri Emmanuel, *Unequal Exchange: A summary*, Brighton: University of Sussex, 1975a.

275 Paul Sweezy, (1942); Paul Baran, *The Political Economy of Growth*, London and New York: Monthly Review Press, 1957; Paul Baran and Paul Sweezy, (1966).

276 Bill Dunn, 'Class, Capital and the Global Unfree Market: Resituating Theories of Monopoly Capitalism and Unequal Exchange' in *Science & Society*, No. 81, 2017.

277 Marx quoted in Enrique Dussel and Aníbal Yáñez, (1990), p. 74.

278 Samir Amin, (1976)

279 Office of Technology Assessment, *International Competitiveness in Electronics*, Washington, DC: US Government Printing Office, 1983.

280 Walter Rodney, (1981) [1972], p. 27.

281 Andrea Ricci, (2021).

282 Stefania Vitali et al., *The Network of Global Corporate Control*, PLoS ONE, No. 6, 2011.

283 Alan Evans, 'On Monopoly Rent' in *Land Economics*, No. 67, 1991.

284 Paul Baran, (1957); Paul Baran and Paul Sweezy, (1966); Samir Amin, (1976).

285 https://ilsr.org/article/independent-business/factsheet-credit-cards/

286 Alan Evans, (1991).

287 Jason Hickel et al., 'Imperialist appropriation in the world economy: Drain from the global South through unequal exchange, 1990–2015' in *Global Environmental Change*, No. 73, 2022.

288 John Smith, (2016).

289 United Nations Conference on Trade and Development, (2015).

290 Trade in Value Added (TiVA) 2023 edition, at https://www.oecd.org/en/topics/sub-issues/trade-in-value-added.html

291 Domestic Value Added data from Bruno Casella et al., (2019).

292 United Nations Conference on Trade and Development, (2015).

293 Kenneth Kraemer et al., *Capturing Value in Global Networks: Apple's iPad and iPhone*, PCIC Working Paper, 2011.

294 Organisation for Economic Co-operation and Development, *Interconnected Economies: Benefiting from Global Value Chains*, Paris: OECD Publishing, 2013.

295 Federico Riccio et al., 'The labour share along global value chains: perspectives and evidence from sectoral interdependence' in *Review of World Economics*, No. 161, 2022.

296 Organisation for Economic Co-operation and Development, *In it Together: Why Less Inequality Benefits All*, Paris: OECD Publishing, 2015; Ernesto Crivelli et al., *Base Erosion, Profit Shifting and Developing Countries*. Washington, DC: IMF, 2015; Alex Cobham and Petr Janský, 'Global distribution of revenue loss from corporate tax avoidance: re-estimation and country results' in *Journal of International Development*, No. 30, 2018.

297 Jason Hickel, (2017); International debt statistics, at https://datatopics.worldbank.org/debt/ids/regionanalytical/lmy/counterpartarea/wld

298 Jason Hickel, (2017).

299 Zak Cope, (2019).

300 Jason Hickel, (2017).

301 Jason Hickel, (2017); Zak Cope, (2019).

302 Official development assistance, at https://data.one.org/topics/official-development-assistance/

303 Walter Rodney, (1981) [1972].

304 Kebede Gebru et al., 'The commodification of social relationships in agriculture: Evidence from northern Ethiopia' in *Geoforum*, No. 126, 2021.

305 David Harvey, *A Brief History of Neoliberalism*, Oxford: Oxford University Press, 2005.

306 Pun Ngai and Jenny Chan, 'Global Capital, the State, and Chinese Workers: The Foxconn Experience' in *Modern China*, No. 38, 2012.

307 Ertuğrul Ahmet Tonak, *The Rate of Exploitation (The Case of the iPhone)*, Tricontinental, 2019.

308 André Campos et al., *Labour conditions at foreign electronics manufacturing companies in Brazil.* Amsterdam: SOMO, 2017.
309 Ertuğrul Ahmet Tonak, (2019).
310 David Harvey, *The New Imperialism*, Oxford: Oxford University Press, 2004; Bill Dunn, (2017).
311 Marx, *Grundrisse*, Miscellaneous, Notebook VII, The Chapter on Capital / Bastiat and Carey, Interest and profit. – Carey. Pawning in England.
312 Otto Bauer, (2000) [1924]; Henryk Grossman, (1992) [1929]; Arghiri Emmanuel, (1972); Samir Amin, (1974).
313 Lefteris Tsoulfidis and Persefoni Tsaliki, (2019); Andrea Ricci, (2021).
314 John Brolin, (2021).
315 The kernel (e.g., Linux), often shared among different operating systems (e.g., Ubuntu or Debian), serves as the computer's core that bridges hardware and software, while the operating system includes additional tools and interfaces that allow users to interact with the computer.
316 Arghiri Emmanuel, (1972).
317 Carl Nordlund, (2014).
318 Arghiri Emmanuel, (1975a); John Brolin, (2007); John Bellamy Foster and Hannah Holleman, (2014).
319 Bas van Bavel, *The Invisible Hand?: How Market Economies have Emerged and Declined Since AD 500*, Oxford: Oxford University Press, 2016.
320 Emmanuel, (1972); Zak Cope, (2019).
321 Samir Amin, (1974).
322 Guglielmo Carchedi and Michael Roberts, 'The Economics of Modern Imperialism' in *Historical Materialism*, No. 29, 2021.
323 Emmanuel, (1972).
324 Enrique Dussel and Aníbal Yáñez, (1990), p. 84.
325 Paul Sweezy, (1942).
326 Arghiri Emmanuel, (1975a), p. 22.
327 Carl Nordlund, (2014).
328 Arghiri Emmanuel, (1975a).
329 Andrea Ricci, (2021)
330 https://www.freedomofmigration.com/wp-content/uploads/2012/02/Friedman-20061016.pdf
331 Torkil Lauesen, (2025).
332 Otto Bauer, (2000) [1924]; Henryk Grossman, (1992) [1929].
333 Arghiri Emmanuel, (1972).
334 John Brolin, (2007).
335 Arghiri Emmanuel, (1972).
336 John Brolin, (2007); Andrea Ricci, (2021); Lefteris Tsoulfidis and Persefoni Tsaliki, (2019); Torkil Lauesen, (2025).
337 Enrique Dussel and Aníbal Yáñez, (1990).
338 Otto Bauer, (2000[1924]); Henryk Grossman, (1992) [1929].
339 However, this entails two possibilities. First, more constant capital might be deployed in the centres, signifying that an equal number of workers will be more productive. Alternatively, an increase in constant capital in the centre could also imply that it operates with a constant capital of a higher value than the periphery, in which case productivity is not necessarily greater. Let us assume the former.
340 Arghiri Emmanuel, (1972).
341 Otto Bauer, (2000) [1924].
342 Marx, *Capital*, Vol 3, Part III, Chapter 14.
343 Ernest Mandel, (1999).
344 Marx, *Works of Karl Marx 1848*, On the Question of Free Trade.
345 See for example Richard Bernal, 'Emmanuel's Unequal Exchange as a Theory of Underdevelopment' in *Social and Economic Studies*, No. 29, 1980.

346 Arghiri Emmanuel, *Unequal Exchange Revisited*, Brighton: University of Sussex, 1975b.
347 Samir Amin, *Imperialism and Unequal Development*, London and New York: Monthly Review Press, 1977.
348 Arghiri Emmanuel, (1972).
349 Jason Hickel et al., (2024).
350 A lower organic composition (OC) may suggest lower productivity, but not always. In broad unequal exchange, lower constant capital in the periphery indeed reduces OC and productivity; in strict unequal exchange, higher variable capital in the centre lowers OC without affecting productivity.
351 Marx, *Capital*, Vol 3, Part I, Chapter 3.
352 Emmanuel's original scheme combined higher wages in the centre with lower wages in the periphery, creating the misleading impression of a causal link. To avoid this, John Brolin begins from equal variable capital. Also, unlike Emmanuel – who raises v and lowers c by an equal amount to hold total investment (C) constant – I do not, so as to avoid conflating productivity and wage differentials. In this respect, I follow Brolin's revision of Emmanuel's scheme (Table 9 in John Brolin), without altering Emmanuel's underlying logic. See: John Brolin, (2007), pp. 180–181.
353 Arghiri Emmanuel, (1972), p. 38.
354 Arghiri Emmanuel, (1975b), pp. 53–54. Quoted in Torkil Lauesen, (2025).
355 Arghiri Emmanuel and Charles Bettelheim, 'International solidarity of workers: Two views' in *Monthly Review*, No. 22, 1970. Interestingly, Marx (*Capital*, Vol 3, Part II, Chapter 8) also argued that in a 'less developed' economic context (Marx compares the 'European' with the 'Asian'), the rate of surplus value will typically be lower, and the organic composition will be lower too; because of the latter, however, the rate of profit may well be higher, despite the former.
356 See further details in 'The End of a Debate' in Samir Amin, (1977).
357 See also Tables 10 and 11 in John Brolin, (2007), pp. 182–183.
358 Michael Webber and Simon Foot, 'The Measurement of Unequal Exchange' in *Environment and Planning A: Economy and Space*, No. 16, 1984.
359 Emmanuel, (1972), (1975).
360 Walter Rodney, (1981) [1972], p. 173.
361 Baidyanath Ghosh, *Dependency Theory Revisited*, London: Routledge, 2019 [2001].
362 Marx, *Capital*, Vol 3, Part III, Chapter 14.
363 Vladimir Lenin, (2010) [1917].
364 https://unequalexchange.org/2023/07/06/emmanuel-and-us/
365 John Brolin, (2007).
366 Bill Dunn, (2017).
367 Paul Sweezy, (1942); Paul Baran and Paul Sweezy, (1966).
368 Andrea Ricci, 'The Political Implications of Unequal Exchange: Towards a Common Agenda for Global Social Movements' in *Capitalism Nature Socialism*, No. 35, 2024
369 Arghiri Emmanuel, (1972).
370 Bill Dunn, (2017).
371 Paul Sweezy, (1942).
372 Arghiri Emmanuel, (1972).
373 Paul Sweezy, (1942).
374 As mentioned, one could of course interpret strict unequal exchange as stemming from the centre's monopolisation of high-wage labour markets, but this was not the monopoly school's critique. See: John Brolin, (2007).
375 Enrique Dussel and Aníbal Yáñez, (1990)
376 Torkil Lauesen and Zak Cope, 'Imperialism and the transformation of values into prices' in *Monthly Review*, No. 67, 2015.
377 Torkil Lauesen, (2025), p. 69.

378 Alf Hornborg, *Global Ecology and Unequal Exchange: Fetishism in a Zero-Sum World*, London: Routledge, 2011.
379 See critique in Alf Hornborg, 'Unequal Exchange is Not Primarily About Monetary Value' in *Nature Communications*, No. 16, 2025.
380 Arghiri Emmanuel, (1972); Walter Rodney, (1981) [1972]; Samir Amin, (1974).
381 Stacy Maddern, 'Emmanuel, Arghiri and "Unequal Exchange"' in *The Palgrave Encyclopaedia of Imperialism and Anti-Imperialism*, Cham: Palgrave Macmillan, 2021.
382 Walter Rodney, (1981) [1972].
383 Arghiri Emmanuel, (1972); John Brolin, (2021).
384 James Steinhoff, (2021).
385 Arghiri Emmanuel, (1972).
386 Communist Working Group, (2025) [1986]; Zak Cope, (2019); Jason Hickel et al., (2024).
387 Arghiri Emmanuel, (1972); Samir Amin, (1974); Zak Cope, (2019).
388 Jason Hickel et al., (2024).
389 Communist Working Group, (2025) [1986].
390 Marx, *Capital*, Vol 1, Part VII, Chapter 25.
391 John Brolin, (2007).
392 Communist Working Group, (2025) [1986].
393 Andrea Ricci, (2021).
394 Arghiri Emmanuel and Charles Bettelheim, (1970).
395 Ruy Mauro Marini, (2021) [1973].
396 Enrique Dussel and Aníbal Yáñez, (1990).
397 See Table 11 in John Brolin, (2007), p. 183.
398 Bill Dunn, (2017).
399 Gernot Köhler, 'Estimating Unequal Exchange: Sub-Saharan Africa to the World', in *Accounting for Colonialism*, Cham: Palgrave Macmillan, 2023
400 See also the example of the pencil, at https://fee.org/ebooks/i-pencil/
401 Roy Bhaskar, *A Realist Theory of Science*, Brighton: Harvester Press, 1978.
402 Input-output tables are economic tools that represent the flow of goods and services between sectors within an economy, detailing how the output from one industry is an input to another.
403 Each country was assigned to the income cluster they belonged to in 2022, based on GDP (constant 2015 US$), at https://data.worldbank.org/indicator/NY.GDP.MKTP.KD Income Classification (World Development Indicators), at https://datatopics.worldbank.org/world-development-indicators/stories/the-classification-of-countries-by-income.html
404 Labour force (total, in full-time equivalent), at https://data.worldbank.org/indicator/SL.TLF.TOTL.IN Average annual hours worked by persons engaged for 1990-2018, at www.ggdc.net/pwt, then linearly extrapolated for 2019-2022.
405 Andrea Ricci, 'Unequal Exchange in the Age of Globalization' in *Review of Radical Political Economics*, No. 51, 2019.
406 Crelis Rammelt, 'Two Sides of the Same Coin: A Synthesis of Economic and Ecological Unequal Exchange' in *Capitalism Nature Socialism*, No. 05/11, 2025.
407 Gross National Income (current PPP$), at https://data.worldbank.org/indicator/NY.GNP.MKTP.PP.CD; Gross National Income (current US$), at https://data.worldbank.org/indicator/NY.GNP.MKTP.CD
408 I clustered countries into the three regions based on 2022 data, and used a WITS query to calculate the total import and export flows between them: Trade Data (UN Comtrade), at https://wits.worldbank.org/WITS/
409 Jason Hickel et al., 'Plunder in the post-colonial era: quantifying drain from the global south through unequal exchange, 1960–2018' in *New Political Economy*, No. 26, 2021.
410 With average working hours of 1,726 hours in the average centre country in 2022 (based on my clustering).

411 Labour force (total, in full-time equivalent), at https://data.worldbank.org/indicator/SL.TLF.TOTL.IN

412 Similarly, Jason Hickel and colleagues estimate that 46 per cent of the North's total consumption of labour was net-appropriated from the South in 2021. Source: Jason Hickel et al., (2024).

413 Gernot Köhler, 'The Structure of Global Money and World Tables of Unequal Exchange' in *Journal of World-Systems Research*, No. 4, 1998; Barry Finger, 'Unequal exchange, Dependency Theory and the Exploitation of Nations' in *International Socialist Review*, No. 107, 2017; Akiko Nakajima and Hiroshi Izumi, 'Economic Development and Unequal Exchange among Nations' in *Review of Radical Political Economics*, No. 64, 1995; Jason Hickel et al., (2024).

414 Christian Dorninger et al., (2021); Jason Hickel et al., (2022).

415 Andrea Ricci, (2023).

416 Gernot Köhler, (1998).

417 Paraphrasing Gernot Köhler, at https://anti-imperialist.net/blog/2022/11/06/interview-with-gernot-kohler-on-unequal-exchange-and-global-apartheid/

418 Andrea Ricci, (2024).

419 Exchange rates (indicator), at https://data.oecd.org/conversion/exchange-rates.htm#indicator-chart

420 Purchasing power parities (PPP), at https://data.oecd.org/conversion/purchasing-power-parities-ppp.htm#indicator-chart

421 Price level ratio of PPP conversion factor (GDP) to market exchange rate, at https://data.worldbank.org/indicator/PA.NUS.PPPC.RF

422 Gernot Köhler, (1998); Jason Hickel et al., (2021).

423 https://medium.com/@monetarypolicyinstitute/rip-ppp-purchasing-power-parity-b8c8dc7d5c3c

424 Andrea Ricci, 'Global locational inequality: Assessing unequal exchange effects' in *Environment and Planning A: Economy and Space*, No. 54, 2022.

425 Christopher Olk, 'How much a dollar cost: Currency hierarchy as a driver of ecologically unequal exchange' in *World Development*, No. 180, 2024.

426 Christopher Olk, (2024).

427 Gernot Köhler, (1998).

428 Gernot Köhler, (1998).

429 Marx, *Capital*, Vol 1, Part VI, Chapter 22.

430 Gernot Köhler, (1998).

431 Manfred Lenzen et al., 'Mapping the structure of the world economy' in *Environmental Science & Technology*, No. 46, 2012.

432 The method was proposed by Andrea Ricci, (2025). Data sources: Gross National Income (current PPP$), at https://data.worldbank.org/indicator/NY.GNP.MKTP.PP.CD Gross National Income (current US$), at https://data.worldbank.org/indicator/NY.GNP.MKTP.CD

433 Andrea Ricci, (2019); Jason Hickel et al., (2021).

434 Guglielmo Carchedi and Michael Roberts, (2021).

435 Gernot Köhler, (1998).

436 Gernot Köhler, (1998), p. 145.

437 Andrea Ricci, (2021), p. 161.

438 https://wageindicator.org/about/overview-wageindicator-newsletters/news/2017

439 Andrea Ricci, (2025).

440 For further explanations on the equations, see: Crelis Rammelt, (2025).

441 This matches with a recent estimate from Andrea Ricci: In 2019, the average person in the global centre received $3,810 in value transfers from the periphery, including $1,174 through global value chains. Western Europeans saw the biggest benefit, getting an impressive $576 per person, per month. Source: Andrea Ricci, (2021).

442 Michael Webber and Simon Foot, (1984); George Joseph and Mark Tomlinson, 'Testing the Existence and Measuring the Magnitude of Unequal Exchange Resulting from International Trade: A Marxian Approach' in *Indian Economic Review*, No. 26, 1991 Jason Hickel et al., (2021); Torkil Lauesen, (2025).

443 Labour income share (as a percent of GDP), at https://data.socialjustice.ilo.org
444 Torkil Lauesen, (2025), p. 116.
445 Zak Cope, (2019).
446 Torkil Lauesen, (2025), p. 126.
447 Based on a world average of 2,035 hours worked per year, using the datasets mentioned earlier.
448 https://dqydj.com/2022-income-percentile-calculator/
449 Arghiri Emmanuel, (1972); Arghiri Emmanuel, (1975a).
450 Arghiri Emmanuel, (1972), p. 131.
451 Andrea Ricci, (2021).
452 Noelle Robbins, 'Flushing Forests' in *World Watch Magazine*, No. 23, 2010.
453 It has also prompted the development of alternative energy theories of value, which I won't deal with in this book. For detailed discussions, see John Bellamy Foster and Paul Burkett, *Marx and the Earth: An Anti-Critique*, Leiden and Boston: Brill, 2016.
454 Rikard Warlenius, 'Linking ecological debt and ecologically unequal exchange: stocks, flows, and unequal sink appropriation' in Journal of Political Ecology, No. 23, 2016.
455 Andrea Ricci, (2023).
456 Walter Rodney, (1981) [1972], p. 22.
457 Nicholas Georgescu-Roegen, The Entropy Law and the Economic Process, Cambridge: Harvard University Press, 1971.
458 Marx, *Grundrisse*, Notebook III.
459 Based on: WU Vienna, *Material flows by material group, 1970-2024. Visualisation based upon the UN IRP Global Material Flows Database*, Vienna: Vienna University of Economics and Business, 2024; United Nations Environment Programme, *Assessing global resource use: A systems approach to resource efficiency and pollution reduction*, Nairobi: UNEP, 2017.
460 Dennis Meadows et al., (1972); Gaya Herrington, (2021).
461 Joyeeta Gupta et al., 'A just world on a safe planet: a Lancet Planetary Health–Earth Commission report on Earth-system boundaries, translations, and transformations' in *The Lancet Planetary Health*, No. 8, 2024.
462 Katarzyna Tokarska et al., 'The climate response to five trillion tonnes of carbon' in *Nature Climate Change*, No. 6, 2016.
463 Paul Burkett, 'The value problem in ecological economics: lessons from the physiocrats and Marx' in *Organization & Environment*, No. 16, 2003; Paul Burkett and John Bellamy Foster, 'Metabolism, energy, and entropy in Marx's critique of political economy: Beyond the Podolinsky myth' in *Theory and Society*, No. 35, 2006; John Bellamy Foster and Paul Burkett, 'Value Isn't Everything' in *Monthly Review*, No. 70, 2018.
464 The following is based on: Crelis Rammelt, 'How entropy drives us towards degrowth' in *Real World Economics Review*, No. 117, 2024.
465 Nicholas Georgescu-Roegen, (1971).
466 Herman Daly, 'Sustainable Development – Definitions, Principles, Policies' in *The Future of Sustainability*, Dordrecht: Springer, 2006.
467 Marx, *Capital*, Vol 1, Part V, Chapter 16.
468 Charles Eisenstein, (2013), p. 35.
469 Felix van Hoften, 'Elke innovatie leidt tot uitsterving van een soort' in *Waardenwerk*, No. 93, 2023.
470 wrld.bg/ybEL50ykTbd
471 Brett Clark and John Bellamy Foster, 'Ecological Imperialism and the Global Metabolic Rift, Unequal Exchange and the Guano/Nitrates Trade' in *International Journal of Comparative Sociology*, No. 50, 2009; John Bellamy Foster, 'Marx and the Rift in the Universal Metabolism of Nature' in *Monthly Review*, No. 65, 2013.
472 Johan Rockström et al., (2009); Joyeeta Gupta et al., (2024).
473 See debates in Paul Gellert, 'Bunker's Ecologically Unequal Exchange, Foster's Metabolic Rift, and Moore's World-Ecology: Distinctions With or Without Difference?' in *Ecologically Unequal*

Exchange: Environmental Injustice in Comparative and Historical Perspective, Cham: Palgrave Macmillan, 2019; Kai Heron, 'Dialectical Materialisms, Metabolic Rifts and the Climate Crisis: A Lacanian/Hegelian Perspective' in *Science & Society*, No. 85, 2021.

474 David Montgomery, *Dirt: The Erosion of Civilizations*, Oakland: University of California Press, 2012; Gabe Brown, *Dirt to Soil: One Family's Journey into Regenerative Agriculture*, Vermont: Chelsea Green Publishing, 2018.

475 Kwame Nkrumah, (1965).

476 Joan Martinez-Alier, 'The Ecological Debt' in *Kurswechsel*, No. 4, 2002.

477 Stephen Bunker, 'Modes of extraction, unequal exchange, and the progressive underdevelopment of an extreme periphery: the Brazilian Amazon, 1600-1980' in *American Journal of Sociology*, No. 89, 1984; Stephen Bunker, 'Toward a Theory of Ecologically Unequal Exchange' in *Ecologically Unequal Exchange: Environmental Injustice in Comparative and Historical Perspective*, Cham: Palgrave Macmillan, 2019 [1985]

478 Stephen Bunker, (1984); Stephen Bunker, (2019) [1985].

479 Pablo Alonso-Fernández and Rosa Regueiro-Ferreira, 'Extractivism, ecologically unequal exchange and environmental impact in South America: A study using Material Flow Analysis (1990–2017)' in *Ecological Economics*, No. 194, 2022; Yikang Bai and Jennifer Givens, 'Ecologically Unequal Exchange of Plastic Waste? A Longitudinal Analysis of International Trade in Plastic Waste' in *Journal of World-Systems Research*, No. 27, 2021; Juan Infante-Amate and Fridolin Krausmann, 'Trade, Ecologically Unequal Exchange and Colonial Legacy: The Case of France and its Former Colonies (1962–2015)' in *Ecological Economics*, No. 156, 2019.

480 Stephen Bunker, (2019) [1985], pp. 28–29.

481 Arghiri Emmanuel, 'The Socialist Project in a Disintegrated Capitalist World in *Socialist Thought and Practice*, 16, 1976, p. 72.

482 Samir Amin, (1977), p. 212.

483 Alf Hornborg, 'Towards an ecological theory of unequal exchange: articulating world system theory and ecological economics' in *Ecological Economics*, No. 25, 1998; John Bellamy Foster and Paul Burkett, (2018).

484 John Brolin, (2021); Andrea Ricci, (2023).

485 Marx, *Critique of the Gotha Programme*, Part I.

486 Marx, *Capital*, Vol 1, Part VII, Chapter 24, Section 4.

487 Pierre Jalée, *How Capitalism Works*, New York: Monthly Review Press, 1977.

488 Ernst Schumacher, *Small Is Beautiful: A Study of Economics As If People Mattered*, London: Blond & Briggs, 1973, p. 11.

489 Herman Daly and Joshua Farley, (2011), p. 32.

490 John Bellamy Foster and Paul Burkett, (2018)

491 Marx, *Capital*, Vol 1, Part I, Chapter 3, Section 2.

492 https://www.resilience.org/stories/2022-05-19/the-great-simplification-full-movie/

493 Giorgos Kallis and Erik Swyngedouw, (2018).

494 John Bellamy Foster and Paul Burkett, (2018).

495 https://www.resilience.org/stories/2022-05-19/the-great-simplification-full-movie/

496 Joan Martinez-Alier, (2002), p. 218.

497 Alf Hornborg, 'Why economics needs to be distinguished from physics, and why economists need to talk to physicists: a response to Foster and Holleman' in *Journal of Peasant Studies*, No. 42, 2015.

498 Nicholas Georgescu-Roegen, 'The Entropy Law and the Economic Problem' in *Valuing the Earth: Economics, Ecology, Ethics*, Cambridge: MIT Press, 1993 [1971], p. 80.

499 John Gowdy and Susan Mesner, 'The Evolution of Georgescu-Roegen's Bioeconomics' in *Review of Social Economy*, No. 56, 1998.

500 Nicholas Georgescu-Roegen, Energy and Economic Myths: Institutional and Analytical Economic Essays, Oxford: Pergamon Press, 1976, p. xiv.

501 Paul Burkett, (2003), p. 140.
502 Nicholas Georgescu-Roegen, (1976).
503 Crelis Rammelt, (2024).
504 Andreas Malm, *Fossil Capital: The Rise of Steam Power and the Roots of Global Warming*, London: Verso, 2016.
505 Marx, *Capital*, Vol III, Part VI, Chapter 38.
506 Nicholas Georgescu-Roegen, (1976).
507 Paul Burkett, *Marx and Nature: A Red and Green Perspective*, Cham: Palgrave Macmillan, 1999.
508 Marx, *Capital*, Vol III, Part VI, Chapter 38.
509 Nancy Fraser, (2017).
510 Marx, *Capital*, Vol I, Part VIII, Chapter 26.
511 Torkil Lauesen, (2025).
512 Guy Shrubsole, *How We Lost Our Green & Pleasant Land & How To Take It Back*. Glasgow: William Collins, 2019.
513 Marx, *Capital*, Vol 1, Part VIII, Chapter 26.
514 https://vividmaps.com/british-empire-at-its-territorial-peak/
515 David Harvey, (2004).
516 Walter Rodney, (1981) [1972].
517 https://grain.org/en/article/7136-the-bunong-people-s-land-struggle-with-socfin
518 Walter Rodney, (1981) [1972].
519 Herman Daly, *Sustainable Development: Definitions, Principles, Policies*, Washington, DC: World Bank, 2002.
520 Joan Martinez-Alier, (2002). Brett Clark and John Bellamy Foster, (2009).
521 James Rice, 'Ecological Unequal Exchange: International Trade and Uneven Utilization of Environmental Space in the World System' in *Social Forces*, No. 85, 2007.
522 Alf Hornborg quoted in Siem Rothengatter, *The Impact of Ecological Unequal Exchange on Population's Ability to Access Minimum Needs in Resource-Drained Countries*, Amsterdam: University of Amsterdam, 2024, p. 107.
523 Christian Dorninger et al., (2021).
524 Alf Hornborg, (2025).
525 Jennifer Givens quoted in Siem Rothengatter, (2024), p. 73.
526 Andrea Ricci, (2023).
527 Walter Rodney, (1981) [1972].
528 https://archive.org/details/michael-parenti-lecture-1986-yellow-parenti
529 Stephen Bunker, (1984); Stephen Bunker, (2019) [1985]; Roldan Muradian and Joan Martinez-Alier, 'Trade and the environment: from a "Southern" perspective' in *Ecological Economics*, No. 36, 2001; Alf Hornborg, 'Identifying ecologically unequal exchange in the world-system: implications for development' in *A Modern Guide to Uneven Economic Development*, Cheltenham: Edward Elgar, 2023.
530 Andrea Ricci, (2023); Andrea Ricci, (2024).
531 Jason Hickel et al., (2022).
532 Alf Hornborg, (2023).
533 Martin Oulu, 'The unequal exchange of Dutch cheese and Kenyan roses' in *Ecological Economics*, No. 119, 2015; Andreas Roos, 'Global asymmetries in the rise of solar power' in *Ecological Economics*, No. 199, 2022.
534 About 1,736,100 joules are consumed in extraction, production, and transportation, while the battery itself contains only 14,400 joules. Sources: Ramsay Hamade et al., 'Life Cycle Analysis of AA Alkaline Batteries' in *Procedia Manufacturing*, No. 43, 2020; https://engineering.stackexchange.com/questions/35660/understanding-the-total-energy-in-a-aa-battery
535 For reviews, see: John Brolin and Astrid Kander, 'Global trade in the Anthropocene: A review of trends and direction of environmental factor flows during the Great Acceleration' in *The*

Anthropocene Review, No. 9, 2022; Giulio Corsi et al., 'Uneven development and core-periphery dynamics: A journey into the perspective of ecologically unequal exchange' in *Environmental Science & Policy*, No. 157, 2024.

536 WU Vienna, (2024).

537 Heinz Schandl et al., (2018).

538 Thomas Wiedmann et al., 'The material footprint of nations' in *Proceedings of the National Academy of Sciences*, No. 112, 2015.

539 WU Vienna, (2024).

540 https://www.dw.com/en/how-big-is-your-water-footprint/a-61171792

541 Adapted from: Heinz Schandl et al., (2018); Pablo Alonso-Fernández and Rosa Regueiro-Ferreira, (2022); Crelis Rammelt and Raimon Cardelus Ylla-Català, (2025); Fridolin Krausmann et al., 'Material Flow Accounting: Measuring Global Material Use for Sustainable Development' in *Annual Review of Environment and Resources*, No. 42, 2017

542 Justin Kitzes, 'An Introduction to Environmentally-Extended Input-Output Analysis' in *Resources*, No. 2, 2013; Anke Schaffartzik et al., 'Environmentally Extended Input-Output Analysis' in *Social Ecology Working Paper*, No. 154, 2014.

543 Justin Kitzes, (2013); Anke Schaffartzik et al., (2014); Christian Dorninger and Alf Hornborg, 'Can EEMRIO analyses establish the occurrence of ecologically unequal exchange' in Ecological Economics, No. 119, 2015.

544 Joan Martinez-Alier et al., 'Changing social metabolism and environmental conflicts in India and South America' in *Journal of Political Ecology*, No. 23, 2016.

545 Christian Dorninger and Nina Eisenmenger, 'South America's biophysical involvement in international trade: the physical trade balances of Argentina, Bolivia, and Brazil in the light of ecologically unequal exchange' in *Journal of Political Ecology*, No. 23, 2016; Pablo Samaniego et al., 'Commercial and biophysical deficits in South America, 1990–2013' in *Ecological Economics*, No. 133, 2017; Juan Infante-Amate and Fridolin Krausmann, (2019); Pablo Alonso-Fernández and Rosa Regueiro-Ferreira, (2022).

546 WU Vienna, (2024).

547 Christian Dorninger et al., (2021); Jason Hickel et al., (2022); Crelis Rammelt and Raimon Cardelus Ylla-Català, (2025); Crelis Rammelt, (2025).

548 Louison Cahen-Fourot and Nelo Magalhães, 'The accumulation–metabolism nexus: internationalization, labour–capital relations, and material flows of French capitalism since the post-war era' in *Socio-Economic Review*, No. 22, 2024; Pablo Alonso-Fernández and Rosa Regueiro-Ferreira, (2022); Pablo Samaniego et al., (2017).

549 For example, a study by Daniel Moran et al., 'Does ecologically unequal exchange occur?' in *Ecological Economics*, No. 89, 2013 was later corrected by Christian Dorninger and Alf Hornborg, (2015).

550 Luisa Rivera-Basques et al., 'Unequal ecological exchange in the era of global value chains: the case of Latin America' in *Ecological Economics*, No. 180, 2021.

551 See overviews in John Brolin and Astrid Kander, (2020); Giulio Corsi et al., (2024)

552 Christian Dorninger et al., (2021).

553 Jason Hickel et al., (2022); Energy Institute, *Statistical Review of World Energy 2023*, London: Energy Institute, 2023.

554 Christian Dorninger et al., (2021); Jason Hickel et al., (2022).

555 Serge Latouche, 'La décroissance comme condition d'une société conviviale', in *L'Économie*, L'Esprit du temps, 2005.

556 Yang Yu et al., 'China's unequal ecological exchange', in *Ecological Indicators*, No. 47, 2014; Pablo Alonso-Fernández and Rosa Regueiro-Ferreira, (2022).

557 Rikard Warlenius, (2016).

558 Mount Everest weighs approximately 162 Gt (Quora). See also: Crelis Rammelt and Raimon Cardelus Ylla-Català, (2025).

559 Christian Dorninger et al., (2021); Jason Hickel et al., (2022).

560 Alf Hornborg, (1998); John Bellamy Foster and Hannah Holleman, (2014); Alf Hornborg, 'Ecological economics, Marxism, and technological progress: Some explorations of the conceptual foundations of theories of ecologically unequal exchange' in *Ecological Economics*, No. 105, 2014.

561 Alf Hornborg, (1998); Alf Hornborg, (2009); Rikard Warlenius, (2016); Jennifer Givens and Xiaorui Huang, 'Ecologically Unequal Exchange and Environmental Load Displacement: Global Perspectives on Structural Inequalities and the Environment' in *Handbook of Environmental Sociology*, Cham: Springer Nature, 2021.

562 John Shandra et al., 'Appetite for Destruction? China, Ecologically Unequal Exchange, and Forest Loss' in *Rural sociology*, No. 85, 2020; Jamie Sommer et al., 'India, Palm Oil, and Ecologically Unequal Exchange: A Cross-national Analysis of Forest Loss' in *Sociological Perspectives*, No. 63, 2020; Gabriel Weber and Ignazio Cabras, 'Environmental Justice and Just Transition in the EU's Sustainability Policies in Third Countries: The Case of Colombia' in *The International Spectator*, No. 56, 2021; Samia Tasmim et al., 'Feed me! China, agriculture, ecologically unequal exchange, and forest loss in a cross-national perspective' in *Environmental Policy and Governance*, No. 32, 2022.

563 Yang Yu et al., (2014); Benedikt Bruckner et al., 'Ecologically unequal exchanges driven by EU consumption' in *Nature Sustainability*, No. 6, 2023.

564 Manfred Lenzen et al., 'International trade drives biodiversity threats in developing nations' in *Nature*, No. 486, 2012.

565 Amanda Irwin et al., 'Quantifying and categorising national extinction-risk footprints' in *Scientific Reports*, No. 12, 2022.

566 Yikang Bai and Jennifer Givens, (2021); Kate Tong et al., 'Ecological unequal exchange: Quantifying emissions of toxic chemicals embodied in the global trade of chemicals, products, and waste' in *Environmental Research Letters*, No. 17, 2022.

567 Virginia Rodríguez García et al., 'Long- and Short-Run Forest Dynamics: An Empirical Assessment of Forest Transition, Environmental Kuznets Curve and Ecologically Unequal Exchange Theories' in *Forests*, No. 12, 2021; Jared Fitzgerald and Daniel Auerbach, 'The Political Economy of the Water Footprint: A Cross-National Analysis of Ecologically Unequal Exchange' in *Sustainability*, No. 8, 2016.

568 Joan Martinez-Alier, (2002); Rikard Warlenius, (2016).

569 Jason Hickel, 'Quantifying national responsibility for climate breakdown: an equality-based attribution approach for carbon dioxide emissions in excess of the planetary boundary' in *The Lancet Planetary Health*, No. 4, 2020.

570 https://news.virginia.edu/content/microplastics-are-our-food-water-and-air-should-we-be-worried

571 Yang Yu et al., (2014); Yulong Zhang et al., 'Ecological unequal exchange between China and European Union: An investigation from global value chains and carbon emissions viewpoint' in *Atmospheric Pollution Research*, No. 14, 2023; Gül Tunç et al., 'Ecological unequal exchange between Turkey and the European Union: An assessment from value added perspective' in *Ecological Economics*, No. 192, 2022; Eunice Oppon et al. 'Modelling Multi-regional Ecological Exchanges: The Case of UK and Africa' in Ecological Economics, No. 147, 2018.

572 Feng Hao, 'A study of ecologically unequal exchange for 89 countries between 1990 and 2015' in *The Social Science Journal*, No. 57, 2020.

573 https://news.virginia.edu/content/microplastics-are-our-food-water-and-air-should-we-be-worried

574 Jason Moore, *Capitalism in the Web of Life: Ecology and the Accumulation of Capital*, London: Verso, 2015.

575 David Korten, *When Corporations Rule the World*, Boulder: Kumarian Press, 1995.

576 Howard Odum, *Environmental Accounting, Emergy and Environmental Decision Making*, New York: Wiley, 1996; Alf Hornborg, (1998).

577 Howard Odum, (1996); Howard Odum, 'Emergy accounting' in *Unveiling Wealth: On Money, Quality of Life and Sustainability*, Dordrecht: Springer, 2002.

578 Enrico Sciubba, 'Why Emergy-and Exergy Analysis are non-commensurable methods for the assessment of energy conversion systems' in *International Journal of Exergy*, No. 6, 2009.
579 Marta Pérez-Soba et al., *The emergy perspective: natural and anthropic energy flows in agricultural biomass production*, Luxembourg: Office of the European Union, 2019.
580 Howard Odum and Elisabeth Odum, *A Prosperous Way Down: Principles and Policies*, Denver: University Press of Colorado, 2001.
581 Torbjörn Rydberg, 'Emergy and trade: Exploring a Measure of Equitable Exchange' in *International Trade and Environmental Justice: Toward a Global Political Ecology*, New York: Nova Science Publishers, 2010.
582 Howard Odum, (1996); Howard Odum and Elisabeth Odum, (2001).
583 Enrico Sciubba, (2009); Crelis Rammelt, (2024).
584 Göran Wall, 'Exergy conversion in the Swedish' in *Resources and Energy*, No. 9, 1997
585 Luis Carmona et al., 'Resource use and economic development: an exergy perspective on energy and material flows and stocks from 1900 to 2010' in *Resources, Conservation and Recycling*, No. 165, 2021.
586 Enrico Sciubba, (2009); Mei Liao et al., 'Decomposition of embodied exergy flows in manufactured products and implications for carbon tariff policies' in *Asia Europe Journal*, No. 11, 2013.
587 Alf Hornborg, (1998); Alf Hornborg, (2009).
588 Mei Liao et al., (2013).
589 https://exergyeconomics.wordpress.com/selected-publications/; Luis Carmona et al., (2021).
590 Some propose adjusting the emergy approach to use exergy, interpreting 'available energy' in Odum's writings as 'exergy.' Others argue this would be inconsistent with the second law of thermodynamics. For more on this debate, see: Simone Bastianoni et al., 'Emergy as a function of exergy' in *Energy*, No. 32, 2007; Enrico Sciubba, (2009); John Bellamy Foster and Hannah Holleman, (2014); Alf Hornborg, (2015).
591 https://www.epa.gov/pollinator-protection/colony-collapse-disorder
592 https://www.resilience.org/stories/2022-05-19/the-great-simplification-full-movie/
593 John Brolin, (2007); Rikard Warlenius, (2016); Andrea Ricci, (2023).
594 Julien-François Gerber and Arnim Scheidel, 'In search of substantive economics: Comparing today's two major socio-metabolic approaches to the economy–MEFA and MuSIASEM' in *Ecological Economics*, No. 144, 2018; Christian Dorninger and Andreas Roos, 'Quantifying ecologically unequal exchange: Reviewing methodological trends, underexplored options, and future directions' in *18th Conference of the International Society for Ecological Economics and 11th International Degrowth Conference*, Oslo, Norway, 2025.
595 Andrea Ricci, (2024).
596 Göran Wall, (1987).
597 Based on Christopher Olk, (2024).
598 Andrea Ricci, (2023).
599 Others arrive at slightly higher ratios, using different country clusters, datasets and years: Christian Dorninger et al., (2021); Jason Hickel et al., (2022); Crelis Rammelt and Raimon Cardelus Ylla-Català, (2025).
600 Crelis Rammelt and Raimon Cardelus Ylla-Català, (2025).
601 Marx, *Critique of the Gotha Programme*, Part I.
602 Andrea Ricci, (2023).
603 Andrea Ricci, (2023).
604 Crelis Rammelt, (2025).
605 In his research, Ricci employs emergy, with NELT expressed in emergy joules per hour (emJ/h). I use tons of raw material equivalents (RME) – not because I believe it measures EUE more accurately, but because it has sufficient data and is slightly easier to interpret. What emergy does for energy, RME does for matter: both seek to capture the original natural use-values.

606 By dividing NELT by MELT, Ricci calculates an emergy-money ratio (EMR) – the relationship between biophysical resources and money. Since Ricci expresses NELT in emergy joules per hour (emJ/h) and MELT in dollars per hour ($/h), the resulting EMR is naturally expressed in emergy joules per dollar (emJ/$). Ricci's EMR is equivalent to the inverse of my measure of the monetary compensation per unit of biophysical resources (1 / MEN). I have therefore inverted Ricci's algebra without altering its logic.

607 In Ricci, EMR decreases as per capita income rises, primarily due to the significant growth in MELT in the denominator of the EMR ratio, which outpaces the growth in NELT in the numerator.

608 Crelis Rammelt, (2025).

609 Jennifer Givens quoted Siem Rothengatter, (2024), p. 73.

610 Pablo Alonso-Fernández and Rosa Regueiro-Ferreira, (2022).

611 https://debtjustice.org.uk/press-release/rising-debt-locks-global-south-countries-in-fossil-fuel-production

612 Christopher Olk, (2024).

613 Andrea Ricci, (2024), p. 9.

614 Noelle Robbins, (2010).

615 Allan Schnaiberg and Kenneth Gould, *Environment and Society: The Enduring Conflict*, New York: St Martin's Press, 1994.

616 James O'Connor, 'Capitalism, nature, socialism: a theoretical introduction' in *Capitalism Nature Socialism*, No. 1, 1988.

617 Julien-François Gerber, 'The second contradiction of capitalism' in *The Journal of Peasant Studies*, No. 52, 2025.

618 https://www.wto.org/english/res_e/statis_e/trade_evolution_e/evolution_trade_wto_e.htm

619 Jason Hickel et al., (2021).

620 Fred Magdoff and John Bellamy Foster, *What Every Environmentalist Needs to Know about Capitalism: A Citizen's Guide to Capitalism and the Environment*, New York: Monthly Review Press, 2011.

621 Paulo Freire, *Pedagogy of the Oppressed*, London: Penguin, 1996, p. 62.

622 Terry Eagleton, (2018).

623 Pierre Jalée, (1977); Ben Fine and Alfredo Saad-Filho, *Marx's 'Capital'*, London: Pluto Press, 2010; Michael Wayne, *Marx's 'Das Kapital' For Beginners*, Hanover: Steerforth Press, 2012; Hadas Thier, (2018).

624 Donella Meadows and Diana Wright, *Thinking In Systems: A Primer*, London: Earthscan, 2008.

625 George Box, 'Science and Statistics' in *Journal of the American Statistical Association*, No. 71, 1976.

626 Paul Smaldino, 'Models Are Stupid, and We Need More of Them' in *Computational Models in Social Psychology*, New York: Psychology Press, 2016.

627 Andrea Ricci, (2024).

628 Karl Marx, *Economic and philosophic manuscripts of 1844*, Moscow: Progress Publishers, 1959 [1932].

629 https://www.bbc.com/news/articles/c9qy98gp474o

630 https://doi.org/10.64628/AAJ.3shrfyuy5

631 Torkil Lauesen, (2025).

632 George Monbiot, (2003); Benn Steil, (2013).

633 Torkil Lauesen, (2025).

634 Samir Amin, 'A Note on the Concept of Delinking' in *Review (Fernand Braudel Centre)*, No. 10, 1987; Walter Rodney, *Decolonial Marxism: Essays From the Pan-African Revolution*, London: Verso, 2022.

635 Arghiri Emmanuel, (1972), p. 146.

636 Andrea Ricci, (2025).

637 Abraham Maslow, *The Psychology of Science: A Reconnaissance*, New York: Harper & Row, 1966, pp. 15–16.

638 Stephanie Kelton, *The Deficit Myth: Modern Monetary Theory and the Birth of the People's Economy*, New York: PublicAffairs, 2020.
639 Jason Hickel, 'Could money be the ultimate decolonizer?' in *New Internationalist*, No. 533, 2021; Christopher Olk et al., 'How to pay for saving the world: Modern Monetary Theory for a degrowth transition' in *Ecological Economics*, No. 214, 2023.
640 https://www.taxresearch.org.uk/Blog/2024/06/27/economics-is-not-alchemy/
641 Christopher Olk et al., (2023).
642 Jason Hickel, (2021).
643 Christopher Olk et al., (2023).
644 Andrea Ricci, (2024).
645 Sabelo Ndlovu-Gatsheni, (2015).
646 Nelson Maldonado-Torres, (2007), p. 243.
647 Sabelo Ndlovu-Gatsheni, (2015).
648 Stephen Bunker, 2019 [1985], p. 253.
649 Inês Cosme et al., 'Assessing the degrowth discourse: A review and analysis of academic degrowth policy proposals' in *Journal of Cleaner Production*, No. 149, 2017.
650 Blake Alcott, 'The sufficiency strategy: Would rich-world frugality lower environmental impact?' in *Ecological Economics*, No. 64, 2008.
651 Dario Krpan et al., 'Assessing public support for degrowth: survey-based experimental and predictive studies' in *The Lancet Planetary Health*, No. 9, 2025.
652 John Kenneth Galbraith, *A Tenured Professor*, Boston: Houghton Mifflin, 1994, p. 34.
653 Fred Magdoff and John Bellamy Foster, (2011), p. 32.
654 Andrea Ricci, (2025).
655 José Fevereiro and Benjamin Lowe, 'Macroeconomic implications for the Global South of a green transition in the Global North' in *Ecological Economics*, No. 237, 2025.
656 Markus Wissen and Ulrich Brand, *The Imperial Mode of Living: Everyday Life and the Ecological Crisis of Capitalism*, London: Verso, 2021; Andrea Ricci, (2025).
657 Torkil Lauesen, (2025).
658 Fred Magdoff and John Bellamy Foster, (2011), p. 42.
659 Barry Finger, (2017).
660 Julien-François Gerber, (2025).
661 Walter Rodney, (1981) [1972], pp. 10–11.
662 Erik Olin Wright, 'The Continuing Relevance of the Marxist Tradition for Transcending Capitalism' in *tripleC*, No. 16, 2018, 490–500.
663 Yannis Varoufakis, *Technofeudalism: What Killed Capitalism*, New York: Melville House, 2023.
664 Erik Olin Wright, *Envisioning Real Utopias*, London: Verso, 2010.
665 https://theanarchistlibrary.org/library/tom-wetzel-erik-olin-wright-on-the-transition-to-socialism
666 Charles Eisenstein, (2013), p. 26.
667 J.K. Gibson-Graham, *A postcapitalist politics*, Minneapolis: University of Minnesota Press, 2006; Samuel Alexander et al., *Post-Capitalist Futures: Paradigms, Politics, and Prospects*, Cham: Palgrave Macmillan, 2022.
668 Erik Olin Wright, (2010).
669 Terry Eagleton, (2018).

INDEX

www.ingramcontent.com/pod-product-compliance
Ingram Content Group UK Ltd.
Pitfield, Milton Keynes, MK11 3LW, UK
UKHW060919150926
475447UK00003B/28

9 780850 368086